DATE DUE

NEW BEDFORD'S CIVIL WAR

THE NORTH'S CIVIL WAR
Paul A. Cimbala, series editor

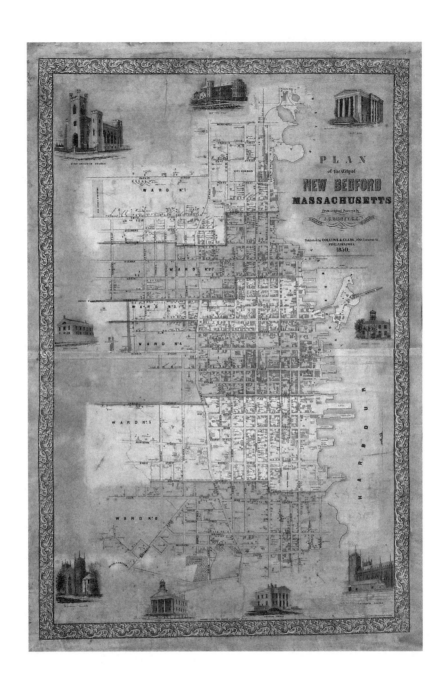

PLAN
of the City of
NEW BEDFORD
MASSACHUSETTS
From original Surveys by

Published by COLLINS & CLARK, 100 Chestnut St.
PHILADELPHIA.
1850.

New Bedford's Civil War

Earl F. Mulderink III

Fordham University Press
New York   2012

Frontispiece: Map of New Bedford, 1850.

Library of Congress Cataloging-in-Publication Data

Mulderink, Earl F.
    New Bedford's Civil War / Earl F. Mulderink III.—1st ed.
        p.   cm.— (The North's Civil War)
    Includes bibliographical references and index.
    ISBN 978-0-8232-4334-1 (cloth : alk. paper)
    1. New Bedford (Mass.)—History—19th century.   2. Massachusetts—History—Civil War, 1861–1865—Social aspects.   3. New Bedford (Mass.)—History, Military—19th century.   4. New Bedford (Mass.)—Social life and customs—19th century.   5. United States—History—Civil War, 1861–1865—Social aspects.   I. Title.
F74.N5M85   2012
974.4′85—dc23

2011046355

Printed in the United States of America
14 13 12   5 4 3 2 1
First edition

Contents

List of Figures   ix
Acknowledgments   xi

Introduction | 1

1   "A Burning and Shining Light":
Prosperity and Enlightened
Governance in Antebellum
New Bedford | 10

2   "The Nearest Approach to Freedom
and Equality": African Americans
in Antebellum New Bedford | 32

3   "Suppression of an Unholy
Rebellion": Wartime Mobilization
on the Home Front | 53

4   "Citizen-Soldiers of Massachusetts":
New Bedford's Volunteers in
the Civil War | 77

5   "Boys, I Only Did My Duty": New
Bedford's Black Soldiers in the Fifty-
Fourth Massachusetts | 99

6   "Worthy Recipients": New Bedford's
Black Veterans and the Web of Social
Welfare | 119

7   "Business Is Extremely Dull":
Whaling and Manufacturing in
Wartime New Bedford | 138

8   "The Position of Our City Has
Materially Changed": Public Costs
and Municipal Governance during
the Civil War | 164

9   "The Great Hope for the Future":
New Bedford in the Postbellum
Era | 184

10   "On the Altar of Our Common
        Country": Contested
        Commemorations
        of the Civil War | 201
        Epilogue | 219

        Notes   *223*
        Index   *299*

Figures

Map of New Bedford, 1850 — Frontispiece

Union Street looking east, circa 1849 — 18

Abraham Howland, New Bedford's first mayor — 25

Liberty Hall, circa 1868–70 — 34

Rodney French, mayor and antislavery leader — 49

Quaker attire, photographed October 12, 1863 — 55

The Reverend William J. Potter, influential local leader — 66

View of Fort Phoenix from Palmer's Island — 70

George Howland Jr., mayor during the Civil War — 78

William Logan Rodman — 82

African-American war hero William H. Carney, circa 1900 — 111

Post One veterans, Grand Army of the Republic, 1898 — 129

Captains of the Stone Fleet, circa 1861 — 140

Sinking the Stone Fleet in Charleston Harbor — 143

New Bedford wharf scene, circa 1868 — 175

View of County Street, circa 1867–77 — 181

Coopering on the wharf, circa 1868 — 190

Wamsutta Mills and mill operatives, circa 1870–80 — 194

Post 190 veterans, Grand Army of the Republic, circa 1893 — 212

Acknowledgments

Many thanks, first of all, to Paul Cimbala, who provided encouragement (and procured a contract) that compelled me to complete this project. I appreciate his work as editor and Fordham University Press for publishing their excellent series The North's Civil War. FUP staff have been most helpful throughout a lengthy process. Wil Cerbone shared detailed comments and insights about the manuscript; FUP director Fred Nachbaur offered judicious encouragement; and Eric Newman shepherded the book through the publication process. Kate O'Brien-Nicholson and Katie Sweeney demonstrated their considerable skills in the realm of marketing. Michael Koch was gracious and thorough in copy editing the entire manuscript, no easy task. Outsider reader Michael Frisch provided sensible, extensive, and helpful criticism of the entire manuscript, as did an anonymous reviewer. While I remain solely responsible for any errors, this book is stronger because of the expertise rendered by the entire FUP staff.

A second round of thanks is directed to librarians and archivists. Topping the list is Paul Cyr, Special Collections Librarian at the New Bedford Free Public Library, who generously proffered sources, leads, and insights, along with reviewing a draft of the manuscript. I doubt that anyone knows more than Paul about New Bedford's history, and he and the NBFPL remain treasures of the Whaling City. Janice Hodson provided timely assistance in obtaining appropriate images for the book, and I thank her and the Trustees of the NBFPL for granting permission to reproduce them. Gratefully, I acknowledge assistance from the staffs of the New Bedford Whaling Museum, the Baker Library at the Harvard University Business School, the Boston Public Library, the Massachusetts Historical Society, the National Archives, and the State Historical Society of Wisconsin. Southern Utah University's interlibrary loan staff, notably Phil Dillard, had a perfect record in obtaining scholarly books and articles.

A variety of colleagues at Southern Utah University have provided encouragement and even inspiration. Special thanks are due to Jim Aton for his continuing friendship and our ongoing conversations about history, writing, and academic life. Both Jim Aton and Mark Miller read an early version of the full manuscript and furnished perceptive comments. By churning out meaningful scholarship despite heavy teaching loads, fellow SUU historians—Curtis Bostick, Wayne Hinton, Mark Miller, Ryan Paul, Larry Ping, and Jim Vlasich—

provide proof of our department's high standards. I am grateful for travel and research support from several sources at SUU: the Department of History and Sociology, the College of Humanities and Social Sciences, and the Provost's Fund for Faculty Development. Extended funding allowed me to hire an excellent research assistant, Kristen Fowler, whose varied efforts improved this book immeasurably. Her cheerful, can-do attitude was an added bonus. Rudia Williams deserves recognition for effectively managing our department and student assistants. One more institutional plug goes to the Mystic Seaport Museum and their fine staff, especially Dr. Glenn S. Gordinier, who helped me to stay informed about historical issues tied to race, ethnicity, gender, and power in maritime America.

I am pleased to publicly acknowledge friends and family for their support over many years. Most of them learned, eventually, to stop asking when this book would be completed. I offer heartfelt "thank-yous" to fellow professors Jerry Kapus and Tom Mondschean, along with George Pacocha, David "Doc" Shuster, Greg Surufka, and Paul Zega. I appreciate advice and encouragement from graduate school colleagues, particularly Nancy Isenberg. I want to thank my mother, Margaret Grish, and my siblings (and their families): Steve Mulderink, Peg Newcomb, and Doug Mulderink. All of these folks, and many others, have helped me to endure the trials of an academic career.

My professional odyssey landed me far from New Bedford in the landlocked desert of southern Utah. For the past decade and a half, my sojourn here has been enriched beyond belief by my wife, Rita Osborn, and daughters, Alyson Osborn and Amy Osborn. Despite the challenges of doing scholarly work in the midst of extremely busy lives, my efforts were buoyed in multiple ways by all of the "Mulderborns" (including Shadow). While I proudly take full credit for finishing this book, I want to extend my gratitude to Rita, Alyson, and Amy for making it all possible and more pleasurable.

In closing, I feel compelled to quote one of New Bedford's local chroniclers, Daniel Ricketson. Writing in 1858 about his serialized articles published in the *New Bedford Daily Mercury* (and reprinted in his book, *History of New Bedford*), Ricketson explained: "I am aware that much of the material of this history is wanting in arrangement, but it should be remembered that I have been obliged to collect my information from a great variety of sources, and at different times during a period of many years" (vii). Concluding his labors with some satisfaction, he added, "If I have succeeded in saving from oblivion a considerable portion of our history, which I have in many instances received . . . from old and scattered records, I shall feel that my time has not been misspent, or my labors in vain" (408).

My sentiments exactly.

Introduction

A s an antidote to the gloom of war in September 1864, New Bedford residents organized a gala bicentennial celebration to honor the incorporation of Dartmouth township, the city's political precursor. This impressive civic event illuminated contemporary perceptions of the city and its citizens in wartime. City Hall hosted a banquet for six hundred guests where speaker after speaker connected New Bedford with national leaders and pressing issues of the war. Addressing New Bedford's unique historical context and praising city leaders for their cooperation with President Lincoln and Massachusetts Governor John A. Andrew, speakers also highlighted the ordinary men fighting for the Union cause. C. B. H. Fessenden offered a typical sentiment in declaring "*all honor* to the brave and gallant soldiers and sailors, the true peacemakers." The Reverend William J. Potter, a former chaplain in the Union army, emphatically commended the Union troops who were defending the "free church, the free school, and the free ballot." Former governor and local luminary John H. Clifford flattered his townsmen for being "steadfast and uncompromising in maintaining the 'Liberty and Union, now and forever,' of their common country."[1]

New Bedford Mayor George Howland Jr., a scion of old whaling wealth, offered the day's most personalized observations. Recalling his childhood when New Bedford was home to three thousand people, the young Howland was schooled about public service by his grandfather, a strong-minded Quaker named John Howland. Asked by the elder Howland if he had attended a town meeting earlier that day, young George said "no" and questioned why. His grandfather replied, "in the style peculiar to that day, 'Go to larn,'" the mayor explained. With forebears who believed that "there was something for every one to do, and that it behooved every one to do something," the adult Howland had filled his business and political life with meaningful service, as did his peers. Although he complained about the "incubus" of the "wicked rebellion," Howland looked optimistically to the future, pointing to wonderful technologies on display in his city that included the steam engine, the telegraph, and a photography exhibit by the Bierstadt Brothers. Asking rhetorically if New Bedford would continue to confront the challenges of the Civil War, Howland responded, "The only answer I can make to the query is the real Yankee one, 'Why not?'"[2]

Howland's cheering comments about New Bedford were complemented by local attorney William W. Crapo. His labored and lengthy treatise drew upon the city's historical ties to traditional New England notions of religious freedom and political democracy. Praising the dissenting nature of founding Puritans, Quakers, and Baptists, Crapo proudly claimed that "The most perfect democracies that mankind has ever known are found in the early New England towns." But New Bedford's residents went further than many New Englanders by establishing a "city of refuge and safety" for African Americans. Black residents of the city were fortunate to find "the encouragements of quiet homes, the benefits of education, and the rewards attending fidelity of labor and diligence in business." Crapo lauded the black mariner and sea captain Paul Cuffee as one of the area's "industrious, thoughtful, earnest" forefathers. "Many of us here present are of the old stock," Crapo continued, "Let us acquit ourselves as worthy sons of noble sires."[3]

New Bedford's leaders demonstrated a keen sense of civic identity centered on patriotism, optimism, and egalitarianism during the Civil War. Their pronouncements reflected the sentiments of some 22,000 people who lived in this vital northern port city as they confronted the vagaries of war. When fighting erupted in 1861, New Bedford stood as the world's whaling "capital" and was home to one of the North's most significant and sizeable black communities. Like their northern counterparts, New Bedford's citizens wrestled with wartime demands and disruptions in all spheres of life, often with a local twist. For example, most of the city's Quaker leaders abandoned pacifist principles to actively support the Union effort, with many pushing for the enlistment of black soldiers. The city's far-flung whaling industry was threatened by wartime events, yet locals cheered the sinking of the so-called Stone Fleets in Southern harbors in the late fall of 1861. New Bedford did not experience boom times during the war, but local business leaders found new opportunities through military mobilization and manufacturing. Even in a city known for its tolerant environment, New Bedford experienced wartime tensions and threats of racially motivated draft riots in July 1863 like those of New York City. Moreover, wartime financial and fiscal disruptions undercut the city's long-standing patterns of public largesse. The war's wide swath touched the home front in numerous ways and shaped the city's subsequent development into the twentieth century.

New Bedford's Civil War contributes to an emerging field termed "Civil War cities" by historian J. Matthew Gallman. Through the imaginative investigations of cities north and south, of varying size and significance, historians have addressed multiple questions about the Civil War and broader patterns in the nineteenth century. In some ways, this book offers a traditional approach—that of a "city biography"—in exploring New Bedford's history as its people faced economic, political, and social changes. Despite New Bedford's uniqueness as a whaling entrepôt, the city's wartime history upholds Gallman's observation that "cities and communities across the North shared similar subnarratives despite their differing circumstances." In devoting attention to military recruiting, enlistments, and ongoing connections between home front and battlefield, this book addresses the late Peter J. Parish's concern that historians had neglected the war's "most important" aspect, namely how Northerners sustained a "will to win" as the war persisted. Urging that closer attention be paid to the "grass roots" level, Parish also reinforces Gallman's important point that the Civil War was a "national war fought by local communities."[4]

Historians who have explored local efforts during the war years have tended toward truncated and focused studies that begin with Fort Sumter's fall in April 1861 and terminate in 1865. One aim of *New Bedford's Civil War* is to connect this city's wartime experiences with longer-term patterns, partly prompted by Peter J. Parish's suggestion that historians cut across boundaries to link the war with "major, long-running issues in the history of the United States during the nineteenth century."[5] From the late 1850s through the 1870s, New Bedford faced continuing assaults on the whaling enterprise and some local capitalists embraced textile manufacturing as their economic salvation. As another example of the war's longer-term impact, veterans shaped their memories and meanings of the Civil War long after it ended. They supported each others' claims for military pensions and gathered in local GAR posts to share comradeship well into the twentieth century. Although the war concluded in 1865, its multiple and differential consequences stretched for decades in New Bedford, as in the nation.

Research for this book was spurred two decades ago when historian Maris Vinovskis famously asked, "Have social historians lost the Civil War?" Although this national conflict proved to be the deadliest of all American wars, Vinovskis questioned then why so few social historians, most notably those who studied American communities between 1850 and 1880, had analyzed the impacts of the war.[6] Vinovskis singled out Michael Frisch as one historian who had addressed relevant topics, although now he could add a number of accomplished works on Northern communities that include J. Matthew Gallman on Philadelphia, Ernest McKay and Edward K. Spann on New York City, Thomas H. O'Connor on Boston, Theodore J. Karamanski on Chicago, and Russell L. Johnson on Dubuque, among others. Certainly, this book's inclusion in the

Fordham University Press series The North's Civil War, edited by Paul Cimbala, suggests a newfound appreciation for "the war at home."[7] In trying also to heed Vinvoskis's call, *New Bedford's Civil War* draws upon the tools and resources of social history to examine an important northern home front during the Civil War era.[8]

In exploring the war's many, multifaceted aspects, this study upholds Reid Mitchell's contention that "community values" were "crucial to the way in which Americans made war from 1861 to 1865." But, "community values" could be fragmented and contested.[9] Historian Thomas Bender's conception of "community" as "network of social relations marked by mutuality" helps in understanding the multiple "communities" that comprised the larger urban polity of New Bedford.[10] This perspective builds upon James McPherson's insight that wartime military enlistment patterns reinforced community ties and sustained tight connections between men at war and their families and townsmen on the home front.[11] Community ties were reinforced—and also fragmented—by ethnic and racially segregated military units, such as the Fifty-Fourth Massachusetts Colored Infantry. *New Bedford's Civil War* pays particular attention to an African-American community that, as Ira Berlin and his colleagues stated so well, "fought a different Civil War" than did native-born white Americans.[12]

This book focuses on broadly construed communities within New Bedford, similar to Thomas O'Connor's approach in looking at "groups" within Civil War Boston.[13] One group comprised the city's economic elite, the business leaders and entrepreneurs whose intermarried families dominated the profitable whaling industry before the war. Many of these individuals and families put whaling profits to work in other endeavors such as banking, insurance, and, eventually, textile manufacturing. A second community, spawned from and intertwined with the business community, consisted of political leaders who served in a variety of elected and appointed roles. Individuals such as George Howland Jr., five-term mayor of New Bedford, shaped the city's public policies and municipal governance throughout the Civil War era. These white men, many of Quaker heritage, shared a liberal or progressive view of city governance that upheld New Bedford's national reputation as an antebellum haven for fugitive slaves and free blacks. The city's African-American residents comprise a third community and focal point of this book, a group noteworthy for its size, visibility, and sense of empowerment before the war. During the Civil War, a number of men served with valor and distinction in the Fifty-Fourth Massachusetts Infantry, the "brave black regiment," and they helped to shape national debates over black military enlistment, equal pay, and notions of citizenship.

To explore the business, political, and black communities, this book investi-gates four interrelated issues that remained central in the Civil War era. The first is that of economic change and challenge. As the world's whaling capital in the antebellum era, New Bedford's aggressive commitment to the global expansion of whaling enriched the city's merchants and provided employment for thousands of people. Even before the war, however, some questioned the city's economic dependence on whaling and began to experiment with industri-alization, principally in textile manufacturing. Both whaling and textile indus-tries were disrupted by the war, which served further to accelerate changes to the city's economic and social landscapes. A second issue centers on the politics and policies of city leaders. Antebellum New Bedford was governed by men of wealth and mainly antislavery views who promoted "enlightened governance." The disruptions of the Civil War prompted debates and policy decisions by municipal leaders, and after their war New Bedford's urban milieu was charac-terized by large-scale industrialization and its attendant problems. A third focus in this book is on racial dynamics and New Bedford's African Americans who enjoyed a relatively favored position in what Kathryn Grover termed "the fugi-tive's Gibraltar."[14] Black residents of New Bedford enjoyed unique opportuni-ties and visibility in the antebellum era, and their status was enhanced during the war by military service. After the war, African-American veterans and the larger black community extended the meaning and history of the Civil War through public events and a collective memory that reiterated their wartime valor. A fourth issue, often implicit throughout the book, is that of New Bed-ford's multiple contributions to state and national efforts during the war. Like other northern communities, New Bedford supported and shaped a national victory by the Union in significant ways that went beyond sending men off to military service.

New Bedford's primacy in the global business of whaling prompted some con-temporaries to call it the country's "richest city." During a ninety-year period from 1816 to 1906, New Bedford was responsible for more than 45 percent of total American whaling output.[15] Besides providing an overview of whaling in the antebellum era, chapter 1 investigates networks of capitalism, manufactur-ing experiments, and the city's municipal organization, political leadership, and governing practices. Moving from economic to political realms, chapter 1 builds upon the detailed findings of Kathryn Grover (*The Fugitive's Gibraltar, Escaping Slaves and Abolitionism in New Bedford, Massachusetts*), who offers insights about white Quakers and African Americans. Grover suggests that New Bedford's commitment to racial toleration and antislavery agitation made it different from "most other New England places." This book builds upon Grover's contention that New Bedford was often identified by its radical abolitionism whether or not the stories were true. More than most northern communities, the city stood as a relative haven for African Americans in the mid-nineteenth century.[16]

Chapter 2 examines the freedom, political empowerment, and economic opportunities enjoyed by black residents through the 1850s. New Bedford's African-American community stood out for its size and its diversity, constituting the highest proportion of black citizens in any New England urban area between 1850 and 1880. This account follows the lead of historians such as James Horton and Lois Horton who have written extensively about free black communities in the North, including Boston's. The Hortons offer a helpful definition of *community* as "both institutions (social, political, economic, and religious) and sentiments based on shared experience and a sense of common destiny that bound community members together." New Bedford's black community, like others in the North, included networks among family, friends, and coworkers that "were both based in and transcended geography."[17] Still, the city's role as the world's primary whaling port through the 1850s did not necessarily create a favorable labor market. Frederick Douglass lived in New Bedford upon his escape from slavery in 1838 where he experienced discrimination despite his training as a skilled ship caulker.[18] Douglass learned much in New Bedford and joined others in working collectively to end slavery, support fugitive slaves, and agitate for the full citizenship of all black Americans. Chapter 2 surveys church life, demographic patterns, and connections between New Bedford's black community and others in Massachusetts and New England.

Moving into the war years, several chapters explore the conflict as it impacted New Bedford after war erupted in April 1861. Chapter 3 offers an account of wartime patriotism and mobilization by looking at military recruitment, Home and Coast Defense, operations of the Provost Marshal General's office, and the maintenance of civic pride. Local, state, and federal records help to document New Bedford's involvement in and contributions to the national struggle.[19] Although most citizens proudly supported the Union cause, city authorities and residents did not always speak in unison as the casualties and costs of war continued to climb. New Bedford's experiences highlight the effective mobilization of resources and cooperation among an array of local, state, and federal officials who created new policies and bureaucracies. Still, the war provoked anxieties about inadequate coastal protection, fears over attacks by Confederate raiders, and worries about racially motivated riots in July 1863, similar to those of New York's infamous Draft Riots.

Many works that make up the new social history of the Civil War pay close attention to the soldiers and sailors who fought on both Union and Confederate sides.[20] Chapter 4 details New Bedford's "citizen-soldiers," the predominantly white military units that represented the city and state in fighting for the Union. As Reid Mitchell, James McPherson, and others have suggested, community identification was reinforced by military enlistment patterns as men fought with others they had known as civilians. This chapter analyzes enlistment patterns, describes military units associated with New Bedford, investigates the backgrounds of the city's soldiers, offers a focused look at Irish and Irish-American soldiers, and concludes with an assessment of mortality patterns among New Bedford's men who died during the war.[21] New Bedford's leaders were justly proud of their men who went off to war on behalf of the Union.

Black army enlistees from New Bedford are the focus of chapter 5. These men, like other African Americans throughout the country, fought a "different Civil War" than whites as they battled against racism and for equal pay for black soldiers. New Bedford's black and white communities allied in agitating for emancipatory war aims and the full inclusion of blacks as citizens. In exploring the recruitment and military experiences of the Fifty-Fourth Massachusetts Infantry, the chapter pays particular attention to the assault on Fort Wagner, the emergence of a local black war hero, William Carney, and the soldiers' quest for equal pay. In an influential work about military service, Gerald Linderman noted that community values were extended to war, and that home front and battlefield were often linked inextricably.[22] Such was the case for African-American enlistees from New Bedford who had their own chronicler, James Henry Gooding of the Fifty-Fourth Massachusetts, whose published letters home have been superbly edited by Virginia Matzke Adams. Gooding's "eloquence helped persuade Congress to equalize the pay of white and black soldiers in 1864," according to James McPherson, and the corporal's death at the notorious Andersonville Prison in July 1864 symbolized the ultimate price paid by many black Union enlistees and their families.[23] This account is indebted to the work of numerous historians who have written about black soldiers during the Civil War, among them Noah Andre Trudeau, John David Smith, Edwin S. Redkey, Donald Yacovone, Wilbert L. Jenkins, and Joseph Glatthaar.[24]

Chapter 6 scrutinizes social welfare practices and payments during and after the war by focusing on black poor aid recipients and veterans. This chapter addresses other "costs" of the Civil War by examining a web of welfare that extended from local to state to national resources. This close examination addresses Michael Katz's plea that "the history of dependence in American [history] needs to be rewritten from the bottom up, that is, through an analysis of the lives and experiences of the poor themselves."[25] As documented in local

Overseers of the Poor records and federal military pensions, black individuals and families faced hardships that stretched their own resources. At the same time, the Civil War brought about an intrusion of the federal state into the lives of civilians and soldiers, a process perpetuated by veterans' applications for, and their dependence upon, military pensions. Some scholars, most notably Theda Skocpol, have examined the military pension system to understand the underpinnings of the modern welfare state, and historian Patrick Kelly has explored the concept of "martial citizenship" and welfare in his important work.[26] More than additional income, pension payments were considered part of a contractual bond between Union soldiers and sailors and the federal government. This belief cut across the lines of race, class, gender, and military rank, and was demonstrated in persistent patterns of veterans' mutual support long after the war had ended.[27]

The Civil War disrupted New Bedford's maritime economy, as detailed in chapter 7. Whaling's decline was poignantly illustrated by the sinking of the so-called Stone Fleets in Southern harbors in 1861, and by the ample destruction wrought by Confederate raiders as the war progressed. The Stone Fleets brought national attention to New Bedford, but the sinking of these ships served as a metaphor for a declining industry that faced unique struggles in wartime. Depredations by the CSS *Alabama* and *Shenandoah* and increased competition from petroleum dealt a double-whammy to New Bedford's whaling economy.[28] To understand local business leaders and the wartime context in which they worked, this chapter examines whaling agents and outfitters who persisted (and even prospered) through the war years. Other entrepreneurs turned to textile manufacturing and to new modes of industrial production that included twist drills, shoes, and bakeries. Business and economic changes of the Civil War years pointed to a more diverse and industrialized economy that accelerated after the war.

The costs of war were found not only within business endeavors, and chapter 8 details efforts by public officials to confront wartime challenges of fiscal management and public governance. This chapter examines community debates over wartime costs, maintaining public services, and planning the city's postwar future. New Bedford's local officials coordinated with agents of state and national governments to meet unprecedented military expenses such as bounties. Despite the pressures of an uncertain war and an economic downturn, New Bedford avoided large deficits by cutting costs in key areas like public schools and collecting taxes with great efficiency. The city's wartime mayors and treasurer viewed New Bedford's scrupulous attention to fiscal and budgetary matters as an additional wartime cost that served also as a patriotic contribution to the national war effort. The issue of supplying New Bedford with fresh water, and its huge price tag, divided business and political leaders during a wartime referendum in 1864.

Chapter 9 surveys the city's embrace of manufacturing in the postwar era, a transition prompted by the whaling industry's continuing decline and the apparent promise and profits of textile production. Although some feared changes in the city's economy, influential local visionaries contended that economic challenges would be overcome by the active development of textile manufacturing. In turn, the city opened to new sources of immigration from French Canada, the Azores, and later, southern and eastern Europe. As New Bedford shed the mantle of the "Whaling City," its boosters touted a new identity of "Mill City" that claimed a population of 100,000 at the turn of the twentieth century. With the memory of the Civil War receding into the past, residents surveyed a landscape of textile factories, smokestacks, and tenement housing within a diverse and industrialized city. By the late 1800s the sons and grandsons of whaling oligarchs maintained oversight of business and civic life in an overgrown urban environment marked by ethnic diversity and growing class-based rifts between workers and employers.[29]

The Civil War can be viewed from another perspective, from the vantage of myth- and memory making that followed in its wake. Chapter 10 builds upon scholarly contentions that the creation of memory is a historically constructed process that is both a collective and individual act. David Blight's *Race and Reunion: The Civil War in American Memory* provides an unsurpassed overview of Civil War memory making in the North and South. His work adds to insights from David Thelen who noted that "Memory is not made in isolation but is created within the contexts of community, broader politics, and social dynamics."[30] New Bedford's postbellum patriots claimed to organize the state's first substantial "Memorial Day" in 1866, and their celebrations upheld community pride, notions of equality, and depictions of civil religion. The city's black community joined their one-time neighbor, Frederick Douglass, to use the memory of the war and of African Americans' participation in it to push for full equality through the nineteenth century. Douglass sought to "forge memory into action that could somehow save the legacy of the Civil War for blacks," David Blight noted.[31] Through their impoverished all-black GAR post, and with the stirring example of local war hero Sergeant William Carney, New Bedford's black community sought to sustain wartime sacrifices amid growing indifference by whites. The racially segregated nature of many postbellum events and rituals highlights an unfulfilled assimilative quest by African Americans through the nineteenth century.

1

"A Burning and Shining Light": Prosperity and Enlightened Governance in Antebellum New Bedford

New Bedford was widely known in the antebellum era for its whaling, wealth, and staunch antislavery environment. The city's mayors stood as virtuous leaders who opposed slavery, favored temperance, and believed that public funds should be used to help the destitute—within reason. Local philanthropic organizations reflected religiously oriented and interdenominational values, embodied best in the New Bedford Port Society. The New Bedford Free Public Library and generous poor relief stood as evidence of the liberal views of city leaders. New Bedford was a port city with a diverse population, some of it transient and poor. Periodic urban disorders suggested underlying tensions within the changing environment, and the occasional outbursts of collective vigilantism suggested a potential for greater conflict. Order was maintained by whaling prosperity, the prevalence of diverse religious organizations, the proactive governance of city authorities, and residents' appreciation of their city as a haven.

At mid-century, the recently incorporated city of New Bedford enjoyed prosperity matched by few other communities in the United States. Charles Francis Adams had noted in 1835 that County Street, the city's most majestic thoroughfare, was home to "more noble looking mansions than any other in the country." Herman Melville sang similar praises in his novel, *Moby-Dick*: "The town itself is perhaps the dearest place to live in, in all New England . . . nowhere in America can you find more patrician-like houses; parks and gardens more opulent, than in New Bedford." To underscore the whaling-based wealth of the town, Melville wrote that "they have reservoirs of oil in every house, and every night recklessly burn their lengths in spermaceti candles."[1] A local citizen, Nathaniel Parker Willis, boasted that New Bedford was the country's wealthiest city on a per capita basis. "What do you think of a town," Willis asked, "in which if the property taxed in it were equally divided, every man, woman, and child in its population would have over $1,000?"[2] According to the Hartford *Courant,* based on the number of adult male voters (4,315) and the total of real and personal taxable property ($25,809,000) in 1855, each voter was worth about $6,000. The Civil War would have a dramatic impact on New Bedford's wealth, however, as city's total value dropped from over $24 million in 1860 to a little more than $20 million in 1865.[3]

At the height of its antebellum prosperity, the city was "redolent of oil and bursting with promise," wrote local resident Henry Beetle Hough. Whaleship spars stood "thick as a forest" along more than two dozen wharves stacked with casks of oil.[4] Just a year prior to the Civil War, *Harper's New Monthly Magazine* described New Bedford as "Mecca, or Holy City of the whale-hunters" where a visitor "stumbles at every step upon the spoils of the great deep." Docks and streets lay "covered with anchors, rusty cables, harpoons, hoops, and lances; staves and empty oil-casks sounding the blows of the cooper." Prosperous banks and insurance companies stood near the wharves, a short stroll to dance halls, bars, and brothels with names like The Marsh, The Buckingham, The Star of the Sea, and Old Forty. Returning whalemen wore caps and adornments of various foreign places, and bustling gangs of caulkers and riggers worked on ships soon to return to the Arctic or Antarctic Oceans. Casks of "oleaginous cargo" covered the wharves with their "golden liquid treasure," soon to be set upon by "gaugers, clerks, supercargoes, oil-fillers, bung-starters, and scrapers."[5]

The wharves, not only the center of New Bedford's commercial activity, were also the heart of the global whaling enterprise. Some twenty-six wharves and three slips comprised the city's waterfront in 1859, stretching northward from east of the Friend's Burial Ground to the drawbridge that connected New Bedford with Fairhaven across the harbor. The largest merchants operated out of counting rooms on Commercial Wharf, Central Wharf, Rotch's Square, and nearby docks. The city's fourteen attorneys and three law firms were concentrated on Water Street. Most of the six large oil or candle manufacturing companies operated a block from the harbor, parallel to the wharves. At least two dozen saloons (including a "billiard saloon" and "bowling saloon") were located mainly on South Water Street, with two others on Steamboat Wharf.[6]

As Herman Melville wrote, New Bedford's "brave houses and flowery gardens came from the Atlantic, Pacific, and Indian oceans."[7] The whaling industry was the major employer in New Bedford. *National Magazine* reported in 1845 the capital invested in New Bedford's 251 whaling ships amounted to over $7.5 million, and 7,000 men toiled in whaling-related activities.[8] Whaling continued to add great value to New Bedford's economy through the antebellum era. In 1858, for example, 65 whaling ships were filled with nearly $2 million worth of goods that ranged from 13,650 barrels of flour to 78,000 pounds of cheese to 205,000 yards of canvas. The whaling industry paid advance wages that year in New Bedford amounting to $130,000.[9] Tables 1-1 and 1-2 illustrate

Table 1-1. New Bedford Whaling, 1841–76

Year	No. Vessels Returning	Import Whale Oil, Barrels	Import Bone, Pounds	Total Valuation, US Imports	New Bedford Tonnage
1841	57	49,555		7,125,970.88	
1842	63	51,112		4,379,812.03	
1843	56	40,922	409,220	6,293,680.21	69,708
1844	76	102,992	978,592	7,875,970.38	76,784
1845	68	83,724	1,006,007	9,283,611.75	82,633
1846	62	80,812	456,900	6,203,115.43	82,701
1847	79	98,735	1,568,200	8,419,288.49	80,947
1848	75	115,436	621,900	6,819,442.78	81,075
1849	64	72,961	797,300	7,069,953.74	77,138
1850	64	91,627	1,081,500	7,564,124.72	81,442
1851	94	155,711	2,349,900	10,031,744.05	94,642
1852	59	42,352	925,600	5,565,409.89	104,006
1853	91	118,673	2,835,800	10,766,521.20	107,512
1854	113	175,336	1,669,200	10,802,594.20	105,459
1855	78	102,968	1,460,500	9,413,148.93	107,702
1856	79	81,783	1,087,600	9,589,846.36	114,364
1857	105	127,362	1,350,850	10,491,548.90	110,267

1858	80	103,105	1,184,900	7,672,227.31	107,931
1859	89	121,522	1,608,250	8,525,108.91	103,564
1860	88	90,450	1,112,000	6,520,135.12	98,760
1861	85	72,134	724,434	5,415,090.59	86,971
1862	68	61,056	297,600	5,051,781.64	73,061
1863	66	43,191	307,950	5,936,507.17	64,815
1864	77	35,883	224,250	8,113,922.07	58,041
1865	57	51,693	376,450	6,906,650.51	50,403
1866	40	44,513	392,100	7,037,891.23	53,798
1867	62	72,108	731,146	6,356,772.51	52,652
1868	69	49,939	667,507	5,470,157.43	50,628
1869	59	54,566	471,495	6,205,244.32	50,775
1870	59	49,563	569,861	4,529,126.02	50,213
1871	56	55,710	560,993	3,691,469.18	40,045
1872	33	15,573	177,868	2,954,783.00	36,686
1873	39	25,757	150,598	2,962,106.96	32,556
1874	32	26,349	321,637	2,713,034.51	29,541
1875	53	25,067	359,973	3,314,800.24	31,691
1876	55	20,535	93,484	2,639,463.31	30,464

Source: Leonard Bolles Ellis, *History of New Bedford and Its Vicinity: 1620–1892* (Syracuse, NY, 1892), 390.

Table 1-2. New Bedford and American Whaling, 1816–1905

Period	Total Tons	N B Tons	N B % of Total
1816–20	18,389	6,650	36.1
1821–25	37,161	13,162	35.4
1826–30	47,953	23,885	49.8
1831–35	92,750	46,659	50.3
1836–40	133,897	56,585	42.5
1841–45	185,678	73,007	39.3
1846–50	208,347	82,659	39.7
1851–55	195,938	106,105	54.2
1856–60	195,692	109,805	56.1
1861–65	116,565	77,734	66.7
1866–70	79,870	60,127	75.3
1871–75	55,354	46,020	83.2
1876–80	45,655	40,503	88.7
1881–85	40,278	27,365	67.9
1886–90	31,566	11,028	34.9
1891–95	25,194	4,648	18.6
1896–00	17,605	3,185	18.1
1900–05	11,017	3,101	28.1

Source: Lance E. Davis, Robert E. Gallman, and Karin Gleiter, *In Pursuit of Leviathan: Technology, Institutions, Productivity, and Profits in American Whaling, 1816–1906* (Chicago: University of Chicago Press, 1997), 343.

the expansion and contraction of the whaling industry when New Bedford dominated the industry during the nineteenth century.

Despite heady profits and global expansion, some signs of distress in traditional whaling practices emerged before the Civil War. Volatile prices went along with risky and uncertain voyages. For example, of sixty-eight whalers that arrived at New Bedford and its harbor neighbor of Fairhaven in 1858, forty-four had unprofitable voyages, mostly due to price declines for sperm oil and whale oil. A brief, 100 percent rise in whalebone prices between 1855 and 1858 proved a temporary boon. As an industry, whaling was marked by traditional practices among its investors, ship captains, and crew. Typically, two-thirds of a whaling vessel was comprised of unskilled seamen, "green hands," or "boys," and their high rates of labor turnover contributed to the industry's status as a "laggard" compared with other sectors of the American economy such as manufacturing and transportation. As an industry with a constant incursion of new and unskilled workers, whaling faced diminished productivity throughout the nineteenth century, and it was unique also for its "mobile" capital stock and labor.[10]

From modest and old-fashioned enclaves, whaling merchants divvied up vessel ownership and profits among partners and family members.[11] Whaling agents, the "moving spirit of the industry," were epitomized by such leading merchants as George Howland Sr. When he died in 1852, Howland left an estate of $615,000, a fleet of nine whaling vessels, a countinghouse, a wharf, and a candle factory. Howland enjoyed a typical profit on returning voyages between 6.5 and 14 percent. As a successful and long-standing merchant, Howland would have several vessels at sea at any one time that increased his annual returns to upwards of 20 percent per year. Other income came through fees charged for provisioning vessels and guarantees for oil and bone sales. In the mid-1850s, a merchant with four vessels at sea was likely to make $24,000 per year, almost the income of the president of the United States or ten times the salaries of federal district judges.[12] With these types of returns, and clear dominance of the global whaling enterprise, New Bedford's whaling agents and merchants had little reason to alter their profitable practices.

By the 1850s, however, whaling merchants began to depend on labor recruiters known as *crimps*. Similar to patterns in other maritime labor markets uncovered by historian Jeffrey Bolster, the crimps reflected a change in New Bedford's racial dynamics and social relations. Crimps, primarily owners of taverns or boardinghouses within the city, helped to "whiten" the labor market at mid-century by neglecting native-born black seafarers.[13] New Bedford's crimps emerged as an institutionalized group in 1859 when they formed an "Association of Outfitters." Known locally as "landsharks," these individuals supplied whalers with men and materials. *Harper's New Monthly Magazine* in 1860 described the city's "sharks" as "pirates," calling them a "set of small traders, agents, and owners of groggeries, boarding-houses, pimps, etc., etc., who trade in the necessities or pander to the vices of the outgoing or returning seamen."[14] New Bedford's newly established association demonstrated a change in class relations and power in the city and its labor market, suggesting a decline in local Quaker control as whaling operations expanded around the globe.[15]

Whaling and Manufacturing

New Bedford's whaling enterprise generated a variety of supportive and profitable manufacturing enterprises. Within the region, for example, shipbuilding was farmed out to surrounding areas such as Padanaram, Mattapoisett, and Marion, all of which enjoyed prosperous years before the Civil War.[16] Within the city, a major sign of industrial growth could be seen in the construction of the New Bedford and Taunton Railroad that stretched twenty miles and had been constructed at a cost of $400,000. New Bedford's whaling agents managed the company and owned nearly all the railroad's stock.[17] Oil refineries and candle makers stood out among the more specialized manufacturing enterprises. In 1855 the city's oil and sperm candle enterprises employed over 120 workers and the total manufactured value of oil and candle production was estimated at over $3.2 million. All together, eighteen oil and candle manufactories had a capital investment of nearly $1.4 million.[18]

Sperm oil and whale oil refining was a local "art" in New Bedford, dominated by a few firms, some of which stretched back to the 1830s.[19] Sperm oil was used primarily for oiling machinery and for lighthouse illumination through the 1860s. Whale and other heavy oils were similarly processed to generate a form of stearine used in soaps with the consistency of tallow. Whale oil was used as an illuminant, fish oil was used in mines, and soapy byproducts were used in citrus groves of California and Florida. Stearine had applications in textile and clothing manufacturing, as it was used in mills as sizing for yarns, mixed with soap, and exported for smearing sheep prior to shearing.[20] New Bedford's oil refining and manufacturing enterprises reflected problems encountered by the whaling industry. Whalefishery products dominated at the start of the 1850s, but at the end of the decade, the whaling industry's share of illuminants and lubricants had dropped by two-thirds, mostly because of competition from petroleum and other products. Over the next fifteen years, only the sustained demand for whalebone helped to extend the American whaling industry beyond the "near total collapse of the markets for oil," according to a recent analysis.[21]

By the mid-1850s, Samuel Leonard had emerged as the most prominent oil manufacturer in the city and the world, and his company's fortunes reflected the challenges faced within the industry. Originally a lumber merchant, Samuel Leonard maintained a counting office and works on Rotch's South Wharf and his whale oil refinery on Acushnet Street became the nation's largest producer in the 1850s.[22] The economic recession of 1857 hit hard, and by 1858 the company faced financial distress and was forced to reorganize the following year. The Leonard Company's short recovery ended in 1861 when the business failed and was taken over by Jonathan Bourne Jr. and Charles H. Leonard.[23] Other whale and oil manufacturing firms faced similar challenges during whaling's downturn in the late 1850s and into the war, and the industry continued to rely on primitive practices for several decades.

Outside of oil refining and candle manufacturing, rope making remained one of New Bedford's most successful whaling-related businesses. Whaling outfitters and crews preferred ropes from New Bedford not only for rigging ships but for securing harpoon lances to the whale boat. "No whaleman would ever use a tub line that was made anywhere outside of the New Bedford cordage works," local authors claimed with pride, for "whalemen knew the New Bedford company's rope could be trusted."[24] Established in 1842 by leading Quaker merchants Joseph Ricketson, William J. Rotch, and Benjamin S. Rotch, the New Bedford Cordage Company incorporated four years later with capitalization of $60,000, and then expanded again three years later with a value of $75,000 when Leander A. Plummer joined the board. These men were wealthy through astute business dealings and marriage. Benjamin Rotch had married a daughter of Abbott Lawrence and was a partner of Almy, Patterson, & Company in Boston. William J. Rotch, active in real estate and shipping, became New Bedford's mayor in the early 1850s when he was described as "making money and is good as anybody" with an estate taxed for over $161,000 in 1860. Enjoying an excellent reputation and dishing out steady dividends, the New Bedford Cordage Company endured for decades beyond the Civil War as a profitable enterprise even as the whaling industry continued to shrink.[25]

New Bedford's Antebellum Economy and Occupational Distribution

Three other industries profited from strong connections to whaling. In 1855, in whaling's boom-days, seven bakeries with 45 workers churned out breads and hardtack for lengthy voyages, together producing $182,662 in manufactured products. A dozen cask manufactures were in operation in 1855, and their 115 workers produced over $154,000 in barrels, staves, and casks, and related goods. Blacksmithing employed 74 men in at least a dozen firms that created over $121,000 worth of goods. Sail lofts employed over 100 men, and the New Bedford Cordage Company was credited with a workforce of 60. All together, manufacturing entities tied to whaling produced an estimated value of $3.7 million (and more than the twice the estimated value of capital invested in these concerns). In these manufacturing and industrialized pursuits, about 625 workers, all men, were employed, less than 10 percent of the number of whalemen at sea.[26]

In addition to the Wamsutta Mill's extensive operations, a number of smaller firms employed a handful of workers.[27] Many were artisans operating from shops out of their homes or near the waterfront. In terms of manufactured value, the three largest industries ranked by their estimated products were two brass foundries with 26 workers ($95,000); a dozen tin ware producers with 32 employees ($72,000); and 1 rivet manufacturer with 8 employees ($70,000). Together, all of these smaller, non-whaling-related manufactures employed 314 men and only 4 women, the latter listed as makers of snuff, tobacco, and cigars.[28]

City directories from the 1850s help to flesh out occupational patterns. In 1859 more than 500 laborers toiled in New Bedford (the single largest category of workers), followed by 342 mariners and smaller numbers of coopers, shipwrights, and master mariners. New Bedford's role as regional center of commerce and trade employed a large number of clerks (244), merchants (86), and bookkeepers (47). City directories certainly undercount less stable jobs and businesses. Together skilled, semiskilled, and unskilled laborers comprised more than half of all occupations, and maritime workers constituted 18.5 percent of all workers. The 1859 city directory also shows that of 174 firms, mercantile businesses predominated (85), followed by maritime and whaling firms (51), transportation and other manufacturing (17), construction (15), and professional firms (6).[29]

Early Industrialization: The Wamsutta Textile Mills

Despite whaling prosperity and profits through the 1850s, some local capitalists and commentators viewed manufacturing as an antidote to the city's

First known photograph of New Bedford: Union Street looking east, circa 1849. (Copy print from original daguerreotype by Morris Smith. Courtesy of the Trustees of the New Bedford Free Public Library.)

dependence on its far-flung industry. Nathaniel Parker Willis opined in 1851 that "some new industry must be grafted on the habits of the place . . . independent of the precarious yield from following the sea."[30] Although the city's first textile factory, the New Bedford Steam Mill Company, failed in 1852, several prominent capitalists incorporated the Wamsutta textile mill in 1848. This profitable business influenced the city's long-term transition to manufacturing despite the carping of conservatives. Some citizens continued to "look backward" by scorning factories as "they clung to the oily tradition of the city," wrote one local resident. Other objections came from those who feared corporations in place of partnerships, as when local lawyer Henry H. Crapo commented that "The public opinion of New Bedford was strongly against 'corporations' of any kind." Crapo explained also that the city's workingmen resented the prospect of regimented labor in factories and that merchants objected to importing overseers and operatives instead of using local labor. Some whaling merchants viewed cotton manufacturing as a "hazardous voyage" in comparison with whaling, and they may have turned up their noses at an expected rate of return of only 6 percent per year when whaling profits were immense.[31]

The chartering and founding of the Wamsutta Mills pointed to a new economic direction for New Bedford, one that would continue through and beyond the Civil War. Future Mayor Abraham H. Howland joined his brothers-in-law, Henry Wood and Joseph C. Delano, to obtain a state charter in 1846 for "a corporation by the name of the Wamsutta Mills for the purpose of manufacturing cotton, wool and iron in the town of New Bedford." Howland's plans found a willing ear and deep pockets in the person of congressman Joseph Grinnell, although the two men would later have a falling out. With an estimated worth of $150,000 in the mid-1840s, Joseph Grinnell was well-positioned to take business risks. Another prime mover was Thomas Bennett Jr., a native of Fairhaven of modest means who was exposed to the cotton business while living in Louisiana. Initially planning a factory in Georgia, Bennett sought investors starting with Grinnell who wondered why the mill could not be built in New Bedford. After others gave their approval, Grinnell and Bennett plunged forward to secure the charter of incorporation from Abraham Howland and began to raise funds for the Wamsutta Mills.[32]

New Bedford's foray into textile industrialization arrived later than in other New England communities (such as Lowell) because whaling had been dominant and profitable. Whaling profits poured into the planned factory came from many of the city's wealthiest individuals and families.[33] These adventurous investors did not speak for all of the city's wealthy residents, as some still preferred to avoid incorporated businesses and textile production. Even so, business diversification by whaling merchants demonstrated much foresight within the business community.[34] Because the site chosen for the mill was near the railroad depot on the city's northern outskirts, the company built its own housing for operatives along with a three-story cotton mill that alone cost nearly $40,000. Finished in the summer of 1848, the Wamsutta Mill Number 1 received its first bales of cotton in early fall.[35] By May 1849 over 107,000 yards of cloth were woven and superintendent Bennett proposed to raise $140,000 in more capital to expand equipment and production. With new capital, Bennett ordered other equipment to expand Mill Number 1 to over 12,660 spindles. The company declared its first dividend, of 5 percent, in January 1850, and in February stockholders expressed satisfaction with Bennett's management and opted to close subscriptions for new stock sales.[36]

Wamsutta's fine cotton cloth acquired a solid reputation and its use of slave-produced cotton appeared to engender few debates in the city's antislavery circles. Using high-quality cotton known as *benders* from the Mississippi River delta, Wamsutta produced profitable and unique textiles advertised as "fine cotton shirtings and sheetings." With annual dividends of around 5 percent per year, contented stockholders voted to nearly double the company's capital stock to $300,000. By January 1853, substantial profits prompted stockholders to build a second factory and stock sales doubled the company's capitalization to $600,000. After the Mill Number 2 was completed in the fall of 1854, Wamsutta operated some thirty thousand spindles and six hundred looms. Five years later, the Wamsutta Company expanded to become a million dollar corporation in 1860. That same year, a majority of stockholders showed awareness of the changing market for illuminants when they voted for gas instead of whale oil lighting inside the factory. When war erupted in 1861, the Mill Number 3 would stand unused for four years. For all the optimism, expansion, and steady production prior to 1861, Wamsutta's directors did not anticipate the lengthy slowdowns prompted by war.[37]

Ably managed by Thomas Bennett Jr., the Wamsutta Mills prospered in the 1850s. By 1851 Bennett had established a profitable relationship with Boston merchant John A. Burnham who worked with the firm of Greenleaf and Hubbard, commission merchants in New Orleans who specialized in the cotton trade.[38] The company's business success and reputation was reflected in glowing R. G. Dun credit reports of A1 rating beginning in 1854. Owned by "v[ery] substantial men mostly in New Bedford," the Wamsutta company made superior cloth, made money, and paid semiannual dividends around 6 percent.[39] In mid-December 1859, amid growing sectional mistrust between North and South,

Bennett reported that enough cotton was on hand to last through the first months of 1860.[40]

The company provided routes of upward mobility for those not born to wealth, such as Thomas Bennett Jr. and Andrew G. Peirce, and offered jobs and opportunities for a burgeoning population of Irish immigrants.[41] The Irish influx contributed to the city's 25 percent gain in population in just five years after 1850. A correspondent for the Boston *Pilot*, New England's most influential Roman Catholic newspaper, noted on October 8, 1860, that "several hundred operatives, mostly Irish girls are now employed in the mill, and they receive high wages."[42] By 1855 nearly 70 percent of the city's 2,900 foreign-born residents hailed from Ireland when the Irish immigrant community eclipsed the black population as the city's largest minority group. Nearly 2,000 Irish-born residents outnumbered New Bedford's population of native-born blacks of 1,657 at mid-decade. But because the Wamsutta Mills factory and housing were built on the northern outskirts of the city, the Irish immigrants tended to live further from the central businesses and wharves of New Bedford, and so, despite their numbers, Irish immigrants remained largely "invisible" in the city's political and cultural spheres into the early war years.[43]

New Bedford's turn to foreign-born operatives conforms to broader patterns found in New England's textile factories and urban areas in the 1840s and 1850s.[44] Still, New Bedford's immigrant influx paled compared with Lowell and Boston. Lowell's foreign-born population jumped to about 40 percent of the total population in 1855, while Boston's mostly Irish immigrant community totaled 60,000 out of a city population of 160,400, or about 37.5 percent of the total.[45] According to the 1860 census, Massachusetts ranked first of all states for its percentage of Irish population, with just over 15 percent claiming Irish birth, compared with about 5 percent nationally. In 1855 New Bedford was the seventh most populous city in Massachusetts, and its percentage of all foreign-born residents was about 15 percent, or 2,875 individuals in a city of 20,389 people.[46] At the time of the Wamsutta Mill's incorporation, the textile industry had largely transitioned from a labor force comprised of native-born females to one of mainly Irish-born immigrants, including men, women, and children.[47]

Networks of Capitalism

Wealthy merchants, many of them linked by birth or marriage ties, dominated the city's economic, political, and social spheres. The families, and their patriarchs, enjoyed whaling profits that were poured into other enterprises such as oil and candle manufacturing, textile manufacturing, and railroads. About a dozen families, many of them intermarried Quakers, controlled the whaling trade and its riches. Their names formed a "Who's Who" of New Bedford: Russells, Rotches, Rodmans, Howlands, Arnolds, Grinnells, Parkers, Bournes, and Hathaways.[48] New Bedford's whaling wealth astounded others. In proclaiming New Bedford as probably the "wealthiest place" in the United States, the *New York Times* reported in 1853 that thirty-eight estates were taxed for a value over $100,000.[49] In 1855 New Bedford's whaling agents had an assessed average wealth of $65,000 per person or firm, and agents who had twenty or more voyages before 1856 had an estimated worth of more than $112,000.[50]

The whaling elite established links marked by kinship, shared values, and ownership and management of other capitalist concerns. The networks among these business leaders were dense, as would be expected in a relatively small city with a high level of mercantile and financial activity. In 1859 New Bedford was home to at least five banks, five insurance companies, and nine incorporated firms. Of the ten men listed as officers of the Bedford Commercial Bank in 1859, five of them also served as trustees of the New Bedford Institution for Savings while six sat as directors of at least one of five insurance companies. William J. Rotch stood out among all of the city's capitalists in not only sitting on boards of one bank, one savings institution, and two insurance companies, but also being the president of the New Bedford Cordage Company and a director of both the Gosnold Mills and the New Bedford Gas-Light Company.[51] The business community was not monolithic, however, as networks or cliques of business leaders competed against each other. Four banks, all established before 1832, had an average of between nine and ten directors, and none of the nine directors of the Merchants' Bank sat on the board of the Bedford Commercial Bank, for example. Similar patterns and rivalries could be seen among directors of savings institutions, maritime insurance companies, and several incorporated companies.[52]

New Bedford's capitalists illustrated an emerging business class in the North who established banks to support their enterprises. As economic historian Peter Temin observes, mid–nineteenth-century banks were established "more like an investment club than a bank of today." In an era that preceded a national banking system, local banks generally followed an accepted practice of "insider lending" as bank loans were distributed to the institution's own officers and directors. This practice was neither illegal nor unethical; it was the primary way of doing business and raising capital in the United States at the time. This system worked adequately until the Civil War and the National Banking Act of 1864 brought federal oversight and greater regulation.[53]

As one example of a local bank's growth and support, the Bedford Commercial Bank was chartered in 1816 with capital of $100,000. George Howland became its first president, joined by other elites as directors: John Avery Parker, Cornelius Grinnell, Gideon Howland, Seth Russell Jr., James Arnold, Joseph Ricketson, Thomas Nye, and Samuel Rodman Jr. Similar patterns of growth were seen in other antebellum banks, such as the Mechanics' Bank, the Merchants' Bank, and the Marine Bank.[54] During the Civil War, the Bedford Commercial Bank was organized as the National Bank of Commerce on December 19, 1864, and a decade later it claimed a capitalized value of $1 million. Eager perhaps to encourage thrift among the city's less wealthy residents, New Bedford established one of the state's earliest savings banks, the New Bedford Institution for Savings, in 1825. Its founders claimed to have "no motives of self-interest, and no expectations of personal gain." Later, wealthy Quakers founded the New Bedford Five Cents Savings Bank that encouraged a minimum of five cents per deposit with the aim of appealing to a "different class in the community." The bank's first president, George Howland Jr., served for thirty-seven years while also sitting as a trustee on the board of the New Bedford Institution for Savings and wartime mayor of the city between 1862 and 1865.[55]

New Bedford Becomes a City

New Bedford's prosperity went hand-in-hand with population growth. In 1830, the town claimed just under 7,600 residents, a figure that climbed to 12,087 a decade later. Upon incorporation as a city in 1847, the municipal population was estimated at 16,000. Prior to the Civil War, the number of New Bedford residents rose to 22,300 in 1860, a high point until the state census of 1875 that counted 25,895 city residents.[56] An antiquated system of town governance could not keep pace with economic and demographic pressures, and in the 1840s citizens clamored for a city charter. At a special town meeting in January 1847, twenty prominent men were selected to create a charter for the city's incorporation that was later approved by referendum. Adopted on March 18, 1847, and implemented over the next few months, the charter specified a new city government divided into six wards, each with one alderman, four councilmen, one assessor, one overseer of the poor, and three School Committee members. The mayor, to be elected on a city-wide annual ballot, oversaw the city's major functions with the aid of ward-based aldermen, while the Common Council elected its own president.[57] Upon incorporation, citizens joined with the *New Bedford Mercury* in cheering: "Success to the city of New Bedford! May she ever be foremost in good works, ever be eminent as the friend of freedom, liberality, good will, education, and Christianity! To the latest generation may she be a burning and shining light!" That very year, residents saw their modern city fulfill those wishes: a novel magnetic telegraph was displayed, a publicly funded almshouse opened at Clark's Point, Hawes and Brothers began to produce daguerreotypes "of great merit and beauty" at their offices in Liberty Hall, and news from Europe traveled to New Bedford in a mere twenty-eight days. An estimated ten thousand people crowded into New Bedford for the city's first official Fourth of July celebration that concluded with a rousing fireworks demonstration. In the following year, one Abraham Lincoln spoke in defense of the Whig presidential candidate Zachary Taylor. His words are not known, but the *New Bedford Mercury* reported that Liberty Hall's "attentive audience" was delighted by Lincoln's "frequent flashes of genuine racy Western wit."[58] By all contemporary accounts, New Bedford was moving with optimism into a new era of prosperity and enlightened governance.

New Bedford's Enlightened Governance

New Bedford's nineteenth-century political community was dominated by white men with abolitionist sentiments. As noted by Kathryn Grover, during its first ten years as a city, New Bedford was "headed almost exclusively by abolitionists or men from abolitionist families." As an example of city leaders' liberal sympathies, particularly toward African Americans, city funds were used in the late 1850s to pay for the funeral of a fugitive slave, Daniel Drayton, and to defray the cost of Emancipation Day festivities slated every August first.[59] George Howland Jr., born in 1806 to Quaker wealth, represented the city's leaders in the antebellum and war years. Schooled at the Friends Academy, Howland started working in his father's office at the age of fourteen and persisted in whaling for sixty years. His public service began in 1840 when Howland was elected to the General Court, followed by election victories as mayor and on the Common Council, where he was selected its president in 1858, 1861, and 1862. He donated his mayoral salary during the Civil War to the New Bedford Free Public Library while continuing to amass wealth through shrewd business dealings. By March 1864, Howland was described as "very safe & rich," with over $100,000 in assets and expected inheritance of $50,000 from the estate of Sylvia Howland. By October 1866 Howland's whaling businesses had grown to a value of $250,000, mostly through whaling.[60]

New Bedford's wealthy residents, many of them Quakers, devoted care to the less fortunate, stamping the city with an enlightened air. Sundry organizations catered to the spiritual, literary, moral, and financial uplift of citizens from every class and background. A correspondent for *National Magazine* in

Abraham Howland, New Bedford's first mayor. Oil on canvas, circa 1847, William Allen Wall. (Gift of Mary Tucker Howland. Courtesy of the Trustees of the New Bedford Free Public Library.)

1845 reported that few communities could match New Bedford "where so liberal an outlay in every branch of public expenditure has uniformly been made.
No department has been neglected." Further, he wrote, "the public buildings,
the arrangements for the support and comfort of the poor and the sick, the
means of public education, the condition of the streets and highways, and the
state of the fire department, manifest unequivocal evidence of a liberal expenditure, and a careful and discreet supervision." New Bedford's citizenry supported generous public relief that stood as an "ornament" to their "enlightened
liberality."[61]

As a major port city home at any one time to hundreds of transient whalemen, New Bedford established private and public benevolent institutions that
reached out to the unchurched and provided a measure of social control. The
interdenominational New Bedford Port Society offered religious instruction
and services to sailors and operated a clothing store that sold items made by
wives, widows, and daughters of seamen. Founded in 1830, the Port Society
drew its leadership and funding from the city's wealthiest families. Members
and managers pledged to "protect the rights and interests of seamen and to
furnish them such moral, intellectual, and religious instruction as the Board of
Managers deem practicable."[62] In pursuing its agenda of enlightened governance and moral guidance, the Port Society hired capable chaplains, such as
the Reverend Enoch Mudge, who served from 1832 to 1844. Often presumed to
be Melville's inspiration for the character of Father Mapple in *Moby-Dick*,
Mudge was chaplain when the still unknown writer visited New Bedford and
the "Whaleman's Chapel" in late December 1840. An indefatigable, conscientious, and inspiring leader, Mudge raised money for the construction of a
chapel, the Seaman's Bethel, dedicated in May 1832, and later he actively promoted temperance while administering a growing enterprise. During his dozen
years of service, Mudge enjoyed positive, even enthusiastic relations with the
Board of Managers who viewed him as the "sailor's friend."[63]

The Port Society's major source of income starting in 1837 was a tonnage tax
paid by ship owners in New Bedford and neighboring Fairhaven, with additional income contributed by wealthy benefactors.[64] Elite women of New Bedford established a Ladies' Branch of the Port Society in 1833. In January 1851
Sarah Rotch Arnold donated her father's mansion to the society along with a
bequest of $10,000 upon her death in 1860. After the Arnold mansion was
moved to a new site of Johnny Cake Hill, the building became the Mariners'
Home and a focus of women's benevolent activities. In 1859 affluent women
directed the Ladies Branch, led by Mrs. James Arnold, president; Mrs. Thomas
A. Greene, secretary; and Miss Eliza Howland, treasurer. Some of these women

also participated in the Benevolent Society and the Dorcas Society that aimed to relieve the destitute and suffering in a "quiet and unobtrusive way."[65]

City officials also used municipal funds for public works. During the 1850s, New Bedford's officials promoted and built one of the nation's first free public libraries that, its trustees proclaimed, was "for the people." They averred that the library would be open to everyone, similar to public schools and public roadways. Trustees reported that the New Bedford Free Public Library had inspired other communities to build similar libraries, and it helped to "diffuse among all classes and conditions the inestimable treasures of knowledge, and the elevating influence of a healthy literature."[66] Another significant use of public funds was to build institutions and a municipal infrastructure to help the less fortunate. The city's Overseers of the Poor liberally disbursed public aid into the 1880s. The municipal welfare system was established upon New Bedford's incorporation as a city in 1847 and paralleled the city's structure of governance in which one overseer governed in each of the city's six wards. The city-funded Overseers of the Poor superseded an ineffective private effort, the New Bedford Benevolent Society, which had struggled since its founding in 1840.[67] This new welfare system found favor with civic leaders like Daniel Ricketson who expressed sympathy for the "worthy" poor, including Irish immigrants and fugitive slaves. Private and public relief functions continued to operate alongside each other, as several groups headed by women included the Orphan's Home, the Dorcas Society, and the Ladies' Benevolent Society.[68]

The city-sanctioned Overseers of the Poor granted wood for cooking and heating purposes, provided vouchers at local grocers, paid for new shoes, reimbursed doctors who made sick calls, covered the burial expenses of indigent people, and decided who would be sent to the State Almshouse. The ward-based system led to generous relief payments through the Civil War and into the 1880s, possibly because the individual overseer knew many in his ward community and may have been subjected to political pressures from poor constituents.[69] Debates about aiding the city's poor resonated through the antebellum era. In 1860 the Overseers commented that "It is difficult to distinguish between the really worthy and those who are only apparently so." They worried that "out of door aid" encouraged "the habits of the lazy and dissipated" in contrast to housing at the almshouse that at least extracted labor from able-bodied residents.[70] Yet, some Overseers held that poverty was often beyond anyone's control, particularly in the late 1850s when New Bedford was afflicted by the "continued depression in the business of the place." Unskilled workers were most affected, such as those engaged in "comparatively unimportant work, such as washing, house-cleaning, and small jobbing, or rather work requiring no especial skill, and may be done by the employers themselves." Among poor families headed by widows or common laborers, "such men and women appeared to be 'worthy' in that they were *willing* to work, if work were available," the Overseers reported. In characterizing these "worthy" poor, they drew explicit parallels between African-American and Irish poor by noting that "some are fugitives from the slavery of monarchies as well as republics." This public attention to "fugitives" suggests that the city's relief system upheld a long-standing tradition of benevolent paternalism practiced by New Bedford's leaders.[71]

Religious Life and Reform

The city's rich church life was noted in an 1845 account that reported that "the adherents of almost every shade of religious belief are to be found in New Bedford." Methodists claimed five separate churches, including one black congregation and another of "Reformed Methodists," and single churches could be found among the Baptists, Society of Friends, Episcopalians, Unitarians, Universalists, Roman Catholics, and Mormons. Two of the five Christian churches were "owned and occupied by societies of coloured persons." Other groups include the Millerites and the Come-outers, along with a small gathering of Friends known as Hicksites.[72] New Bedford's religious and church history in the antebellum era reflected schisms within congregations and the impact of population growth. On the eve of the Civil War in 1860, at least two dozen different churches were dispersed throughout New Bedford and created a wide swath of religious-based benevolence.[73]

Despite internal schisms and membership losses, the Society of Friends (Quakers) cast a long shadow over the city's religious, political, and business communities. In 1849 many of the estimated 445 Quakers in the city were among New Bedford's most prominent and wealthy citizens who shared an enlightened political bent. Following a separation in 1847, the Society of Friends had two meetings: one in a large brick meeting house on Spring Street between Sixth and Seventh Streets, the other occupied a meetinghouse on Fifth Street. Some disputes stretched back to conflict between "New Lights" and "Old Lights" in the 1820s, and, over time, the Friends lost many of their "more prosperous and reform-minded members," according to Kathryn Grover. In the decade after 1845, the number of Friends in New Bedford dropped from nearly 600 to 267. Still, wealthy and influential Quakers included George Howland Sr., George Howland Jr., Samuel Rodman Jr., and William C. Taber.[74] Writing in the late 1850s, Daniel Ricketson attributed to the Quakers the "industry and enterprise [and] the present prosperity of New Bedford."[75]

Public Order in New Bedford Through the 1850s

Besides encouraging moral rectitude, city officials began to modernize the police force following New Bedford's incorporation in 1847. Previously, a small police was supplemented by a night watch and a private force of influential citizens, the New Bedford Protecting Society, formed in the aftermath of the "Ark Riots" of the 1820s.[76] In the mid-1830s, following similar unrest, the Protecting Society urged boardinghouse owners to restrict liquor and impose curfews. New Bedford was similar to other nineteenth-century municipalities in moving slowly to a professionalized and well-trained force, most of which would develop after the Civil War. For a sizeable city with a large transient population of sailors and lodgers, antebellum New Bedford was not home to excessive violence or disorder despite some periodic flare-ups.

New Bedford was transformed by a growing class and geographic divide in the antebellum era as wealthier residents moved away from the waterfront and its troublesome areas. One account suggests that New Bedford became a "city divided with the conservative and wealthy members of the community looking down, literally and figuratively, on the festering trouble spots along the waterfront." A municipal survey in 1852 showed that there were seventy-eight "liquor shops" and fifty-six "houses of ill repute" in the city. Of these, thirty-seven liquor stores and twenty-one brothels were located in Ward 4, the city's commercial district and home to predominantly working-class families.[77] Because of an increase in population density, in that same year the City Marshal's Office was expanded to six officers and a night watch comprised of twenty men paid for part-time work. New police stations were constructed in 1857 and 1858 with operations centralized at City Hall on South Second Street. Generally, police officers and marshals dealt with drunkards and transient lodgers who had come in search of employment. In 1859, for example, city authorities provided food and lodging for 1,554 lodgers, 10 percent of them females.[78]

With a population of about sixteen thousand people, a number of them transient seafarers, New Bedford did have its share of disorder, some of it class or racially motivated. An African-American minister from Providence, Rhode Island, was attacked by "rowdies" in July 1852, and homes, barns, or businesses of black individuals were likely arson targets in 1855, 1856, 1858, and 1859. The most glaring case of probable arson arose in April 1860 when a fire destroyed an uninsured AME Bethel Church on Kempton Street; a fire two years later destroyed the church vestry.[79] The most significant threat to public order before the Civil War emerged in the Howland Street riot of 1856 when an "organized mob" of upstanding residents directed their rage at a neighborhood "infested with a dangerous class of citizens." Howland Street was known for its "moral pesthouses," the dance halls, saloons, gambling dens, and brothels that catered to seamen and lower-class people. The murder of a man named Rogers set off a wave of vigilante justice that the city's marshals could not contain.[80] Over three hundred individuals participated in an attack on April 19, 1856, that convened at City Hall Square. Rioters torched two houses and prevented the fire department from doing its work. Facing a crowd that had grown to three thousand, Mayor Howland called out Captain Timothy Ingraham and the city guards who stood "fully armed and equipped for serious work." Although several individuals were arrested, none were brought to trial in the last case of urban disorder before the Civil War.[81]

Besides the threats of social unrest, officials also contended with an omnipresent fear of fire in a city filled with countless casks of whale oil and other flammable materials. Major fires in the fall of 1854 destroyed Liberty Hall, host since 1838 to political meetings, entertainments, and lectures by the likes of William Lloyd Garrison, Wendell Phillips, Theodore Parker, Henry Ward Beecher, and Frederick Douglass. Called a "forum for the anti-slavery gospel" by the Reverend William J. Potter, Liberty Hall was quickly rebuilt on the same site.[82] Three years later, the largest fire in New Bedford's history swept through. Whipped by strong winds from the southeast, the fire started at William Wilcox's planing mill on Water Street during the early afternoon. At the wharves, the ship *John & Edward* was enveloped in flames and created "literally a sea of fire." Desperate measures followed: several ships were saved by pushing them into the harbor, and city officials blew up a building on the corner of Second and North Streets to obstruct the fire's path. At North Water and North Streets, a brigade of broom-wielding citizens brushed away burning cinders from fourteen thousand barrels of oil stored under seaweed, valued at $200,000. By nightfall, the fire was largely contained, although fire companies mopped up overnight amid occasional explosions of bomb-lances on partially destroyed ships. All together, fire losses were estimated at $254,575, with less than $7,000 covered in insurance. The city of New Bedford would soon purchase steam engine–powered fire equipment and take steps to professionalize its fire-fighting forces.[83]

Summary

As a well-known and prosperous city, New Bedford claimed a unique place in nineteenth-century America as the center of the global whaling enterprise. Following traditional and profitable practices, the whaling industry brought wealth into the city and provided employment for thousands at home and abroad. When signs of economic trouble surfaced in the late 1850s, however, many business and political leaders persisted in their heavy reliance on whaling. A few began to view textile manufacturing as an alternative path and invested in the Wamsutta Mills. With its robust and diverse religious organizations, antebellum New Bedford was characterized by a spirit of racial tolerance and generosity, much of it prompted by leading Quaker merchants. Sundry benevolent organizations illustrate efforts by the city's elites to help the less fortunate, particularly fugitives from slavery. No community better appreciated New Bedford as a home than its sizable population of African Americans, many of whom moved there with a realistic belief that they would find opportunities not found in other northern cities. Indeed, the size, visibility, and empowerment of New Bedford's black community served as ample proof of the city's enlightened governance. The next chapter closely examines the experiences of black residents of New Bedford, some of them fugitive slaves like Frederick Douglas who lived in the city from 1838 to 1841. During the Civil War, Douglass would visit New Bedford numerous times to join forces with whites and blacks in calling for black military enlistment and emancipatory war aims.

2

"The Nearest Approach to Freedom and Equality": African Americans in Antebellum New Bedford

The former fugitive slave Frederick Douglass recalled that his one-time home of New Bedford had offered the "nearest approach to freedom and equality that [he] had ever seen."[1] New Bedford's magnetic pull for southern-born blacks was illustrated by a dozen fugitive slave narratives, including Douglass's famous *Narrative*, associated with the city, as Kathryn Grover has noted.[2] African Americans enjoyed a relatively privileged position throughout the antebellum era as they created their own organizations, participated in political events of the day, and stepped into public roles tied to growing antislavery sentiment. Writing in the late 1850s, Daniel Ricketson observed that "the number of the colored population of New Bedford has always been large, and has increased proportionally with the growth of the place." Moreover, Ricketson contended that New Bedford's African Americans were "among our most respectable and worthy citizens, and in their general character, as a whole, remarkable for their morality, industry, and thrift."[3] Building upon their growing numbers, African Americans escalated their efforts in calling for an end to slavery and for full citizenship rights for all blacks. Working out of local antislavery groups and all-black churches, New Bedford's African Americans contributed significantly to regional and national debates over the issue of slavery.

Historians who have examined northern free blacks in the nineteenth century have tended to neglect New Bedford's black community in favor of larger cities. Kathryn Grover's superb work on antebellum New Bedford stands out. James and Lois Horton published their comprehensive account of *Black Bostonians* in 1979; more recently, they concluded that northern "African Americans were never isolated, they were never passive, and they were never a monolithic group."[4] Black citizens of New Bedford worked together with New England's African Americans and all "operated within a cultural and intellectual milieu shared with their oppressors," as Patrick Rael suggests. Rael concludes that black leaders, particularly members of the clergy, newspaper editors, and abolitionists, made fervent appeals to "cherished American values" in an effort to promote racial equality and an end to slavery.[5] In New Bedford, members of the black community joined their counterparts throughout the North in pushing toward increased militance in the 1850s as they confronted political, legal, and economic challenges. The heavy and continuing influx of southern-born blacks intensified New Bedford's antislavery environment, especially among its African-American residents.

Demographics and Economic Opportunities

Since 1840, the city's black population had grown at a faster rate than the white (see Table 2-1). The Whaling City's black population grew nearly 50 percent in the 1850s, and from 6.3 to 6.8 percent of the total population, as black migrants were drawn by the city's reputation, established institutions, family connections, and economy.[6] In both absolute and relative terms, the city's African-American population was larger than that found in nearly all northern cities, and New Bedford contained 9 percent of the state's native-born African Americans in 1850. The city's black community swelled from 1,008 in the 1850 federal census to 1,527 in the state census of 1855. Five years later, according to 1860 census figures, only one northern city, Philadelphia, contained a higher percentage of black residents than New Bedford, and no city in Massachusetts came close.[7] New Bedford's reputation as a haven for fugitive slaves contributed to this population surge, and Kathryn Grover suggests that more than 300 and as many as 700 fugitive slaves lived in New Bedford at different times between 1845 and 1863.[8]

Both the pace of growth and size of the black community were noteworthy. By the late 1850s, about one out of six people of color in Massachusetts (16.7 percent) lived in New Bedford where they were dispersed throughout the city's six wards. Heavier concentrations of blacks were found in Wards 3 and 4, the historic heart of the city, where about one-half of the city's African Americans lived.[9] Black-owned homes and businesses tended to be in the older, settled parts of the city, with sizeable pockets located along South Water Street. Most black-owned businesses congregated near Union Street in a five-block square area bordered by School Street on the south and Middle Street on the north. Small businesses, such as Polly Johnson's confectionery establishment, worked out of home, suggesting a distribution similar to that of other northern cities.[10] The size of the city's black community provided substantial support for a growing number of all-black churches that sustained a burgeoning antislavery movement.

The city's black population grew partly because of waterborne links and escape routes from slavery. New Bedford merchants had maintained ties to southern counterparts through the coasting trade and maritime commerce. In

Liberty Hall stood at the corner of William and Purchase Streets, circa 1868–70. (Stephen Adams, photographer. Courtesy of the Trustees of the New Bedford Free Public Library.)

the early 1800s, for example, the African-American shipowner and captain Paul Cuffe sailed a schooner that reached as far south as Norfolk, Virginia, and Savannah, Georgia. A white merchant, Joseph Rotch, traded sperm and whale oil with North Carolina merchants who sent in exchange, tobacco, pork, and naval stores. Norfolk, Virginia, was about a four- to five-day sailing voyage from New Bedford, and North Carolina's coastal towns were another day away. Maritime trade provided slaves and free blacks with skills, knowledge, and opportunities to leave the South, and New Bedford's African Americans were more likely to have southern origins than counterparts in other cities. Of three

Table 2-1. New Bedford Population, 1790–1920

Year	New Bedford Population	African-American Population	African-American % of Total
1790	3,313	38	1.14
1780	4,361	160	3.66
1810	5,651	190	3.36
1820	3,947	210	5.32
1830	7,592	383	5.04
1840	12,087	767	6.34
1850	16,443	1,047	6.36
1860	22,300	1,518	6.80
1870	21,320	1,460	6.84
1880	26,845	1,541	5.74
1890	40,733	1,699	4.17
1900	62,442	1,685	2.69
1910	96,562	2,855	2.98
1920	121,217	4,998	4.12

Source: Federal population censuses, 1790–1920.

thousand black men from New Bedford who sailed on foreign voyages between 1809 and 1865, at least 17 percent or five hundred of them claimed southern birth.[11] Nearly 30 percent of the city's blacks claimed a southern birthplace in 1850, and only Philadelphia among northern cities had a higher share of southern-born blacks. Some seventy-five black men and women who informed census enumerators in 1850 they did not know their birthplace probably sought to disguise their southern slave origins.[12]

New Bedford's economy provided employment opportunities through maritime trade that connected merchants with Atlantic coastal cities and whaling that linked the city with the world.[13] For black seamen, whaling vessels featured integrated environments where they could earn wages equal to white sailors of the same rank. Seafaring offered an adequate wage, room and board, employment for several months (or years) at a time, and a sense of camaraderie and egalitarianism that countered heavy racist proscriptions in the larger American society.[14] Although the vast majority signed on as common mariners or seamen, some African Americans worked as boat captains, stewards, steerers, and pilots. A common if romanticized sentiment was expressed by a reporter in 1860: "[It] matters little what may be a man's nationality, his color, his language, or religion, . . . the only questions to be asked are, has he the arm to pull an oar, the eye to aim a harpoon, the heart to face a wounded whale in his stormy wrath[?]"[15]

The racial dynamics of whaling changed as the enterprise expanded globally in the 1840s. New Bedford's whaling merchants turned increasingly to *crimps* to procure crews and outfit ships. The enlarged role of crimps (or "sharks" in the local vernacular) corresponded with a decrease in the number of native-born black men employed in the city's whaling industry. One contemporary observer, City Treasurer James B. Congdon, concluded that the percentage and number of black men on whaling ships had declined in the 1840s and 1850s. Looking back and writing in 1863, Congdon could remember when "every ship had more or less of the crew colored. . . . The proportion gradually diminished until in a majority of cases the cooks and stewards only were colored." Congdon's own father-in-law owned a vessel manned by twenty black men in a crew of thirty, and Congdon blamed "prejudice of the whites" for the decline of black seamen, presumably referring to the changes in labor recruitment fostered by crimps.[16] Through the hiring of crimps, owners sought relief from "onerous and tedious detail," but black American mariners found that crimps raised barriers to continued employment.[17]

As Congdon's comments suggest, fewer native-born African Americans were employed over time in the more skilled positions of boat captain, steerer, and pilot. Of the 3,189 identifiable black men who shipped on New Bedford's vessels between 1803 and 1860, the vast majority signed on as common mariners or seamen, and the number of black mariners shrank between the 1830s and the 1850s.[18] Kathryn Grover estimates that black mariners declined from 35.6 percent of all black workers in 1836 to 14.9 percent twenty years later, a drop that coincided with a huge growth in the black community. Crimps factored in this transition, and the whaling labor market paralleled skilled trades in which black men found reduced opportunities on land. In a census sample of 1860, black men were not employed as master mariners, boat builders, riggers, shipwrights, or spar makers. Only two black men worked as a rope maker or sailmaker, compared with twenty-four and thirty-four white men, respectively, in an 1860 census sample.[19]

Racism remained a prevalent force in the New Bedford labor market, not unlike other northern cities. For example, Frederick Douglass had been a caulker in Baltimore before escaping to New Bedford where, he explained, racial prejudice among white caulkers prevented him from plying his craft. Douglass was compelled to work a number of menial jobs at one-half a caulker's wages. In New Bedford as of 1860, caulking was a small pocket of opportunity as eight southern-born black caulkers comprised 3.7 percent of all black male workers, although they owned on average less than $36 in personal property and no real estate. In comparison, white caulkers on average possessed $225 of personal property and nearly $570 in real estate.[20] Black business leader Ezra R. Johnson confirmed in 1855 that black workers faced limited opportunities in skilled occupations. He wrote that apprenticeships were hard to come by, and "there is little or no disposition to encourage colored men in business." Johnson even suggested that a few black men who had acquired capital and experience in California's Gold Rush opted to go back to California rather than do nothing in New Bedford. In reporting that "our colored mechanics are principally from the south," Johnson indicated that these workers probably lacked the education, skills, and capital to compete with white workers in a competitive capitalistic economy.[21]

Fugitive slave George Teamoh may have captured best the limited economic opportunities for black men and women in New Bedford. Although pleased with his freedom, Teamoh claimed "I was doomed to share a hard lot in that wealthy city. Once there you were 'free indeed,' and then thrown upon your own resources after a few weeks of indulgence." He found it difficult to compete with other workers, and he refused to beg.[22] New Bedford's labor market for black workers paralleled patterns in other northern cities where opportunities were located typically on the bottom rungs of the economic ladder. In 1850, 85 percent of New Bedford's African Americans were employed in unskilled, semiskilled, and service jobs, a higher percentage than New York, Brooklyn, Providence, and Boston. On the positive side of the labor ledger, New Bedford's black artisans and skilled workers were 9.3 percent of the total black working population, a higher figure than any other northern city. Joining together artisans, entrepreneurs, and professionals between 1845 and 1855, New Bedford's people of color comprised 21 percent of those jobs, compared with 10.4 percent in New York, 16.1 percent in Boston, and 12.8 percent in Providence. The influence of whaling is shown by the presence of black men in oil and candle manufactories, for example, as five men of color worked at the works of George T. Baker and Son in 1856.[23]

One well-documented case of an important and skilled black artisan centers on blacksmith Lewis Temple, who died in the 1850s. Temple's career and life suggest some of the opportunities open to black workers in New Bedford prior to the Civil War. Born around 1800 in Richmond, Virginia, Temple made his way to New Bedford by the 1820s and worked along the wharves and gained smithing skills. By the mid-1830s, Temple had become an established citizen and operated a whalecraft shop on Coffin's Wharf. For the next decade, Temple plied his trade, paid his poll tax every year, and probably participated in abolitionist activities. Frederick Douglass was a nearby neighbor between 1837 and

1839, and the Douglass and Temple families attended the same church and probably socialized together. By 1845 Temple had built a blacksmith shop on the Walnut Street Wharf where, around 1848, he invented the "Temple Toggle Iron Headed Harpoon" that was quickly adopted by most whalemen. Whaling historian Clifford W. Ashley credits Temple with the "most important single invention in the whole history of whaling," the toggle-iron harpoon that replaced a standard whaling implement that had endured for centuries.[24] Eventually, the harpoon head would be known variously as "Temple's Toggle," "Temple's Gig," and "Temple's Toggle-Iron." Never patented, the name remains Temple's "sole royalty."[25]

Besides fulfilling whaling contracts, Temple forged tools for New Bedford's maintenance crews. Among surviving documents is a receipt from the ship *Arabellar* that paid Temple $57.88 for a variety of goods, including $2.75 for one head spade; $5 for five cutting spades; $3.75 for five lances; and $40 for "40 Togel irons at $1.00" each. The illiterate Temple signed the receipt with his mark. In July 1853, along with a thousand others from New Bedford, Lewis Temple signed a temperance petition to the city's mayor. The firm of Delano and Pierce began in January 1854 to construct a sizeable brick blacksmith shop near Steamboat Wharf at the foot of School Street. However, while walking home a few months earlier in 1853, Temple was injured on a city sidewalk and later successfully sued the city for $2,000 in damages. At the time of his death in May 1854, Temple had not yet collected on the award. Temple's estate had included two buildings plus the unfinished blacksmith shop, worth $700, and $300 of supplies. Once Temple's creditors were paid, nothing was left from his estate for his widow and son, Lewis Temple Jr. The family's simple gravestones indicate their poverty and the fact that Lewis Temple never cashed in on his significant invention that revolutionized the whaling industry.[26]

The picture of occupational opportunities for black men and women in New Bedford in the antebellum era is a mixed one. For example, African Americans were not present in significant numbers in the transportation trades, a pattern similar to Boston but not Philadelphia. Kathryn Grover suggests that the whaling sector's need for skilled labor opened a door for black workers: some skilled black mariners were welcomed, and white workers could leave unskilled jobs to others, including native-born African Americans. Still, closer comparisons between white and black workers in New Bedford suggest a racially segmented labor force. The most detailed analysis shows that in 1836, 71.2 percent of the black workers toiled in unskilled positions, compared with 17 percent of whites. Nearly 37 percent of whites were employed in skilled occupations, compared with less than 10 percent of people of color.[27] These patterns remained consistent at least until the Civil War as found in a sample of eleven thousand entries from Wards 2, 3, and 4 in the 1860 federal population census. As shown in Table 2-2, black men were underrepresented in the higher status and higher wealth categories and overrepresented in the category of semi- and unskilled workers. The most glaring discrepancy was among the white-collar ranks of clerks, dealers, and shopkeepers where only three blacks were to be found, less than 2 percent of all black workers in the sample.[28]

New Bedford did provide favorable opportunities for a few black individuals and families, especially of the professional class, based on 1860 federal census data. Black physician Ezra Johnson owned $30,000 in real estate and another $5,000 in personal estate. New Bedford's only black dentist, Thomas Bayne, claimed personal wealth of $1,000, and four black clergymen held a per capita worth of $400 in personal estate and $450 in real estate. Still, black men were excluded from clerk positions in whaling agents' offices, banks, insurance companies, and retail stores. In this sample of 190 black male workers in Wards 2, 3, and 4, only one man worked respectively as a butcher, baker, and grocer. The lone black butcher (a C. H. Williams) claimed $100 in personal wealth and no real estate; Richard H. Carter, a mulatto baker, owned $500 of real estate and no personal property; and grocer Solomon Peneton, a long-standing member of the African-American community, reported $2,500 in real estate and $800 in personal property in 1860.[29]

Other patterns suggest an exclusionary labor market. As seen in the 1860 census sample of Wards 2, 3, and 4, no black men were employed as blacksmiths, cabinetmakers, carriage makers, coopers, painters, printers, or tinplate workers. Barbering was the one trade dominated by African-American men,

Table 2-2. Black and White Men's Occupational Distribution , 1860

	Black Men		White Men	
Occupational Distribution 1860	*Number*	*Percent*	*Number*	*Percent*
Merchants and Professionals	7	3.7	215	7.8
Clerks, Dealers, and Shopkeepers	3	1.6	358	12.9
Skilled Workers	33	17.4	778	28.1
Semi- and Unskilled Workers	105	55.3	566	20.4
Maritime Occupations	41	21.6	703	25.4
Farmer/Farmhand	1	0.5	28	1.0
Miscellaneous	0		124	4.5
Total	190		2772	

Source: 1860 Census Sample (Wards 2, 3, 4).

similar to other cities, and black barbers constituted almost 10 percent of working black men in this sample. The most successful black tradesmen were shoemakers Henry Freeman, Alfred Swan, and Thomas Crouch, who together
owned a total $5,500 in real property. Altogether, 33 black tradesmen were
greatly outnumbered by 778 whites. According to the census sample of Wards
2, 3, and 4, 4 out of 10 black men in New Bedford were unskilled laborers,
compared with one in ten white men. Just as Ezra Johnson had suggested that
apprenticeships were closed to blacks, only one black male was employed as
an apprentice, to a blacksmith, while forty-two white men were apprenticed to
masons (8), carpenters (7), blacksmiths (4), painters (5), coopers (3), and thirteen other occupations.[30]

Census data also reveals disparities between African-American and white
women in New Bedford. First, black women worked for wages more than did
white women. In this sample, women comprised nearly one-third (31.2 percent)
of all black workers, while white women were about one-fifth (20.1 percent)
of all white workers. (Note that this sample excludes Wards 1, 5, or 6, where more
workingwomen would be found, particularly in Ward 1, home to the Wamsutta
Mills.) Second, black women were disproportionately employed in domestic
service. Of eighty-six working black women, sixty-six (nearly 77 percent) were
domestics, washwomen, or worked out. Occupations that employed some
skilled black women included dress making, millinery, and seamstresses (14
total, or 16.2 percent of working women), along with nurse (1), cook (2), waiter
(2), and hair dresser (1). No black women were employed as teachers, clerks,
saleswomen, or as operatives. Although black men faced economic challenges
and hardships, black women occupied the bottom rung of the occupational
ladder and claimed far fewer resources than did men. Similar to patterns in
other northern cities before the Civil War, black men and women were
employed in low-wage occupations that constrained their opportunities for
property ownership and occupational mobility.[31]

From an economic perspective, New Bedford offered black men and women
only marginal opportunities for employment compared with other northern
urban areas before the Civil War. In his survey of fifteen antebellum cities, Leonard Curry affirmed that free blacks were "able to grasp but the shadow of the
[American] dream." African Americans toiled in poorly paying jobs, lived in
substandard housing, lodged in almshouses, and encountered high rates of vice
and crime.[32] Other scholars point to similar patterns. Kenneth Kusmer suggests
in his study of Cleveland that, by 1870, the formative process of the "ghetto"
had begun, and David Katzman depicts nineteenth-century black residents of
Detroit facing diminished opportunities compared with recently arrived white
immigrants who obtained better jobs and newer housing.[33] The Philadelphia

Social History Project (PSHP), led by Theodore Hershberg, examined the city's "opportunity structure" of the nineteenth century to find that African Americans historically were denied equal access to jobs, housing, transportation, and public and private services.[34] Studies of African-American social mobility before 1880 in Poughkeepsie, New York, and Boston, Massachusetts, suggest a similar and dismal pattern.[35] When viewed as a labor market, New Bedford was not appreciably better than other northern cities for black workers, despite its reputation as a haven for fugitive slaves.

Church Life: Community and Autonomy

New Bedford's African Americans could choose among several churches for their religious life, including the Society of Friends. All-black churches built upon the Whaling City's robust religious life and illustrated the black community's growth, autonomy, and desire for self-expression. Prior to the Civil War, African Americans established five all-black congregations in total: the African Christian Church (1826); the Bethel African Methodist Episcopal Church (1842); the Second Baptist Church (1844); the Zion Methodist Episcopal Zion Church (1850); and the Salem Baptist Church (1858). Local churches, aligned with regional and national efforts by black Americans to create their own religious bodies, offered friendship, financial assistance, spiritual sustenance, and opportunities for social and political empowerment. Congregants built and sustained their own churches often at great financial sacrifice. Unlike political parties controlled by white elites or other public associations that may have relegated blacks to the back rows or secondary positions, black churches offered opportunities for leadership and stood as the preeminent expressions of community life.

The founding of black churches and denominations throughout the North was prompted in part by the failure of major Christian denominations to denounce slavery and their continued embrace of racist practices and beliefs. Frederick Douglass experienced first-hand such racism when he attended a revival meeting in New Bedford's First Baptist Church in 1838. Upon entering the church, a deacon informed Douglass that "we don't allow niggers in here." Rebuffed, Douglass then attended the integrated Elm Street Methodist Church where "about a half dozen colored members" sat in segregated pews distant from the church altar. Douglass related how the sacrament was first served to white congregants by "Brother Bonney—pious Brother Bonney." Douglass described black church members waiting for their turn "like sheep without a shepherd," and he later lambasted these "poor, slavish souls." Eventually, after attending other churches with similar experiences, Douglass found his spiritual home in a Zion Methodist congregation where he first spoke publicly about his life in slavery.[36]

In New Bedford and throughout the North, black churches served as a nucleus for the community. Black churches offered an outlet for those with leadership aspirations, provided a worldview for combating racist oppression, and crafted a theology that inspired hope for a better afterlife. Most major black leaders of the nineteenth century (apart from Frederick Douglass) made their names and careers from the pulpit. Generally, African-American religious leaders remained conservative in their approach to religion, emphasizing a theology that incorporated nonviolence and patience. Most mainstream African-American ministers viewed their mission to inculcate the values of self-help and Christian forbearance. Historian James B. Stewart has argued that some free black churches remained conservative in their antislavery stance because they did not want to jeopardize their own standing within their communities or they relied upon white patronage for financial and other support.[37]

The issue of slavery remained at the forefront of American politics through the 1850s, and many black church leaders and congregations became more militant through the antebellum period. They recoiled at the indifference of mainstream (white) denominations to the horrors of bondage. Frederick Douglass again provides an instructive example as he moved into the antislavery crusade following his "happiest days" spent serving his church at the schoolhouse on Second Street. After filling several positions as sexton, steward, class leader, clerk, and local preacher, Douglass was urged in late 1840 by the Reverends William Serrington and Thomas James to pursue a ministerial calling. Abetted by his recent exposure to the William Lloyd Garrison's antislavery newspaper, *The Liberator*, Douglas spoke publicly with first-hand knowledge about the horrors of slavery. William C. Coffin heard Douglass preach in the spring of 1841 and invited him to speak to a larger audience at the annual meeting of the Massachusetts Anti-Slavery Society in Nantucket. Douglass would soon become the nation's best known black activist and fugitive slave, highlighted by the publication of his *Narrative* in 1845.[38]

The history of New Bedford's black churches through the Civil War years reflected both self-determination and discord. Congregations formed and split over a variety of differences, some theological, others financial and personal. When the African Christian Church was founded in 1826, elders William Quint and Charles Cook wanted to establish "the best manner of improving the condition and promoting the spiritual interests of their colored brethren in this town." When they dedicated a house of worship on Middle Street in June 1830, they expected their black adherents to worship "according to the dictates of their own consciences." Organized as a nonhierarchical congregation in which ministers and members stood as equals, the church extended its goodwill through a conscious emphasis on "brotherly love" and nonviolence.[39] A decade later, this body was reorganized as the Third Christian Church, its pulpit filled by Elder Hervey Sullings, followed by another rupture in 1844 when at least eighteen parishioners departed to form the Second Baptist Church.[40]

This new Baptist Church was founded with the approval, if not some financial support, of white leaders in New Bedford. Pastors and delegates from white Baptist churches in the region convened in New Bedford in January 1845 to dedicate this church headed by Thomas T. Allen and Edmund Kelly. William Piper, the first deacon of the Second Baptist Church, had been employed by the Quaker leader William R. Rodman, and he, like his employer, was known for his "honorable name" and for his "integrity and great fidelity." The Second Baptist Church grew to 130 members within ten years of its founding.[41] As with black churches typically throughout the North, segregated fellowship came at a cost and black Baptists shared privations not known to white members of that faith. By 1857, the (white) First Baptist Church claimed 267 members, while the (black) Second Baptist Church claimed 168. The white church outnumbered the black in students, teachers, and library volumes. Following a small revival in 1857 that landed fifteen new baptisms, the Second Baptist Church pleaded for help from sister churches to build a new house of worship. The cost of religious autonomy was seen in collection figures; in one year the white First Baptist Church's collections totaled over $2,000 while the black Second Baptist Church took in only $69.04, a figure that underscored the relative poverty of black church members.[42]

More trouble lay ahead in the late 1850s when internal disputes led to another offshoot, the Salem Baptist Church, organized on December 7, 1858. Led by the Reverend William Jackson, ninety-five parishioners told the Second Baptist Church "that they could not live together in peace and harmony" and demanded separation and an equitable division of church funds. The splinter congregation was recognized by an ecclesiastical council that met in New Bedford's First Baptist Church. At least two members of the new church, William Bush and Peter Nelson, had been deacons in the Second Baptist Church. Pastor William Jackson demonstrated tenacity that would serve him well later as the official Chaplain of the Fifty-Fifth Massachusetts Colored Regiment.[43] Four black men (James Collins, John Sullings, James Luscomb, and Isaac Bly) assumed legal and financial responsibilities for building the new church on North Sixth Street at a cost of $4,500. Despite irregular payments occasioned by the intervening Civil War, these men rendered the church debt-free by 1868.[44]

New Bedford's black Baptist ministers and churches built regional and national influence into the Civil War years, particularly in the area of missionary efforts in Africa. Local men and women supported the American Baptist Missionary Convention (ABMC) first formed in 1840 to promote Christian outreach in Sierra Leone. The national ABC convention met in New Bedford in 1847 and in 1853 at the Second Baptist Church, and in 1861 at the Salem Baptist Church. The Reverends William Jackson and Edmund Kelly of New Bedford remained prominent in this national cause. Jackson led the Second Baptist Church when it was admitted to the ABMC in 1845, the ninth church to affiliate with leading black churches from New York City and Philadelphia. Female members of Second Baptist Church organized one of twelve women's auxiliaries, known as the Daughters of Convention. These women's efforts paralleled those of groups found in the larger cities of Philadelphia, New York, Washington, DC, Baltimore, and Boston. After Jackson established the Salem Baptist Church, his new church joined the ABMC in 1859 and persisted with missionary efforts.[45]

For northern African Americans, new religious denominations emerged by the 1840s as alternatives to the Baptist faith. New Bedford's Bethel African Methodist Episcopal (AME) church, established in 1842, hosted the First Annual Conference of the New England AME Conference eight years later. A dozen men and women, "many of the most respectable" of the city's black population, raised nearly $2,000 to fund a new building. By the early 1850s church members had made plans to enlarge a worship house that already seated over four hundred people.[46] In June 1852 the Bethel church again hosted the annual meeting of the New England AME Conference and welcomed Bishop Daniel Payne, a towering figure in the African-American religious establishment. Payne sermonized about the themes of moral and educational uplift, the quest for equal treatment of black Americans, and the virtue of leading Christian lives. Sounding like a latter-day John Winthrop, Payne reminded his listeners that "the eyes of New England are upon you, . . . the eyes of angels are upon you, . . . the eyes of God himself are upon you . . ."[47]

New Bedford's Bethel AME Church became the preeminent AME congregation in New England. Of all New England AME churches, the Bethel AME Church paid their preachers the highest salaries and usually donated the largest sums for the Bishop's salary, ministers' salaries and expenses, and charitable causes. The Bethel Church consistently ranked first in membership among sister churches through the duration of the Civil War, peaking at 246 members in 1859. Significantly, as they grew in number, Bethel's voices and views became more militant in criticizing slavery. In early June 1860, for example, delegates to the New England AME Conference refused any "connection or sympathy with slaveholders, their apologist churches, ministers, or members, whether they be white or black."[48]

Despite evidence of success, Bethel's black Methodists faced hardships that were not uncommon for northern African Americans, even in a tolerant environment like New Bedford. They faced arson, meager finances, and competition with other black churches. The Bethel house of worship burned in 1854, apparently at the hands of an arsonist. Although church members began to rebuild in 1855 when the Reverend Joseph R. Turner laid a cornerstone, seven years elapsed into the Civil War with no further progress. A diffusion of authority within the congregation and pressing economic difficulties of the late 1850s undermined fund-raising efforts. Eventually, the Reverend Henry J. Johnson, long a pillar of the church and New Bedford's African-American community, created the One Object Society whose goal was to construct a church building. Aided by generous public contributions to fund construction costs of $4,500, the Bethel AME Church's new place of worship seated 450 persons when it was dedicated after the Civil War on June 10, 1866.[49]

New Bedford's religious vitality was illustrated yet again when black congregants organized an African Methodist Episcopal Zion (AMEZ) Church in March 1850. The AME and AMEZ denominations held similar but not identical beliefs. The AMEZ Church opposed life-long appointments for their bishop, preferring a more democratic mode of four-year terms elected by active church members. Similarly, on the local level, elders were chosen for four-year terms. Growing too large for Joseph Harrison's house, the small AMEZ group moved to a schoolhouse on the corner of Seventh Street and Mechanics Lane. In the summer of 1851 they moved into a new church, built at a cost of $2,000 and described as a "plain, neat structure situated in close proximity to the residences of the majority who worship there, and will seat nearly five hundred."[50] Leadership opportunities opened for men and women who successfully incorporated their church in January 1859, a body sustained through 1924 when parishioners honored Frederick Douglass by renaming their church the Douglass African Methodist Episcopal Zion Church.[51] New Bedford's support for two substantial African-American Methodist churches illustrates the religious fervor and organizational talents within the black community.

Antislavery Agitation

As New Bedford's black churches and church memberships multiplied, they contributed to the escalating antislavery crusade. New Bedford was home to a

robust antislavery movement, with support from both a growing black population and from sympathetic white leaders able to exercise political power and
influence. As with Boston's antislavery movement, New Bedford's African-
American abolitionists acted autonomously to form the city's first antislavery
group and then inspired whites to follow suit. In October 1833 William P.
Powell established the New Bedford Union Society along with the Reverend
Jacob Perry of the African Christian Church, Lewis Temple, John C. Briggs,
and Richard Johnson and his sons Richard C. Johnson and Ezra Johnson. New
Bedford's black activists initially followed the lead of Boston's Massachusetts
General Colored Association by remaining separate from white antislavery
activists. Still, within a year, in July 1834, New Bedford's white antislavery lead-
ers, under the guidance of President William Rotch Jr. founded their own Anti-
Slavery Society of New Bedford.[52]

As the antislavery movement grew in the 1830s, a backlash emerged when a
group of merchants and attorneys organized an antiabolitionist movement.
Blacks responded with renewed self-determination in quest for equal rights.
Black leader Ezra R. Johnson directed a petition in 1837 to Massachusetts's legis-
lators signed by over one hundred African-American women, the majority
from New Bedford. They opposed any policies that hampered the rights of fugitives and free blacks, such as the Negro Seamen's Acts passed in South Carolina.[53] The intensity of antislavery zeal could be seen in the treatment accorded
Nathan Johnson, Frederick Douglass's benefactor when the latter first arrived
in New Bedford. Johnson was accused of slave kidnapping in 1839, prompting
several of the town's white leaders to intervene. A special committee of The
Young Men's Anti-Slavery Society exonerated Johnson by finding him innocent
of all "charges," as reported in local and regional newspapers and front-page
coverage in the *Liberator* in March 1840.[54]

Antislavery meetings were integrated as early as the 1830s, and many of the
city's leading residents supported fugitive slaves and called for an end to slavery.
An increasingly militant stance was upheld in both public and private endeavors. "Liberty Hall," dedicated in 1838, stood as the most potent symbol of the
city's antislavery ardor and provided an integrated public space for preaching
the "anti-slavery gospel."[55] While speaking in New Bedford in 1842, Frederick
Douglass reported that "New Bedford has never been so favorable [*sic*] aroused
to her anti-slavery responsibility as at present." Douglass described his and
Charles Remond's efforts on behalf of George Latimore, a fugitive slave, as they
spoke "almost day and night" in both public and private meetings. At three
Sunday meetings in New Bedford's City Hall, Douglass stated proudly that he
saw no "prejudice against color." "There were neither men's side nor women's
side; white pew, nor black pew; but all seats were free and all sides free."[56]

New Bedford's reputation as a sanctuary for fugitive slaves gained greater currency after passage of the Fugitive Slave Law of 1850. Prominent merchant Charles W. Morgan predicted in his diary in early October that should there be an attempt to extricate fugitive slaves, "bloodshed will ensue for they are a powerful body and determined to be free or die, and I hope they will carry it out."[57] Daniel Ricketson likewise condemned the "odious" law and added that "it is thought that the rendition of a fugitive from our city could not be effected."[58] White and black residents continued to welcome fugitive slaves into New Bedford. Estimating the city's fugitive slave population at seven hundred, a "wealthy Friend (Quaker) of New Bedford" wrote to a Boston correspondent about their safety. Not only would these "good citizens" find protection in New Bedford, but "here we intend they shall stay." Local women protested by gathering 1,729 signatures on a petition demanding the Fugitive Slave Act's repeal. Rodney French forwarded the petition to Horace Mann, claiming that it bore names of the city's "most respectable ladies." He added, "Very few indeed, who were called upon, declined signing it." An estimated nine hundred blacks gathered to talk and pray after the city faced a false alarm of slave catchers in the city, and afterwards, Mayor Abraham H. Howland convened a public meeting to discuss opposition to the Fugitive Slave Act.[59]

Protests escalated in Massachusetts after fugitive Anthony Burns was remanded into slavery from Boston in 1854. At least one New Bedford church tolled its bells and black residents publicly promised to practice "the art of using firearms" for self-defense. By October 1855 New Bedford's people of color pledged "to hold themselves in readiness at all times for the protection of the civil rights of the community." As of that date, no fugitive slave had been apprehended in New Bedford. The Reverend William Jackson took up collections in his church to assist refugees and by March 1856 he had established the Vigilant Aid Society. This group soon criticized another black church, the African Methodist Episcopal Church on Kempton Street, for refusing to help "even their own mothers, fathers, sisters, brothers, uncles, and aunts." Apparently, the AME's clerk had refused to hold a public meeting within the church. In this bitter conflict, the AME congregation was criticized as "anti-Christian, a blind guide, a synagogue of Satan, a cage of unclean birds."[60] This turf battle within the black community illustrated the intense passions roused by the antislavery movement.

New Bedford's public antislavery events solidified ties among most white and black leaders. When Frederick Douglass returned to the city in 1856 for an Emancipation Day celebration, Samuel Rodman observed that the platform of black speakers addressed a "gratified audience of about a thousand people, a majority of whom were white and more than half women."[61] Following the

Dred Scott decision of 1857, Daniel Ricketson commented that there was "hardly a house in the place which had not given shelter and succor to a fugitive slave." In addition Ricketson claimed that "there is but little prejudice against color, and a general willingness and desire that the colored population may enjoy equal rights and privileges with themselves." Ricketson described New Bedford's African Americans as "among our most respectable and worthy citizens," and pointed to the city's integrated public schools and to the heritage of Paul Cuffe as evidence of his community's racial egalitarianism.[62] The common interests of antislavery whites and blacks would find common expression again during the Civil War in the cause of black military enlistment.

Growing Militancy

New Bedford's black leaders and community members began to demonstrate increased militancy in the 1850s. A turning point came in 1854 when, prompted by the Anthony Burns case in Boston, New Bedford's black community declared that a forcible response to slave catchers was justifiable. African Americans agreed to practice the defensive "art of using firearms." A few weeks later, blacks announced plans to create the Union Cadets and "to hold themselves in readiness at all times for the protection of the civil rights of the community," a surge of militance that extended into the Civil War.[63] When the city's "colored military company" was renamed the "New Bedford Independent Blues" by October 1855, Massachusetts's state laws prohibited the admission of black men into the all-white state militias. Ironically, the state's attorney general was New Bedford lawyer John Henry Clifford, who refused to allow a Boston black military company to borrow state arms and equipment.

The particular contribution of New Bedford's black militias, detailed by historian J. R. Kerr-Ritchie, was to uphold their collective defense and vigilance against the apprehension of fugitive slaves. Offering more than public displays of pomp in parades and Emancipation Day celebrations, black militias became vital components of transnational assaults against slavery with their militant and militaristic assertions of natural rights. By bearing arms and marching in public, black militias defended their community and projected militancy into the public arena. New Bedford African Americans' prewar militarism upholds Kerr-Ritchie's assertions that such black militias served as a "rehearsal" for the Civil War in which black men were eventually accorded the rights to bear arms as citizen-soldiers.[64]

New Bedford's black residents continued to enjoy support from many leading white citizens. For example, City Hall was opened in 1858 for the Convention of the Colored Citizens of Massachusetts that convened on August 1, the

Rodney French, one-time mayor and antislavery leader, circa 1861. (Courtesy of the Trustees of the New Bedford Free Public Library.)

traditional Emancipation Day celebration held locally since at least 1844.[65] New Bedford's 1858 gathering was an offshoot of a National Negro Convention Movement that began in the 1830 and organized statewide in Massachusetts in 1854.[66] New Bedford's 1858 convention escalated the protests for equal rights and against slavery, led by local leaders such as barber Bela C. Perry, who joined Session President William Wells Brown. Brown proclaimed "to the world that we have rights, not granted by the American Government, but by the Creator;

they cannot be taken from us by any Congress or Legislature." Militant rhetoric accompanied peaceful public militia displays and parades. Twenty black militians of the New Bedford Blues marched and saluted the Boston Liberty Guards, numbering some twenty-five muskets. A separate procession of "colored seamen" made their way to Dunbar's Grove on the south end of the city for a clambake accompanied by the all-black Rhode Island Brass Band of Providence.[67]

Speeches during the convention contained strident calls for full equality. For example, Charles L. Remond offered a "defiant position towards every living man that stood against them," listing state legislatures, courts, and Judge Roger B. Taney as chief among their enemies. Remond wanted "black men stand up for and by themselves." Robert Morris of Boston brought the audience to its feet with his pledge to aid fugitive slaves: "If any man comes here to New Bedford and they try to take him away, you telegraph us in Boston, and we'll come down 300 strong, and stay with you; and we won't go until he's safe."[68] Other participants drew on historical and legal precedents for the citizenship rights of all African Americans, symbolized by Crispus Attucks as the "first martyr" of the American Revolution. As historian Mitch Kachun has explained, by the late 1850s Crispus Attucks emerged among African Americans as a heroic figure, a "black Founder" whose memory was invoked in making claims to American citizenship.[69] Denouncing the Dred Scott decision and the Fugitive Slave Bill as "greatest wrong and the most high-handed injustice ever inflicted upon any class of people," convention participants vowed their opposition at "whatever cost."[70]

Like most antislavery events in New Bedford, this August 1, 1858, gathering opened its doors and platform to white and black alike. An afternoon session featured several white Quakers: William Penn Howland and Mr. and Mrs. Matthew Howland of New Bedford, and Mrs. Mary Nichols of England. Mrs. Howland made a "marked impression" on the audience by speaking in a "spirit of Christian love." Later, lively debates surfaced between black abolitionists Josiah Henson, who resided in Canada, and Charles Remond from Boston who contended that he would remain in the United States to fight for freedom rather than move elsewhere. Robert Morris urged conventioneers to vote and to take advantage of integrated schools. "Let the children, black and white, be educated together, and prejudice is conquered," Morris stated. At a wrap-up session on Tuesday, August 2, members urged that other residents and state officials oppose enforcement of the Fugitive Slave Act.[71]

Two years' later, New Bedford's blacks hosted a similar convention. Moved probably by the death of John Brown six months earlier, the 1860 organizing

committee refused to endorse a typical "parade, pic-nic, and oration." Reflecting internal dissension among black community members, two sets of events
took place, a procession and picnic on August 1 and a separate convention (of
which no records have been reported or located). Black lawyer William Henry
Johnson spoke publicly about Crispus Attucks and other black men who had
served their country, his words no doubt supporting the New Bedford Attucks
Frontiers, a militia company founded in June 1860. William H. W. Gray, later
a sergeant in the Fifty-Fourth Massachusetts Infantry, served as the parade's
Chief Marshal. This integrated public event was denigrated by a *Boston Pilot*
correspondent who described New Bedford as the "very Sebastopol of Niggerdom" in decrying the elevated status of blacks in the city. Later that year, following John Brown's execution in Virginia, black residents thanked some of
the city's churches for tolling their bells and Ezra Johnson described Brown as
a proponent of "practical" abolitionism.[72]

On the eve of the Civil War, African Americans in New Bedford had demonstrated their antislavery sentiments and organized militias to defend their community. Following Abraham Lincoln's inauguration in early March 1861,
outspoken antislavery activist Wendell Phillips spoke a month later at New Bedford's Lyceum and again stirred controversy.[73] No stranger to the city or to
public debates, the staunch antislavery activist argued against any concessions
to the South. Opposing all compromises, Phillips believed that New England
could claim the right of secession and he found receptive listeners in New Bedford who favored an aggressive posture against the South, secession, and slavery.[74] In a private letter to antislavery comrade Deborah Weston, Joseph
Ricketson claimed that "nine tenths" of all those who heard Phillips in New
Bedford agreed with his views. "How gratifying it must be to him to know that
the great truths he utters are beginning to be so well appreciated," Ricketson
added.[75]

Summary

Through the 1850s, New Bedford's social fabric was transformed into one of
greater diversity and decidedly rougher cloth. Irish Catholic immigrants had
begun to make their presence felt after 1845, and they competed with native-
born blacks for jobs, opportunities, and acceptance by the larger society. For
their own part, blacks built and sustained their own churches, families, and
sense of community. African Americans were prominent, politically potent,
and "protected" by strong antislavery sentiment and equalitarian beliefs of
leading white citizens. In their annual celebrations of August 1, black residents

of New Bedford not only opposed slavery but held out for full political, social, and economic equality and joined hands with counterparts across the nation. The throngs of people who gathered annually to celebrate Emancipation Day in New Bedford during the 1850s comprised some of the largest peaceful meetings in the antebellum United States. In 1853 they applauded William J. Watkins who declared, "we intend to agitate, agitate, agitate." New Bedford's black community supported several independent militias to uphold their claims to "manhood, independence, and self-defense," as J. R. Kerr-Ritchie has written. By demonstrating connections between bearing arms and citizenship rights, black militias brought together the black community and aroused local support for the enlistment of black soldiers once war came. The next chapter examines the start of the Civil War and mobilization on the home front in which whites and blacks quickly prepared for war. Despite earnest offers from New Bedford's African Americans, however, the war would begin with only white soldiers allowed to fight for their country.

3

"Suppression of an Unholy Rebellion": Wartime Mobilization on the Home Front

During the secession winter of 1860–61, many of New Bedford's residents supported the victorious Republican Party while expressing anxiety about the prospects of war. When new Massachusetts Governor John Andrew offered his inaugural address on January 5, 1861, he advocated military preparations because fewer than 6,000 men stood on active volunteer duty out of 155,000 enrolled in the state's militia. Privately, Andrew sent dispatches to each of the New England governors warning them of his worries about war.[1] In New Bedford, Matthew Howland privately wrote about the "great excitement" over Southern secession and complained that his city faced "great stagnation in trade & business of all kinds." Howland wrote of "gloom and uncertainty" after the Confederate States of America organized by early February 1861.[2] Local attorney and former Governor John H. Clifford worked behind the scenes after learning of rumored plans by Confederate sympathizers to take over the nation's capital before Lincoln's election on March 4. Clifford had visited with Edwin Stanton in Washington, DC, and upon his return to Massachusetts he quietly informed Governor Andrew who then called the Massachusetts legislature into a secret session to request $100,000 for the state's defense. Stanton later wrote to Clifford, after the capital was adequately defended, that "affairs in this city wear, just now, a better aspect than when you were here."[3]

The Civil War began officially after President Lincoln sought to resupply the federal Fort Sumter in Charleston's harbor on April 12, 1861. South Carolinians fired the first shots and were viewed by Northerners as the aggressors from the outset. Fearful of an imminent Confederate attack on Washington, DC, the War Department asked Northern governors to send troops immediately. Governor Andrew convened a "Council of War" that called for four regiments to assemble at the Boston Common on April 16. In New Bedford "the greatest excitement prevailed" where Colonel David Wardrop of the Third Regiment and Captain Timothy Ingraham of the City Guards mobilized their men. Soon, the New Bedford City Guards and others poured into Boston, and by early April 16, more than thirty companies had arrived. These citizen-soldiers were cheered by thousands who braved a cold rain, and war began with enthusiasm and optimism on both Northern and Southern sides.[4]

A martial spirit pervaded New Bedford as women began raising funds for departed troops and meeting publicly at City Hall to sew clothing. Prominent women like Rachel Howland and Sally Anthony procured lint to make bandages while doing "all these things and many others" to support military mobilization. Hundreds of residents turned out to City Hall for an immense meeting on the evening of April 17, 1861. Presiding officer Charles B. H. Fessenden urged the assemblage to uphold "a love of country" and other speakers addressed the necessity of nonpartisan loyalty. William Logan Rodman interrupted to read two dispatches about the New Bedford City Guards who paraded through Boston in "good spirits" while receiving cheers from all. Former governor John H. Clifford linked New Bedford's soldiers and civilians with their counterparts across the North in declaring that "our hopes and fears" were with the "gallant men who have gone out from among us in answer to the call of their country." His former political adversary Rodney French also spoke of fighting for a common cause and wished "God speed" to the City Guards. French expected that the city's soldiers would have "a pleasant voyage, easy work, and a speedy return to their homes." The assemblage selected wealthy citizens Jonathan Bourne, Joseph C. Delano, and Edward C. Jones to forward unanimous resolutions to city officials that underscored their support for the Union.[5]

Meeting early the next morning, the City Council appropriated substantial funds for the "suppression of an unholy rebellion." The City Guards were to receive $5,000 and another $10,000 was pledged for the Home and Coast Guard. City leaders announced that the American flag would be displayed at City Hall until ordered otherwise.[6] From the first sign of war, the city's generosity and alacrity in responding to the challenges of war remained a source of great civic pride, especially when compared with the antiwar stance of New Bedford's Quakers during the war of 1812.[7] Quakers retained a great deal of economic, social, and political power within New Bedford and several stalwart Quakers served in leadership roles during the Civil War, including Mayor George Howland Jr.[8] Although Joseph Ricketson tried to adhere to his "nonfighting principles" as a pacifist Quaker, he confessed privately to being moved by the singing of "The Star Spangled Banner" in the Unitarian Church. Also, he was moved a "rouser of a sermon" by the Reverend William Potter who had declared that "we must fight in order to get peace."[9] As the war unfolded, New Bedford responded in two principal ways: first, by actively recruiting soldiers and sailors, and second, by defending their home front against feared Confederate naval attacks.

Quaker attire worn by children Lucy Merrihew and Nathan Hathaway, both of New Bedford, photographed October 12, 1863. (George Parlow, photographer. Earle Wilson Collection. Courtesy of the Trustees of the New Bedford Free Public Library.)

Recruiting Locally for State Quotas and National Needs

New Bedford's first direct contributions to the war were centered on the New Bedford City Guards, Company L of the Third Massachusetts Regiment. These men mobilized quickly when Governor Andrew's made his first call for troops on April 15. Officially organized in 1852, the City Guards had been commanded since 1854 by Captain Timothy Ingraham and were known for their proficiency in drill. Adorned in gray, black, and gold uniforms like those of West Point Cadets (where Ingraham's son was enrolled), the Guards departed New Bedford at midday on April 16 with a "fitting public demonstration of patriotic feeling," no doubt encouraged by former governor Clifford's pledge of the "united support of the entire community." As the first men of more than two thousand from New Bedford who enlisted in military service, the guards received Clifford's reassurances that "your fellow-citizens will see to it that those you leave behind shall want nothing while you are gone." Clifford expected them to return home with "untarnished glory, to be received by your fellow-citizens with heartfelt joy and honor!"[10]

New Bedford's City Guards provided significant leadership and patriotism at the outset of the war that solidified the military mobilization of both the state and national governments. All but two of the field staff and officers of the "Minute Men of '61" hailed from New Bedford, including Colonel David W. Wardrop and Major John H. Jennings. After receiving their colors from Governor Andrew at Boston's Statehouse on April 17, the regiment embarked with sealed orders for Virginia, where they arrived at Fortress Monroe on April 20. Setting off later that day for Norfolk, Virginia, with the aim of destroying "everything possible that could serve the rebels," this regiment claimed to be the "first northern volunteer troops to land aggressively on southern soil." After returning to Fortress Monroe on April 21, the men performed mostly garrison duty that ruined their fancy and costly uniforms. Men were cheered by reminders and support from home that included letters, clothing, and gifts sent by the New Bedford's Ladies' Soldiers' Relief Society and a $600 donation from Edward C. Jones. The men's three months of active service came to end in mid-July, and the Third Massachusetts traveled back to Boston and mustered out of service on July 22. Of the 500 or so men in the regiment, 160 reenlisted before the close of 1861.[11]

During the initial wave of pro-Union sentiment and optimism about a short war and sure Northern victory, Company L and the "Minute Men of '61" were considered heroes for having saved the country. As the first northern troops deployed to the South, the men of Company L were lauded by a "popular ovation" at New Bedford's city hall with fulsome speeches by Mayor Isaac Taber and John H. Clifford. Contemporaries and historians concurred that the regiment may have prevented an outright Confederate victory in the opening days of the Civil War. Leonard Ellis believed that "A delay of a half hour in the arrival of the Minute Men in Washington would have found our capital and the archives of our government in the hands of the rebels, who would at once have been recognized by England and France." Edward A. Horton captured popular sentiment in "The Vanguard Volunteers" that described the men as "saviors." He declared that the regiment's "alacrity of response" united the North and "impressed the South." Like all "Minute Men of '61," the New Bedford City Guards gave "hope to the dismayed North," provided time for the Union to organize its defenses, and created "memories and inspirations" that would endure among Massachusetts's "greatest treasures."[12] For decades, citizens of New Bedford persisted in claiming that local soldiers in the state's regiments had preserved the nation.

As the war progressed, New Bedford's military recruitment moved from enlisting earnest volunteers to the payment of substantial bounties at local, state, and national levels. By the end of 1861, Mayor Isaac C. Taber proudly declared that the city had recruited 500 men in the army, and over 1,600 men had enlisted in the navy. By the war's end, nearly 3,000 men were credited to New Bedford as soldiers and sailors, or 1,110 more than were required by the state thanks to the allowance of naval enlistment credits.[13] By maintaining up-to-date records of all enlistments in New Bedford, city officials showcased citizens' loyalty and helped to ensure that the city received full reimbursements and credits from state and federal officials. Eventually, sizeable bounties encouraged volunteer enlistments with the aim of minimizing the negative impacts of conscription. Historian James W. Geary contends that early patriotism among Northerners gave way to financial inducements as early as fall 1862.[14] Emily J. Harris found in her insightful analysis of Deerfield, Massachusetts, that bounties comprised more than 10 percent of the town's total expenditures for 1861, and town expenses jumped 61 percent in the next two years and then doubled again between 1863 and 1864.[15]

New Bedford's local bounties were paid mostly in the war's first and second years, and before national conscription became fully operational. The city's first bounty payments of $15 each went to men who enlisted in Company D of the Twenty-Third Massachusetts Volunteer Infantry, the "Clifford Guards," along with those who volunteered for the Fifth Massachusetts Battery and Company B of the Twenty-Eighth Massachusetts Volunteer Infantry. In 1861 the city paid out $4,605 in bounties. Costs increased dramatically between 1862 and 1863 when bounties jumped to an average of $200 per man, and the city's total payout in 1862–63 exceeded $141,000. New Bedford's military expenses prompted officials to issue bonds worth $147,000 and procure an additional loan of $26,000. In addition to direct bounties, at least $25,000 had been paid out by the city to persons dependent on support from military volunteers, with reimbursement expected from the state, a small portion of the $3.2 million distributed by Massachusetts as allotments and bounties throughout the war.[16] City Treasurer Congdon wrote in June 1863 that he had distributed funds to "father, mother, wife, brother, sister, friend, savings bank &c. &c. the whole process involving a great amount of labor but securing thousands of dollars to the dependents of the Volunteers. . . ." By late 1863 New Bedford had paid bounties of nearly $140,000 to 481 men in nine months regiments and 244 who volunteered for three years of service. The city's total cost of mobilizing troops was more than $176,000 by the middle of the war, most of which would be reimbursed later by Massachusetts.[17]

The Provost Marshal General's Office

Local authorities worked diligently with state officials to meet the manpower needs of the federal government. The dynamic relationship among government

Table 3-1. Bounties Paid by New Bedford, 1862–63

Unit/Individual Bounty Payment	Total Bounties Paid to Unit ($)
18th Regiment (mostly $100; some $250)	5,200
38th Reg., Co. H ($100)	3,350
33rd Reg., Co. I ($100)	4,540
41st Reg.	5,750
41st Reg., Co. A ($250)	25,500
47th Reg., Co. D ($200)	12,900
47th Reg.	3,000
3rd Reg., Co. G ($200)	19,100
3rd Reg., Co. F ($200)	11,900
3rd Reg., Co. E ($200)	19,600
Miscellaneous ($200)	2,600
Subtotal paid as of 11/10/1862	**113,440**
Co. F (no unit)	50
47th Reg., Co. D	150
38th Reg., Co. H	50
48th Reg. ($200)	2,200
Mass. 2nd Cav. ($200)	25,800
Subtotal paid through 12/16/1862	**28,250**

Source: New Bedford, Mass., Treasurer, Account of Bounties Paid to Enlistees in Massachusetts Regiments, New Bedford, 1862–63; Boston Public Library, Rare Books, Ms. Am. 2383 (1–2).

entities upholds James Geary's astute observation that "the Civil War represented a watershed between the transition from localism to the nascent nation-state." States' rights were replaced by the federal control and centralization of military affairs, fiscal policy, and other areas.[18] New Bedford became the center of recruiting for Massachusetts' First Congressional District as the local headquarters of the Provost Marshal General's (PMG) office, headed by Captain A. D. Hatch. The PMG's office enrolled and recruited soldiers, planned and implemented conscription, and located and arrested deserters. New Bedford's experiences were similar to those of Springfield, Massachusetts, and other Northern communities. Historian Michael Frisch explained that "the complex business of raising troops and avoiding the draft was the war's most direct manifestation, reaching deeply into almost every aspect of community life."[19] Hatch and his charges were efficient. By the fall of 1864, the First District was credited with enlisting some 8,000 soldiers and seamen, a figure enhanced by the district's 2,306 naval enlistments credited in July.[20]

In one of his typical trimonthly reports to superiors in Washington, DC, Captain A. D. Hatch reported in May 1863 that the "enrollment in this District is progressing to a speedy termination." Hatch's unprecedented military and police powers were often directed at deserters whose apprehension paid thirty dollars per head. Between June 20, 1863, and February 20, 1865, the date of Hatch's final report, the PMG's office arrested seventy-two deserters in the First District. Only three men were caught after May 1864, a busy month that included oversight of a draft between May 13 and May 20, 1864. New Bedford's transient population and maritime economy posed some problems for the PMG, and Hatch reported more than once that drafted whalemen were away at sea. Even as late as February 1865, Hatch reported that some draftees were only "now returning home." By war's end, Hatch claimed that the First District "held to service" about one-half of all men, a higher percentage than found nationally.[21] Elsewhere in Massachusetts, the percentage of men "held to service" was about 25 to 30 percent of all names called, with about 10 percent of them drafted.[22]

The PMG's visibility in New Bedford was reinforced by daily meetings of the Board of Enrollments at 4 P.M., by public gatherings and announcements, and by the active vigilance of hired deputies. Superior officers kept Hatch on his toes, too. Captain W. R. Pease dressed down Hatch in September 1863 because "the small number of deserters arrested in your district since April 24th last indicates a neglect of duty on your part or on the part of your Special Agents." Claiming that the country was "swarming with deserters," Pease told Hatch and his "detectives" to be more zealous.[23] Detailed letters, telegrams, and reports indicate that army authorities in Washington and in Boston paid close attention to the capture of deserters. A "Descriptive List of Deserters" for the First District names 1,367 men between 1861 and 1864, most of them privates who deserted from Southern battlefields. Fewer than forty deserters (of more than 1,300) could be linked explicitly to New Bedford. A few men deserted locally, such as Private John Lowery who deserted on Christmas Day in 1863 and was listed as being in "New Bedford," probably visiting his family.[24] Of the city's known soldiers and sailors, no black enlistees deserted, and white men reported as deserters appear to have been "stragglers" who served in unusual or out-of-state military units. Of 181 men apprehended in the First District between August 1863 and May 1865, an average of ten per month, about one-third of them were arrested in New Bedford. The city's relatively low number of deserters and arrests was due to the city's high level of volunteer enlistments and the lack of conflict over conscription.[25]

Besides serving as an extension of the federal government, the PMG's office provided an economic boost to local residents and businesses. From 1862 through 1865, almost $20,000 was expended in the First District, nearly 11 percent of all PMG funds spent in Massachusetts. Most monies went to employees' salaries ($14,159.19), with smaller amounts allocated for transportation ($3,376.00), rent ($777.50), postage ($544.95), and other clerical expenses.[26] Advertising with Fessenden and Baker of the *New Bedford Mercury* totaled over $330 in a one-year period. A few business owners benefited from extra work, such as Edmund Anthony, publisher of the *New Bedford Standard*, whose advertising and printing efforts generated over $400 of income between September 1863 and January 1864. Levi L. Crane sold tons of coal to the office during the cold months; the New Bedford and Taunton RR was paid to transport men; and other companies sold stationery and clerical supplies.[27] As an example of new employment opportunities during the war, some men became deputies and clerks in the PMG's employ, such as Chief Clerk Cornelius Howland Jr., who earned $100 per month after February 1864. Some men were hired on a temporary basis as agents and guards, and laborers earned up to $3 per day for menial work.[28]

Military Conscription, July 1863

New Bedford's wartime environment was marked by increased efforts by city, state, and federal officials to maintain order while recruiting soldiers and sailors. The city's police force aided the federally funded First District Provost Marshal. In 1862 the city marshal addressed new duties by reporting that his deputies were compelled to provide "efficient service to the government in returning such deserters to camp, and also . . . in aiding and encouraging enlistment."[29] Most operations were overseen by the Board of Enrollments that convened first on May 20, 1863, and persisted with *daily* meetings until June 1865.[30] The board's early business was limited with meetings consisting mostly of reading bureaucratic dispatches. The pace picked up as the office organized for national conscription in the summer of 1863. Locally, Captain Hatch set up the first draft effort on July 13 for subdistricts 1 and 2, followed the next day for subdistricts 3 and 4. By July 15, however, the Board of Enrollments suspended the draft because "the accumulation of names was so large, that more time was necessary to fill out the notices." The state's Acting Assistant Provost Marshal General (AAPMG) ordered that no new notifications be sent to drafted men, and that men presenting themselves should be furloughed until further notice.[31]

These measured bureaucratic reports stand in marked contrast to the experiences in New York City, the site of the nation's worst urban violence during "draft riots" in July 1863. The riots also demonstrated an ugly display of Irish immigrants' animosity toward black Americans, prompting fears in New Bedford and other northern cities about similar threats.[32] In New Bedford and elsewhere, the PMG's staff was instructed to "be careful and employ the right men," and to "take the utmost pain to be guarded in their intercourse with the people on matters pertaining to the business of their office, and are at all times to use the greatest patience, courtesy and civility, to all with whom they may be in communication." The large numbers of men who flooded into New Bedford certainly helped to feed rumors of mob activity, as eventually more than 2,200 men appeared before the Board of Enrollment in July and August of 1863.[33] The fear of draft riots in mid-July 1863 shook residents like no other wartime disturbance, and municipal authorities calmed and controlled the city through the virtual imposition of martial law. This episode illustrated also the continuing solicitude by white leaders toward the city's African Americans.[34]

Wild stories circulated in New Bedford that hundreds of men planned to attack the city and its black residents. Believing that "the peace and quiet of our city were . . . seriously threatened," Mayor George Howland Jr. called out troops to parade through New Bedford on July 13 with an order that they "hold themselves in readiness for duty at any moment." Captain Hurlbut assumed command with forces augmented by a special police squad comprised of members from the Union Drill Club, the City Grays, and the New Bedford Light Artillery. This extraordinary police presence upheld order until all men were discharged eleven days later. After the city expended almost $3,500 for additional police and military protection, Mayor Howland and others were shocked when Massachusetts's officials refused to reimburse the city. State officials claimed the "troops were not called out in accordance with any law which renders their service an expense to the Commonwealth."[35] To his superiors in Washington, DC, Captain Hatch reported simply that there had been "no resistance to the draft," an accurate assessment that failed to convey the anxiety felt by city residents at the time.[36]

Joseph Ricketson compiled the most detailed account of the crisis in several private letters. On July 17, 1863, Ricketson wrote that the "low growling thunder which precedes the storm is and has been heard here for the last few days. But we are prepared for any emergency." Rumors flowed that men from "lower classes" in surrounding towns planned to "burn & pillage New Bedford." He detailed stories of some six hundred to eight hundred men from Fall River, Bridgewater, Wareham and nearby towns "coming here for a Riot, but as I said we are all prepared." The mob's purported targets included the Mansion House, Dunbar's Eating Saloon, and the Provost Marshall's Office at the corner of Union and Purchase streets. Ricketson noted that the local artillery held 150 guns with full cartridges, and two other companies were armed with another 150 guns. He added: "the Dragoons have their sabres sharpened and are armed with carbines[.] One of the companys [sic] of 3rd Reg't. is also here. [W]e have two heavy pieces of Artillery and the Revenue Cutter is at the foot of Union Street, the street we live on, with her guns all shotted." The City Grays defended City Hall, and other public buildings were defended by well-armed troops. Private citizens were also prepared, Ricketson noted, "Our sea captains have revolvers and our citizens are armed." Extra police were posted on the night of the rumored attack, and pickets stretched to the city's outskirts for two or three miles. "*We are determined* there will be no Blank Cartridges," Ricketson concluded.[37]

Racial issues lay at the core of the feared riot, Ricketson and others believed. He reported a "villain" in the city who declared that "he would head the mob and burn the Negro Houses in the west part of town." In response, twenty black men armed with revolvers surrounded the man's house and threatened to shoot him if he appeared. Ricketson revealed strong community support for the city's black residents: "There is but one opinion, *we are going to stand by the Negro in the name of the Lord Jesus Christ.*" Ricketson offered a telling anecdote about the continued paternalism demonstrated by New Bedford's leading citizens toward black residents when the Reverend William Jackson approached a handful of white leaders and asked for a revolver to defend himself. Each man gave Jackson a dollar, while Jonathan Bourne Jr., perhaps the wealthiest man in the city, went to gather more money. In less than ten minutes, sixteen dollars had been raised for the reverend's pistol. Ricketson concluded: "Our first citizens giving readily, this is the feeling here and in Boston. We are now dependant [sic] on the Negro." Ostensibly a Quaker-inspired pacifist,

Ricketson commended the city's militaristic strategy because it had secured peace in New Bedford.[38] Other city leaders agreed with James B. Congdon's contention that the city's "warlike preparation and demonstration saved life, liberty and property."[39]

The 1863 summer draft flooded New Bedford with more than 2,000 men in a two-month period to be examined by the Board of Enrollments, as illustrated in Table 3-2. Of 403 substitutes who enrolled in July and August 1863 in the First District of Massachusetts, 33 men from New Bedford assumed the place of draftees from the same city. The low numbers of local Irish-born men threatened by conscription may also explain that lack of a draft riot in the city. Of the 33 substitutes from New Bedford, 11 were Irish-born, ranging from twenty-year-old laborer Thomas Clifford to a thirty-five-year-old clerk, John Dennison.[40] Nearly 3,000 draftees had been processed by early September 1863 when Captain Hatch summarized that 2,237 men reported and another 679 did not, as most of them were fishermen away at sea.[41] Between July 21 and August 27, on average the board questioned 77 men, exempted 50, commuted 2, passed 13, and provided 11 substitutes. Similar patterns were demonstrated in the state. Within Massachusetts during the July 1863 conscription, 32,079 were called for the state, 22,343 were exempted, 3,044 skedaddled, and nearly 6,700 were "held to service." Over half of Massachusetts' men held to service paid the $300 commutation fee through which the state raised more than $1 million.[42]

New Bedford's role in the 1863 summer draft brought media attention, both negative and positive. Locally, the *New Bedford Mercury* reported that draft proceedings featured a large audience cheering and jeering as if they were "witnessing the drolleries of a first-class comedian." A comic moment came when officials read the name of draftee "Jefferson Davis," who it was hoped could "be in at the death of the other Jeff."[43] New Bedford gained infamy when several draft substitutes escaped from Pierian Hall late on the evening of July 26, 1863. Picking up the story, the *New York Times* dubbed it, "The Draft, A General Skedaddle of Substitutes in New Bedford, Mass." Captain Hatch was encouraged to take photographs of the "next batch of substitutes" should they "stray away."[44] Negative publicity was countered later by both the *Mercury* and the *New York Times* with factual accounts of an orderly enrollment process and the presence of soldiers from the city's Fort Taber. By the end of July 1863 public commentary focused on "the most perfect good order" that prevailed in New Bedford and the belief that conscription was "not much of a hardship after all" because of the numerous exemptions granted to many men.[45]

Public opinion was undoubtedly shaped by the strong defense of conscription by the Reverend William J. Potter who announced that he would heed his draft call. His sermon, entitled "The Voice of the Draft," was excerpted in the

Table 3-2. First District Board of Enrollments, July–August 1863

Date	Total	Exempted	Commutations	Passed	Substitutes
July 21	54	51	2	10	0
July 22	36	29	3	3	1
July 24	86	54	16	7	9
July 25	80	51	0	28	1
July 28	99	49	3	35	12
July 29	120	71	4	37	8
July 30	82	39	5	20	18
July 31	119	71	8	13	27
August 1	57	27	4	25	1
August 2	80	58	0	10	12
August 4	100	58	5	17	20
August 5	74	34	0	16	24
August 7	69	38	0	5	26
August 8	120	78	0	42	0
August 10	90	60	0	14	16
August 11	96	62	0	16	18
August 12	86	59	0	3	24
August 13	92	61	1	14	16
August 14	96	66	0	15	15
August 15	91	82	0	9	0
August 17	110	80	1	11	18
August 18	71	54	0	4	13
August 19	45	36	2	2	5
August 20	79	49	1	15	14
August 21	39	31	2	3	3
August 22	62	50	2	7	3
August 24	45	30	1	2	12
August 25	45	32	0	2	11
August 26	37	20	2	0	7
August 27	36	27	2	0	7
Totals	**2,296**	**1,507**	**62**	**385**	**342**

Source: Proceedings of the Board of Enrollments, May 1863 to June 1865, vol. 1, First District, Massachusetts, Entry 853, RG 110, National Archives.

Note: The numbers taper off during the entire month of September, when a total of 173 men were brought before the Board of Enrollments, with no more than a dozen seen in any one day. These records relate to the entire district, yet only 413 men were drafted from the city of New Bedford in July 1863.

New York Times, circulated in the North, and gained the attention of Secretary of War Stanton, who called Potter to Washington, DC. Potter became a consultant, a military chaplain, and later an agent for the Sanitary Commission.[46] In offering the "word of a conscript to his fellow-conscripts," Potter urged all men to accept the draft with "cheerfulness." Calling the war a "holy cause," Potter viewed the draft and military service as democratizing elements that upheld the "sublimity of self-sacrifice, of the nobleness of doing and dying for one's country." Potter contended that commutation fees of $300 were reasonable because working men of moderate means could support the war without enlisting. He criticized substitutes as mostly foreign-born men who lacked a patriotic commitment to the Union cause. Referring to the earlier episode of escaped substitutes from Pierian Hall, Potter denounced them as "swindlers, perjurers, *runaways.*" Viewing the Civil War as a "just and sacred cause," Potter expected full participation by the North's "better and more enlightened men." He smoothed over class-based contentions about the draft and the war by urging cooperation among everyone, the "rich and the poor, the educated and the uneducated, the man who labors with his hands and the man who labors with his brains."[47] Potter's defense of conscription influenced other Northerners to view the draft and the war in a more positive light.

Following the draft of July–August 1863, city authorities established the New Bedford Recruiting Committee that met between November 20, 1863, and July 25, 1864. Consisting of the mayor, two aldermen, and four city council members, the committee approved financial inducements for "any person who shall bring a recruit to the office." They established a recruiting office under Major J. F. Vinal and authorized a five-dollar fee on December 3 that tripled to fifteen dollars on December 26. The committee's work came to an end in July 1864 because New Bedford could then claim naval enlistments against their military quota, thanks in large part to Governor John A. Andrew.[48] Andrew's letter-writing and lobbying campaigns prompted Congress to pass legislation on July 4, 1864, that allowed coastal communities to claim previous naval enlistments. Andrew soon joined New Bedford's John H. Clifford as two commissioners who determined the state's naval credits amounted to more than 22,300 Union sailors who had enlisted between April 13, 1861, and February 24, 1864. A team of two dozen clerks worked double shifts for several weeks to complete the state rolls before September 5, 1864, the date of the next draft.[49] Because of this federal legislation and massive clerical effort, Mayor George Howland Jr. proudly reported that New Bedford obtained a credit of 1,188 men who enlisted in the naval service. Although New Bedford no longer had to actively recruit soldiers or sailors to meet its quota, Howland urged the city's "good and loyal citizens" to support "their country and their country's cause" as the war entered its final year.[50]

The Reverend William J. Potter, an influential local leader during the Civil War, circa 1880–90. (Headley & Reed, photographers. Courtesy of the Trustees of the New Bedford Free Public Library.)

Home and Coast Defense

When war erupted and the city leaders called a massive rally on April 17, 1861, John Henry Clifford worried aloud about the city's vulnerability to "piratical craft" commissioned by the Confederacy's "bastard government." "Let us have a home force immediately," he stated to loud applause. Fearing Confederate attacks on their wealthy city, local leaders joined with state and federal officials to defend New Bedford. Mayor Isaac Taber requested a $10,000 appro-priation on April 18 to protect the "defenceless" city. Across the harbor in Fair-haven, Fort Phoenix was renovated and an earthworks battery was planned at the harbor's southern reaches at Clark's Point. Although some skeptics publicly questioned the imminent danger of a Confederate attack, others believed that "reckless adventurers" might be "stimulated by the love of booty" and attack the Whaling City. The *New Bedford Standard* advocated a "strict guard" in all coastal communities and encouraged a naval blockade of southern ports to pre-vent hostile vessels from going to sea.[51] A newly established Committee on Home and Coast Guard praised the "hearty co-operation of a generous public" that quickly raised three military companies of sixty-seven men each, plus an artillery company of forty men. Within two weeks of the firing on Fort Sumter, New Bedford's Home and Coast Guard was functional under the command of General James D. Thompson. On April 25, 1861, the Committee for the Relief of the New Bedford City Guards and the Committee for Home and Coast Defence merged into the Joint Special Committee, chaired by Mayor Taber, that over-saw the city's military defense.[52]

At the time, public actions and private musings illustrated great anxiety about a feared Confederate attack on the state's coastal cities. Massachusetts Adjutant General Schouler outlined the dire situation: "The entire coast of Massachusetts was open to attack from sea; not a fort or an earthwork or a gun was in proper condition. There were neither officers nor troops in garrison." Governor Andrew complained throughout the war of inadequate coastal defenses. Mayor Taber dispatched former governor Clifford to Boston to ask for state or federal officials to supply defensive cannons. Wealthy merchant Joseph C. Delano wrote to his Boston counterpart J. M. Forbes asking for weap-ons stored at the Springfield Armory. Delano added, "We want also two of those guns lying at Springfield for our own defenceless harbour to place behind breast works at Clark[']s Point."[53] At the end of April, Joseph Ricketson com-mented that "we look very warlike here" and noted six guns ready at the Fair-haven fort and men were laboring on a Sunday to complete the battery at Clark's Point. New Bedford's home front and coastal defense began as a city-sponsored enterprise because both state and federal governments were not up to the task.[54]

By the start of May 1861, residents felt some relief because Fort Phoenix stood in a "completed state." Starting at 3 P.M. on May 3, 1861, the Fairhaven fort was garrisoned officially with a lavish flag-raising ceremony. Mayor Taber reported that volunteers "were all uniformed in a neat and substantial manner," furnished with "good muskets," and equipped to use the city's light brass field artillery pieces. Soon, three guns of twenty-four pounds each were moved from Fort Phoenix to Clark's Point under the direction of the aptly named Mr. Cannon, supplemented there by two twelve-pound rifled brass guns lent by the state.[55] At the harbor's southern reaches of Clark's Point, the newly christened Fort Taber emerged out of a sand and earthwork battery. Despite the fears of attack and public pomp, the home front duties at Forts Phoenix and Taber proved inconsequential. A soldier's typical day centered on eating well, dressing up, drilling frequently, taking target practice, and assembling for dignitaries. A member of Company C wrote about a festive day in which "revel-ee was soon followed by revel-ree for Fisher arrived with Pork & Beans, Indian Pudding and oh goody! such brown Breads."[56] New Bedford resident Lydia Davenport visited Fort Phoenix in mid-June 1861 and reported that it presented "quite a business like appearance" with "soldiers marching, drilling, and senti-nels standing or walking the parapet." But, she added, "of course it is mere play compared with the Soldiers duty at the seat of war."[57]

The proximity of forts to their homes allowed New Bedford's volunteer sol-diers to move easily between military and civilian roles. Some men went back and forth to town because of sickness or, in the case of Private Russell and Corporal Cook, to attend the theatre. A Private Burt humorously described daily rituals. The men awoke at 4 A.M. to the "noise of the big gun," followed by roll call at 5 A.M. and cleaning of the barracks. A 6 A.M. breakfast concluded with the formation of a "clamming squad" that "marched to the scene of action on the beach" and then a return to the fort with "captured prizes." At 8 A.M., the unit practiced artillery drill for an hour, followed by drill at 10 A.M. The noontime dinner "was thickly interspersed with jokes cheers & laughter, guar-anteeing that no one could possibly be troubled with 'dyspepsia,'" Private Burt reported. The men gathered again for a dress parade and drill at 4 P.M., with supper served two hours later. A steady stream of visitors kept the men amused and alert. If any one theme predominated among the volunteers, it was "A Sol-dier's Life is Always Gay," a song penned by the garrison's Arthur Ricketson. Some soldiers and observers believed that the troops could serve better else-where and avoid the "irksome" or "needless" duty of home and coast defense.[58]

As New Bedford weathered the first months of war, the Committee on Home and Coast Guard supervised Fourth of July events with martial solem-nity. Companies of the Home and Coast Guard formed at Market Square to parade through the city's streets, accompanied by the New Bedford Brass Band.[59] That same day, Lydia Davenport confided in her journal that "we are in the midst of a civil war with all its dread realities; the day has been celebrated with a new interest by our citizens; the military display seems to have a meaning to it, that we never felt before." Two weeks later in the aftermath of the Union's defeat at Bull Run, Davenport spoke for many Northerners: "I feel heart sick, I have no strength for anything." She worried that the Confederate States would triumph.[60] Throughout the North, the sober recognition of war's costs led to debates in mid-July 1861 after President Lincoln had asked for $400 million. The local *Standard* editorialized that "A great national debt is one of the greatest evils that can befall a nation." Fearing a protracted war with massive debt and fraud, they expressed a common northern sentiment that war be a quick one. "We do not believe there is the slightest necessity for any three years' war," opined the *Standard*. "The rebellion can be suppressed within one year if the government puts forth all its energies." People would not support and pay taxes for a "desultory and indecisive war of two, three or four years," the writer predicted.[61]

Concerns over the costs and necessity of home defense occupied residents through the summer of 1861. One writer to the *New Bedford Standard* cleverly turned around "anti-fort" sentiment by suggesting that Forts Phoenix and Taber were "really economical investments" during wartime. Both forts served, first, as a line of defense and, second, as "camps of instruction" where men could train in "practical military science" in a small and hospitable encampment. The fort's closeness to New Bedford minimized transportation costs because the garrison's soldiers could travel to the city at any time if their businesses or families needed them. Furthermore, the hometown environment of family and friends helped soldiers to avoid the "excesses and immoralities" found in larger or distant military encampments. New Bedford remained vulnerable to "pirate-privateer" ships, it was believed. A final argument favoring home defense was an economic one. Most of the forts' construction was done by "our own people, many of whom were at the time wholly destitute of employment," and thus home defense provided jobs and honest labor instead of forcing the destitute to seek private or public charity.[62]

When it seemed less likely that New Bedford would be attacked by late summer 1861, Fairhaven authorities withdrew from the joint Home and Coast Guard. Fort Phoenix was vacated in October 1861 and Company C marched out at quick step as a "solitary gun thundered its last farewell." One soldier bid farewell to Forth Phoenix by writing, "Hushed is the evening tattoo and the voice of the sentry calling the midnight hour!" In future years, he predicted, the fort's defenders would enjoy showing their children "where in the great rebellion of '61 they spent the pleasant days of a garrison life within thy walls."[63] As the Civil War's military campaigns moved into a winter lull, city authorities reduced the local costs of home defense. By early December 1861 Companies A, B, and C were excused from active garrison duty at Fort Taber, and two weeks later, the Joint Committee disbanded all three companies and returned the city's weapons and equipment. Captain Bourne thanked his men for their "universal good conduct" when discharging them on Friday, December 20. A small garrison maintained the fort through the winter. By the end of 1861 some $16,500 had been appropriated locally for Home and Coast Defense despite growing recognition that military protection should be a state and federal responsibility.[64] Nearing one year into the war in April 1862, the Home and Coast Guard discharged the garrison at Fort Taber, leaving behind one man to protect the property.[65]

As New Bedford's officials withdrew from full support of home defense, state officials prodded the federal government for more funding and attention. They pointed to New Bedford's neglected fort at Clark's Point, designed after Fort Adams in Newport, Rhode Island, that was supposed to contribute to a line of coastal defense from Portland, Maine, to Long Island.[66] Wartime construction at Clark's Point had slowed because of inadequate stone delivery and the illness and death of the US Army engineer in charge of the works. In 1862, after granite was procured from a Quincy quarry, Lt. Henry Martyn Robert renewed construction efforts. Governor John Andrew continued to complain about his state's weak defenses through correspondence and speeches. He wrote to President Lincoln in April 1863, for example, requesting an iron-clad vessel

View of Fort Phoenix from Palmer's Island, circa 1861. Drawing by Edward Rodman. (Courtesy of the Trustees of the New Bedford Free Public Library.)

to protect Boston's harbor. In late February 1863 Andrew visited New Bedford to inspect the city's military installations. A salute of thirteen guns awaited Andrew's party as they toured Clark's Point, and two thousand people turned out in the evening to honor the guests at the city council chambers. In a public address, Governor Andrew declared that the "Quaker city of Massachusetts had never faltered" and its Friends "were all loyal to the core." After praising the gallantry of local hero Colonel Alberto Maggi, Governor Andrew spoke also of enlisting black soldiers by stating that "any loyal man, of whatever color, is a welcome recruit." His visit galvanized local recruiting efforts for the Fifty-Fourth Massachusetts Colored Infantry and inspired hopes of raising artillery companies to defend the state's coastal communities.[67]

By the end of March 1863 Massachusetts appropriated $1 million for home defense that accelerated the construction of coastal fortifications at New Bedford with an earmark of $150,000 for the fort at Clark's Point. Governor Andrew also dispatched emissaries to Europe and to Washington, DC, to procure more and larger weapons. Andrew's anxieties rose in late May 1863 upon hearing from Boston's Robert C. Winthrop about British naval plans. From a kinsman who served as the American consul at Malta, Winthrop learned that British naval vessels were ordered to Halifax, Nova Scotia, with orders to attack Portland, Boston, and Newport if war broke out between the United States and England. In response, Andrew ordered Boston's harbor to be fortified and its forts connected by telegraph. Local boosters in New Bedford supported an upsurge in recruiting efforts with larger federal bounties of $100 and state payments of $50. "We are called upon by the General Government to raise a Company for home defence," New Bedford's Joint Committee declared, "and we have faith to believe our citizens will promptly respond to the call."[68] Newspapers urged Massachusetts men to volunteer because their enlistment rates lagged behind other New England states.[69]

During this season of heightened anxiety, Governor Andrew authorized eight companies of heavy artillery to protect the state's coastal communities.[70] By the summer of 1863, New Bedford's Clark's Point fort contained ten casement-mounted guns, and the fort's first tier was finished by 1864. Although readied for action, the garrison's military preparations were for naught.[71] Reporting at the end of June 1863, Captain John A. P. Allen of the Sixth Company stated that his four officers and ninety-eight enlisted men still lacked small weapons. He wrote, however, that the "Post is being greatly improved through seven 10 in[ch] Columbiads [that] have been mounted in the new fortification, and are ready for any emergency." More than eleven feet long, the Columbiad cannons discharged a shell and shot that weighed 120 pounds with a range of two miles. One month later, the company was equipped with Springfield rifles, and some men were dispatched to Fairhaven's Fort Phoenix. Regular target practice allowed the men to hone their artillery skills, provided they did not use more than one hundered shots each month. Former barracks at Fort Taber were transformed into a twenty-bed hospital overseen by local physician Surgeon John H. Mackie who reported that "No death, and but little sickness, has occurred since the post has been garrisoned." The fort's officers made efforts to be "very polite and attentive to visitors" who drove their carriages around the Clark's Point Road.[72]

Between the summer of 1863 and the end of the war, home front military service remained uneventful apart from a minor controversy in April 1864. When the Sixth Company was ordered to Washington, DC, many soldiers and civilians in New Bedford raised a "great deal of dissatisfaction" because the soldiers enlisted believing that they would be used only for garrison duty and only in Massachusetts. Still, their subsequent service in the nation's capital was quiet until the unit mustered out in September 1865.[73] Overlapping military units provided harbor defense following departure of the Sixth Company. The Fourth Company of Unattached Infantry mustered in during April and May 1864 for ninety days. Their captain, Alphonse J. Kilbourn (or Alpheus J. Hillbourn), noted at the end of June that reinforcements arrived from the Thirteenth Unattached Massachusetts Volunteers. The addition of ninety men meant new drills and inspections, followed by the arrival of another contingent in two months, Company B of the First Battalion Massachusetts Volunteer Heavy Artillery, commanded by Captain Caleb E. Niebuhr. Niebuhr's dispatches reflect mundane routines and occasional desertions at Clark's Point. When the 150 soldiers mustered out in June 1865, only one man had local ties, a twenty-four-year-old spinner named James Fanin who had enlisted just four months earlier.[74] Fanin and his predecessors faced no hostile action through the war years, and only a handful of men died at the Clark's Point fort, either from illness or accident.

Policing the Home Front

Although home and coast military protection shifted away from the city's supervision, the maintenance of social order within New Bedford continued to fall on local policing by the city marshal and his staff. Since New Bedford's municipal incorporation in 1847, the city marshal oversaw policing functions that included daily beat coverage and a night watch.[75] Serving before the advent of professional urban police forces, the assistant marshals and night watch dealt lightly with their neighbors by promoting solicitude in dealing with drunkenness, the primary criminal offense in the mid-1800s. Before the war, Marshal William S. Cobb instructed officers to not arrest inebriates unless they were a threat to themselves or others. Cobb's successor, Elias W. Terry, complained about the difficulty of enforcing liquor laws, suggesting that "moral remedies" would prove more effective than "all the officers in Christendom."[76] New Bedford's relative "peace and good order" was tied to benevolent policing performed by local men who were typically attired in civilian clothes and adorned with beaver hats. The informality of the mid–nineteenth century police force was illustrated in an account that "it was not an uncommon sight to see an officer pushing a drunk to police headquarters in a wheel barrow."[77]

New Bedford's city marshal and city residents faced a changing urban environment marked by the dislocations of war and the continuing influx of military enlistees. The city marshal highlighted some challenges in 1862 when he commented about the "perplexing" duties of apprehending military deserters. Urban order was aided, he noted, by a safety valve of military enlistment that drew off unemployed men.[78] Once war commenced, police prosecutions averaged just over 555 per year, with the most obvious pattern shown in increased arrests for females (see Table 3-3). During 1861 the city marshal commended the "quiet and tranquility of our city," with similar reports following through 1865. One major change during the war was the substantial drop in the number of lodgers, transient men and women who sought overnight accommodations under the public charge. In 1862, for example, lodgers' applications numbered seven hundred, nearly one-half of the previous year's figures. That decrease,

Table 3-3. **Police Prosecutions in New Bedford, 1860–70**

Year	Totals	Male	Female
1860	505	359	146
1861	595	445	150
1862	508	321	187
1863	586	381	205
1864	581	377	204
1865	511	367	144
1866	490	389	101
1867	397	317	80
1868	493	381	112
1869	603	473	130
1870	485	385	100

Source: Reports of the City Marshal, 1860–70, NBCD, reel 2.

plus a decline in the number of police prosecutions, was attributed to the city's loss of population siphoned off through generous inducements for military enlistment. By enlisting in the Union cause, the marshal suggested, some men were removed "from a life of dissipation, and placed them under proper discipline, and more healthful influences." Even as New Bedford witnessed frequent military processions and war rallies after 1861, the city remained "unusually quiet" according to the marshal.[79]

At the war's midpoint in 1863, New Bedford experienced increased disorder judging by the number of arrests and lodgings. Arrests for alcohol-related offenses climbed from 282 in 1862 to 370 in 1863, spurred by Mayor Howland's directive that "all parties arrested for drunkenness should be prosecuted." Temperance enforcement coincided with the arrival of many men for the draft in the summer of 1863, reflected in nearly 1,000 lodgers provided board under city expense. About one-quarter of the lodgers were military substitutes granted temporary accommodations and food. As another indication of wartime transiency, during 1864, the captain of the night watch, Thomas Howland, reported that they assisted 612 lodgers, 94 of them female, 101 deserters from the army, and 21 army substitutes.[80] Between 1864 and the war's end, New Bedford's social order was marked by a "rapid advance in the direction of peace and general good order," according to the city marshal.[81]

Some aspects of New Bedford's home front wartime environment are captured in figures for arrests and lodgers. Drunkenness remained the primary criminal offense. Between 1861 and 1866 alcohol-related arrests comprised at least 40 percent of all arrests, rising to over 60 percent of all arrests in 1863 after Mayor Howland's edict that the laws be enforced. The most surprising pattern is the decline of sex-related vice crimes from prewar highs of over thirty arrests per year to a low of just ten in 1862. The decline of whaling prosperity and exodus of men for military service may have reduced the number or type of men who patronized disorderly houses. Elsewhere, a consistent decline in truancy arrests reflected city efforts to prevent truancy rather than punish it (see Table 3-4).[82] New Bedford also witnessed reduced numbers of lodgers, typically transient men and women in search of employment (see Table 3-5). During the economic downturn of the late 1850s, for example, the number of city lodgers jumped to 1,554 in 1859, 10 percent of them females. The number of lodgers during the war vacillated but never came close to prewar highs.[83] On the whole, New Bedford's home front appeared to be relatively stable, and the city's arrest patterns run counter to Philip Shaw Paludan's comments that in the North "general disorder increased as the number of arrests went up in cities."[84]

Table 3-4. Arrests in New Bedford, 1859–68

Arrests	1859	1860	1861	1862	1863	1864	1865	1866	1867	1868
Alcohol-Related	331	128	244	282	370	308	238	195	188	297
Assault Crimes	158	170	150	104	10	09	096	102	88	78
Theft and Property	86	81	89	63	55	69	93	104	49	56
Disorderly Crimes	63	85	73	32	40	65	67	62	42	40
Sexual and Vice	30	32	16	10	17	20	9	9	11	13
Miscellany	22	9	16	17	4	26	8	18	17	9
Totals	**690**	**505**	**588**	**508**	**586**	**578**	**511**	**490**	**395**	**493**

Source: Reports of the City Marshal, 1859–68, NBCD, reel 2.

Table 3-5. Lodgers in New Bedford, 1860–70

Year	Total	Male	Female	Military
1860	1,784	1,605	179	
1861	1,327	1,162	165	
1862	700	543	157	
1863	985	607	137	241
1864	612	396	94	122
1865	505	446	59	
1866	543	492	51	
1867	624			
1868	672			
1869	565			
1870	606			

Source: City Marshal Reports, 1860–70, NBCD, reel 2.

Summary

Noted before the war for a strong antislavery stance, New Bedford's leaders fully embraced the Union cause by promoting patriotism, military enlistment, and defense of their home front. Some Quakers encountered conflicts between pacifism and militarism, although the issue of conscientious objection to the war never became a significant public issue in New Bedford.[85] Joseph Ricketson, who described New Bedford as the "godly Quaker City" in July 1863 commented privately that his brother, Daniel, had become angry about the Quaker "indifference" to the war and its antislavery import. Daniel became a "Quaker preacher," according to his brother, and sermonized in church meetings to "infuse life & vigor into the Society."[86] Most Quakers in New Bedford publicly supported the war, if not through active military service then by substantial donations to recruiting funds, to soldiers' relief, and to public events and commemorations. New Bedford's leaders did well in upholding William Crapo's remonstrance in 1864 that they act as "worthy sons of noble sires." Through the war's duration, New Bedford proved up to the challenge of supporting the Union. The next chapter explores the city's men who fought in the war while representing their home, state, and country.

4   "Citizen-Soldiers of Massachusetts": New Bedford's Volunteers in the Civil War

When William Logan Rodman died in May 1863 at Port Hudson, Louisiana, fellow officer Frank Loring wrote a letter of condolence to Rodman's family in New Bedford. As the Lieutenant Colonel was ordering his men to advance, Loring related, Rodman was shot through the heart, "dying instantly and without pain." Officers and rank-and-file soldiers of the Thirty-Eighth Massachusetts held their lieutenant-colonel in high regard and his death prompted an unusual degree of sadness and regret. "To the regiment his loss will be irreparable," Loring continued. "Its excellent reputation for discipline and morals was due chiefly to him and his just and determined efforts to reward and bring forward merit, no matter where it was to be found." Enlisted men, whom Loring described in class-based terms and in quotations as "democratic volunteers," valued Rodman for his qualities of justice, kindness, and "high-minded sense of honor." For himself, Loring claimed to be more close to Rodman than any other officer in the regiment, and he learned "how sad a thing it is to say, 'I've lost a friend.'" Loring hoped that Rodman's family would find solace that their son and brother died with an excellent reputation. Ultimately, Loring wrote of his comrade, "He fell nobly and in a noble cause."[1]

William Logan Rodman did not become a national hero, but he was New Bedford's most prominent casualty during the Civil War. His military experiences and exalted death illustrate the tragic and transformative nature of the war and its multiple impacts on the home front. Rodman, a Quaker from old whaling wealth, was transfigured by the war, his personal and political beliefs shaped by changing events and opportunities for leadership and demonstrations of manly courage.[2] By the time the Civil War ended two years after Rodman's death, New Bedford had been credited with nearly 3,000 soldiers and sailors who secured the Union victory. They were white, black, native- and foreign-born men of all classes and occupations. Most served and died with a minimum of fame or recognition beyond their immediate families and community. Throughout the war and long afterwards, city officials, civic boosters, and local historians missed no opportunity in proclaiming that New Bedford

George Howland Jr., New Bedford mayor during the Civil War. (Courtesy of
the Trustees of the New Bedford Free Public Library.)

had recruited a surplus of more than 1,000 men, and they took pains to officially recognize more than 250 military casualties from the city.[3]

William Logan Rodman and the Thirty-Eighth Massachusetts

The forty-year-old volunteer William Logan Rodman was not a typical soldier because of his age, wealth, or single status, but his observations at home
and in the field spoke of common wartime perceptions and experiences. After

Fort Sumter's fall in April 1861, Rodman commented on the "stirring times" that he believed would be followed by a "severe accounting." As an escort to the New Bedford City Guards when they departed for Boston on April 16, 1861, Rodman was moved by the large and solemn crowd where "tears rolled down many a rough face." Within the next month, Rodman became active in the Home and Coast Guard's Company C where he enjoyed military drills and garrison duty at Fort Phoenix. His home front military service combined social events with military training, leading him to pronounce: "We had, upon the whole, a good time." Three weeks later, Rodman evinced a growing seriousness about the war when he proudly described his company's diligence and "soldierly bearing." Anticipating a longer war, he began to foresee his own involvement at the front. "If my fellow citizens think this soldiering [is] a necessity," he wrote, "I am willing to take my part of it."[4]

As the war moved into the summer of 1861, Rodman began to explore more purposeful endeavors beyond New Bedford that befitted a man of his status and connections. Governor Andrew asked him to serve as quartermaster in any regiment of Rodman's choosing, but he declined. Rodman thought the regrettable loss at Bull Run in July 1861 might actually have good consequences because of a renewed northern commitment to the war effort. Rodman traveled to Washington, DC, in September to seek an appointment and even met with President Lincoln whom he described as "no beauty" attired in a "tumbled shirt," no waistcoat, and a "$1.25 brown brim coat." Despite the president's rough appearance, Rodman praised Lincoln as a man who was "doing his work well." Rodman's visit to the nation's capital inspired in him a "new love for my country and new confidence in our rulers." Elected to represent New Bedford in the State Legislature in November, Rodman was appointed to its very active Committee on Finance. In the following month, Rodman's home front military service ended when the Home and Coast Guard disbanded, some calling it a "foolish" operation. For his part, Rodman enjoyed serving in Company C. "We began with a good spirit at a time when we thought we might be of service," Rodman related. "We have had a tolerable drill & have out of it a pretty good time."[5]

As the war moved into its second year, Rodman's legislative session ended on April 30, 1862. New Bedford, like other Northern communities, began more active recruiting efforts and Rodman took a leadership role. First striving to raise a company over the summer, Rodman was eventually commissioned major of the Thirty-Eighth Massachusetts on August 19, 1862, and the unit left the state a month later. Sent initially to Baltimore, the regiment sailed for New Orleans to join General Banks's expedition in mid-November. Writing with characteristic modesty, Rodman said of himself: "I am green as a leek, but pick up constantly, and manage pretty well." Subsequent letters and diary entries show his development as a soldier, an officer, and a strong supporter of black troops. As a representative of the Quaker elite, he noted in a letter home on December 4, 1862, that he would resign as secretary of the New Bedford Friends' Academy but retain his trusteeship. Rodman asked that his military rank be added to the academy's records and added, "It will be the first instance of such a record among the Quakers."[6]

When mustered in for three years in early August 1862, Company H of the Thirty-Eighth Massachusetts Volunteer Infantry became the most acclaimed regiment of New Bedford's white soldiers. Other officers besides Rodman included Timothy Ingraham, Thomas R. Rodman (William Logan's cousin), and Charles C. Howland. First sent to Baltimore, Maryland, the regiment later sailed to Louisiana where it joined the Banks' Corps. Moving between Baton Rouge and New Orleans, the men faced their first combat on April 12. During the first assault on Port Hudson in late May, Lieutenant Colonel William L. Rodman and two enlisted men were killed. In July 1864 the Thirty-Eighth moved to Virginia and became part of the army of the Shenandoah. Some losses followed at engagements at Winchester, Fisher's Hill, and Cedar Creek. The regiment moved southward again to Savannah, Georgia, in January 1865, largely serving as guards of Sherman's supply lines until the war ended. Remnants of the regiment were paid off and mustered out of the US service in Boston on July 13, 1865.[7]

This regiment captured New Bedford's attention during the war, partly because of its patrician leadership and the death of William Logan Rodman. Rodman's background precludes him from being considered a typical New Bedford man who served in the Union cause. But, as a scion of an established whaling family, and as an individual whose life was dramatically changed and ended by the war, Rodman's military service offers insights into the many influences of the war. First, as he moved from a pampered civilian life to a soldier at the front, Rodman found the "nobler opening of a new career," as Higginson noted. In an early letter from the field, Rodman expected no "picnic party" and planned to experience his share of "hard knocks before I see New Bedford again." Yet, he professed to be unconcerned about threats or danger, and he described the "strange mental change" that came after his enlistment. "Being bound to go where sent, and resolved to do one's best, seems to calm one's excitement," he explained. In mid-April 1863 he similarly commented of having no fear despite having rode astride his horse in the midst of battle where bullets "whistled round." He worried more about his horse. Camp life kept Rodman busy, as he wrote in February 1863 that he was "never so contented as when attending to my duties here." He was living and viewing the world as a soldier.

In the same letter he complained about "stay-at-homes" who offered "twad-dle" and "infernal humbug" about political and military affairs.[8]

Rodman experienced also the challenge becoming an effective officer. While his privileged background and recruiting efforts led to original commission as the regiment's major, Rodman worked diligently to serve as an exemplary leader. He complained in January 1863 of having to attend a court martial because it took him away from his regiment, "and I am losing the invaluable opportunity of making myself a good commander." When a general twice com-mended his unit in the following month, Rodman explained these "little things" that proved "gratifying to officers and men." He sustained regimental pride through skillful training and concern for his troops. Rodman described with relish and precision a variety of troop movements, tactics, and military maneuvers. His leadership was recognized by General W. H. Emory in mid-April who rode alongside Rodman and said, "You did elegantly, elegantly." Emory later consoled Rodman's father by extolling the son's excellent leader-ship in commanding with "signal success" the Thirty-Eighth Massachusetts in making it "one of the best" regiments in Union service.[9]

When killed at Port Hudson on May 27, 1863, William Logan Rodman had just turned forty-one years old and found a calling in military service despite his Quaker heritage. He was the city's highest-ranking officer to die in the war, and Joseph Ricketson spoke for many when he wrote that Rodman "died a hero." Ricketson also noted that Rodman's "conservative views had become much changed." Also, Rodman served in a unit with neighbors and relatives. When killed, Rodman was barely three feet away from his cousin, Captain Thomas Rodman, who was compelled to lay alongside the corpse for six hours in a blistering sun under constant Confederate fire.[10] Rodman's death, the return of his body, and his iconic status all shaped local commemorations of this regiment and the larger meaning of the Civil War. When remaining men of the Thirty-Eighth returned home from war on July 14, 1865, they were met by a marching band, throngs of celebrants at City Hall, and "hearty cheers and a shower of bouquets" from children.[11]

New Bedford's Other Soldiers

Like other northern communities, New Bedford adhered to national pat-terns suggested by James McPherson in which states, cities, and individuals raised troops in the place of the national government. Army companies and often entire regiments consisted of men recruited from a specific locale, such as a township, city, or county.[12] By early 1862, when the Union had enlisted

No. 706.

William Logan Rodman. (Courtesy of the Trustees of the New Bedford Free
Public Library.)

around 700,000 soldiers, New Bedford men were drawn by generous state and local bounties. Enthusiasm ebbed and flowed with the news of battlefield victories and defeats, and policy changes such as bounty payments and emancipation also shaped enlistment patterns. New Bedford sustained large enrollments in short-term infantry units during 1861, particularly in the Third Massachusetts Volunteer Militia (combining both three months and nine months service). Heavy enlistments persisted through 1862 when nearly one-half (725 of 1,553) of all soldiers from New Bedford joined army service. After some 1,188 naval credits were allowed for New Bedford in the summer of 1864, city officials crowed about the city's surplus of 1,100 men more than required by state and federal enlistment quotas. At war's end, more than nine out of ten (95 percent) of New Bedford's soldiers served in state units, drawn no doubt by bounties and heavy community recruitment efforts.[13]

New Bedford's soldiers represented a cross-section of the community in patterns that mirror other Northern communities. Most studies of Civil War soldiers, particularly on the Union side, agree with James McPherson that "the Union army appears to have been quite representative of the Northern population."[14] James Geary followed McPherson's lead and used a similar methodology in analyzing soldiers' prewar occupations to argue that the Civil War was not a "rich man's war and a poor man's fight." Conscription, in fact, proved to be a "fair" method of encouraging enlistments; because of policies that allowed commutation and substitution, only 46,347 men became federal conscripts, less than 1 percent of men of military age in the North.[15] In an influential article, W. J. Rorabaugh asked who fought for the North in the Civil War and concluded that property ownership was a key variable. He suggested that Union enlistees "were disproportionately propertyless youths and young men from all occupations except the mercantile and professional elite; propertied small shopkeepers, clerks, and skilled workers in their twenties; and skilled workers in their thirties."[16]

A more recent investigation by John Robertson notes that the "Union Army of 1861 was the most socially representative army in United States history," with relative higher proportions of skilled and white-collar men in the soldiers' ranks. Ultimately, Robertson emphasizes economic and material motives as the primary force in explaining initial enlistments and subsequent reenlistments. As the war progressed, Robertson suggests that laborers were twice as likely to reenlist as white-collar and skilled workers. Following reenlistment, Robertson writes, "more than half of the remaining soldiers were either laborers or without a listed occupation, and almost four-fifths were rural." Military service provided steady work for those on the bottom rungs of the social ladder. In

Table 4-1. **Enlistments According to 1865 "Army and Navy Register"**

Military Branches	Number
Infantry	1,004
Cavalry	403
Navy	274
Artillery	183
Battery (mostly Light Artillery)	92
Clerical, Other, Miscellaneous	35
Total	**1,991**
Army Officers' Ranks Above Private	
Major	2
Colonel	3
Lieutenant Colonel	6
Lieutenant	13
1st Lieutenant	25
2nd Lieutenant	17
Captain	32
Sergeant	44
Corporal	59
Total	**201**
Other Army Ranks (incomplete)	
Orderly Sergeant	3
Quarter Master	9
Musician	5
Assistant Surgeon	3
Hospital Steward	4
Private or no rank, Infantry	835
Private or no rank, Cavalry	369
Private or no rank, Artillery	158
Private or no rank, Battery	78
Total	**1,464**
Navy Ranks (incomplete list)	
Seaman	61
Landsman	23
Acting Master	23
Ensign	16
Acting Ensign	15
1st Class Boy	8

Table 4-1. (Continued)

Military Branches	Number
Paymaster's Clerk	6
Acting Master's Mate	4
Sailing Master	4
Ordinary Seaman	3
Boatswain	3
Engineer	3
2nd Class Boy	2
Master's Mate	2
Assistant Surgeon	2
Boatswain's Mate	2
Sailmaker	2
Pilot	1
Blank or No rank listed	27
Total	**207**

Source: 1865 Army and Navy Register, *1865 City Directory.*

contrast, men from urban and higher-class backgrounds enjoyed more economic and occupational opportunities. Robertson found that over half of the enlistees he examined in Pennsylvania were farmers or laborers, and the remainder shared 137 different occupations (not unlike Bell Wiley's observation of 300 occupations among soldiers in 123 different companies).[17]

In an effort to determine the backgrounds of New Bedford's enlisted soldiers, a database was created of more than one thousand men, a sample that constitutes about 65 percent of all men credited for army service from New Bedford.[18] This is not the place to enter into a discussion of occupational methodology except to note that New Bedford's labor market necessitated the creation of an additional class of "maritime" workers. Sailors and seamen fit into this broader classification of skilled maritime workers, along with other land-based occupations such as boat builder, caulker, and rope maker.[19] Judging by their backgrounds, New Bedford's soldiers reflected the society from which they came. In terms of age, the men in this sample ranged from fourteen (a musician, Charles G. Allen, in the Third Massachusetts) to a fifty-year-old merchant, Timothy Ingraham, New Bedford's City Marshal who enlisted as Captain of Company L of the Third Massachusetts Volunteer Militia (MVM), a nine months' unit (see Table 4-2). Taken together, the average age of all men in the sample was nearly twenty-seven years at the time of enlistment, and almost half of all enlistees were in their twenties.[20]

Table 4-2. MSSCW New Bedford Units Summary, Massachusetts Units Only

Branch/Unit Name/Company	No.	Term	Muster In Date	NB Bounty (Avg)	Killed/Died	Deserted	MIA/POW	Avg. Age
Infantry								
3rd MVM, Co. L	71	3 mos	4/23/1861	0	0	0	0	26.7
18th MVI, Co. A, F, H	50	3 yrs	8/24/1861	130**	9	3	1	26.2
23rd MVI, Co. D	86	3 yrs	9/28/1861		11	0	2	26.4
28th Ma, Co. B	10	3 yrs	12/13/1861	15	2	4	0	25.0
33rd MVI, Co. I	39	3 yrs	8/5/1862	100	4	3	0	27.5
38th MVI, Co. H	36	3 yrs	8/12/1862	100	9	1	0	29.1
47th MVM, Co. D	68	9 mos	9/20/1862	200	2	13	0	28.5
3rd MVM, Co. E	98	9 mos	9/23/1862	200	0	0	0	23.9
3rd MVM, Co. F	58	9 mos	9/23/1862	200	0	0	0	26.8
3rd MVM, Co. G	97	9 mos	9/23/1862	200	0	1	0	28.5
54th MVI (Col), Co. C	34	3 yrs	3/30/1863		4	0	3	26.3
26th Unattached MVI	33	1 yr	12/13/1864	100	0	0	0	24.1
Cavalry								
3rd MA Cav, Co. A	118	3 yrs	8/31/1862	250	21	7	0	26.8
Artillery								
5th Battery LA	90	3 yrs	12/3/1861		8	4	0	28.3
3rd HA, Co. B	119	3 yrs	5/19/1863		6	14	0	25.4
Totals	**1,007**				**76**	**50**	**6**	**26.7**

* 0 bounty for first enlistees; $325 or more for later enlistees.

** Bounties ranged from $100 to $250, with an average of $130.

Source: Massachusetts Soldiers and Sailors in the Civil War.

Note: Subtracting the naval enlistments (1,188) and Others (159) from the total of 2,900 military enlistments credited to New Bedford leaves 1,553. The database of 1,007 men listed in MSSCW thus constitutes almost 65 percent of all men credited for army military service from the city. "New

Civil War soldiers' backgrounds and motivations have intrigued many scholars. Reid Mitchell emphasizes that both the Union and the Confederacy "created mass armies out of an overwhelmingly citizen population." Because soldiers "probably represented the majority attitudes of each society as a whole," the study of men at war tells much about culture and politics in the United States, Mitchell contends.[21] Earl J. Hess contends that Northern soldiers were motivated by a similar ideology, religion, support from home, and comradeship. Remaining proud of their military service and sacrifices, Hess suggests, the majority of Union veterans sustained a positive perspective over four years of war.[22] Moving away from ideology as a motivating force, John Robertson contends that economic concerns and financial need prompted most men to enlist and reenlist. By pointing out that more than half of men who reenlisted were laborers and almost 80 percent were rural, Robertson contends that material conditions rather than ideology or group loyalty shaped Union forces.[23] At the risk of stating the obvious, we cannot know why any individual enlisted without more direct evidence from them, although substantial quantitative evidence can lead to solid speculation.

More troublesome is the dearth of written evidence (for example, letters and diaries) from the many enlistees who were not of advanced education and socioeconomic standing, such as Lieutenant Colonel William Logan Rodman. In looking at New Bedford's first wave of soldiers, the New Bedford City Guards, these men rushed to Boston in April 1861 and then to the South to serve for ninety days. Early expectations of a quick victory were shown by President Lincoln's call for seventy-five thousand soldiers to serve only three months. Joining other "Minute Men of '61," Company L of the Third Massachusetts Volunteer Militia (MVM) Infantry gained fame in a unit laden with professionals and merchants (almost 16 percent of New Bedford's men in the unit) and shopkeepers and clerks (another 26.8 percent of the city's men). They carried out their duties without any bounty payment and with an expectation that the war would be a short one. Commenting later on the state's three-months' enlistees, William Schouler wrote that they "proved the sterling worth" of the state's volunteer militia. Their composition was decidedly top heavy on white-collar workers, a pattern that would not be replicated by any other army unit.[24]

Despite good intentions, the soldiers of the Third Massachusetts were not the kind needed to defeat the Confederacy. After dilatory recruiting efforts among federal officials, President Lincoln asked on May 3, 1861, for forty-two thousand new troops, all three-years' men. And, after the subsequent debacle at Bull Run in July, Congress authorized the recruitment of another five hundred thousand Union men. In this context, New Bedford officials toiled diligently to recruit men and offer bounty money. In the early summer of 1861, the Eighteenth Massachusetts drew fifty enlistees from New Bedford through an attractive city bounty that averaged $130 per man. Members of the Eighteenth constituted the highest percentage of skilled workers (42 percent) and farmers and farm laborers (12 percent) of any army unit in the sample through the war's duration. No merchants or professionals signed up. Enlisting for three years, these men would see tough service after mustering in during August. Of fifty men, nine were killed in battle or died in service, and another one went missing at Fredericksburg and died as a prisoner of war in South Carolina.[25]

Later that summer, Governor John Andrew addressed the "citizen-soldiers of Massachusetts" in proclaiming that "Duty, honor, the clearest sentiments of patriotic love and devotion, call for your hearts and unconquerable arms." State and city officials worked assiduously to promote enlistments, and by the end of the year, Massachusetts had raised over forty-two thousand soldiers and sailors. This number was more than twice the number of men in the US Army before the Civil War.[26] In the fall, New Bedford's first war casualty was announced: Sergeant Herbert Handley of the Twentieth Massachusetts Volunteer Infantry, Company G, who was killed by a horse in Providence, Rhode Island. New Bedford contributed mightily to substantial state and federal military recruitment in the summer of 1861, particularly as men who had served for three months were recruited in July and August 1861 for units like the Twenty-Third Massachusetts Volunteer Infantry. Its Company D was mainly comprised of New Bedford men and led by Captain Cornelius Howland Jr., First Lieutenant Samuel C. Hart, and Second Lieutenant Anthony Lang. These enlistees were mostly blue-collar workers, with nearly 35 percent skilled tradesmen, over 25 percent semi- and unskilled workers, and almost 13 percent engaged in maritime work.[27]

The composition of the Twenty-Third illustrated how civilian occupation and military ranks were often connected, as five merchants held the rank of Corporal or higher. In New Bedford and throughout the North, Union military rank bore rough approximation with antebellum status and occupation. Historian John Robertson has written that "prewar demographic data" could help in predicting "wartime decision making" among enlistees. Similarly, Teresa A. Thomas contended that "social class colored the experience of war," and that infantry units were drawn mainly from the farming and mechanic classes. Looking to the larger sample of 1,007 New Bedford enlistees, 11 of 24 merchants (nearly one-half) entered military service as commissioned officers, and 6 others (one-fourth) as noncommissioned officers. Only 7 merchants enlisted as privates. For the rank-and-file, prewar status also served as a rough barometer of military rank. Of New Bedford's 106 laborers in the sample, 96 joined as privates, 5 as corporals, and 1 as sergeant. Closer analysis reveals a decline in enlistments by merchants and professionals once the excitement of war dwindled, and a growing percentage of semi- and unskilled men made up the ranks of units established later in the war.[28]

In an effort to examine any differences between men's experiences in different army branches, two artillery units were examined, one from 1861 and the second from 1863. The Fifth Battery Volunteer Light Artillery was formed in early fall of 1861 for three years' service under the leadership of Captain Max Eppendorf, a former artillery officer of the Saxon army. Eppendorf's short command ended in early 1862. New Bedford's contributions to this unit were mainly of working-class men who received an initial fifteen dollars local bounty upon enlistment. Almost half (48.9 percent) of the city's ninety enlistees were semi- and unskilled workers, probably drawn by the prospect of steady income at thirteen dollars per month for privates. Less than 15 percent of all recruits from New Bedford came from other than the ranks of skilled, semiskilled, and unskilled workers. This unit saw heavy action, ranging from Sharpsburg in October 1862 to Fredericksburg in December and Gettysburg in July 1863. They endured the Battle of the Wilderness in May and the Battle of the Crater in late July 1864, and men who did not reenlist were sent home on October 3, 1864. Of New Bedford's known ninety volunteers in this artillery unit, thirteen men mustered out in October 1864 after serving three long years while two dozen men reenlisted and served through the war's duration that included laying siege to Petersburg in early April 1865 and service at City Point until early May.[29]

As 1862 opened, New Bedford's John H. Clifford was elected President of the Massachusetts Senate and praised the "gallant sons of Massachusetts, native and adopted, of every class and condition" who marched into war as a "band of brothers" in defending their common flag. Northern communities rallied to raise troops and recruitment picked up in 1862. On July 4, 1862, President Lincoln called for another three hundred thousand men to serve three years—or for the war's duration. By then, the army of the Potomac had failed to capture the Confederate capital of Richmond, although General Burnside had captured Newbern and General Benjamin Butler occupied New Orleans. When President Lincoln called in August 1862 for three hundred thousand more men to serve nine months, Massachusetts Adjutant General Schouler criticized arithmetic "known only to the authorities in Washington" that increased the state's quota and he resisted plans for conscription. Similarly, Governor Andrew believed that more soldiers could be obtained by voluntary enlistment than by a draft, and he added that employers had promised to save jobs for soldiers once they returned home.[30]

In the summer of 1862 a three-years' regiment, the Thirty-Third Massachusetts Volunteer Infantry, was commanded at the outset by Italian-born veteran
Alberto C. Maggi. Nearly forty men from the Whaling City enlisted in Company I, possibly drawn by a local bounty of one hundred dollars. Some of the
men earned distinction, such as Colonel Maggi, bandleader Israel Smith, and
merchant Elisha Doane. In July 1863 the Thirty-Third participated at Gettysburg where they repulsed Confederate attacks at East Cemetery Hill. Later consolidated into the Twentieth Corps commanded by Generals Joseph Hooker
and I. A. Mower, the regiment men joined the Atlanta campaign in May 1864
and took part in Sherman's famous "March to the Sea." In mopping up at war's
end, the men marched through Petersburg, Richmond, Chancellorsville, and
Washington, DC, where the regiment joined the Grand Review of Sherman's
army on May 24. Mustered out on June 10 and paid off on July 2, of New Bedford's thirty-nine enlistees, twenty served and survived the war's duration.[31]

Besides the Thirty-Eighth raised by William Logan Rodman over the summer of 1862, other units were to serve nine months. The Forty-Seventh Massachusetts Volunteer Militia, captained by lawyer Austin S. Cushman and
merchant Joseph Burt, enlisted nearly seventy New Bedford men in Company
D. Older on average than other enlistees at 28.5 years, they may have been
drawn by largest local bounty paid out, about two hundred dollars per man.
One-third of the enlistees had worked in maritime employments, and this unit
also had the highest percentage of farmers and farm laborers (almost 15 percent) of any sampled group of soldiers. Curiously, this unit had the highest
number of desertions, as thirteen men deserted in New England or on Long
Island.[32] In contrast, the Third Massachusetts recruited 253 men from the city
to enlist in Companies E, F, or G, also receiving a bounty of two hundred dollars per man. These units had no desertions, possibly explained by occupational
distributions. Nearly 6 percent were of the merchant and professional class, 17
percent were clerks and small shopkeepers, more than 35 percent had been
skilled workers and tradesmen, 21.7 percent were semi- and unskilled workers,
just over 14 percent had been employed in maritime pursuits, and about 4 percent were farmers or farm laborers. When the Third mustered out in June 1862,
at least 116 of the men reenlisted, the largest number of them (20) headed to
the Fifteenth Unattached Company Massachusetts Infantry (100 days), with 17
more enlisting in the Fifty-Eighth Massachusetts Infantry.[33]

In September 1862 the Union reeled over news from Antietam, the deadliest
day in American history. Although Massachusetts' men suffered "terrible fatali-
ties," Adjutant General William Schouler reported, the battle was still a victory.
Even as wounded and sick men returned home, they offered "cheering words"
and a "buoyant and gallant spirit" with many stories to tell. Examining the

Union mindset in late 1862, Schouler declared: "There was no grumbling, no fault-finding; nor was there any appearance of personal hatred towards the soldiers in the rebel army."[34] At this time in New Bedford, the Third Massachusetts Cavalry (and later the Forty-First Infantry) drew at least 118 men from the Whaling City after mustering in late August. They received the largest bounties offered by New Bedford during the war, $250 per man. The largest number of volunteers were laborers (18), clerks (14), teamers (12), carpenters (8), and seamen (8). By now, enlistment patterns were emerging. Only 2 of 118 New Bedford enlistees were part of the merchant or professional class: forty-two-year-old architect and builder John F. Vinal, also the unit's captain, and banker James W. Hervey, in his mid-twenties, who served as first lieutenant.[35]

Following a "busy and anxious" 1862, the new year opened with celebration of the Emancipation Proclamation that included provisions for military service by African-American men.[36] Among the most storied regiments of the Civil War, the Fifty-Fourth Massachusetts Volunteer Infantry (Colored) was the first military unit comprised of African Americans raised in the North. Undoubtedly some white Northerners would agree with William Logan Rodman, writing from the field in February, who stated: "I can't say I want to have anything to do with black troops." Rodman wished well to the "negro soldier raising" in New Bedford, although he expressed doubts about James Grace as the company's captain. By the end of March, Rodman expressed his hope that "darkies" would fight and thus save white lives and give employment to blacks. He urged that the experiment go forward. "If the blacks won't fight, why then they will be like a great many white men," Rodman wrote. "If they will, then we have material for an army which may whip the world."[37]

Nearly three dozen African-American men from New Bedford enlisted in Company C of the Fifty-Fourth Massachusetts under Captain James W. Grace, a former merchant and fruit dealer. These men held strong ideological motivations and did not receive any worthwhile bounty payments. They fought to prove their status as citizens and to end slavery. Men of this regiment came disproportionately from the ranks of unskilled and semiskilled workers, and the highest-status occupation of the black volunteers was that of barber and waiter. Seventeen (50 percent) of the men were listed as laborers with an average age of almost twenty-seven. Eighteen of the thirty-four men served until the unit was mustered out on August 20, 1865, and of these, at least five were wounded. Four men were known to have died or been killed, while three others went missing and were supposed to have been killed after Fort Wagner. Nine men were discharged before their terms because of disability.[38]

In addition to raising a "model" regiment of black troops, Massachusetts was effective in enlisting thousands of soldiers in 1863. The state recruited 11,538

volunteers for three years' service, plus 16,837 nine-months' men and 3,736
three-months' men. The issue of home and coastal defense remained a lively
one in the spring of 1863, and some men chose to stay close to home by enlisting
in the Sixth Unattached Company Heavy Artillery that joined eight other companies to garrison the state's coastal forts. Additional companies were raised
through the summer of 1864 to create a regiment. By September 1864 officials
established the Third Regiment Massachusetts Volunteer Heavy Artillery under
the command of Colonel Williams S. Albert, a West Point graduate. In New
Bedford, Captain John A. P. Allen led recruiting efforts that netted 119 men.[39]
Undoubtedly, many men enlisted first in the Sixth Company (later Company
B of the Third Massachusetts Heavy Artillery) with the expectation that they
would avoid service at the war front. This unit experienced a high number of
desertions during the war, as nearly 12 percent (fourteen) skedaddled, most of
them at Clark's Point in New Bedford where they faced distractions and entice-
ments. Other explanations for desertions could include the high percentage of
seamen and mariners (nearly 40 percent) and that fifty-five (46 percent) of the
soldiers were aged twenty-two or younger, most of them seamen, farmers, or
farm laborers.[40]

MSSCW Entries in 1860 Census Sample

    As military and social historians can attest, tracking and tracing individuals'
military service is challenging even with access to significant published
records.[41] Men moved in and out of military units, and army units formed and
reformed in response to military events and political decisions. The sample of
1,000 individuals listed in the published *Massachusetts Soldiers, Sailors, and
Marines in the Civil War* (*MSSCW*) rosters were compared with the 1860 federal
population census for New Bedford. The end result was 317 individuals located
in both military and census sources.[42] The sample was distributed through all
six wards: Ward 1 (66), Ward 2 (67), Ward 3 (51), Ward 4 (36), Ward 5 (42), and
Ward 6 (55). The sample is skewed toward white men, as only 9 in the sample
of 317 (less than 3 percent) were listed as black or mulatto.[43]
    Perhaps the most effective analysis is of occupation since it helps to approxi-
mate class standing (see Table 4-3).[44] Sixteen merchants who enlisted included
famous names but these were typically younger sons who lacked the substantial
wealth of older generations. For example, Cornelius Howland Jr., aged twenty-
six and married; Thomas R. Rodman, a decade older and worth at least $10,000
in real property and $5,000 in personal property, also married; and William L.
Rodman, a single man of forty and no property who would become the city's

Table 4-3. MSSCW Occupations by Unit

Unit	Merchant and Professional	Clerk and Shopkeeper	Skilled Worker	Semi-and Unskilled Worker	Maritime Worker	Farmer and Farm Laborer	Student	None or Blank
3rd MVM (3 mos)	15.5%	26.8%	36.6%	11.3%	7.0%	1.4%	1.4%	0.0%
18th MVI, A, F, H	0.0%	16.0%	42.0%	16.0%	12.0%	12.0%	2.0%	0.0%
23rd MVI Co. D	7.0%	14.0%	34.9%	25.6%	12.8%	5.8%	0.0%	0.0%
33rd MVI Co. I	5.1%	12.8%	30.8%	30.8%	7.7%	7.7%	2.6%	2.6%
38th MVI Co. H	5.9%	14.7%	26.5%	41.2%	2.9%	5.9%	2.9%	0.0%
47th MVM Co. D	4.4%	4.4%	17.6%	7.4%	33.8%	14.7%	1.5%	16.2%
3rd MVM (9 mos)	5.9%	17.0%	35.2%	21.7%	14.2%	4.0%	1.6%	0.4%
54th MVM Co. C	2.9%	0.0%	5.9%	61.8%	26.5%	2.9%	0.0%	0.0%
26th Unattach.	0.0%	12.1%	18.2%	36.4%	24.2%	6.1%	3.0%	0.0%
3rd Ma CAV, A1.	7%	18.6%	32.2%	27.1%	12.7%	5.1%	1.7%	0.8%
5th MA Battery	2.2%	3.3%	37.8%	48.9%	4.4%	3.3%	0.0%	0.0%
3rd HA, Co. B	1.7%	1.7%	24.4%	19.3%	38.7%	11.8%	0.0%	2.5%

Source: Massachusetts Soldiers and Sailors in the Civil War.

most prominent war casualty.[45] Carpenters were among the most numerous of skilled workers, and only three of them claimed real property (in amounts of $160, $500, and $1,000, respectively) and only two others possessed personal property.[46] Thirty-three laborers constituted over 10 percent of this sample, the largest single occupational category. The largest group by nativity and marital status consisted of eleven single Massachusetts-born men, followed by ten married Irish-born laborers.[47] About one in seven army enlistees in this sample were mariners or seamen, and they were predominantly Massachusetts-born (35 or 79.5 percent of this group).[48] In comparing enlisted "sons" with "others" and household "heads," the sons averaged 23.2 years of age, only 3 out of 118 owned any property, and 5 were married.[49] Nearly one-half (154 or 48.6 percent) of the men located in the census were married, and 83 percent of them (128) owned nothing, which may explain their material motivations to enlist in military service.[50] While only suggestive, these patterns lend credence to material explanations for soldiers' enlistment and reenlistment during the war, as John Robertson has suggested.

Irish Soldiers from New Bedford

A number of Civil War scholars have analyzed the experiences of foreign-born soldiers and sailors to determine if they were more or less "patriotic" than native-born Americans, judging by enlistment patterns and public declarations of loyalty.[51] The Irish in New Bedford present an interesting case because by the mid-1850s they were the largest minority group in the city, and many found work in the recently established Wamsutta Mills. However, the Irish did not generate much attention before the war, and during the war they lacked the kind of public support generated for black military enlistment. Throughout the North, military service provided opportunities for immigrants to prove their loyalty to their adopted country, to find financial stability through military bounties and income, and, particularly for the Irish, to acquire a "white" racial identity to compete better against black Americans.[52] Most Irish and Irish Americans joined their contemporary Peter Welsh in proclaiming that Union military service would accelerate claims of citizenship within their "adopted country."[53]

New Bedford's Irish-born men had choices for enlisting in the Union cause but few opted to serve in two specifically Irish regiments, the Ninth or the Twenty-Eighth Massachusetts Volunteers. Although their community lacked a chronicler like Peter Welsh, they could read of Irish patriotism and Catholic solidarity in the *Boston Pilot*.[54] On occasion the Irish Catholic newspaper offered insights and insults about New Bedford. For example, readers learned in August 1862 that New Bedford's "Assessors inform us that more patriotism is manifested among the Irish than any other class of citizens." In mid-October 1863, the *Pilot* criticized New Bedford's previous military draft in which large numbers of men paid commutation money or hired substitutes. "This does not speak well for the Sebastopol of niggerdom," the paper declared. Not only was the *Pilot* reflecting its racist worldview but it was making up for scant coverage of Irish patriotism in local newspapers. The *New Bedford Daily Evening Standard* made no mention of Irish Americans until September 16, 1861, when the paper published a letter from Colonel Thomas Meagher who actively recruited for the Twenty-Eighth Massachusetts Regiment. Advertisements for Irish recruits followed in mid-October at the height of enlistment efforts by Edmund H. Fitzpatrick, and only gradually were news items published about Irish and Irish-American efforts during the war.[55]

On the whole, Irish-born soldiers from New Bedford were not segregated into easily identified units and received little local publicity.[56] Of the nearly two thousand New Bedford soldiers listed in the "Army and Navy Register," only four served with the Ninth Massachusetts Volunteers, the state's first "Irish Regiment." Some twenty-eight men enlisted in Company B of the Twenty-Eighth Massachusetts, sometimes called the Taber Guards. Irish citizens of New Bedford held their own war meeting and discussed a possible "pay-off" at the war's end. They spoke of intangible benefits because bounties were limited at the time to only $15 from city authorities, plus promises of a $100 bounty from the state at the "expiration of the campaign."[57] The recruiting drive for the Twenty-Eighth Massachusetts Volunteers featured advertisements framed by an American flag and an Irish harp directed to "Irishmen, and Sons of Irishmen." They were urged to "rally forth for your country's good, at your country's call." Like its cousin, the Ninth Massachusetts, the Twenty-Eighth endured some of the Union's most difficult and deadly battles, among them Second Bull Run, Antietam, Chancellorsville, Gettysburg, and Cold Harbor.[58] Irish-born recruits enjoyed options as to where and when they enlisted. Their service in a variety of regiments beyond the state's two Irish regiments suggests a level of mobility and, possibly, limited loyalty to a city and state that promoted racial equality.[59]

Mortality among New Bedford's Soldiers and Sailors

The private anguish of families who lost husbands, sons, and brothers in the war can never be fully known. With nearly 620,000 deaths through the Civil War, Americans were awash in death and mourning from 1861 to 1865 and beyond.[60] As of January 1865, of the more than 2,000 men who had enlisted at or from New Bedford, at least 163 were listed as dead, killed, or wounded and presumed dead. New Bedford's city council spearheaded a postwar effort to identify all of the city's dead veterans, led by City Treasurer James B. Congdon. Wrapping up his labors in May 1869, Congdon reported that all military veterans who died of war-related wounds had been "martyrs in the cause of their country." By his count, 257 men (216 soldiers and 41 seamen) deserved permanent recognition on the city's "Roll of Honor."[61]

New Bedford's casualties reflected the fluctuations and intensity of war. In 1861 nine men died from New Bedford, but the figure climbed to forty-seven in 1862. With deaths at Gettysburg and other major battles in 1863, New Bedford lost seventy-six men in 1863, yet more would die in 1864 when ninety-three were killed in battle or died of disease. During the last year of the war, twenty-six men perished. Historian James Robertson has raised interesting points about the "clustering" of deaths by noting a positive correlation between combat deaths and desertions. Furthermore, he points out that nearly 95 percent of all combat deaths took place during a period of twenty days clustered around six battles in 1862 and 1863.[62] For New Bedford's fighting men, the single deadliest day came when six men died at Fredericksburg on December 13, 1862. Five men died at the siege of Fort Wagner on July 18, 1863, and another five died at the battle of Cold Harbor on June 3, 1864. Among army deaths, most (164) lacked a rank and presumably were privates. At least thirteen New Bedford men, including Corporal James H. Gooding of the Fifty-Fourth Massachusetts, died in captivity at Andersonville, the notorious Confederate prison in Georgia; six of them died there during October 1864.[63]

In the effort to commemorate deaths and sacrifices from their own community, New Bedford officials did acknowledge those who served out of the state. At least fourteen men (5.5 percent of the total) on the Roll of Honor died serving in units outside of Massachusetts or in the US Navy. Army soldiers comprised 84 percent of all war casualties connected with city residents. Only 50 of the 256 men were buried locally at home, and 5 of these were "monuments" and not graves. New Bedford's soldiers expired all over the South, from Baton Rouge, Louisiana, to Newbern, North Carolina, to Lookout Valley, Tennessee, to Sharpsburg, Maryland. All but one of two dozen prisoners of war had been buried in the South. Only two of forty-one naval deaths, Seaman James T. Jenney and Acting Master's Mate Nathaniel D. Ottwell, were listed as having either a burial or monument in New Bedford. Of New Bedford's more than 250 dead soldiers and sailors, only seven apparently died "at home" in New Bedford, while another five were listed as dying in New Bedford.[64]

All of these numbers point to the problems faced in New Bedford and in the North of honoring men who died and could not be physically buried at home. Again, William Logan Rodman provides an instructive example. Dying a hero's death in battle, Rodman was feted with proper rituals by both military and civilian compatriots. After laying beside his cousin's corpse for hours, Captain Thomas Rodman joined several comrades from New Bedford in riding two miles to a saw mill to obtain wood for a coffin. Rodman's body was transported to a hospital where it was "wrapped in a blanket and the coffin filled and covered with green leaves." The men drove in a mule cart two more miles to bury Rodman in a "beautiful little space near our camping-ground of a few nights previous," next to graves of other soldiers. During a funeral attended by officers, Rodman's body was reported to wear the expression of "perfect tranquility and repose." Rodman's body remained there until cool weather would allow the body to be transported through New Orleans and then shipped home to New Bedford. Rodman's status as an officer and his prominent place in New Bedford ensured that his body would be sent home, and local newspapers reported the corpse's return in late December 1863.[65]

Those who died in the Union cause were feted with public recognition during and after the war, and funerals and commemorations brought together city officials, private citizens, veterans, and civilians. The funeral of Captain Thomas R. Robeson is a good example. Entering the war as a twenty-two-year-old captain, Robeson was shot in the thigh with a minie ball on May 3, 1863 and died three days later. Before his death in a military hospital, Robeson exhibited "gentlemanly & noble traits of character," according to Joseph Ricketson. When the captain's body was received in New Bedford, his coffin was displayed for public viewing, covered with an American flag and flowers. The "solemn & impressive" funeral was officiated by the Reverend William Potter, and an array of visitors included active and inactive military officers.[66] Similar rituals were repeated by the thousands in the North, made especially poignant when brothers Ezra Chase and William Chase were eulogized in New Bedford on October 20, 1864.[67]

Summary

Most of New Bedford's nearly two thousand white soldiers and sailors did not acquire national fame during the war, although a few attracted the attention of Massachusetts Governor Andrew and appeared in local newspaper accounts.[68] William Logan Rodman was feted during and after his death. The state's and city's first Grand Army of the Republic Post, Number One, was named for Rodman, and eventually the fort at Clark's Point was named for Rodman in 1898. Even with substantial documentation drawn from local, state, and federal military records, however, it is challenging to find out more about men's individual experiences during the war. Few first-hand accounts by the city's Civil War veterans survive, and official records are often sparse with personalized details. The Irish military experience reflected a quest for assimilation and full citizenship rights but often with a sense of resentment against black Americans and the Union policy of emancipation. Massachusetts Governor John Andrew joined with enlightened white and black supporters to push black military service, leading to creation of the Fifty-Fourth Massachusetts Regiment, the first such regiment raised in the North and arguably the most significant of all "colored" units. As detailed in the next chapter, New Bedford's enlistees in the Fifty-Fourth Regiment would acquire fame greater than the city's white soldiers as they fought for the Union, for equal pay, and for an end to slavery.

5

"Boys, I Only Did My Duty": New Bedford's Black Soldiers in the Fifty-Fourth Massachusetts

When war began in April 1861, members of New Bedford's black community showed their continuing desires to defend themselves and their city. Just ten days after the Confederate attack on Fort Sumter, Captain Johnson of the New Bedford "Blues" claimed that four hundred black men were "ready to enlist in the service of the government." Meeting at New Bedford's city hall, hundreds of black citizens, men and women, pledged a volunteer militia to "fight for liberty, to be ready at any moment . . . wherever our support may be required." William Henry Johnson declared that New Bedford's black men were "true and loyal citizens" eager to organize for the "security and defence of our city and State against any and all emergencies." Black and white leaders offered strong support, such as New Bedford's former mayor, Rodney French, who was pleased that his "colored fellow citizens had offered . . . to fight this great battle of liberty."[1] Although state and federal authorities were slow to accept the enlistment of black soldiers, New Bedford's black men would eventually provide vital contributions to the Union military victory and add ammunition to arguments for full citizenship for all African Americans.[2]

New Bedford's blacks joined a larger national chorus led by their former neighbor Frederick Douglass who championed black military service at the war's outset. Douglass urged "our people everywhere to drink as deeply into the martial spirit of the times as possible; organize themselves into societies and companies, purchase arms for themselves, and learn how to use them." A prescient thinker, Douglass declared that the war would probably "reach a complexion when a few black regiments will be absolutely necessary." Black men's active participation in the military struggle would prove their valor, demonstrate their manhood, and stake their full claims to citizenship. In May 1861 Douglass declared: "LET THE SLAVES AND FREE COLORED PEOPLE BE CALLED INTO SERVICE, AND FORMED INTO A LIBERATING ARMY. . . ." Other black leaders joined Douglass in attacking racist policies that prevented black men from enlisting in the Union army, and their practical arguments gained weight as the war progressed. "Men in earnest don't fight with one hand when they might fight with two," Douglass wrote in September 1861, "and a drowning man would not refuse to be saved even by a colored hand."[3]

This chapter examines the military experiences of African-American men connected with the famous Fifty-Fourth Massachusetts Volunteer Infantry, the "brave black regiment" that captured the country's attention after it was created in early 1863. More than thirty local residents joined Company C that became "the representative Massachusetts company," according to Luis Emilio, a regimental officer and historian.[4] Scores of New Bedford's black men fought for the Union in other segregated units such as the Fifty-Fifth Massachusetts and the Fifth Massachusetts Cavalry, along with the Union navy. A close examination of the Fifty-Fourth Massachusetts showcases the mostly anonymous black Americans from the Whaling City who, like other African-American soldiers, fought a "different Civil War" than did whites. By focusing on the men of Company C, this chapter highlights links between home front and battlefield, and between white and black communities of New Bedford, as together they experienced the Civil War.[5]

Antislavery and pro-Union sentiment remained fervent in New Bedford, whipped up no doubt by visits from Frederick Douglass several times during the war. During November 1861, for example, Douglass reported a "very large and enthusiastic meeting" of New Bedford's "colored citizens" who asked the Massachusetts state legislature to permit black men's enlistment in the state militias. Mayor Isaac Taber joined prominent white citizens in supporting black enlistment, including Rodney French who urged black citizens to "commence drilling, for he thought that their services would very soon be required by the Government."[6] Public meetings, speeches, and newspaper editorials through 1861 kept up a drumbeat of agitation directed against slavery and the Confederacy. In an editorial of November 7, 1861, the *New Bedford Standard* hoped that Charleston might be "reduced to ashes as a punishment for her many crimes against the Union." A story circulated about South Carolinians who promised to all "Yankee invaders, who remain on our soil, a prison above it or a grave beneath it." Later, in mid-March 1862, public attention focused on an antislavery petition signed by hundreds of New Bedford women and directed to both houses of Congress. Calling for the "extinction of slavery through the country," the petition was supported by the *Standard* and termed slavery the "cruelest form of oppression," its end certain.[7]

New Bedford's citizens continued to push for emancipation as a Union war aim while protesting the exclusion of black men from military service. During the city's traditional antislavery event of August 1, 1862, about one thousand people gathered at Myrick's Station outside the city for a day-long rally. An integrated slate of officers included Frederick Douglass's son, Lewis Douglass, and the elder Douglass's appearance was "cheering to all present." Two days later, ex-slave abolitionist William Wells Brown spoke before the city's largest white church on Sunday, August 3, sermonizing about the right of black men to bear arms for the Union and an immediate end to slavery.[8] Although Lincoln had issued a preliminary emancipation proclamation in September 1862, a *Standard* editorial suggested that the year closed with some "despondency" because of battlefield disasters and depredations by Confederate ships against Union vessels. Commencing on January 1, 1863, the new national policy of emancipation brought optimism, as did larger armies in the field, the construction of new iron clad ships, and "immense preparations" to strike at slavery, the "root of the rebellion." New Bedford's Liberty Hall and numerous churches hosted Emancipation celebrations that linked Northern free blacks with their "soon-to-be-free brethren of the South," noted one local commentator.[9]

Black Military Enlistment

The Emancipation Proclamation legitimized and accelerated the Union's move to enlist black soldiers. At home in New Bedford, black citizens convened at City Hall on January 21, 1863, to hear William Wells Brown explain that military service would allow blacks to prove themselves "valuable citizens." Deeply committed to the cause of enlisting black soldiers, Massachusetts Governor John A. Andrew convinced Secretary of War Edwin Stanton in January 1863 to allow Andrew to enroll volunteers that "may include persons of African descent, organized into special corps."[10] Andrew explained that the state's (and the North's) first "colored regiment" constituted "perhaps the most important corps to be organized during the whole war" and serve as the "model for all future colored regiments." The unit's white officers, according to Andrew, were to be experienced and of "firm antislavery principles, ambitious, superior to a vulgar contempt for color, and hav[e] faith in the capacity of colored men for military service." This regiment's "success or failure will go far to elevate or depress the estimation in which the character of the colored Americans will be held throughout the world," Andrew believed. Contemporary white officials and black allies faced opposition, an "almost impenetrable wall of prejudice" described by Massachusetts Adjutant General William Schouler. Because of the state's relatively small black population, military recruitment spread throughout the North as black leaders and white allies spurred enlistments from Boston to St. Louis.[11]

Recruiting efforts began in New Bedford in mid-February 1863, but enlistments lagged because some feared that African-American soldiers would face discrimination, particularly unequal pay. To allay these fears, Governor Andrew wrote to City Treasurer James B. Congdon that he expected black recruits to collect the same "pay, equipments, bounty, or any aid or protection" as other (white) volunteers. Andrew added that Massachusetts would not enlist African-American men unless the "Government of the United States was prepared to guarantee and defend to the last dollar and the last man, to these men, all the rights, privileges, and immunities that are given by the laws of civilized warfare to other soldiers." In spelling out this contractual bond, Andrew declared that black men "will be soldiers of the Union, nothing less and nothing different." He added: "I believe they will earn for themselves an honorable fame, vindicating their race and redressing their future from the aspersions of the past." To promote recruiting efforts in New Bedford, Andrew explained to Congdon that he sought a "*model* regiment, and as it will be the first so raised, it is my intention to make it also, the *best*, of the regiments to be recruited from the colored population of the country."[12]

New Bedford's Committee on Military Relief reached out to both black and white citizens by circulating a "subscription paper" of wealthy donors that listed some of the state's wealthiest families, many of them prominent in the antislavery movement. New Bedford's elites offered monetary and public support, among them Cornelius Howland, C. B. H. Fessenden, and James B. Congdon.[13] A recruiting office opened on William Street on February 10, 1863, staffed by James W. Grace, a youthful white grocer and lieutenant in the Massachusetts militia. Within two days, Grace enlisted eight men and began to advertise and speak throughout the city, often accompanied by prominent white and black antislavery activists such as William Lloyd Garrison, Wendell Phillips, and Frederick Douglass.[14] Greater civic support came when the city hosted a "Grand Rally" on February 18, 1863, at which black enlistees were promised equal pay, full rations, and family support. William Wells Brown called for volunteers to liberate their "brethren in the South" with the believe that one "Massachusetts colored regiment in South Carolina would make the Confederate government quake with fear."[15]

Recruiting was successful by the third week in February 1863. Grace urged black men to report at once because "many citizens of unquestioned respectability have joined the company, [and] we hope it may be filled during the week." By February 26, the Soldiers' Relief Society reported receiving $139 in contributions for outfitting the company and providing up to $15 in bounty payments per enlistee.[16] James B. Congdon reported that 30 of the city's black men had enrolled, about one-fourth of the estimated 132 African-American men who resided in New Bedford at the time. Quaker Joseph Ricketson reported on "first rate" enlistments in the Fifty-Fourth, and future military hero William Carney recounted that white and black citizens worked "earnestly" to recruit black soldiers. The city's Soldiers' Relief Committee voted in early March to provide up to $50 as individual and family relief, followed by approval of a $25 bounty payment to any man mustered into the regiment.[17] Although these payments reflected the desires of local white leaders to support black troops, they became a source of conflict with state authorities, who had begun to discourage local bounty payments. New Bedford's Common Council urged instead that payments be viewed as relief, not bounties. On March 9, 1863, each of the city's black recruits was granted a one-time payment of $25 "as a measure of immediate *aid* and *relief*," Congdon explained, and a private "Citizens' Gratuity" of ten dollars to each enlistee continued.[18]

Despite these paternalistic and patriotic efforts, recruiting was undermined by a "rougher element" of Northern whites opposed to black enlistment, even in New Bedford. Such conflict showed class and racial antagonisms prevalent in nineteenth-century American society. Luis Emilio recounted that Lieutenant Grace's recruiting efforts in New Bedford were "often insulted by such remarks as, 'There goes the captain of the Negro Company! He thinks the negroes will fight! They will turn and run at the first sight of the enemy!'" Emilio also claimed that Grace's young son was ridiculed in school because of his father's work. To overcome overt hostility, white dignitaries joined African-American leaders in a civic celebration that symbolized the city's sponsorship of Company C. Speakers at a farewell meeting included whites Lieutenant Colonel Hallowell, James W. Grace, and C. B. H. Fessenden, along with black leaders William Berry, the Reverend William Grimes, the Reverend Edmund Kelly, and enlistee Wesley Furlong. The New Bedford contingent left for camp on March 4, 1863, carrying with it the good wishes of many in the city.[19] New Bedford's Soldiers' Relief Society continued to raise money for the "Toussaint Guards" of Company C, and by May 1863 nearly $160 had been received for the purchase of flannel for shirts, yarn for socks, and handkerchiefs. From the perspective of elected leaders and many wealthy whites, the city stood squarely behind its black citizens in sending off men to war, many of them with first-hand knowledge of slavery.[20]

New Bedford Men of Company C

Company C of the Fifty-Fourth Massachusetts Infantry Regiment served as a core contingent in the Union's most significant black regiment. Support from white and black citizens in New Bedford remained strong during the war, as did connections between home front and battlefield. Frederick Douglass's stirring

rhetoric was upheld by the courage of William H. Carney, James Henry Gooding, and others who served in Company C. One-third of the company, thirty-
two black men, enlisted from New Bedford (claims of fifty men were exagger-
ated). Community values were reinforced by the fact that soldiers knew one
another as neighbors, family, and friends.[21] A biographical portrait illustrates
the diversity among them. Of the twenty-four men who enlisted in February
1863, fourteen were single, ten married. More than half (14) listed their occupation as laborer, followed by men who worked as seamen (3), hostlers (2), and
one each as a steward, farmer, waiter, teamster, and barber. Of the second wave
of recruits, eight men who enlisted in March and April 1863, four were single,
two married, and the marital status of two men was unknown or not recorded.
Of the six known occupations for these later recruits, one was a laborer, two
were seamen, and one each claimed to be a caulker, a barber, and a shoemaker.
The company's youngest member was Alexander H. Johnson, a single seaman
who enrolled as a musician at the age of sixteen. Several men were in the forties,
led by Abram Torrence, aged forty-three, a married laborer who enlisted on
February 18, 1863. Samuel Leighton and George Delevan were each forty-one
years old, married, and laborers.[22]

    Just two days before Company C left New Bedford for Camp Meigs at Read-
ville, Frederick Douglass published a front-page editorial entitled "Men of
Color, to Arms!" This stirring plea summarized the major themes behind the
enlistment of black soldiers. Arguments ranged from the practical and political
to the economic and moral dimensions of the conflict. "A war undertaken and
brazenly carried on for the perpetual enslavement of colored men, calls logically
and loudly upon colored men to help to suppress it," Douglass wrote. Black
military service would destroy slavery and sustain the claims of free blacks to
full and equal rights as citizens, he argued. Potential recruits were promised
wages, rations, equipment, and protection equal to those of white soldiers. In
April 1863 Douglass continued his exhortations by writing, "He who fights the
battles of America may claim America as his country—and have that claim
respected." Black men were also defending their "liberty, honor, manhood and
self-respect."[23] At home, the *Standard* printed favorable accounts of black soldiers (mostly former slaves and now termed "contrabands") under the com-
mands of Colonel Thomas Wentworth Higginson and General David Hunter.
Writing from South Carolina, Hunter reported that black soldiers possessed a
"natural aptitude for arms" and he believed that "now is the time appointed
by God for their deliverance." Hunter added that the racial prejudices of white
officers and soldiers were "rapidly softening or fading out."[24]

    Compared with white soldiers in the Civil War, most black soldiers did not
leave behind letters, journals, or other published accounts that provide insights

about their experiences.[25] Company C from New Bedford included an enlistee who would provide a poignant voice, James Henry Gooding, who penned a series of extraordinary letters published in the *New Bedford Mercury* between March 3, 1863, and February 22, 1864. Averaging nearly one each week, Gooding's forty-six letters offered unparalleled insights about black military life. Their publication in a contemporary New Bedford newspaper underscores the strong ties between the white and black citizenry of New Bedford. Born free in Troy, New York, Gooding first made his way to New Bedford in the summer of 1856, where he secured a berth on a whaling voyage. Gooding typified the maritime experiences of black men when he returned to New Bedford in April 1860 to collect his "lay" or wages amounting to $114.42, about $2.50 per month. After a month in the city, Gooding signed on as steward on a bark that shipped to the Arctic in search of right whales, and he later worked as a cook on a merchant vessel bound for South America. Returning home in the summer of 1862, Gooding married Ellen Louisa Allen in the Seaman's Bethel and the couple moved to South Water Street. Gooding's maritime career ended with his enlistment in Company C of the Fifty-Fourth Regiment on February 14, 1863.[26]

Gooding's first letter, printed one day before Company C departed for Camp Meigs, appealed to the black community for more soldiers. "Are the colored men here in New Bedford," Gooding asked, "who have the advantage of education, so blind to their own interest, . . . that through fear of some double dealing, they will not now embrace probably the only opportunity that will ever be offered them to make themselves a people[?]"[27] Writing later from Camp Meigs, Gooding reported that the New Bedford contingent in Company C was the largest in camp. In mid-March Gooding boasted again: "Among the men in this camp the New Bedford men stand A No. 1, in military bearing, cleanliness and morality." Thinking of home, Gooding commented that, "We have prayers every morning and evening," with most of the fervor emanating from men connected with the Bethel Church on Kempton Street. Gooding asked New Bedford's Military Relief Committee to pay the men's families because some of them "needed it very much." Gooding did not want black soldiers' families to become "objects of public charity." "We are all determined to act like men," he continued, "and fight, money or not; but we think duty to our families will be a sufficient excuse for adverting to the subject." New Bedford's soldiers were treated well, especially through hometown gifts forwarded by ladies of the Relief Society who sent shirts, socks, and handkerchiefs. Writing on April 11, 1863, Gooding thanked the women of the city for sending a sewing purse to each man, and he went on to say: "Tell the ladies that our boys think there are no women anywhere so good as the New Bedford ladies."[28]

Conflicts from the home front carried over to military camp among two black pastors with New Bedford ties. Governor Andrew asked the Reverends William Jackson, of the Salem Baptist Church, and William Grimes, of the African Methodist Episcopal faith, to alternate as post chaplains at Readville. The two men highlighted the religious diversity and differences within New Bedford's African-American community.[29] James Gooding felt compelled to clear up "some false impressions" made by Grimes against Jackson, writing that Jackson "did NOT apply, either in person or by letter to the governor, for the chaplaincy of the 54th." "Furthermore," the Reverend Jackson declared through Gooding that, "it was unnecessary for the Pastor of the 'Bethel Church' [Grimes] to publish his resignation when he never held any position to resign." Gooding defended Jackson as the "victim of prejudice," who later was named chaplain of the Fifty-Fifth Massachusetts Regiment where he also faced conflict over his appointment.[30] The Jackson-Grimes dispute had serious repercussions because the Fifty-Fourth went without a full-time black chaplain until the Reverend Samuel Harrison was commissioned on September 8, 1863.[31]

The Fifty-Fourth had been recruited from across the North and its diverse soldiers encountered some conflicts, mostly with racist whites within the camp at Readville.[32] But as soldiers in a "model regiment," men of the Fifty-Fourth knew of their importance and maintained their decorum and soldierly bearing. On April 30, 1863, for example, the men were paraded for a "grand gala" that included Governor Andrew, Treasury Secretary Salmon Chase, and noted reformers Samuel Gridley Howe, Robert Dale Owen, and William Lloyd Garrison. On May 14, 1863, the troops assembled to receive their state bounty payments while waiting for equal military pay from the US government. Gooding believed that his comrades sent home more money than any other regiment in camp.[33] The men's purposeful training and sober actions earned much praise. Surgeon-General Dale of Massachusetts reported that the regiment's barracks, cookhouses, and kitchens were cleaner than any others he had seen. "No regiments were ever more amenable to good discipline, or were more decorous and proper in their behavior than the Fifty-fourth and Fifty-fifth Massachusetts Colored Volunteers," he concluded. Enlisted men shared this esprit de corps. In his last letter from Camp Meigs, Gooding wrote that "most every man in the regiment vies with each other in excellence in whatever they undertake. It is, I think, one of the best guarantees that the 54th will be a credit to old Massachusetts wherever it goes."[34]

The Fifty-Fourth's symbolic importance to the Union cause was poignantly illustrated during the presentation of regimental flags on May 18, 1863. Extra trains ran from Boston to Readville and swelled the crowd to more than one thousand people that included members of Congress, professors at Harvard, and white and black abolitionist leaders. Governor Andrew's words and the ceremonial exchange of flags and banners underscored the importance of the first black regiment raised in the North. "I know not, Mr. Commander," Governor Andrew famously addressed Colonel Robert Gould Shaw, "when, in all human history, to any given thousand men in arms there has been committed a work at once so proud, so precious, so full of hope and glory as the work committed to you."[35] Andrew presented four flags to the regiment: a national flag, a state flag, an emblematic banner with the Goddess of Liberty and the motto, "Liberty, Loyalty, and Unity," and a fourth flag emblazoned with a cross upon a blue field. Steeped in the language of civil religion, Andrew urged the soldiers to protect the flags. The Massachusetts state flag bestowed by the "colored ladies of Boston" was a "sacred charge," he reminded them. Andrew's speech was "never [to] be forgotten by those that heard his voice," related Luis Emilio, who reprinted it in full in his regimental history. This integrated event saluted the Fifty-Fourth with patriotic sentiments and sent them off to war with self-conscious awareness of their important roles.[36]

As the regiment departed Massachusetts, they were cheered by public support but realistic about the challenges they faced. Gooding summarized his and his comrades' sentiments: "There is not a man in the regiment who does not appreciate the difficulties, the dangers, and maybe ignoble death that awaits him, if captured by the foe," Gooding wrote, "and they will die upon the field rather than be hanged like a dog; and when a thousand men are fighting for a very existence, who dare say the men won't fight determinedly?" In the face of some lingering racism toward black soldiers, the regiment marched through Boston's streets on May 18, 1863, and encountered "vast crowds" cheered them.[37] The men of Company C joined others in leaving for the Southern military front with a resolve to accept nothing less than equal pay, a cause taken up by their white officers. On July 2, 1863, Colonel Shaw wrote to Governor Andrew to complain about the "great piece of injustice" to his soldiers, and with uncharacteristic vehemence, he added: "In my opinion they should be mustered out of the service or receive the full pay which was promised them." Shaw's concerns were echoed in James Gooding's published letters sent home to New Bedford.[38]

Events on both home front and battlefield aided the cause of black enlistment and aligned with antislavery fervor. At home, the former slave and author Harriet Jacobs made several wartime visits to New Bedford to raise funds for freed blacks in Alexandria, Virginia. New Bedford's city hall hosted members of the Ladies Educational Commission who packed a box of supplies for Jacobs, who brought ten black children to New Bedford. In the city's North Christian Church, the Reverend D. C. Haynes of the Freedmen's Relief Association spoke about the general destitution of the contrabands, a term applied to recently escaped slaves who found refuge behind Union army lines. In response to a lead story in the *New Bedford Standard* that asked, "Will the negro fight?" an answer came from Port Hudson, Louisiana, where the Second Louisiana Infantry entered the fight with nine hundred men and emerged with three hundred. "Six hundred dead bodies lay upon the field of carnage as evidence of the bravery of the colored soldier," the account read. The Fifty-Fourth would still need to prove their own military valor to dispel any doubts about their manhood, loyalty, or motivation.[39]

The Assault on Fort Wagner

Gooding and fellow soldiers first tasted combat in the middle of July. Union strategy, devised by General Gilmore, centered on attacking Morris Island, a heavily fortified Confederate post that guarded Charleston harbor. The city of Charleston, the symbolic hub of the Confederacy where the first shots of Civil War were fired in April 1861, lay seven miles inland. Army troops were to wear down the Confederate forces at Fort Wagner and Fort Sumter to open the harbor to a full naval assault. But Confederate forces created some of the most sturdily constructed embattlements and fortresses ever built, and difficult terrain made offensive maneuvers more difficult.[40] Corporal Gooding's letters home were complemented by those of white Captain James W. Grace who wrote home on the Fourth of July 1863 from Port Royal promising that readers would "hear of great works in a few days." Grace praised his men over other black soldiers, such as the First South Carolina, where one soldier was shot for desertion and another hung for "inciting mutiny." Grace contended: "The 54th is just as smart as any white regiment in this department. We have been praised everywhere we go for our drill, and soldierly bearing." Boosting his hometown, Grace added, "Company C still ranks among the very first for intelligence, discipline, drill, and fine appearance."[41]

To prepare for the eventual assault on Fort Wagner, the Fifty-Fourth Regiment moved to nearby James Island in a blinding rainstorm on the night of July 8, 1863. On the morning of July 10, the day's mail brought the cheering news of Union victories at Vicksburg and Gettysburg. The Fifty-Fourth battled at Grimball's Landing on July 16, demonstrating their bravery in bloody close combat. The regiment lost fourteen men killed, eighteen wounded, and thirteen missing. In his official report, General Terry commended the "steadiness and soldierly conduct of the Fifty-fourth Massachusetts Regiment who were on duty . . . and met the brunt of the attack." "It is not for us to blow our horn," James

Gooding reported, "but when a regiment of white men gave us three cheers as we were passing them, it shows that we did our duty as men should."[42] This was the first time during the Civil War that a regiment of northern African-American soldiers could be acknowledged for their military gallantry. The fight on James Island was a prelude to the famous but failed assault on Fort Wagner.

"At last we have something stirring to record," wrote James Gooding on July 20, 1863. He had survived the deadly assault on Fort Wagner two days earlier. With only six hundred of the regiment's men present for this engagement, the attack contained no shortage of momentous acts and brave speeches. Before the assault, General Strong proclaimed himself a "Massachusetts man" and knew that troops would fight for their state's honor. Strong called forward the color-bearer and asked, "If this man should fall, who will lift the flag and carry it on?" Standing nearby, Colonel Robert Gould Shaw removed a cigar from his lips and quietly said, "I will" as his regiment cheered. Speaking to his troops with unusual force and drama, Shaw concluded, "Now I want you to prove yourselves men."[43] With darkness approaching, the regiment moved in quick time along the sand toward Fort Wagner. Ordered not to fire, they climbed to the fort's parapet. Within two hundred yards of the Confederate battery, "Wagner became a mound of fire, from which poured a stream of shot and shell," Luis Emilio reported. "A sheet of flame, followed by a running fire, like electric sparks, swept along the parapet." Led by Colonel Shaw, the men plunged forward with fierce hand-to-hand combat. Continuous fire that raked the troops killed Shaw and others. "We met the foe on the parapet of Wagner with the bayonet," James Gooding related, "we were exposed to a murderous fire from the batteries of the fort, from our Monitors and our land batteries, as they did not cease firing soon enough. Mortal men could not stand such a fire, and the assault on Wagner was a failure." Some men died while trying to retrieve Shaw's body.[44]

From a military standpoint, the Union assault on Fort Wagner was a deadly disaster and the Fifty-Fourth Massachusetts Colored Infantry suffered grievous casualties. Combined Union forces counted 1,515 casualties, including 111 officers, among them General Strong, Colonel Putnam, and Colonel Robert Gould Shaw of the Fifty-Fourth. "Such severe casualties stamp the sanguinary character of the fighting," wrote Luis Emilio, describing the failed assault as "one of the fiercest struggles of the war." Of the Fifty-Fourth's enlisted men, 9 were killed, 147 wounded, and 100 went missing. Despite heavy casualties, the regiment's new commander, Colonel Edward N. Hallowell commented that many of the officers "behaved with coolness and bravery" and he commended four enlisted men for "especial merit," among them Sergeant William H. Carney of Company C. Speaking of Carney, Hallowell said: "Of him as a man and soldier,

I can speak in the highest term of praise."[45] Military commanders' compliments and positive newspaper accounts turned a brutal defeat into a political and moral victory for proponents of racial equality.

William H. Carney, War Hero

Black soldiers had proven their courage before horrendous enemy fire, headed by Sergeant William H. Carney of New Bedford. At the time of Carney's enlistment, New Bedford learned that his father had been a fugitive slave from Norfolk Virginia, who saved money through "untiring industry" to purchase his wife's freedom. Eventually, the elder Carney returned to Norfolk and procured his other children, and the family celebrated a joyous reunion in New Bedford during the war.[46] Christian Fleetwood recalled the fateful day at Fort Wagner when the color sergeant was shot and Carney threw away his rifle, snatched the flag, and raced to the parapet. Retreating later under a "storm of shot and shell" with substantial loss of blood and multiple wounds, Carney refused to surrender the flag to anyone. When Carney found his comrades, Fleetwood explained, he said simply: "Boys I only did my duty. The old flag never touched the ground."[47] Carney's defense of the flag and simple explanation for his heroism struck a resonant chord among Northerners. Governor Andrew requested a thirty-day furlough for Carney and asked Secretary of War Stanton, "Can any higher praise be bestowed upon this brave man, than a recital of his noble conduct in the assault upon Fort Wagner?" Carney's visit to family and friends in New Bedford illustrated close and continued ties between men at war and their home communities. Carney returned to his unit and served until a medical disability forced his discharge in June 1864. Like his comrades at the time, Carney had not accepted a single cent of pay from the federal government.[48]

Carney's iconic courage reinforced the accomplishments of his regiment and of black Union soldiers. Popular accounts and military reports fostered a positive assessment of black troops that combated racist beliefs. Luis Emilio's regimental history twice referred to Carney's actions at Fort Wagner, and the illustrated frontispiece of his book features a photograph of Carney holding "the flag he saved at Wagner," along with a caption of his oft-told declaration, "The old flag never touched the ground, boys."[49] Carney's history and exploits were advertised in the *Liberator* on November 6, 1863 when he explained his motives for enlisting. "When the country called for *all persons* [to military service]," he declared, "I could best serve my God by serving my country and my oppressed brothers. The sequel is short—*I enlisted for the war*." He signed

African-American war hero William H. Carney, circa 1900. (Courtesy of the Trustees of the New Bedford Free Public Library.)

himself, "William H. Carney, Sergeant Co. C, 54th Mass. Vols."[50] Led by Carney's exploits, the Fifty-Fourth Massachusetts earned commendations throughout the North following the Fort Wagner assault.

New Bedford learned more about black soldiers' bravery and casualties from James W. Grace. "The regiment did well, and fought most bravely," Grace wrote in a published letter, adding with understatement that "Fort Wagner is a hard place to take." Grace described leading his troops against a furious charge by rebels who came out of their battery to bayonet wounded men. To illustrate his men's "courage and pluck," Grace related an anecdote of the battle's aftermath when he asked the exhausted company who was still willing to attack the Confederate battery. Every man stepped to the front and said they would fight.[51] Besides William Carney, at least eleven other men from New Bedford were wounded, killed, or listed as missing following the failed assault. Missing (and presumed dead) were Joseph R. Campbell, a twenty-three-year-old caulker; Joseph Hall, a single nineteen-year-old laborer; Abram P. Torrence, one of the senior members of the unit; and Treadwell Turner, a single laborer just twenty-one years old. A wounded man, Nathan L. Young, a twenty-one-year-old barber, left behind a wife when he died in the Beaufort military hospital on July 19, 1863. These were the immediate casualties whose families suffered at home. Three men, including Carney, were discharged before the war's end. As testaments to strength, luck, and skill, at least three of the wounded men served until the end of the war, and Cornelius Henson survived a lengthy stint as a prisoner of war and returned home about five weeks before the regiment mustered out.[52]

The regiment settled in for a lengthy siege on Morris Island, and the Confederate battery at Wagner was not captured until early September 1863. Men of the Fifty-Fourth constructed trenches in searing heat and faced nonstop sniping from Confederate guns. High temperatures and heavy rains took their toll, and deaths became so frequent that the regiment ceased to play funeral music because it depressed the soldiers. After reporting on seeing stretchers pass with dead comrades, Gooding commented: "A man dies none the less gloriously standing at his post on picket, or digging in the trench; his country needs him there, and he is as true a soldier as though he were in the thickest fray."[53] The final successful assault made on Fort Wagner came early in the morning of September 7 after Union leaders learned that the Confederates had evacuated. "It was a joyous time," Luis Emilio reported, "our men threw up their hats, dancing in their gladness. Officers shook hands enthusiastically. Wagner was ours at last." James Gooding informed readers at home that the troops had secured Charleston's strongest fortification.[54] African-American soldiers, led by heroes from New Bedford, played a vital role in capturing the prizes of Fort Wagner and Charleston, South Carolina, victories that created a surge of optimism in the North.

Enlistments proceeded in Fort Wagner's aftermath. Massachusetts established "The Fund for Colored Troops" in late July 1863 with the goal of raising at least $50,000 in recruiting funds. A number of New Bedford residents responded, among them George Barney and David R. Greene each for $200, and Jonathan Bourne Jr., Edward C. Jones, Joseph C. Delano, and the Crocker brothers each for $100. Governor Andrew instigated the enlistment drive to meet military exigencies and to elevate the "colored race." At the same time, New Bedford's newspapers featured notices about "Rumsey's Minstrels" at the city's Liberty Hall, a performance that promised "The Essence of Ole Virginny" with plenty of "comicalities." Later, the Massachusetts recruiting drive's aim was increased and renamed the "Hundred Thousand Dollar Fund," and New Bedford's Joseph C. Delano reported that nearly $1,700 was raised locally.[55]

Citizens on the home front continued to learn of the harsh realities of military service in early August 1863. Captain Grace reported with sadness that several men who were presumed missing or prisoners had died, including Corporal Abram P. Torrance and Private Nathan L. Young. Grace regretted that Private Lewis A. Fleetwood's foot was amputated because he "was an unusually smart young man, and it was my intention to have made him a Corporal in a few days." The Fifty-Fourth was subject to continuous enemy fire in extreme heat. Grace claimed that it was so hot that horses brought from the North wilted and died. Yet, of all the Union troops in the area, the Fifty-Fourth was the healthiest and largest contingent with four hundred men ready for active duty. Of Company C, sixty men reported for duty, a drop from the ninety-five that left Readville. They cheered the arrival of the Fifty-Fifth Massachusetts, the state's second black regiment. "We were glad enough to see them, for we are all sick and worn out," Grace commented. Optimistic about capturing Charleston, Grace expected a fight to commence soon, praying "may the God of battles be with us, and give to us the victory."[56]

On the home front, New Bedford's women continued to assist black soldiers and freed blacks. The ex-slave Harriet Jacobs returned to New Bedford in late October 1863 and requested supplies for former slave children from the Relief Society at City Hall. In that same month, black women raised funds on behalf of sick soldiers by sponsoring entertainment at City Hall that called upon the "sympathies of the citizens generally." Black church leaders also worked to retire their debts at the Salem Baptist Church and the AME Zion Church.[57] Sergeant William H. W. Gray's wife, Martha, offered a black woman's most noteworthy wartime contributions. Writing to her congressman for a "small favor," she sought permission to "go south as a nurse for the sick and wounded of the 54th Reg't." Mayor George Howland Jr. supported her mission of "loyalty and humanity," as she explained further: "I have in the 54th Regt. my Husband, two cousins, and no less than seven young men that I have taught in the Sabboth School, these with the three young men that boarded with my Father, (Wm. Bush) is all very near to me, and it makes my heart bleed when I think of them with so many others, suffering for what I could do for them, if I was only permitted to do so." She was most concerned with her husband's health, for she believed "that more men die in Camp for want of proper attention, than from sickness or wounds." Gray declared that she "gave my Husband and Friends up for the good of the Country," but she was "anxious to do all that I can for them, and my country also." With no children, Martha Gray sought to be "useful" by serving in a hospital after bringing medical supplies from New Bedford. After the war, Martha Gray failed in efforts to secure a military pension despite strong support and documentation from allies in New Bedford.[58]

The unique and different aspects of African-American military service were underscored on the one-year anniversary of the Emancipation Proclamation in 1864. Luis Emilio recounted: "We kept up till midnight having a jolly time & then napped off to sleep," only to be awakened occasionally by rats. He viewed Emancipation Day as a "great one for the Black race."[59] Sergeant William H. W. Gray of New Bedford served as one of the day's featured speakers and rejoiced that "the steps we have taken can never be retraced, the mite we have gained can never be snatched from our tenacious grasp, if we but watch the course of events, and remain faithful and true to ourselves, to our God and our country." The regiment closed the ceremony by singing "Battle Hymn of the Republic" in honor of Colonel Shaw, accompanied by "the flourish of bugles, the rolling of drums, and the drooping of colors."[60]

Back home in New Bedford, white and black residents also honored the Emancipation Proclamation in January 1864. Gathering in Pierian Hall, William H. Johnson presided over a fete that included speaker William Wells Brown, a frequent wartime visitor to the city. Ads proclaimed: "Let there be a great gathering of the people from the east, west, north and south, to the first celebration of the African Freedom since the adoption of the Federal Constitution." Besides a public reading of the Proclamation, John Freedom's choir furnished music and the Salem Baptist Sabbath School put on an exhibition. For African Americans in New Bedford and throughout the North, this anniversary was poignant because tens of thousands of black men were armed and deployed in the South while still battling against unjust pay.[61]

Battles for Equal Pay and Equal Rights

The Fifty-Fourth's valor at Fort Wagner helped to alter many white Americans' public opinion about the service of black soldiers and the meaning of the Civil War. William Carney's exploits and those of his regiment provided ample evidence of African Americans' claims for equal pay and full citizenship.[62]

While engaged in exhaustive fatigue work on Morris Island, the Fifty-Fourth's soldiers again confronted the problem of unequal pay when they learned in early August 1863 that their pay would consist of ten dollars monthly payments minus three dollars deducted for clothing. Again, they refused. Ten dollars were paid to contraband laborers, and these men were soldiers. Corporal Gooding addressed the issue over the next few months. When Colonel Littlefield asked if any men would accept lesser payments, Gooding wrote, "not one man in the whole regiment lifted a hand." After waiting five months, Gooding declared, they would continue to wait until Congress remedied the problem. "Too many of our comrades' bones lie bleaching near the wall of Fort Wagner to subtract even one cent from our hard earned pay," Gooding wrote. "If the nation can ill afford to pay us, we are men and will do our duty while we are here without a murmur, as we have done always, before and since that day we were offered to sell our manhood for ten dollars a month." He concluded with a simple statement: "Our motto is work faithfully and willingly."[63]

Gooding's agitation demonstrated close ties between New Bedford's black soldiers at war and prominent white leaders at home. James B. Congdon took up Gooding's cause by forwarding the corporal's letters to Governor Andrew and affirming that Gooding "belongs in this city, and . . . [h]e is intelligent, honest, patriotic." Four months later Congdon forwarded more of Gooding's correspondence in which he disagreed with some comrades' decision to not accept interim payments from the state. Despite internal dissension within the regiment, the men collectively refused payments from the state of Massachu-setts, prompting the governor to complain again about the federal govern-ment's failure to treat black troops as "soldiers of the Union, nothing less, nor more." Andrew attacked the discriminatory pay scheme as "a mistake in law, as well as in justice and policy." While Andrew respected the "manly feeling" that compelled the African-American soldiers to turn down ten dollars per month when they desired thirteen dollars, he agreed with James Gooding that there would have been "no want of dignity" had the men of the black regiments accepted interim payments from his state.[64]

In campaigning for equal pay, James Gooding wrote perhaps the most famous letter written by a black Union soldier during the Civil War. In a mis-sive to President Lincoln dated September 28, 1863, Gooding asked the presi-dent, "Are we Soldiers, or are we Labourers?" Military service held no racial distinctions, he explained. "The Anglo-Saxon Mother, Wife, or Sister are not alone in tears for departed Sons, Husbands and Brothers. The patient, trusting Descendants of Afric's Clime have dyed the ground with blood, in defense of the Union, and Democracy." Gooding contended that Lincoln had issued an order that called upon the Confederates to treat captured black Union soldiers no differently from white ones. "Now if the United States exacts uniformity of treatment of her Soldiers from the Insurgents," Gooding asked, "would it not be well and consistent to set the example herself by paying all her Soldiers alike?" Gooding distinguished soldiers from contrabands, whom he called "menial hirelings." In closing, Gooding wrote: "We feel as though our Country spurned us, now that we are sworn to serve her. Please give this a moment's attention."[65] There is no record that Lincoln read the letter.

Funding problems continued unabated. Writing in November 1863, Gooding noted that black soldiers were men with families to feed, clothe, and keep warm. He believed that the monthly offer of "the ten dollars by the greatest government in the world is an unjust distinction to men who have only a black skin to merit it." Congress had robbed "a whole race of their title to manhood." One month later, the New Bedford Standard reported that the men of the Fifty-Fourth and Fifty-Fifth regiments again refused to accept state pay. Gooding reminded readers that "the 54th is minus the circulating medium" of money in February 1864 when he reported that black soldiers could not purchase "cakes, poultry, eggs, fruit and so on" from ex-slave peddlers.[66] Regimental officers like Luis Emilio lamented in April 1864: "How hard it is on our poor men of the 54th now over a year in service & without a cent of pay! Terrible! Many of their families turned out of doors by their landlords. The poor fellows come to us officers & show us their letters from home. But what can we do for them?" Writing to President Lincoln on May 13, 1864, Governor Andrew complained that the families of black soldiers had been "driven to beggary and the almshouse."[67]

In June 1864 Congress finally passed legislation to bring equal pay to black troops. Men of the Fifty-Fourth Massachusetts took the so-called "Quaker oath" prescribed by Colonel Hallowell, affirming that they had "owed no man unrequited labor on or before the 19th day of April, 1861." When payday came on September 28, 1864, Hallowell commemorated it as "our day of thanksgiving and prayer" and "a victory as important as the conquest of Atlanta."[68] Everyone enjoyed a boisterous jubilee. One officer's journal entry read: "The 54th Regt. paid off. $13.00 from date of enrollment! Victory at last!" The attorney general of Massachusetts called the day "the most memorable day in the history of the regiment," noting that the Fifty-Fourth had been mustered for pay seven times in sixteen months and each time the men refused to accept anything less than equal pay. "They would give their services," the attorney general wrote, "but they would not sell their manhood." Of the $160,000 required to pay all the men retroactively to their enlistment, more than $100,000 was sent home by the men to their families and relations. A white officer underscored the event's significance: "They felt that they were men; they were recognized; their status as soldiers was gained; 'I can send money home at last to my wife, my child!' "[69]

James Henry Gooding never lived to receive equal pay. He was captured in battle at Olustee, Florida, on February 20, 1864, and died at the notorious Andersonville Prison. He had been an important voice in shaping public perceptions of black soldiers in depicting how their experiences were similar to but different from those of white volunteers.[70] Although the battle of Olustee garnered less publicity than the assault on Fort Wagner, it was one of the deadliest engagements for the Fifty-Fourth Massachusetts as the regiment tried to cover a retreat. Losses for the Union side totaled 1,828 casualties. From the Fifty-Fourth Massachusetts, 3 officers were wounded, and of the enlisted men, 13 were killed, 63 wounded, and 8 went missing. The regiment earned praise in some northern newspapers. *The Liberator* reported that the "glourious Fifty-Fourth Massachusetts" saved an entire brigade from capture or annihilation. "If this regiment has not won glory enough to have shoulder straps, where is there one that ever did," asked the reporter.[71] J. Matthew Gallman's recent appraisal of Olustee emphasizes that the battle featured both war-tested and untested black soldiers. By fighting and dying as veteran soldiers, men of the Fifty-Fourth illustrated the transformative nature of the Civil War with still more than another year of war to go.[72]

The Fifty-Fourth Massachusetts capped its wartime exploits with a triumphant procession through Charleston, South Carolina, on February 27, 1865, followed months later by an impressive Fourth of July celebration. Mustered out on August 20, 1865, the men returned home to Boston on September 2 to throngs of cheering people. In an address at the Boston Common, Colonel Hallowell praised the troops' bravery. In paraphrasing the colonel's comments, Luis Emilio emphasized the national impact of the "brave black regiment": "When they left Massachusetts, it was the only State which recognized them as citizens. Now the whole country acknowledged their soldierly qualities. He hoped by good behavior they would show their title to all the privileges of citizenship." Escorted by the Shaw Guards for their trip home to New Bedford, the Fifty-Fourth veterans of Company C were met by many citizens, the all-black Carney Guards, and the New Bedford Band. Twenty-two veterans paraded through crowded streets to City Hall for a reception in their honor, where they heard speeches from long-time supporters William H. Johnson, Henry Harrison, and James B. Congdon.[73]

Summary

New Bedford's black community had contributed a sizable and significant contingent of soldiers to the most famous African-American military unit of the Civil War. Most Northerners concurred with Luis Emilio that the Fifty-Fourth had "wrung justice and equal rights with white soldiers" while creating a new class of "intelligent, educated, and self-reliant" African-American men.[74] This was true generally of blacks' military service, and others from New Bedford served with less fame in segregated military units such as the Fifty-Fifth Massachusetts Regiment and the Fifth Massachusetts Cavalry. At least seventy-six black men connected with New Bedford enlisted in the Union navy, as well.[75] In his last published letter, James Henry Gooding recognized the transformative nature of black military experience. As his regiment passed through Jacksonville, Florida, in early February 1864, Gooding reported that "the faces of the ladies in Jacksonville indicated a sort of Parisian disgust as the well-appointed Union army, composed in part of Lincoln's 'niggers,' filed through the streets." Yet he believed that even these white Confederates offered a begrudging respect to the black soldiers. Women who once greeted the men with "frowns," he wrote, "are treating us with respect and courtesy; in fact more than we should expect in some parts of the free North."[76] Gooding's letter depicted of the revolutionary changes wrought by war and black military service, with key contributions by New Bedford's white and black communities. The next chapter examines black veterans and their families during and after the war as they made claims for full equality.

6

"Worthy Recipients": New Bedford's Black Veterans and the Web of Social Welfare

In August 1864 Fanny Wright applied for aid with New Bedford's Overseers of the Poor. She stated that her husband, John L. Wright, was serving in the war. The Overseers noted that her husband was in the Fifty-Fourth and granted her an order, basically a voucher, for $1.50 worth of provisions from local grocer Robert Luscomb. She followed up in early 1865 by obtaining five dollars in grocery vouchers, two feet of fire wood, and a quarter ton of coal.[1] The aid granted to Fanny Wright in the form of groceries, coal, and fire wood displayed the characteristic benevolence of New Bedford's public welfare system between the 1850s and 1880s.[2] These records also highlight problems faced by impoverished African Americans during the protracted war, a problem addressed in poignant appeals by, among others, James Gooding of the Fifty-Fourth Massachusetts. White leaders such as Massachusetts Adjutant General William Schouler reported that, as a result of the men's refusal to accept unequal pay from the state, "They were greatly in need of money, and their families were suffering at home, yet they resolutely determined to receive no pay unless they received full pay."[3] Family members who cheered military service suffered when the men refused to accept unequal pay, when they were disabled by wounds or sickness, or when they died.

Individual case studies like Fanny Wright's help to address Michael Katz's plea that "the history of dependence in American [history] needs to be rewritten from the bottom up, that is, through an analysis of the lives and experiences of the poor themselves."[4] This chapter examines links between black residents of New Bedford, military service, and an emergent web of social welfare that extended from local to state and federal resources. At the local level, New Bedford's Overseers of the Poor offered the most direct public assistance and displayed persistent generosity during and after the Civil War.[5] Wartime changes redefined the meaning of citizenship so that African-American men eventually could claim full rights as soldiers, veterans, and voters. This process was played out in federal military pension applications that began in July 1862 and were open to black men after they were allowed to enlist in the Union cause. Army or navy veterans disabled because of service-related wounds or disease could apply for pensions, as could widows, dependent children, and other dependent relatives such as mothers and fathers. Payments followed rank. A fully disabled private could receive no more than eight dollars per month, while a disabled general might collect thiry dollars per month. Writing in 1864, the pension commissioner declared that "no other nation has provided so liberally for its disabled soldiers or seamen, or for the dependent relatives of the fallen."[6]

Glimpses into the lives of New Bedford's black Union soldiers and sailors can be found in local poor records and federal military pension files.[7] The pattern of penury among them suggests that military service often brought financial distress rather than material rewards. The original intent of military pensions was to provide assistance to disabled, honorably discharged Union veterans or to family members who had depended financially on them. In his examination of the Twenty-Ninth United States Colored Troops, historian Edward A. Miller described military pension files as "sparse stories" and concluded that payments were inadequate to support most families. Black veterans' lives, he wrote, generally were "without luxury, often without necessities, and frequently full of misery."[8]

Beyond the material support of local welfare and veterans' payments, military pensions were viewed by Union veterans and their dependents as their right. Such disbursements honored the "saviors" of the nation, and military pensions were viewed as part of a contractual bond between Union veterans and the nation. Soldiers and sailors had exchanged military service (and its potential disabilities) for pension assistance from a "patron state." This belief cut across the lines of race, class, gender, and military rank, and it was demonstrated in persistent patterns of families' and veterans' mutual support long after the war had ended. Sociologist Theda Skocpol aptly explains that "U.S. Civil War pensions (and other forms of public help for veterans and dependents) were not conceptualized in socioeconomic terms at all. Instead they were understood in political and moral terms."[9] New Bedford's Elizabeth Carter captured this belief following the death of her son, Miles Carter Jr., a veteran of the all-black Fifth Massachusetts Cavalry. Pursuing a mother's pension for more than a decade, she wrote that "I have become discouraged but I will not give up contending for my rights."[10]

Federal Pay, Local and State Relief

The controversies over black soldiers' pay prompts the question of how the men and their families survived after enlistment without military pay. A Union private received a monthly salary of $13 per month, a sizeable amount for men and women who toiled on the bottom rungs of the occupational ladder. In addition to a promised federal military salary, state aid was paid to a soldier's family up to a maximum of $12 per month, disbursed first by towns and cities and reimbursed later by the state. By the end of the war, William Schouler reported that Massachusetts had expended more than $3.2 million in aid to dependents and state bounties.[11] Compared with black soldiers and sailors elsewhere, black enlistees in Massachusetts probably enjoyed the "greatest chance of community and government support," Richard Reid notes. Still, he suggests, the economic hardships of black families even in New England were "overwhelmingly of a different magnitude than most white families."[12]

Contemporary accounts depicted the suffering of northern black soldiers and families. The *New York Tribune* reported that because the government charged black soldiers more for their clothing than was paid to them, every black man who died in battle or of disease did so in debt. "The men who gave their lives to the country in the memorable assault on Fort Wagner are in debt on the Quartermaster's account for the uniforms which the rebels stripped from their bodies after death," explained one reporter in January 1864. Governor John Andrew wrote to Senator Charles Sumner in May 1864 demanding that Sumner visit President Lincoln to press the issue of pay for black soldiers. Claiming that wives and children of black soldiers had been forced into public almshouses, Andrew wrote, "I have not words to express my feelings of indignation and shame at the fraudulent conduct of our Government in this matter."[13]

In New Bedford, the Civil War created economic and fiscal dislocations that disrupted the city's public welfare system. Judging by Overseers records between 1861 and 1865, the Overseers showed flexibility and generosity in meeting the needs of indigent city residents, white and black alike.[14] In particular, female household heads coped with absent husbands and sons who left for military service, for work elsewhere, or for unknown reasons. Mayor Isaac Taber spelled out the problem in January 1862 that "unusually large portion of our population are at the present time dependent upon the city for support. Many are forced by necessity to make application, who would gladly work, could work be procured."[15] Black residents were viewed as less likely to seek welfare during the war despite their hardships. City Treasurer James B. Congdon offered his perception in 1863 that, "In proportion to their numbers[,] the colored people are less dependent upon public charity than the whites." A black minister, the Reverend Edmund Kelly, concurred that "upon an average [blacks] make fewer applications" for public charity.[16]

Given black soldiers' refusal to accept unequal pay, did they or their families end up in the poorhouse, as some alleged? Patterns and records from New

Bedford suggest not. Nearly two hundred black individuals applied for relief to the New Bedford Overseers of the Poor between 1864 and 1865, mostly after equal pay was finally disbursed to black soldiers in September 1864. Only a handful of local applicants were directly linked to men in military service.[17] In a typical case, Henrietta Williams, the wife of Sergeant Wharton A. Williams, sought relief in September 1864. This twenty-three year-old mother of one child received one order of firewood just two weeks before her husband was paid his soldier's wages.[18] Sixty-three-year-old Nancy Douglas received orders of wood in September 1864 and January 1865 after affirming that a grandson, Emery Phelps, served in the unit.[19] Margaret Harrison claimed not one but two sons in the Union army. In her early fifties, Harrison and her husband had separated after living in New Bedford for eighteen years. She received one order of wood on January 25, 1865.[20] Some women reported meager support and communication from their husbands at war. Elizabeth Lawrence claimed in early 1865 that she had received only five dollars from her husband, Robert, since he last contacted her in May 1864. Urged to apply for state aid as the wife of a soldier, she received a voucher for $1.50 worth of provisions.[21]

At least one veteran of the Fifty-Fourth was forced to apply for public aid before the war's end. George Delevan, wounded at the battle of Fort Wagner on July 18, 1863, was discharged ten months later with disabilities and applied for Overseers' assistance in September 1864. The Overseer duly recorded: "He enlisted in the 54th Regiment[,] returned home sick, wants prov[ision]s. Order on Robt Luscomb [$]2.00." George Delevan's plight illustrated the impact of war wounds because he returned home incapacitated for physical labor, and eventually he secured a federal military pension.[22] Black men who enlisted in the Union navy could apply for pensions, as could their families. Eliza Williams, the mother of Benjamin Williams, received firewood in March 1864 while living alone.[23] Catherine Hill, the mother of seaman Thomson Hill, asked numerous times for public aid. In her late forties and lacking a husband and an able-bodied son, Hill received ten allotments of wood and four quarter-tons of coal between March 1864 and February 1865.[24] The John Tolivar family faced a similar situation because the ailing father could not work and the family's eldest son was away in the navy. The Overseers granted their request for fuel in March 1864.[25]

State payments to the families of men in military service were supposed to alleviate some of these hardships, but family members suffered when men did not apply. Harriet Brown, who had lived with her husband in New Bedford since 1850, reported in March 1864 that her husband "has always followed the sea, is now in the Navy." She claimed to have no half-pay ticket, and that her husband "has been gone nearly a year, & all she has had from him is $11.00, which he sent to her 9 or 10 mo[nth]s ago." To provide for Harriet and her three children, the Overseers granted fuel and provisions no fewer than five times between March 26, 1864, and January 27, 1865.[26] All in all, few records indicate that hardships of military service led directly to applications for Overseers' payments, and most likely, African Americans helped one another through informal forms of mutual assistance.

Federal Military Pensions

Like their white and black counterparts around the country, African-American Union veterans of New Bedford made full use of a military pension system that grew more liberal over time.[27] Begun with a spirit of generosity and accepted by veterans and their dependents as an entitlement, the pension system grew considerably through the nineteenth century.[28] Historian Maris Vinovskis has argued that pension payments for Union veterans "had a profound and long-lasting impact on the lives of veterans," and that the entire system, by 1900, had become "a very extensive and expensive old-age assistance program for veterans."[29] Some scholars, most notably Theda Skocpol, have viewed the Civil War pension scheme as an underpinning of the modern welfare state. By 1900 the United States had spent about $2.5 billion in benefits for nearly one million individuals on the national pension rolls—about one in every seventy-five people. By 1910 over 90 percent of all surviving Union veterans received payments. Pensions constituted the single largest expenditure of the federal government in the fifty years after the Civil War.[30] With respect to black veterans, pensioners together received over $313 million, "a previously little appreciated but sizable infusion of money into the post–Civil War black community," writes Donald Shaffer.[31]

In his authoritative work, Shaffer estimates that the average black pension recipient and family received $3,759 over two decades. Blacks' applications were scrutinized closely, Shaffer notes, because they were often "more complex and difficult to prove" because of missing documents and records. When compared with white applicants, however, blacks "received an inequitable portion of the pension money," Shaffer contends. White widows were more successful applicants than black widows (84 percent to 61 percent), as were white parents to black (70 percent to 36 percent). Black and white dependent children were successful in about half of their pension applications. Pension files demonstrate how military service and its disabilities reshaped lives long after the war had ended, often bolstering long-standing community ties.[32] Patrick Kelly makes

the important point that the pension system strengthened localism because veterans returned home to their communities where they spent pension monies.
And, just as they had formed soldierly bonds as comrades, veterans operated
within a community of their own, fulfilling Thomas Bender's definition of
community as a "network of social relations marked by mutuality."[33] Pension
applications and pension funds helped to sustain black veterans and their families well into the twentieth century. As illustrated in Table 6-1, pension files were
located in the National Archives for forty-one of New Bedford's black Union
veterans.[34]

Lucy Turner's Story

Lucy Turner's case exemplifies the persistence of African Americans in gaining military pension benefits. Her story reveals details about prewar and wartime experiences, her family's employment histories, and their family's relations
among themselves and with others, including well-intentioned whites. Lucy
Turner's young son, Joseph Hall, enlisted in Company C of the Fifty-Fourth
Massachusetts. Soon after arriving at Camp Meigs, Hall sent his mother five
dollars with a letter that read in part: "I want you should use it for yourself
particular to pay your debts. [I]f you need more to settle your debts send to me
immediately [sic] and I will send you some more." Hall signed the allotment
roll so that six dollars would be deducted from his monthly pay for his mother's
benefit. When Lucy visited the regiment's camp in Readville, Massachusetts,
one of Joseph's comrades witnessed him paying his mother out his state
bounty. Lucy's wartime employer, Lydia T. Allen, knew that Lucy was "very
poor" because of an intemperate husband and that Joseph Hall paid his mother's rent or gave her money every week. When Joseph Hall died at Fort Wagner
on July 18, 1863, his death must have been a devastating blow to a mother who
lost a loved son and a vital wage earner.[35]

Although an illiterate woman born into slavery, Lucy Turner proved to be a
relentless pension applicant who sustained her appeals for eight years until
granted benefits in 1877. Similar to many pension applicants, Lucy Turner (and
her attorneys) obtained affidavits, letters, and city records of marriage and
charity payments. The most fascinating evidence centered on her and her children's symbolic emancipation in May 1853 at the hand of Gideon Welles, later
secretary of the navy under President Lincoln. Hoping to aid Turner and her
family as they set off from Hartford, Connecticut, Gideon Welles declared
"Lucy, Ann Elisa, Martha and Joseph, each and all of them Free." After Turner
moved to New Bedford, her young son remained in Hartford to work for

Table 6-1. Black Military Pension Applicants from New Bedford

Veteran	Unit	Type	Date Granted
Fifty-fourth Massachusetts Colored Infantry			
Campbell, Joseph	C	W, M	4/23/1867
Carney, William	C	V, W	12/24/1864
Cooper, Watson	A	V, M	1/6/1893
Craig, Noah	C	V, W	9/23/1889
Delevan, George	C	V, W	10/27/1866
Demory, Francis	C	V, W	10/17/1884
Dixon, Charles	D	V	3/29/1866
Fleetwood, Lewis	C	V	7/11/1864
Fletcher, David	C	W	Not granted
Foster, Richard	C	W	8/27/1868
Furlong, Wesley	C	V	7/7/1888
Gooding, James H.	C	W	5/9/1864
Gray, William H. W.	C	V, W,	9/21/1876
Hall, Joseph L.	C	Mother	3/27/1877
Harrison, Charles	C	V	1/23/1892
Harrison, John	C	W	Not granted
Henson, Cornelius	C	V, W	1/16/1884
Johnson, Alexander H.	C	V	12/24/1890
Lee, George H.	C	V	5/5/1898
Lee, Harrison	D	V	10/17/1890
Nelson, Richard	C	V	Not granted
Phelps, Emery	C	V, W	10/26/1894
Stevens, Robert	C	V, W	Not granted
Torrence, Abraham	C	W	Not granted
Williams, Warton	C	V	6/5/1874
Wilson, Joseph T.	C	V, W	3/15/1867
Wright, John L.	C	V, W	5/19/1890
Young, Nathan	C	W	6/6/1866
Fifty-Fifth Massachusetts Colored Infantry			
Jackson, William		V	5/3/1895
Low, Robert H.	B	V	5/7/1866
Fifth Massachusetts (Colored) Cavalry			
Carter, Miles, Jr.	·	Mother	Not granted
King, Isaiah		V	7/7/1904
Pierce, Frederick		W	8/28/1899

Table 6-1. (Continued)

Veteran	Unit	Type	Date Granted
Union Navy			
Borden, Nathaniel		V	8/14/1888
Dorster, John N.		V, W	5/9/1917
Fuller, James		V	8/2/1907
Handy, John T.		V, W	6/24/1891
Handy, Joshua		Father	3/30/1898
Lee, Luke R.		V	9/16/1912
Smith, Thornton		W	6/13/1891
Turner, Lodrick		V	12/13/1897

V = Veteran/Invalid; W = Widow; M = Minor

Source: Records of the Adjutant General's Office, Record Group 15, National Archives, Washington, DC.

Greenesbury W. Offley, a friend of Welles. Offley explained in an affidavit that Joseph's "mother was entirely destitute at the time and I knew that she was dependent in part on her said son for support." Two or three times Offley sent Hall's wages to his mother, and Offley personally delivered six dollars in wages to her in New Bedford.[36]

Hall's support of his mother persisted in their new home. One of Hall's comrades in Company C, John H. Harrison, attested that in the four years prior to their enlistment he and Hall had worked together in several bakeries. After getting paid each Saturday, Harrison often accompanied Hall home where he saw Joseph pay his mother all his wages, often three or four dollars per week. Susan Stout, a neighbor of Lucy Turner's, affirmed that she had known "the said Joseph L. Hall her son to bring provisions home to his mother[,] meat and flour which he had purchased himself for her support[, and] that he used to give his earnings when he had work to his mother for her support." Joseph Hall told Stout that he tried to give "all the money he could to his mother." Another neighbor, Julia Castle, claimed Lucy Turner "used to speak of what a good son he was to her."

Lucy's son's income helped to compensate for the family's penury. When Lucy Turner married Elisha in May 1859, she was thirty-eight and he was fifty-five and already hobbled by old age. Elisha Turner's income remained meager and inconsistent over the years, and the family received some local welfare payments between 1864 and 1877. In the latter year, Elisha Turner deposed that he had been in "very poor health for the last fifteen years [and] I have not been able to earn more than five dollars per month in any one year, and for the last two or three years not much of anything." Corroborating stories came from former employers and others, and the Turners retained an attorney to coordinate her appeals for a dependent mother's pension. After a lengthy process, Lucy's application was approved on March 22, 1877, with monthly payments of $8 to commence as of March 14, 1869, the date of her original application. In addition, she received nearly $800 in pension arrears. Two years later Turner fought successfully for payments dating back to her son's death in July 1863, netting an additional $550. Although these payments were sizeable, they had been granted only after years of bureaucratic struggles and were probably poor compensation for the loss of her hard-working only son. Lucy Turner's pension battle demonstrated how the Civil War changed conceptions of social welfare and illustrated how African-American veterans and their dependents sought repayment for military service and sacrifices.[37]

More often than not, pension applicants documented their lives of material hardship after the war. Veteran Isaiah King authored compelling letters to the pension bureau and attorneys that detailed his postwar challenges as family breadwinner. He fought for thirteen years to secure a pension. Except for a six- or seven-year stint at sea, King had worked as a laborer in New Bedford after the war ended. In a letter of May 1892 to his attorney in Washington, DC, King wrote about lingering health issues: "I am not able to do hard manual labor on account of my affliction[.] I do what light work I can get to do which is not enough to support my family[.] I have a Wife and four children to suport and have a very hard time of it to get along and am very much in nead of healp." After missing an important physical examination, King followed up with a letter to the Pension Bureau in which he wrote: "I am raising a large family and have not bin able to have the dockter treatment that I nead." Calling himself a "poor fellow" who waited patiently, he asked for help but still waited ten years for a military pension. First receiving a six dollar monthly payment in the 1890s, King later collected seventy-five dollars per month at the time of his death in 1933, some seventy years after he had enlisted.[38]

Casualties of War

The assault on Fort Wagner on July 18, 1863, solidified the reputation of black soldiers but it also led to the first substantial wave of casualties for men of the Fifty-Fourth Massachusetts Regiment. Disabled black veterans from Company C took full advantage of the pension program if medically discharged before the war's end. Lewis Fleetwood, the first black applicant from New Bedford, had been discharged June 8, 1864, with an amputated left foot after nearly a year in military hospitals. After filing for a pension on July 11, 1864, Fleetwood had to wait only until September before obtaining an $8 per month claim retroactive to his discharge date.[39] Most other claimants were like George Delevan who had to wait substantially longer for benefits. Forty-three years old when he first sought an invalid military pension in November 1864, Delevan claimed he was incapacitated by a shell wound to his left shoulder and a spinal wound obtained at Fort Wagner's parapet. After six months in the hospital at Beaufort, South Carolina, Delevan transferred to New York for his discharge in May 1864. Complaining of "severe pain" back home in New Bedford, Delevan received an $8 per month full disability pension starting in November 1866, along with pension arrears of $232 pegged to his discharge date.[40] Yet Delevan's pension case goes on to show the challenges faced by veterans when wounds healed, disabilities disappeared, and payments dropped. In September 1873, following a routine physical examination, Delevan was knocked down to a three-fourths disability, reducing his monthly payments to $6. The fifty-eight-year-old Delevan claimed to be "entirely incapacitated" for all manual labor in his final appeal of 1877, and he died the following year without an increased pension. His widow, Margaret, faced pension rejections through 1901 because her husband's cause of death, nephritis, was not attributed to war wounds.[41]

Even the status of full-fledged war hero did not promise complete satisfaction to pension applicants. William Carney, wounded at Fort Wagner, recuperated in a military hospital through December 1863 and then enjoyed a thirty-day furlough home in New Bedford. Although he rejoined his regiment in January 1864, Carney was discharged on June 30, 1864, because of injuries. The hero of Fort Wagner suffered physically for the remainder of his life, and Carney was awarded a pension more quickly than any other black applicant from New Bedford. Together, he and his widow collected benefits longer than any other local black veteran. Some supporters, like his attorney Edwin L. Barney, claimed that Carney's patriotism was sufficient justification for a pension, apart from his war wounds, an unusual argument for a pension application. After repeating the story of Carney holding aloft the flag at Fort Wagner, Barney declared that Carney "deserves a Pension for that alone aside from the wounds he received." Subsequent applications contained similar accounts and patriotic pleas for greater pension benefits.[42]

Carney's initial disability pension of $5.33 per month was reduced to $4 in March 1866, leading to nearly nine years of frustrated appeals for increased benefits. In 1875 Carney successfully petitioned for a doubling of his pension payments to $8 per month based upon total physical disability and by the early 1890s, he was receiving $12 per month. Carney's postwar penury was offset by at least two jobs that were undoubtedly tied to his wartime heroism and modest character. In 1869 Carney was appointed New Bedford's first black postal employee, and later he was chosen a messenger at the State House in Boston where he died in December 1908 following a freak elevator accident. Carney's death was acknowledged by the lowering of the State House flag. His widow, Susanna, received a widow's pension in 1909 that continued until her own death in January 1916, and together their federal pensions lasted for fifty years.[43]

William Carney was well-known for his wartime bravery and lived a long life, but some of his comrades suffered during the war and faced even greater challenges in securing a military pension. Such was the case with a black prisoner of war, Cornelius Henson, who had enlisted with Carney in the Fifty-Fourth. Taken prisoner after the Fort Wagner assault, Henson survived for nineteen months in the notorious Andersonville prison before his release in a prisoner exchange in March 1865. Discharged at Boston on July 8, 1865, Henson clearly was broken by his prison experiences as explained by friends and his wife and later widow, Mary, whom he married in 1870. George Bailey said of Henson after the war that he "seemed to be weak and broken down and not able to do any hard work." Once a hardy stevedore, after the war Henson found employment at the Macomber brothers' store where a coworker recalled that Henson could barely do "a boy[']s work." Store coowner Pardon Macomber stated that veterans "all conceal their ailments as long as they can work for fear

Post One Veterans, Grand Army of the Republic, 1898. William H. Carney is included in this photograph taken on the steps of New Bedford City Hall, on Pleasant Street. (Rotogravure Collection. Courtesy of the Trustees of the New Bedford Free Public Library.)

of discharge if they are found to be sickly." Mary Henson explained that her husband's other jobs had included running a grocery store and selling newspapers. At the time of his death in 1880, she related, Henson had been selling "life insurance on a small scale, where they pay five or six cents a week."[44]

Henson's status as a prisoner of war meant that he lacked many of the military and medical records that could verify his claims. Still, former comrades rallied to Mary Henson in her attempt to obtain a widow's pension. William Carney deposed in June 1883 that Henson had been "as rugged as any of the rest of us" at enlistment but after his return to New Bedford in 1865, Henson was barely recognizable and looked like a "broken down man." "He seemed to be three times his age," Carney related, "and I attributed his condition to his imprisonment." A Pension Bureau Special Examiner, George W. Parchal, provided an unusually supportive evaluation, noting that Henson had survived as a prisoner of war for nearly twenty months while facing the Confederates' wrath against the "regiment of 'Yankee niggers.'" Declaring Henson's claim meritorious, Parchal concluded "there is no question in my mind" than Henson deserved an invalid pension. These strong statements emerged after Henson died in September 1880, never having received any pension benefits from the United States.[45]

Mary Henson's quest for a widow's pension was taken up by others, including New Bedford Congressman William W. Crapo who had initiated inquiries in early May 1880. Mary Henson followed up by seeking support from coworkers, neighbors, physicians, previous employers, other black Union veterans, and even a former mayor of New Bedford. Finally, in January 1884, Mary E. Henson received a widow's pension of eight dollars per month plus arrears that totaled nearly one thousand dollars. After making another claim for arrears in 1888, Henson received a check for eighty dollars in July and collected her widow's pension until she died nearly two years later.[46] Other widows similarly sought pension payments with varying levels of success. Ellen Gooding, for example, received a widow's pension that provided steady additional income for nearly forty years.[47] Some women did not live long enough to receive pensions, as was the case with the widows of Joseph Campbell and Abraham (or Abram) Torrence. Abraham Torrence's widow, Ann, died before her pension claim was approved, and she left no children.[48]

Applications for military pensions typically provide prosaic details about men's and women's lives in the aftermath of the Civil War. John L. Wright's postwar experiences depicted common problems of declining health, troubled finances, and challenges in connecting postwar disabilities with wartime experiences. Serving mainly as a "colonel's orderly" during the war, Wright applied in 1881 for a pension because of a hernia that he claimed was caused by "forced marches with heavy knapsack, and hard labor in digging trenches & building breast-works." Unfortunately for him, the usually supportive physician Dr. John Mackie disagreed: "Applicant has no rupture or any weakness. . . . He is an ignorant negro who has been told by some irregular practitioner that he is ruptured." Dr. Mackie's diagnosis derailed Wright's pension application. Wright applied again seven years later, and gained Mackie's support because of blindness in one eye. In 1894 the local medical examining board commented that "this colored soldier seems to be better preserved for his age than most men of his race."[49] Wright also had the distinction of marrying a war widow, Caroline Jackson, in 1879, after his second wife but first legal one, Fannie, died in July 1878. By the time Caroline died, she was receiving twenty dollars per month and had outlived two black veterans and at least two of her children.[50]

Extending the Veterans' Community

Pension applications depict long-standing ties of comradeship and community among veterans. When Noah Craig complained of rheumatism in 1885, he was backed up by former sergeant Wesley Furlong, who filed his own claim for the same reason. Furlong drew upon three black veterans from New Bedford— John Wright, Charles Harrison, and William Carney—for affidavits on his behalf. Harrison, for example, deposed that "I also was acquainted with [Furlong] and lived near him for a few years after we were discharged, and I know that he was troubled with stiffness and lameness more or less during that time."[51] Similarly, Furlong was supported by Charles H. Harrison, also a veteran of the Fifty-Fourth Massachusetts who served after the war as commander of the New Bedford's all-black Grand Army of the Republic post. Harrison spent the bulk of postwar life in New Bedford, save for a stint as a teacher in Georgia from 1869 to 1875. Upon his death in 1927, Harrison had the distinction of providing affidavits for more black applicants' pensions applicants than any other veteran in New Bedford.[52]

Even when men moved out of New Bedford, they showed support for former comrades and extended their veterans' community. Alexander Johnson and Emery Phelps both moved to Worcester, Massachusetts, where they maintained active memberships in their local GAR post. One of the original drummer boys in the Fifty-Fourth Massachusetts and a New Bedford native, Johnson moved to Worcester in 1868, where he remained until his death in March 1930.[53] A shoemaker before the war, Emery Phelps moved to Worcester also in 1868 with his new wife, Abby, and found employment as a gardener and waiter. Phelps reported that he saw Johnson two or three times a week at their GAR post, worked together for twenty years, and knew intimate details of Johnson's medical complaints. Phelps's first pension application of 1891 was rejected despite support from Johnson and their former captain, James W. Grace. Grace recalled events of thirty years earlier when he assigned Phelps to clerical work because the soldier's health had begun to fail: "I gave him light duty to perform as he did not want to give up. . . . Private Phelps was a good sold[i]er and did his duty faithfully until he was taken sick in July with rheumatism in his limbs and hands." Phelps eventually received a pension of $8 per month and arrears of $336 in October 1894, and he and Johnson remained steadfast friends.[54]

The community of black veterans encompassed men who served the Union cause in military units other than Company C of the Fifty-Fourth Massachusetts Infantry. At least three men served in other companies in the Fifty-Fourth: Watson Cooper of Company A, and Charles Dixon and Harrison Lee of Company D.[55] Two men with differing ties to New Bedford enlisted in the Fifty-Fifth Massachusetts Regiment: the Reverend William Jackson, a regimental chaplain who lived in New Bedford after the war, and Robert Low, whose adventures took him in and out of New Bedford, where he died in his late nineties. At least four men from New Bedford enlisted in the Fifth Massachusetts Cavalry: Miles Carter Jr., Isaiah King, Frederick Pierce, and William S. Jackson (the first husband of Caroline Wright, the widow of John Wright of the Fifty-Fourth). Finally, a number of black navy veterans also called New Bedford home.

Interlaced with supporting details and affidavits, pension files show solid support among veterans in dealing with the pension bureau and its white agents. Such was the case with Harrison Lee, who had served in Company D of the Fifty-Fourth Massachusetts Regiment and died in 1907 while living alone in a shanty. Beginning in 1880, Lee turned to his comrades for assistance, particularly after Dr. John Mackie reported that Lee's wartime "wounds" were not from battle but resulted from wood falling on his leg. Charles Harrison twice claimed to have seen Lee wounded at the battle of Fort Wagner, followed up with a letter to the pension commissioner in 1885 that read:

> Sir
>
> As far as Records I know not but recolection is what I go by[.] [H]e was wounded in the right leg on the calf[.] [H]e's very bad off now as he with us all is growing old[.] [H]e cant do much labor as a man[.] [W]e will soon be gone to our long Home from Poor Houses. [I]f their is no aid is Secured we die, unacounted for and uncared for[.] [P]lease to give this your careful attention for there is but a few living for witnesses[.]

William Carney also provided an affidavit, as did Charles Ellis, formerly of New Bedford, who reported that Harrison Lee was wounded at Honey Hill, not Fort Wagner, further confusing Lee's pension claim.[56]

Because of conflicting information, the Pension Bureau dispatched Special Examiner George Eells in November 1888. He interviewed Charles Harrison, Charles L. Ellis, William Carney, and Harrison Lee. Of Lee, Eels commented: "He is an ignorant colored man and seemed to be reasonably [sic] straight forward and candid in making his statement." Eells injected a hint of racism by reporting that Lee "bears a good reputation for truth and veracity and sobrietty [sic] for a colored man." Charles Ellis explained that his previous testimony may have been conflicted because he had "been drinking a little that day and was not as careful as he would have been if he had been sober." William Carney reiterated his prior claim to have seen Lee in the medical hospital in the aftermath of Fort Wagner. Charles Harrison retreated from earlier claims about knowing where or when Lee was wounded, but he was certain of seeing "blood oozing out" from Lee's wound. Lee himself claimed that he was hurt outside of Battery Wagner while on guard duty, "bunked down under cover of the magazine when a shell was shot from Fort Craig and exploded right amongst us wounding one man to death . . ." Lee complained that his "army troubles" forced him to rely on "chore work as I can pick it up." Although he lived by himself in a shanty, Lee secured helpful testimonials from comrades to obtain a pension until his death.[57]

A surviving veteran and regimental chaplain of the Fifty-Fifth Massachusetts Infantry, the Reverend William Jackson, endured difficulties in securing a military pension despite strong support from others. Jackson had sparred with the Reverend William Grimes over their shared leadership as chaplains for the Fifty-Fourth during training in Readville. Jackson was named chaplain of the Fifty-Fifth, but did not earn wide praise during his military career. His initial claim for a pension in 1890 was rejected when Jackson was in his mid-sixties and in declining health. The main problems centered on the lack of medical and military records to prove wartime injuries, and Jackson's explanations stretched credulity. Appearing before the city's Medical Examination Board in July 1890, Jackson contended that his eyestrain was caused by "franking letters" in military service and his reported hernia was caused by an accident with a bicycle. Despite his poverty, the church leader counted on supportive comrades three decades after the war. During the 1890s the reverend's pension appeals were supported by veterans from other units, such as Charles Harrison of the Fifty-Fourth Massachusetts and Isaiah King of the Fifth Massachusetts Cavalry. When the pension bureau awarded Jackson a windfall pension payment in 1901, he had died two months previously.[58]

Although the primary focus here has been on men and families connected with soldiers in the Fifty-Fourth Massachusetts, some black men enlisted in the Union navy. The city's role in the whaling industry provided employment opportunities for men of color, and pension files for black Union navy veterans suggest that they were more footloose than the city's soldiers. In a small sample of navy veterans, only one settled permanently in New Bedford. These veterans did not maintain the tighter community relationships as did those connected with army service, particularly in the Fifty-Fourth Massachusetts. Most naval veterans were like James E. Fuller who was one of the first black Americans to enlist in the Union cause in September 1861. Following his discharge in 1864 as a landsman, Fuller moved around to various port cities that included New Bedford, New Orleans, Philadelphia, and Portsmouth, New Hampshire. Fuller's file lacked corroborating evidence from comrades, family, or friends, suggesting that his wanderings prevented him from maintaining closer contacts.[59] Seaman Nathaniel Borden's story was similar. Borden enlisted in New Bedford in July 1861, served three years and then reenlisted again in New Bedford. Claiming San Francisco as his home in 1892, Borden had no contacts with anyone in New Bedford.[60]

Mobility and hardship seemed to be the hallmarks of postwar lives for other black navy veterans from New Bedford.[61] Brothers Joshua and John T. Handy also joined the navy. Joshua, the elder of the two, enlisted in New Bedford on September 10, 1861, and died of tuberculosis thirteen months later. John Handy described how he and his brother entered naval service: "[W]hen we were old enough we went on a whaling voyage, Joshua went first and I never saw him afterwards. I sailed sometime after my brother sailed, and when I came home from whaling I learnt that Joshua had come home from his whaling voyage and had shipped in the United States Navy in 1861. . . . I enlisted in the U.S. Navy in 1863." The younger Handy survived the war and established deep roots in New Bedford by working as a carpenter and marrying in 1868. He was a life-long member of the Kempton Street African Methodist Episcopal Church. When Handy died in 1920, his widow, Rachel, filed for a widow's pension with plentiful support. Henry Scarborough Jr. attested to having known John and Rachel Handy for forty-five years; David Piper claimed to have known the Handys for fifty years; Emma Kimball had known John Handy for sixty years; and Henrietta Price claimed ties dating back sixty-five years as "near neighbors." John Handy and his family had maintained a vibrant community with yet another reminder that New Bedford offered blacks a haven of freedom, friendship, and opportunity.[62]

Scandal Within the Black Community

Pension applicants were required to prove their physical disabilities, but in some cases they were expected to demonstrate their morality, as well. Pension laws prohibited women from retaining a widow's pension if they remarried, so a woman's remarriage or adulterous cohabitation to evade the law made their claims fraudulent. Historian Michelle Krowl explored black women's pension applications and suggests that "racial prejudice" may have prompted white pension agents to doubt black women's veracity. Formal investigations also exposed private lives and forced women (and some men) to "explain publicly their postwar sexual behavior."[63] New Bedford's black community experienced a scandalous case that involved pension claims by the widow of Frederick Pierce, formerly of the Fifth Massachusetts Cavalry. This wayward ex-soldier compiled a less-than-distinguished military record after enlisting in January 1865 in the all-black Fifth Massachusetts Cavalry. Before mustering out ten months later, Pierce was absent without leave for one month after in April, and hospital records document that he was treated for syphilis. Returning to New Bedford after the war, Pierce sought work as a shoemaker but departed the city and his wife by the early 1870s and died of pneumonia in 1883.[64]

Fourteen years after Pierce's death, his widow, Missouri Pierce, applied for a pension in December 1897. She complained of poverty caused by her husband's desertion. "Utterly destitute," Missouri Pierce supported her family as a laundress and by "any other kind of work that I can get to do." Her application was undercut by another woman, Sarah Townsend, who claimed that Missouri had cohabited with a boarder named Taylor Watkins. Townsend added, "It had been talked quite awhile that he and Missouri had been intimate, that he was going there when Mr. Pierce was away. . . . Everybody there knew about it." Sarah Townsend's son, William, recalled that Frederick Pierce "claimed that when he would come home from work [and Missouri] would not have anything ready for him to eat, that he was making pretty good wages shovelling coal . . . and he said she was spending his money on some other man, . . . So he 'kicked' and left her." Sarah Townsend's own father contradicted her by confirming that Missouri Pierce was of "good character," having known her for forty years. The Reverend Johnson opined that Frederick and Missouri Pierce had been "happily together until Mr. Pierce went to war," and his desertion was no fault of hers. Frederick Pierce's uncle and aunt, Mr. and Mrs. Lucius Pierce, confirmed the real story: Frederick "became infatuated with the Townsend woman & run away with her." Ex-soldier Pierce committed adultery with Sarah Townsend and moved away from New Bedford, his wife, and their children.

Although Special Examiner Fairbanks reported that a "score of reliable witnesses" had attested to Missouri's good character, she was compelled in 1899 to refute Townsend's charges to claim her widow's pension. Missouri attested that the laborer Watkins had boarded with her for three years, but she turned him out after he "got to drinking." When asked specifically if she had had "sexual intercourse" with him, she replied: "No sir. I did not. He was a boarder and I had nothing to do with him." She added that, "no one can say that I have cohabited with any man & tell the truth." Taylor Watkins explained his boarding arrangement with Pierce: "I paid her three dollars a week for my board, and she did my washing & mending & I paid her extra for that." Asked if they had sexual relations, he replied, "No sir. I never had sexual intercourse with the cl[aiman]t. She was an excellent woman and a woman of good character." Julia Knox, a congregant in Missouri's church, attested that Missouri was always "a hard working woman and a good woman, a christian woman."

The case of Frederick and Missouri Pierce demonstrates that women who opened their homes to boarders could be subject to gossip or hints of sexual misconduct. Missouri Pierce's "worthiness" as a pension applicant was scrutinized closely. Frederick Pierce's deportment rankled some members of the black community, as did the actions of Sarah Townsend and her friend, Elizabeth Sisco. Frederick Pierce stands out among the postwar black veterans not only for his adulterous relations with Sarah Townsend, but because so few of the men under study led impious or improper lives after the Civil War. While some ex-soldiers suffered from poor health and poverty, many African-American veterans carried themselves with dignity and adhered to proper social norms. Frederick Pierce's widow, Missouri, must have felt relief and vindication when the Pension Bureau upheld her claim by awarding her an eight dollars monthly widow's pension in August 1899.[65]

Summary

New Bedford's black soldiers and sailors pursued military pensions for the same reasons as did white veterans. They sought federal payments to compensate for war wounds and military disabilities, to provide additional income, and to reap their reward for saving the Union. Some did suffer because they lacked adequate military, medical, or family records. Historian Robert Reid explains that the groups least able to benefit from the military pension system were the poor, the uneducated, and the ill informed. Black Americans were "overrepresented in all these categories, so it is not surprising that fewer black veterans applied and fewer were successful," Reid concludes.[66] Just as black Americans fought a "different" Civil War than whites, their pension files illustrate unique challenges they faced after the conflict, particularly in the South. Sergeant William H. W. Gray of the Fifty-Fourth Massachusetts decamped from New Bedford with his wife, Martha, and settled on Wadmalow Island, off the coast of South Carolina. His death in July 1881 created hardship for his widow. Because her husband's death was attributed to dropsy and deemed unrelated to Gray's army service, Martha Gray could not obtain a widow's pension despite heartfelt pleas sent directly to the Pension Bureau Commissioner. She concluded with a poignant appeal: "I consider my self a worn out Soldier of the U.S. I was all a round the South with the Regt. adminstring to the wants of the sick and wounded, and did bare the name of the Mother of the Regt." A pension bureau special examiner dispatched to interview Martha Gray appeared too late for she had died in August 1890. Martha Gray never received any pension benefits, nor did her children, and her story of wartime sacrifice and postwar hardships lay hidden in military pension records. Still, her experiences as "Mother of the Regiment" and her campaign for a widow's pension embody the transformative nature of Civil War and of new notions of citizenship for black Americans.[67]

7   "Business Is Extremely Dull": Whaling and Manufacturing in Wartime New Bedford

The Civil War brought economic dislocations to New Bedford, most obviously to the whaling enterprise. Local historian Leonard Ellis wrote of residents' "forlorn hope" as they feared becoming "an abandoned seaport" like Nantucket. At war's end, Ellis wrote: "Our idle wharves were fringed with dismantled ships. Cargoes of oil covered with seaweed were stowed in the sheds and along the river front, waiting for a satisfactory market that never came."[1] The war did not destroy the whaling industry, but it accelerated its decline after the "golden days" of the 1850s. Outspoken Unitarian minister William J. Potter declared in 1863 that the city's prosperity had ended before the Civil War, a decline he blamed on a conservative reliance on whaling. In trying to spur manufacturing and other commerce, Potter explained that the "depressed condition of business here is not in any thing extraneous, but in the business itself." Writing privately in early January 1862, Matthew Howland, the brother of Mayor George Howland, complained that "business is extremely dull." More than one hundred whaling vessels were already removed from the fleet and would never be fitted again. Although New Bedford's whaling economy had suffered, Howland added that the "Rebellion . . . seriously effects most every kind of business in the country."[2]

Historians who have analyzed the economic consequences of the Civil War emphasize its differential impacts on regional and local economies. The prevailing interpretation is that the war slowed the rapid economic growth of the North. But, as Phillip Shaw Paludan observes, "the evidence from local and from national analysis is conflicting as to what the war did to urban economies." Cincinnati's economy was "profoundly energized" by wartime changes and Chicago was "forever transformed," according to Paludan. J. Matthew Gallman's incisive study of Philadelphia concluded that war did not bring major economic changes or growth to that city, apart from a boom in textile manufacturing and construction. Extending his purview to New York City and to Massachusetts, Gallman contended that the Civil War did not accelerate economic growth or change fundamental economic structures. In his overview of

New England's economy, Peter Temin concluded that war played only a "minor role" in the region's industrialization between 1830 and 1880.[3]

New Bedford's economy was affected more negatively by the war than other Northern communities because of the city's dependence on whaling. Although a valuable industry in 1860 with an annual output of almost $8 million and ranked among the top fifty industries in the United States, whaling was a vulnerable enterprise when the war began.[4] Whaling was hammered during the Civil War as insurance rates climbed to peak prices, lays were renegotiated, and ship owners stopped outfitting vessels and transferred ownership. The average annual tonnage of the whaling fleet that fell by nearly half in the war years of 1861–65. The industry never revived, even as New Bedford's whaling merchants continued to dispatch whaling ships through the end of the century. Economic historians Lance Davis, Robert E. Gallman, and Karin Gleiter concluded that the Civil War "drew the final curtain on the Golden Age" of whaling. Whaling merchants faced the capture or destruction of forty-six whalers by Confederate ships, and another forty sunk by Union naval authorities in southern harbors.[5] Although some merchants remained tied for decades to the moribund whaling industry, many of New Bedford's capitalists began to eagerly embrace manufacturing during the war.

The Stone Fleets

During the war's first year, New Bedford's whaling merchants played a novel role by selling old vessels to be sunk in southern harbors known as the *Stone Fleets*. Union naval authorities, led by Gustavus Fox, pursued ambitious plans to block the key harbors of Savannah, Georgia, and Charleston, South Carolina.[6] George D. Morgan, the navy's civilian ship purchasing agent in New York, believed that aging blunt-nosed whaling ships from New England were perfect and could be obtained cheaply. Of two dozen whalers purchased by the Union navy, seventeen hailed from the New Bedford area with prices ranging from just over $3,000 to $5,500. To prepare the Stone Fleets federal military spending poured directly into New Bedford and the city's harbor bustled with activity for more than two months in the late fall of 1861. The local firm of I. H. Bartlett & Sons worked with contractor Richard H. Chappell to outfit ships at four leased wharves north of Union Street. Some 7,500 tons of stone came from former fences on local farms and, at fifty cents per ton, stone had "suddenly become an irresistible money crop," according to one wag.[7] As the ships filled with stone, they were stripped of all but necessary sails, ropes, and fittings. Piled in an open square, the vessels' extra gear was later sold at auction and, as one source reported, "Many were the bargains secured by local whaling men."[8]

The Stone Fleets brought a temporary economic boon to the Whaling City and helped to solidify residents' patriotic contributions to the Union cause. New Bedford's first fleet set forth on November 20 led out of the harbor by the federal revenue cutter *Varina* and saluted by thirty-four guns as it passed the garrison at Fort Taber. Amid an enthusiastic "regatta atmosphere" in Buzzard's Bay, thousands of citizens cheered and waved handkerchiefs as the vessels rounded Clark's Point. Setting southward under full sail and sealed orders, the Stone Fleet's captains learned on November 21 that they were heading to Savannah, Georgia, to report to the blockade squadron. Captain Willis of a Fairhaven ship, *Rebecca Sims*, claimed later that the voyage was dangerous because rough seas could have sunk the heavy vessels. "I have often thought that we men of the Stone Fleet deserved a pension," Willis stated later, "for I never realized the

Captains of the Stone Fleet, circa 1861. *Standing left to right*: Capt. Beard, Capt. Gifford, Capt. Swift, Capt. Childs, Capt. Stoll, Capt. Rodney French, Capt. Wood, Capt. Cumiski, Capt. Willis, Capt. Bailey; *seated left to right*: Capt. Malloy, Swift, Brown, Howland, Capt. Worth, Capt. Tilton, Capt. Braydon, Capt. Taylor, Capt. Chadwick. (Courtesy of the Trustees of the New Bedford Free Public Library.)

danger we were in until the trip was all over." He returned home safely as a hero on January 2, 1862.[9]

New Bedford's ships soon contributed to military and naval preparations against Charleston, South Carolina, the center of Southern secession. The *New Bedford Standard* reported in late November about a Captain Marwick out of Boston who had witnessed twelve of the ships, "the roughest looking craft he ever saw afloat, bound South with a fair wind and going in fine style." He learned they were the "Rat-hole squadron, bound South with sealed orders." The *New York Times* reported on the "Great Stone Fleet" on November 22, 1861, and expected the rebels to view the fleet with "terror and dismay."[10] Contemporary depictions included a Bierstadt Brothers photograph of the stoic seated captains and a lithograph by Benjamin Russell of the fleet as it departed New Bedford with a caption, "Boarding their vessels for a one-way passage into history." The fleet's limited usefulness was reflected in the self-appointed leadership of former mayor Rodney French whose reputation among city leaders was less than stellar. After French ordered a gun fired when his vessel entered Savannah harbor, a naval officer asked who had done so. French replied it was the "Commodore of the stone fleet, Rodney French." A displeased officer replied, "There is only one Commodore in these waters, and he is Flag Officer DuPont of the South Atlantic Blockading Squadron. Don't fire that gun again!"[11]

Back home in New Bedford, a second fleet of seven vessels was prepared like the first and sailed from the city on December 9, 1861. With a total tonnage of 6,400 tons, New Bedford's ships joined six from Boston, five from New London, and two more from New York City. Ordered to report to Admiral DuPont at Port Royal, South Carolina, two early-arriving ships of the second Stone Fleet joined fourteen First Fleet ships under the direction of Captain Henry Davis.[12] The ambitious effort to seal Charleston's harbor commenced late on December 19, 1861, and ended on December 20, the first anniversary of South Carolina's secession from the Union. Captain Davis planned to sink the ships in checkerboard fashion across the harbor's main channel. On the day after Christmas, the *New York Times* headlined its front page, "The Sunken Fleet, The Main Channel to Charleston Harbor Destroyed." Sixteen stone-filled ships, "the queerest, quaintest specimens of ship-building afloat," were sunk as a measure of "righteous retribution." With detailed stories and illustrations, the *Times* described the sinking of "queer old tubs, with queer fittings up, and quaint names." Herman Melville offered a fitting epitaph in his poem, "The Old Sailor's Lament," in which he wrote of the stone whalers, "They sunk so slow, they died so hard, but gurgling dropped at last."[13]

Despite New Bedford's local pride and national attention surrounding the Stone Fleets, Charleston did not fall to Union forces for two more years. Letters home to New Bedford from Charleston described "a lull, like a great calm" when no major military assault went forward. While the Stone Fleets might be called a failure or boondoggle, they generated great publicity about the importance of a naval blockade in defeating the Confederacy.[14] In New Bedford and a few other northern port cities, the Stone Fleets also provided additional income to whaling ship owners, to farmers with stones to sell, and to a variety of workers who outfitted the ships. The Stone Fleets' primary significance may have been to generate active patriotism in support of the Union military effort. "Commodore" Rodney French returned home to showcase a number of what he described as "interesting relics from Dixie," including shells, shots, and pieces of a palmetto tree. His exhibition joined other curiosities displayed in the window of E. N. Burt & Company that included a musket made at Harper's Ferry left behind by a rebel soldier at Port Royal. When the remaining officers and crews of the Stone Fleets arrived home in mid-February 1862, they enjoyed glowing reports about their heroic actions in the South. In New Bedford, salutes of thirty-four guns were scheduled in Rotch's Square to commemorate battlefield victories and the Stone Fleets' heroes.[15] Civic boosterism associated with the Stone Fleets helped New Bedford's leaders to maintain a solid pro-Union and prowar home front.

Confederate Privateers and Raiders

As the war stretched on New Bedford's whaling enterprise paid dearly because of persistent and successful attacks by Confederate privateers. These costly depredations prompted anger, anxiety, and substantial financial losses for the city's whaling merchants. At the war's outset, Confederate States President Jefferson Davis had declared his intentions to provide letters of marquee and reprisal for private armed vessels to harass the superior Union navy and the North's substantial merchant marine. By the end of 1865, Confederate privateers destroyed two dozen New Bedford whalers and disrupted northern commerce and trade.[16] Just as southern authorities had anticipated, Confederate naval attacks created psychological and economic challenges for the North while offsetting the Union's strong naval, whaling, and merchant fleets. A major target was the large "Yankee" whaling fleet of New England. Some Southerners hoped that repeated and costly attacks on whaling and merchant fleets would compel Northern commercial interests to beg for peace.[17]

Sinking the Stone Fleet in Charleston Harbor. Cover of *Harper's Weekly*, January 11, 1862.

Nearly a year and a half into the war, stories and rumors began to circulate in the Northern press about the CSS *Alabama*. Union naval authorities dispatched from New York several steamers, ships, and men-of-war to capture the destructive foe.[18] New Bedford learned in December 1862 of the *Alabama*'s successful capture of the *Levi Starbuck* when the second and third mates returned home. First spied about six miles away from their own ship, they reported that the *Alabama* appeared four miles out with an American flag but then closed within a half mile, hoisted Confederate colors, fired a gun, and claimed the *Levi*

Starbuck as a captured prize. In less than a half hour, the Confederate crew stripped the *Starbuck* of its nautical instruments and provisions, and then covered its deck in tar so it could be torched at night and sunk. After watching their own ship's sinking, captured crew members witnessed the *Alabama*'s take of another northern vessel, the *T. B. Wales* out of Boston. Firsthand accounts like these confirmed Northerners' worst fears about Confederate privateers.[19]

The *Alabama* proved to be an effective, efficient, and feared enemy vessel. By Christmas 1862, the *Alabama* had attacked twenty-six Yankee merchant ships, destroying twenty-two of them and releasing the other four on ransom bond. After four months of its aggressive campaign, the aggregate value of the *Alabama*'s captures was $1,542,211, six times the ship's original purchase cost. Captain Hagar of the *Brilliant* out of New York sensationalized the *Alabama*'s destructive capacity by claiming that under steam power it could reach fifteen knots and its awesome fire power included three 32-pounders, a 100-pound rifled pivot gun, and a 68-pounder on the main deck. Adding to the vessel's fearful reputation, Captain Semmes reportedly disguised the *Alabama*'s appearance by lowering its telescoping smokestack, or unfurling black sails, or displaying a British flag and using boarding officers in Royal Navy uniforms. The *Alabama* was certainly the world's most famous ship in 1864 when it steamed into Cherbourg, France, having overhauled nearly thirty northern vessels valued over $5.1 million. The *Alabama* had cost the North millions of dollars, about thirty times the original cost of building, arming, and outfitting the raider.[20] Northerners in general and New Englanders in particular despised the *Alabama*'s Captain Semmes, and he gladly reciprocated the animosity.[21]

Led by the *Alabama*, Confederate raiders became the stuff of legends and inflicted significant damage to Northern merchants. The privateers forced Northern ship owners to change trade patterns and transfer ownership to foreign flags, and compelled the Union navy to dilute its blockade by diverting at least two dozen vessels to hunt for the *Alabama* and its sister ships. The already agitated residents of New Bedford faced reports of new "pirate" ships in January 1863 when the *Oreto* evaded the Union blockade at Mobile, Alabama, and was soon rechristened as the CSS *Florida*.[22] Three whalers and a merchant ship were destroyed in April 1863, including the *Oneida* of New Bedford, a converted whaler caught en route from Shanghai to New York. Owned by T. and F. S. Hathaway, the ship was carrying valuable tea and was valued at $30,000 and insured locally for only $25,000. Other local ships were captured or destroyed: the bark *Lafayette* of New Bedford, the brig *Kate Cory* of Westport, and the schooner *Kingfisher* of Fairhaven. Heavy losses angered the city's merchants. "Why is it that the administration does nothing, nothing whatever, to endeavor at least to put a stop to these depredations?" asked the *New Bedford Standard* on June 1, 1863. Navy Secretary Gideon Welles was urged to retire to private life rather than have this "disgraceful indifference and inaction continue longer."[23]

While the *Alabama* and the *Florida* garnered headlines and inflicted much damage, the subsequent depredations by the CSS *Shenandoah* proved more costly to New Bedford. More galling, the *Shenandoah's* attacks took place *after* Robert E. Lee's surrender in April 1865, but before ship captains operating in the far-flung Arctic Ocean had heard such news. Captained by James Waddell, the *Shenandoah* was purchased by the Confederates and fitted out as a warship in October 1864. By the time Waddell returned his ship into Liverpool, England, in November 1865, its voyage of destruction was extraordinary. The *Shenandoah* traversed sixty thousand miles around the globe and burned thirty-two vessels, ransomed six, captured over one thousand prisoners, and destroyed cargoes and vessels estimated at $1.5 million. New Englanders were incensed to learn that the *Shenandoah's* main target was their whaling fleet. Confederate naval commander James Bulloch ordered Waddell to visit the Pacific Ocean and other areas "frequented by the great American whaling fleet, a source of abundant wealth to our enemies and nursery for their seamen." Even if Waddell could not "utterly destroy" the whaling fleet, he was encouraged to "damage and disperse" it.[24] As an aside, some merchants in New Bedford were tipped off that a new and fearsome vessel was to be unleashed. New York merchant W. E. Watson informed New Bedford's firm of J. & W. R. Wing about the raider but asked that the privileged information not be disclosed, possibly hoping for inflated market prices once the *Shenandoah* finished its mission.[25]

Arriving in the Arctic in June 1865, after the Civil War's end, the *Shenandoah* attacked twenty-four whalers, nearly two-thirds of all vessels captured during her entire career. An ice-bound New Bedford ship, the *Brunswick*, unknowingly served as stagnant prey while selling off gear and cargo. Approaching under steam in a calm sea, the *Shenandoah* quickly dispatched eleven vessels worth nearly half a million dollars. Captain Ebenezer F. Nye, of New Bedford's *Abigail*, became a hero for ordering two of his whaleboats to notify other vessels of threats by the *Shenandoah*. At one point, a passing brig, the *Kohola* of Honolulu, informed Captain Waddell that the war was over, to which he allegedly responded, "You go to Hell." Waddell could not have known that the Confederate naval commander in London, James D. Bulloch, had issued orders on June 19, 1865, for the *Shenandoah* to terminate its actions. Eventually, Waddell disarmed his ship, logged about ceasing hostilities, and set course for Australia. Fearing capture by the US Navy, he reset his ship's course for England and next touched land at Liverpool on November 5, having traveled seventeen thousand miles directly from the Arctic without dropping anchor.[26]

Newspapers around the world printed angry headlines and editorials about the *Shenandoah's* destructive swath. After the bonded *Milo* reached San Francisco on June 20, one account screamed, "TERRIBLE HAVOC BY PIRATE SHENANDOAH!" In New Bedford, the *Standard* first reported about the *Shenandoah* in late January 1865. Nearly every weekly issue starting in August 1865 focused on the ship's "terrible blow" to the city's whaling interests.[27] The *Shenandoah* destroyed nearly $900,000 worth of whaling vessels, outfits, and cargo from New Bedford alone, and most residents believed that Captain Waddell and the Confederates had willfully ignored the end to war. The *Whalemen's Shipping List* of August 4, 1865, stated that "the pirate ship was advised of the surrender of Lee and the murder of the President. . . . But [the captain] doubted the first, though believing the last and went on about his devilish work." A photograph of victimized whaling captains circulated widely with a telling caption that their ships had been destroyed by the "rebel Cruiser Shenandoah: the last act of an expiring insolence." Altogether the *Shenandoah* and other Confederate raiders captured forty-six Northern vessels, of which twenty-five hailed from New Bedford. Total direct damages to the Whaling City's fleet neared two million dollars, fueling further pessimism about the future of the whaling enterprise.[28]

Whaling During the Civil War

Whaling was a vulnerable enterprise when war began. "No commercial interest of the North, perhaps," wrote local historian Leonard Ellis, "was in a more unfortunate condition at the time when Sumter was fired upon." Even with wartime dislocations and uncertainty, however, reports about profitable voyages kept many in the whaling business. The *Young Phoenix*, for example, returned home in August 1861 laden with more than two hundred barrels of sperm oil and five hundred barrels of whale oil. Over the course of its eight whaling voyages, the *Phoenix* had yielded a gross return of nearly $1 million, an average of more than $100,000 per voyage. In 1862 New Bedford outfitted nearly sixty whaling ships, of which fifty-seven sailed. Twenty went to the Atlantic, nineteen to the North Pacific, nine to the Pacific, three to Hudson's Bay, three to the Indian Ocean, two to the Atlantic and Indian Oceans, and one to the South Pacific. When the *George Howland* left in early June 1862 for the North Pacific Ocean, all but two men of the thirty-man crew hailed from New Bedford, suggesting that the war or fear of Confederate privateers did not dim their hopes for profitable voyages. Locals pointed to other promising indicators such as high prices for whalebone in 1862 when New Bedford merchants sold their entire stock.[29]

Warning signs for the whaling business were present for those who looked. In the first ten months of 1862, for example, seventy-eight whaling vessels were withdrawn nationally, half of them from New Bedford alone and another eleven from across the harbor in Fairhaven.[30] Confederate raiders made their mark as eleven whaling vessels were destroyed in 1862 by either the *Alabama* or the *Sumter*. By the midpoint of the Civil War, the ports of Fall River, Orleans, Mystic, and Coldspring Harbor gave up entirely on whaling, and Boston's and Salem's whaling fleets dropped to five and one vessel, respectively. High insurance premiums and fear of wartime destruction encouraged owners to withdraw their whaling vessels. Over the first two years of war, the number of imported barrels of whale oil had dropped by more than 50 percent, and whalebone imports dropped in half from over one million pounds in 1861 to 488,750 pounds in 1863.[31]

As the war continued, the whaling industry continued to suffer on a national level and New Bedford's whaling-based economy experienced considerable damage. Between January 1861 and January 1866, the total tonnage of whaling vessels in the United States (nearly two-thirds of them sailing out of New Bedford) fell from almost 160,000 tons to 68,000 tons. Although the American whaling fleet declined in size almost every five-year period from 1855 to 1906, the war years of 1861–65 brought a 40 percent decline in tonnage and a 52 percent decline in revenue compared to the five-year period before the war. Just ten years after reaching its peak in 1857, the whaling industry had contracted by 70 percent. As Teresa Hutchins noted perceptively, whaling expansion that had taken place over the course of three decades was snuffed out in one decade. The overall impact could be seen in New Bedford's "valuation" of taxable property that dropped from about $24 million in 1860 to $20,525,790 in 1865. The Civil War's disruptions and Confederate privateers accelerated the decline of the American whaling enterprise.[32]

New Bedford's Business Health and R. G. Dun Credit Reports

Despite a downward slide for the whaling industry during the war years, a closer analysis of New Bedford whaling firms indicates that some larger firms not only survived but also saw their values increase. These values should be read with care, for they also reflect the ravages of wartime inflation. Throughout the North, historian Mark Wilson estimates that wartime prices rose by 75 percent between 1861 and 1864, fueled by the printing and circulation of paper money. An authoritative study by John J. McCusker indicates that prices nearly doubled during the five-year period of the war.[33] In an effort to determine the

Table 7-1. Whaling Statistics, 1856–76

Year	No. Vessels Returning	Import Sperm Oil, Barrels	Import Whale Oil, Barrels	Import Bone, Pounds	Total Valuation, US Imports ($)	New Bedford Tonnage
1856	79	52,885	81,783	1,087,600	9,589,846.36	114,364
1857	105	48,108	127,362	1,350,850	10,491,548.90	110,267
1858	80	46,218	103,105	1,184,900	7,672,227.31	107,931
1859	89	64,327	121,522	1,608,250	8,525,108.91	103,564
1860	88	43,716	90,450	1,112,000	6,520,135.12	98,760
1861	85	47,404	72,134	724,434	5,415,090.59	86,971
1862	68	36,529	61,056	297,600	5,051,781.64	73,061
1863	66	42,458	43,191	307,950	5,936,507.17	64,815
1864	77	48,172	35,883	224,250	8,113,922.07	58,041
1865	57	21,292	51,693	376,450	6,906,650.51	50,403
1866	40	21,345	44,513	392,100	7,037,891.23	53,798
1867	62	24,552	72,108	731,146	6,356,772.51	52,652
1868	69	31,841	49,939	667,507	5,470,157.43	50,628
1869	59	32,673	54,566	471,495	6,205,244.32	50,775
1870	59	42,886	49,563	569,861	4,529,126.02	50,213
1871	56	30,654	55,710	560,993	3,691,469.18	40,045
1872	33	33,021	15,573	177,868	2,954,783.00	36,686
1873	39	30,229	25,757	150,598	2,962,106.96	32,556
1874	32	25,480	26,349	321,637	2,713,034.51	29,541
1875	53	34,430	25,067	359,973	3,314,800.24	31,691
1876	55	30,233	20,535	93,484	2,639,463.31	30,464

Source: Leonard Bolles Ellis, *History of New Bedford* (Syracuse, NY: Mason, 1892), 390.

impact of the war at the level of individual businesses, R. G. Dun credit reports were scrutinized for scores of firms in New Bedford from the 1840s to the 1870s.[34] Of fifty-four firms or individuals in the whaling business that endured beyond the Civil War, forty-three of them showed an increased value during the Civil War.[35]

A representative case study is that of Sylvanus Thomas & Company, whaling agents who branched into oil manufacturing and real estate. By August 1862 the firm was "making nothing" but still held $150,000 in stock and real estate. Sylvanus Thomas took over as sole proprietor in March 1863 with an individual worth estimated at $40,000. He had the good fortune to buy one-quarter ownership in a lucrative whaling vessel that in October 1863 made "the best voyage ever made here." Thomas also benefitted from federal government contracts to manufacture and supply oil for illuminating lighthouses. Through 1864, Thomas's firm earned a "very large profit" of over $100,000. Thomas's "venturesome" character propelled him to buy up the sperm oil market in 1866 and again reap "very large" profits. As the owner of New Bedford's largest oil manufacturing concern, Thomas was estimated to be worth between $100,000 and $200,000 just before his death on November 21, 1866. But, the volatile nature of the business was illustrated the following year after former employee George Homer took over the firm and lost "all he had" in 1867.[36]

As suggested in the Dun credit reports, highly capitalized firms and families stood the best chance of surviving the Civil War. The eleven whaling-related firms or individuals that suffered wartime declines in value were relatively smaller firms with none having a peak value greater than $175,000.[37] Of the forty-three firms in Table 7-2, eighteen enjoyed a peak value between 1861 and 1865, and twenty-two had peak values between 1866 and 1875. The increased value during the war years may have reflected both inflation and gains through diversification. For example, J. S. and F. S. Hathaway saw their firm's estimated value rise from $300,000 in 1862 to $500,000 in 1864. Despite the loss of three ships to Confederate raiders, the firm branched out in trade to Asia and was described in November 1865 as being "Good sound & rich." By May 1867 the firm was worth over $1 million, and T. S. Hathaway was described as the "richest man" in New Bedford in 1872.[38] Another man occasionally termed the city's wealthiest, Jonathan Bourne Jr., parlayed his largely self-made success into a fortune that extended beyond the war. With modest beginning in the 1830s, by June 1842 Bourne was worth an estimated $20,000, a figure that increased twelve-fold by 1855. By the end of the war in 1865, Bourne's wealth was estimated at $500,000, and when he retired in the late 1860s a Dun reporter valued Bourne's wealth at $750,000.[39]

Table 7-2. R. G. Dun Whaling Valuations, Sorted by Peak Value in Current Dollars

Name	Other Businesses	Duration	Peak Credit Rating	Peak Value	Peak Year
Howland, Isaac Jr. & Co.		23	A No. 1	$2,000,000.00	1858
Jones, Edward C.	Investments	37	A No. 1	$1,200,000.00	1874
Arnold, James		25	A No. 1	$1,000,000.00	1856
Bourne, Jonathan Jr.		25	A No. 1	$750,000.00	1867
Crocker, George O. & Co.		33	A No. 1	$600,000.00	1869
Hathaway, J. S. & F. S.	Asian Trade	36	A No. 1	$500,000.00	1864
Greene, David & Co.		37	A No. 1	$400,000.00	1867
Tucker, Charles R. & Co.	Bank	32	1st Rate	$300,000.00	1867
Wood, James B. & Co.	Outfitting	30	No. 1	$300,000.00	1867
Tillinghast, Pardon		26	A No. 1	$300,000.00	1864
Howland, Edward W.	Bank	22	1st Rate	$300,000.00	1864
Swift & Allen	Outfitting	15	A No. 1	$300,000.00	1875
Thomas, Sylvanus & Co.	Oil	12	Good	$300,000.00	1856
Howland, Edward		23	None	$300,000.00	1864
Howland, George & Sons	Oil	29	A No. 1	$250,000.00	1866
Rotch, William J.	Manufacturing	34	No. 1	$200,000.00	1863
Gifford, William & Son		29	A No. 1	$200,000.00	1866
Seabury, O. & E. W.	Outfitting	28	A No. 1	$200,000.00	1866
Nye, Thomas & Asa	Bank	22	A No. 1	$200,000.00	1864
Barker, Abraham & George	Store Owner	20	A No. 1	$200,000.00	1864

Name	Business	Age	Rating	Amount	Year
Wing, Joseph & William R.	Outfitting	24	A No. 1	$200,000.00	1865
Swift, William C. N.		15	No. 1	$200,000.00	1864
Allen, Gideon		32	Good	$150,000.00	1866
Howland, Abraham	Coal Oil	23	A No. 1	$150,000.00	1866
Perry, Ebenezer		15	No. 1	$150,000.00	1867
Hicks, John	Merchant	18	No. 1	$125,000.00	1867
Cook & Snow		40	A No. 1	$100,000.00	1864
Brownell, William O.		29	Good	$100,000.00	1864
Rodman, Samuel	Manufacturing	28	No. 2	$100,000.00	1866
Watkins, William	Outfitting	27	Good	$100,000.00	1870
Howland, William Penn	Petroleum	25	A No. 1	$100,000.00	1862
Bartlett, Ivory & Sons	Bank	28	No. 1	$100,000.00	1866
Philips, William & Son		24	Good	$100,000.00	1866
Hawes, Charles E.	Daguerrotypist	31	Good	$75,000.00	1871
Kollock, Lemuel	Manufacturing	21	Good	$75,000.00	1864
Maxfield, Edmund		20	Good	$75,000.00	1864
Taber, Henry H. & Co.	Outfitting	28	Good	$50,000.00	1867
Slocum, Cunningham & Co.	Outfitting	14	Good	$50,000.00	1867
Ashley, Abraham		10	Good	$50,000.00	1864
Thompson, James D.		14	No. 2	$50,000.00	1865
Thomas, Henry F.	Petroleum	16	No. 2	$42,000.00	1861
Kempton, David B.		25	No. 2	$40,000.00	1865
Reynard, William H.		13	None	$40,000.00	1870

Source: R. G. Dun & Co. Collection, Baker Library Historical Collections, Harvard Business School.

Clearly, some of New Bedford's leading merchants enjoyed individual success despite the gloomy statistics of whaling's wartime demise. The firm of Joseph and William R. Wing expanded during and after the war, growing from a fleet of five vessels in 1861 to sixteen in 1866. Although William R. Wing claimed that the costs of outfitting a ship in New Bedford increased by 75 percent between 1863 and 1865, the Wings enjoyed steady profits that continued through the late nineteenth century. Between 1880 and 1910, the Wing firm owned the largest single fleet of whalers in the world. The Wings were risk takers, sound businessmen, and lucky. During the 1860s, the firm's whalers realized a net return of more than $93,000, plus an additional $42,233 in agents' commissions, as twenty-nine of thirty-two whaling voyages concluded successfully, a ratio of nine successes to each loss. Their success came at a time when other firms were pulling out of whaling, and they prospered from a 94 percent increase in sperm oil prices between 1861 and 1866. Only one Wing vessel was destroyed by a Confederate raider, and fifteen whalers sent out during the war years returned with profits, ten of them yielding returns "100 percent above what it required to outfit the vessels," according to Martin Butler. The Wings' eagerness to remain in whaling was not matched by others, as the nation's whaling fleet in early 1865 was the smallest in twenty-five years.[40]

The Wings stayed true to their calling despite higher wartime costs for outfitting and insurance. Outfitting expenses rose dramatically, from between $10,000 and $15,000 per ship in the early 1860s to between $20,000 and $40,000 in the latter part of the decade. Increased costs were attributed to soaring inflation, the scarcity of high-quality southern timber and naval stores, and higher insurance rates. One local ship owner complained that a barrel of tar that sold for less than one dollar before the war cost $25 by 1863. Wartime taxes increased costs, as did a 6 percent premium charged by New Bedford insurance underwriters in early 1863. Insurance premiums rose more than 10 percent that year, forcing smaller whaling firms, or those less averse to risk, to opt out of the business. The Wings' persistence was rewarded when two whalers returned home in 1866 with sizable catches that brought a five-fold return on investments. Despite falling prices for sperm oil and accumulating stocks of unsold oil in the late 1860s, the Wings sent out six whalers in 1865, four in 1866, four again in 1867, and six in 1868. Although most whaling merchants foresaw a "bleak outlook" for their enterprise by the end of 1869, the Wings did not feel the pinch until the 1870s.[41]

The challenges of wartime whaling were met through diversification. The Wings' began to focus on outfitting ships and pursuing opportunities in banking, insurance, real estate, and manufacturing. Their outfitting trade netted sales over $80,000 in both 1864 and 1865, with an average annual gain of $18,000 per year between 1860 and 1866. The Wings joined local insurance and banking

firms to protect and manage their investments. In 1863 Joseph Wing became a
director of the Commercial Mutual Marine Insurance Company, and William
followed a similar path in 1864 when he was named to the board of the Ocean
Mutual Insurance Company. When the Merchants Bank was reorganized as a
national bank in 1865, the Wing brothers purchased stock, and in January 1866,
William was elected to the bank's Board of Directors, a seat held until his death,
the last of the whaling merchants to serve. Other wartime diversification
included stock purchases (not always profitable) of steamboat lines, a local tan-
ning company, a shoe factory, and mining operations associated with the Com-
stock Lode. As part of the "last generation of whaling merchants," the Wings
owned nine vessels by 1908, the world's largest fleet in a moribund industry.
The Wings showed foresight in buying stock in the Potomska Mills in 1876,
which they found to be a "most rewarding" investment after the Civil War.[42]

The Wings were joined by other successful whaling merchants who made
rational adjustments to their traditional practices. *The Whalemen's Shipping List*
reported on January 13, 1863, that ship owners were fitting out only "suitable"
vessels of "proper size, and only such as may be built expressly for the business,
and that can sail at a comparatively low figure." Individual decisions by whaling
merchants collectively shrunk the fleet's total tonnage and output during the
war. Many sought investments in manufacturing and nonwhaling businesses.
Leading members of the Rotch family, for example, invested in railroads, toll
roads, banks, insurance companies, and real estate. One of the city's wealthiest
individuals, Charles W. Morgan, invested in iron works in Pennsylvania. The
Howlands diversified into railroads and were active in establishing the profitable Wamsutta Mill in the late 1840s.[43] Wartime disruptions and uncertain and
fluctuating whaling prices prompted merchants toward the steadier returns
from manufacturing throughout the 1860s.[44] The *Whalemen's Shipping List* of
February 1, 1870, reported that out of more than one hundred returning whale
ships, only one in four had turned a profit. Three years later, following whaling
disasters in the Arctic Ocean, the newspaper reported that whaling had become
"too hazardous, and its results too uncertain to continue it." The "safer
employment" of capital and "surer rewards" for investors were found not in
whaling the world's oceans but in New Bedford, where the output from two
large textile firms was nearly equal to the total annual value of all whaling
imports.[45]

New Manufacturing in New Bedford

Dislocations to whaling during the war helped to speed a broader transition
to manufacturing in New Bedford. Similarly, in the commonwealth of Massachusetts at least two hundred new manufacturing corporations emerged during

the war, the bulk of them devoted to textile and woolen production.[46] Within New Bedford, at least fifteen manufacturing firms or corporations (excluding whaling oil manufacturers) survived the war. These ranged from the heavily capitalized Wamsutta Mills to short-lived companies like the New England Gutta Percha Roofing Company, led by Mayor John Perry but defunct by 1866. The Wamsutta Mills faced wartime slowdowns in their textile production, but still paid dividends to their shareholders. Similarly, rope making experienced a slowdown during the war as the New Bedford Cordage Company went to "half-time" in August 1861 but still managed to pay 10 percent dividends in 1862. The company purchased a new steam engine in the spring of 1864 when it employed scores of workers. This "good incorporated company" purchased everything with cash and still had an excellent credit rating from Dun reporters; by 1867 the company was making sound profits once again.[47]

Shoemaking was an important industry in Massachusetts and found a congenial home in New Bedford. New technology and mostly women workers churned out millions of pairs of shoes in the 1860s. With a sewing machine, one worker could finish hundreds of pairs of shoes per day, one hundred times faster than by hand. In Lynn, Massachusetts, the number of shoemakers dropped by two thousand between 1855 and 1875 while output increased by seven million pairs of shoes.[48] New Bedford's second-largest manufacturing firm, the New Bedford Union Shoe Company, expanded during the war into a million-dollar corporation. Organized as a joint-stock company, its shares were held widely among local investors and the firm was "by far the best & strongest establishment of the kind" in the city at the war's midpoint in July 1863. Prosperity continued after the war, when shares sold for $500 each. By 1871 some 461 stockholders shared ownership of a company worth between two and three million dollars.[49] A competitor, the New Bedford Shoe Factory, commenced in 1861 under the leadership of Joseph McConnell and Edwin P. Baylor. Full operations in 1862 led to capitalization of $30,000 when stock sold at $65 per share. One year later stock prices soared to $113, and by October 1866 the company was doing $150,000 per year in business.[50]

One individual business that clearly profited through wartime government contracts was that of David Snell's "mechanical bakery." Before the Civil War, bread baking in New Bedford was a competitive industry of small producers. Whaling voyages required ship bread that might last for three or more years, so it was made of hard-tack without moisture and baked in ovens and cured over weeks until it was "seasoned." David Snell became the best known of New Bedford's bakers by the late 1850s and overcame the decline of whaling by securing war contracts for his "mechanical bakery" in the former oil refining factory of Samuel Rodman. He developed a revolving wheel within the ovens that sustained high-volume bread production. Local historian Zephaniah Pease wrote that Snell's bakery produced "tons of army bread . . . packed by the deft fingers of a small army of boys and girls."[51] In February 1863, Snell's mechanical bakery secured a contract to furnish 100 tons of army bread, one of the few documented cases of a government contact issued to a local business. Dun reporters took note in 1865 when Snell was described as having a very good credit rating after making a "g[oo]d deal of money by Govt. contracts." Most of Snell's small business competitors failed while he profited by meeting military needs.[52]

Wartime provided opportunities in other areas, and several large manufacturing firms began their operations in New Bedford. An enduring and successful firm, the Morse Twist & Drill Machine Company, opened in 1864 as a joint-stock company established under general incorporation laws. Capitalized at $30,000 under the direction of President and Treasurer Nathan Chase, this company would become one of New Bedford's most successful manufacturers in the late nineteenth century. By March 1872 the company's stock was selling 40 percent to 50 percent above par value as the firm's operations expanded.[53] Another new corporation, the New Bedford Copper Works, began in 1861 and did solid business through 1863 with capitalization estimated at $300,000. The company's stock prices dropped to $60 by 1866 when the firm was "losing money," and both income and profits were limited into the early 1870s when the firm paid no dividends.[54] These companies contributed to the sizeable increase in manufacturing value in New Bedford between 1855 and 1865.

The largest positive change in the city's economy between 1855 and 1865 was seen in the growth of manufacturing not related to whaling. The number of nonwhaling-related manufacturing firms climbed from 63 in 1855 to 145 a decade later, an increase of 230 percent. The value of their manufactured products increased 464 percent, from $630,660 in 1855 to nearly $3 million in 1865. The amount of capital invested increased more than three times to over $1.1 million in the war's last year. Finally, over 300 women workers made their way into a number of small and often poorly capitalized manufacturing businesses, a significant increase in numbers from 4 female workers listed in 1855. Most women worked in clothing production (199), while smaller numbers labored as "daguerreotype artists," manufactured boots and shoes, produced rope, and toiled at Morse's Patent Twist Drill Company. Handfuls of women engaged in light manufacturing that produced candies and confections, tobacco and cigars, hoop skirts and boxes. By 1865 women workers predominated at the Wamsutta Mills, a million-dollar corporation. Women's wages in New Bedford reflected regional and national trends, as their earnings in blue-collar industries increased by less than half as those for men, and some women saw drops in wages during the war.[55]

Whaling-related manufacturing enterprises were unique to New Bedford and the war had a mixed impact on them. Of the city's five largest whale oil manufacturing concerns in the antebellum era, two went belly-up before the war. Firms that persisted into the war years included Charles Leonard and Samuel Leonard & Son, and their individual histories demonstrate the vagaries of a volatile business. Oil merchant and manufacturer Charles Leonard possessed an estimated wealth of $150,000 in 1856, but his worth dropped 50 percent by 1863.[56] Samuel Leonard & Company was once the largest oil manufacturing company in the country with annual profits in 1854 estimated at $40,000. The slowing economy in the late 1850s forced the firm to compromise with creditors in 1859. By August 1861 the failed firm was assigned to Jonathan Bourne Jr. and Charles Leonard, and two years later, business connections with a Boston firm improved the company's operations and profitability. In April 1865, when the war ended, the company was described as "improved, made money, & now good." Samuel Leonard Jr. took the company's reins in 1866 after his father's retirement, only to see the company go under when its Boston counterpart failed in 1869. Losses were estimated at $125,000. Despite the younger Leonard's excellent character and reputation, the firm could not survive declining prices for whale and sperm oil after 1865.[57]

Whale oil manufacturing was not destined for long-term survival because of better competing products, particularly petroleum oil. Whale fishery oil products dominated the domestic illuminant and lubricant markets at the start of the 1850s, but by the end of the decade the whaling industry's share of these markets had dropped by two-thirds. Economic historians Davis, Gallman, and Gleiter explain: "During the heyday of whaling at most four thousand barrels of oil were returned by any one voyage, even after three or four years. In one day three thousand barrels of [petroleum] oil were pumped from just one Pennsylvania well." In its most productive year, the whale fishery produced more than thirteen million gallons of whale and sperm oil; the petroleum industry surpassed that in its second year alone. Even more telling, during the first six years of crude oil production (which coincided with the Civil War years), the total amount of processed petroleum exceeded the output of all sperm and whale oil over the previous ninety years. Petroleum dealt the "coup de grace" to whale oil as an illuminant in the early years of the Civil War. Prices reflect this pattern, as sperm oil peaked at $2.55 per gallon in 1866 and dropped to $1.36 by 1870; whale oil was priced at $1.45 per gallon and fell to 82 cents in 1868. By the early 1870s whale oil prices dropped to less than half their 1865 level, further reducing incentives to pursue whaling.[58]

Table 7-3. Manufacturing in New Bedford, 1865

Manufacturing	Number	Mf'd Value	Capital	M Employ	F Employ
Whalefishery Vessels	173	$5,647,509	$4,723,000	1,981	20
Whaling Spin-Offs					
Cordage	1	$400,000	$75,000	80	
Sperm & Whale Oil manufactured	6	$4,227,970	$968,000	79	
Casks	13	$145,220	$44,100	61	
Blacksmiths	17	$62,100	$23,800	56	
Sail Lofts	7	$135,300	$30,000	40	
Bakeries	6	$131,500	$30,300	39	
Ship Yard—Ships Launched	2	$44,800	$4,500	30	
Soap and Tallow Candles	7	$45,228	$43,000	23	
Boat and Ship Building	5	$23,165	$9,900	21	
Masts and Spars	3	$12,000	$9,500	11	
Oil and Sperm Candles	5	$107,848	$46,000	10	
Blocks and Pumps	4	$5,717	$1,400	8	
Totals for Whaling Spin-Offs	**76**	**$5,340,848**	**$1,285,500**	**458**	**20**
Textile Manufacturing					
Cotton Mills	1	$1,383,000	$1,000,000	220	300

Table 7-3. (Continued)

Manufacturing	Number	Mf'd Value	Capital	M Employ	F Employ
Other Manufacturing					
Boots and Shoes		$141,889	$44,555	109	21
Metal Sheathing of all kinds	1	$601,772	$300,000	100	
Railroad Cars, Coaches, Wagons	8	$44,517	$42,800	70	
Steam Engines and Boiler	1	$27,350	$40,000	55	
Clothing	20	$23,883	$11,600	50	199
Kerosene or Refined Petroleum	4	$416,820		50	
Flouring Mills	2	$598,064	$210,000	45	
Rolling, Slitting, and Nail Mills	1	$170,757	$80,000	40	
Tin Ware	9	$22,100	$19,600	38	
Daguerreotype Artists	12	$53,740	$22,400	38	37
Furnaces for Hollow Ware	2	$65,160	$20,000	34	
Printing and Newspapers	2	$45,800	$31,600	32	
Tanneries	1	$57,000	$50,000	32	
Looking-glasses, Picture Frames	5	$16,800	$3,350	27	
Shot and Shells manufactured	1	$7,200	$4,000	20	
Master Builders	40	$15,000		18	
Brass Foundries	2	$90,000	$23,000	17	
Saddle, Harness, and Trunk	4	$15,720	$5,000	17	
Chemical Preparations	1	$30,000	$15,000	15	
Ice	2	$9,000	$25,000	12	
Twist Drill (Morses's Twist Drill)	1	$8,000	$30,000	12	15
Gas	1	$22,000	$130,000	11	
Confectionery	3	$91,120	$19,000	9	4
Marble and Other Kinds of Stone	3	$7,823	$7,600	7	
Coffins	2	$6,339	$5,000	5	
Book Binderies	3	$5,668	$2,050	5	13

Snuff, Tobacco, Cigars	1	$6,150	$2,600	5	3
Box manufacturing	2	$3,660	$3,600	4	4
Cement Pipes	3	$1,215	$2,800	3	
Iron Railings and Iron Fences	1	$1,800	$1,000	3	
Sashes and Door Blinds	1	$2,500	$1,300	3	
Mattresses	1	$800	$300	2	
Salt	1	$500	$2,000	1	
Photograph Albums	1	$1,875	$1,000	1	8
Lumber for Market	1	$3,500	$3,000	1	
Copper Manufactories	1	$300,886			
Hoop Skirts	1	$5,000	$2,500		11
Piano and Musical Instruments					
Watches, Chronographs, Jewelry					
Upholstery					
Hat and Cap					
Mathematical Instruments					
Building Stones Quarried					
Wooden Ware					
Firewood for Market		$4,312			
Steam Mills for grinding paints					
Steam Mills for planing					
Machine Shops					
Rivet Manufacturing					
Saleratus Manufactory					
Totals for Other Manufacturing	**145**	**$2,925,720**	**$1,161,655**	**891**	**315**
Totals (not including Whaling and Coastal Trade)	**222**	**$9,649,568**	**$3,447,155**	**1,569**	**635**

Source: 1865 state census.

Some contemporaries recognized that coal and petroleum oil, not Confederate ships, posed the greatest threat or business alternative to whaling. "When man can get oil by tapping the earth or pumping it up like water from a well," the Reverend William J. Potter noted astutely in 1863, "he will not make the perilous search of the sea to give battle to the leviathans of the deep for it."[59] New Bedford's capitalists paid close attention to the emergent petroleum industry in Pennsylvania during the Civil War. A few local businessmen experimented with oil and kerosene even before petroleum oil was discovered in Pennsylvania in 1859. Weston Howland's New Bedford Coal Oil Company drew investments from some of the city's wealthiest whaling merchants when he purchased Fish Island in August 1860 and built one of the country's first factories to refine Pennsylvania petroleum. Despite an explosion in 1861 that destroyed the works and killed two employees, Howland rebuilt immediately and continued a profitable business for several years.[60] In fact, Weston and Isaac Howland closed their ship chandlery in 1862 to devote full attention to the coal oil business, and they were joined by new company manager and former New Bedford mayor Abraham H. Howland when his whaling business was "going astern." Valued at $100,000 at its inception, the Howland oil refinery operation was sold in 1863 and went out of business seven years later. The Howlands' petroleum operation shows diversification in the face of whaling's decline, and perhaps added to its demise.[61]

Wamsutta Mills: Short-term Slowdown, Long-term Gain

New England's textile sector, the North's number one industry, was hit hard by the war and the Confederate embargo on cotton. Some stockpiles of cotton had allowed manufacturing to continue into the first years of war, and many mills operated on two-thirds time in 1861. By June 1862 more than 3 million of 4.5 million spindles in the Northeast were not operating, and mills functioned at about one-fourth time. Cotton became more available as the Union army and navy advanced into the Confederate states and textile manufacturing increased incrementally. New Bedford's Wamsutta Mills faced similar challenge after 1861. Company directors approved plans in 1860 to increase the company's stock to $1 million and to build a third mill with 16,000 spindles. When completed in the summer of 1861, the new mill was nearly as large as the two other buildings combined. Despite their business acumen and deep pockets, the Wamsutta Mills directors did not figure war into their calculations.[62] Wamsutta Mills went on "short time" in May 1861 when the cotton supply was reduced to a trickle. Although spindles and looms arrived in summer 1862 for installation in Mill Number 3, the building remained idle through late 1865. Like other northern textile factories, Wamsutta lacked cotton and workers. Cotton prices jumped from less than ten cents per pound before the war to sixty cents per pound in early 1862, and the company made do with small, fluctuating, and substandard supplies through the war. An inadequate labor pool was solved by recruiting French Canadian workers and hiring more women.[63]

Despite slowdowns and challenges, Superintendent Bennett and the Wamsutta Mills enjoyed some prosperity during the war. Drawing on a salary of about $10,000 through the late 1860s, Bennett purchased one of the city's finest mansions on County Street, the one-time home of John Avery Parker, a "whaling capitalist of the old regime." As local resident and company historian Henry Beetle Hough noted, Bennett's change in residence was "an outward sign, a proof of the transfer of ascendancy from whaling to cotton manufacture."[64] Other company founders did well, also. Joseph Grinnell, the longtime merchant and leading capitalist, had an estate valued at $300,000 in 1871. Another major investor and officer, Edward L. Baker, was president of three companies by March 1862 and earned a good salary from each.[65] R. G. Dun's credit reports noted that Wamsutta was operating four days per week in August 1861, and company stock prices remained high and stable through 1863. As of March 18, 1864, Wamsutta's mills were not running full time but the company was in solid hands with "good men connected." For directors, officers, and investors, the war years did not dent their earnings: an average dividend of 11.88 percent per year was paid between 1849 and 1880, and larger dividend payments were made in 1862 and 1863. By November 1865, the company was capitalized at $1.5 million and a year later its stock sold at 30 percent above par. Once the war ended, a healthy and profitable Wamsutta Mills was poised to lead the city toward a mature industrial economy.[66]

New Bedford's manufacturing enterprises and broader economy were wracked by wartime inflation, illustrated in Table 7-4, and typical of other northern communities. Facing inflated prices in 1865, the lone remaining military officer stationed in New Bedford requested an increased housing allowance. "Here as elsewhere," Major G. N. Mendell noted, "every thing that is bought[,] sold or hired has experienced a great appreciation[,] and even now that the war is over, prices of all kinds are rising and are little less than at the worst period of the war." Inflation led to substantial declines in the real wages of northern workers, estimated by James Geary to be an average drop of 20 percent in real wages by 1863 and 1864. New Bedford's labor struggles during the war were seen briefly in overt support for the ten-hour day in the fall of 1863. An array of mechanics, ship carpenters, caulkers, and joiners formed an

Table 7-4. Civil War Retail Prices in New Bedford, 1861–65 (Prices in Current Dollars and Cents)

Item	11/27/1861 ($)	12/31/1862 ($)	7/1/1863 ($)	12/16/1863 ($)	7/7/1864 ($)	7/5/1865 ($)	% Change, 1861–65
Staples							
Butter (per lb)	0.210	0.280	0.240	0.325	0.400	0.340	161.90%
Cheese (per lb)	0.100	0.130	0.140	0.150	0.205	0.200	200.00%
Eggs (per doz)	0.220	0.290	0.200	0.300	0.320	0.300	136.36%
Fish, Cod	0.035	0.045	0.070	0.065	0.080	0.090	257.14%
Flour (per bbl)	7.625	8.250	8.250	9.125	12.375	9.750	127.87%
Oats (per cwt)	0.540	0.640	0.800	0.850	1.100	0.800	148.15%
Molasses (per gal)	0.620	0.550	0.550	0.660	1.225	1.375	221.77%
Salt (per bush)	0.450	0.450	0.600	0.800	1.000	1.000	222.22%
Sugar (per lb)	0.125	0.145	0.165	0.190	0.350	0.210	168.00%
Meat							
Beef, salt	0.090	0.080	0.100	0.100	0.150	0.160	177.78%
Pork, fresh	0.100	0.100	0.120	0.140	0.150	0.200	200.00%
Chicken	0.125	0.140	0.200	0.180	0.250	0.315	252.00%
Other							
Cement (per cask)	1.500	1.500	1.500	1.850	2.100	2.100	140.00%
Hay, Feed (per ton)	15.500	17.500	17.500	17.500	19.000	18.000	116.13%
Sperm Oil (per gal)	1.750	2.250	2.250	2.250	2.400	2.500	142.86%
Whale Oil (per gal)	0.650	1.100	1.250	1.400	1.500	1.500	230.77%
Petroleum Oil (per gal)	0.500	0.800	0.520	0.750	0.900	0.900	180.00%
Oak Wood (per cord)	4.500	5.000	4.750	7.750	8.250	7.500	166.67%
Average							**180.53%**

Midpoint prices used for range.

Source: *New Bedford Standard* by date as noted above.

association and sought "suitable compensation." Expressing more deference than anger, their published notices proclaimed caulkers' new wages at three dollars per day and the promise of a ten-hour workday that did not materialize.[67] New Bedford's capitalists held the upper hand during the war, but they would encounter significant new challenges in the late 1860s in the growing textile industry.

Summary

Similar to other northern cities, the Civil War had a differential impact on New Bedford's economy. Most obviously, whaling was pushed into further decline as a national industry because of Confederate privateers' attacks and the emergence of petroleum oil as a suitable and profitable alternative to whaling products. The grim statistics from 1855 and 1865 state censuses were revealing. In 1865 the New Bedford whaling enterprise claimed 56 percent of the vessels, 48 percent of the capital, and 29 percent of the employees as it did ten years previously. The continuing contraction of the whaling industry was felt keenly in New Bedford as whaling merchants and leading capitalists pondered their future. An important consequence of the war was a warmer embrace of manufacturing corporations by many of New Bedford's business and political leaders. Despite slowdowns to the Wamsutta Mills and the New Bedford Cordage Company, their directors and investors still received dividends during the war and kept their businesses intact. Other companies, such as Morse Twist & Drills and the New Bedford Union Shoe Company, showcased steady profits through manufacturing. The costs of war were experienced not only within business and economic spheres but also in the public arena as officials contended with the demands of municipal governance during a protracted and expensive war, issues to be explored in the next chapter.

8

"The Position of Our City
Has Materially Changed":
Public Costs and
Municipal Governance
during the Civil War

Looking back over the Civil War, local historian Zephaniah Pease declared
that New Bedford authorities "were most generous in financial support
of all war measures." Writing decades later after the war, he reported
that "New Bedford as a municipality responded nobly to every demand made
upon her generosity and patriotism to aid in a vigorous prosecution of the
war."[1] While true, such idealized sentiments do not convey the difficult choices
faced by city leaders and residents during the war. Mayor Isaac Taber outlined
those challenges in January 1862. "From a variety of circumstances, apart from
those connected with the national struggle in which we are now engaged, the
position of our city has materially changed," the mayor stated. Whaling was
"no longer profitable," unemployment had climbed, and workers who once
had "flourished" in whaling-related trades now looked to military enlistment
or public charity to support their families. Taber noted soberly that city's
extraordinary expenses climbed "in almost inverse proportion" to New Bedford's ability to meet them.[2] The city's business and political leaders, in fact,
viewed their fiscal prudence and responsibility as a vital contribution to the
Union war effort. As they stretched to provide services at a time of competing
needs and troubling economic conditions, leaders confronted issues that went
beyond mundane discussions to embrace debates over New Bedford's future.

The unprecedented war accelerated municipal spending in unforeseen ways.
A decade before the war in 1850, the city expended just over $100,000 in its
annual budget. Five years later as the whaling economy prospered, annual city
expenditures moved beyond $250,000 and then jumped to over $400,000 in the
flush times of the late 1850s (see Table 8-1). By the war's end in 1865, New Bedford witnessed its first annual expenditures of more than $500,000. The city's
pattern was not unlike that of Deerfield, Massachusetts, as analyzed by Emily J.
Harris, in which the town's wartime budget grew 61 percent between 1861 and
1863 and then doubled again between 1863 and 1864.[3] New Bedford's worst wartime budget deficit emerged at the war's midpoint in 1863 and amounted to
about $11,000, a figure one-third of the largest (and aberrant) antebellum deficit
of 1854. After the war, the city's increased population growth helped to push
the annual budget to over $800,000 in 1871. By 1885 New Bedford's annual city

Table 8-1. New Bedford Expenditures and Receipts, 1850–75

Year	Receipts ($)	Expenditures ($)	Budget Gap ($)
1850	100,625.35	100,027.58	597.77
1851	95,008.27	93,202.09	1,806.18
1852	112,335.18	98,532.63	13,802.55
1853	163,392.81	170,541.18	(7,148.37)
1854	224,856.97	257,103.06	(32,246.09)
1855	255,219.66	253,804.03	1,415.63
1856	381,894.65	381,510.13	384.52
1857	421,631.96	417,969.37	3,662.59
1858	400,673.22	402,698.23	(2,025.01)
1859	404,939.93	403,358.48	1,581.45
1860	373,914.74	374,271.18	(356.44)
1861	316,000.89	320,003.34	(4,002.45)
1862	339,256.49	323,413.77	15,842.72
1863	485,054.66	496,087.53	(11,032.87)
1864	401,694.22	405,804.79	(4,110.57)
1865	539,803.65	541,823.03	(2,019.38)
1866	430,841.55	408,456.06	22,385.49
1867	468,454.64	451,266.38	17,188.26
1868	385,926.54	389,734.34	(3,807.80)
1869	561,818.69	582,440.49	(20,621.80)
1870	778,889.29	791,396.45	(12,507.16)
1871	848,235.00	803,266.50	44,968.50
1872	704,252.06	731,902.57	(27,650.51)
1873	891,654.30	790,115.39	101,538.91
1874	760,246.70	784,537.87	(24,291.17)
1875	794,822.88	798,521.28	(3,698.40)

Source: Leonard Bolles Ellis, *History of New Bedford* (Syracuse, NY, 1892), 390.

budget was more than one million dollars, or ten times greater than it was thirty-five years earlier.[4]

Following New Bedford's incorporation as a city in 1847, public authorities demonstrated scrupulous accounting and financial practices that became more sophisticated through the Civil War years. Prior to March 1863, for example, the published annual records of the Finance Committee included minor details such as the names of people paid a few dollars to sweep out a public school. Such antiquarian accounting methods did not survive the Civil War.[5] City officials paid close attention to budget and fiscal matters in meeting novel expenses associated with recruiting troops, paying bounties, transporting soldiers, implementing a military draft, and aiding dependent family members of men at war.

They cooperated with new bureaucracies of local, state, and federal governments during the prolonged conflict. Following the debacle at Bull Run in July
1861, the *New Bedford Standard* took to task the Lincoln administration on July
25 for "too much dilly-dallying and delaying" under a mistaken belief that "this
was to be a rose-water sort of a war." Union forces needed not only the best
weapons and military leaders, but they needed effective spending and efficient
mobilization on all fronts. Similar sentiments circulated locally regarding the
city's commitment to the war effort.[6]

Wartime Costs and Municipal Governance

When Mayor Taber addressed the city's extraordinary costs and challenges
during the first year of war, he mentioned the "probable necessity" of raising
taxes. An early loan of $25,000 to the city council was granted for the relief of
soldiers' families, coast defense, and the formation of military companies. That
sum would prove inadequate, Taber thought, and explained that Overseers of
the Poor would probably need additional funding because of higher unemployment levels and lagging state payments for military enlistment. During 1861, city
officials appropriated $5,000 for the relief of the families of the New Bedford
City Guards, and another $10,000 was budgeted for home and coast defense.
On top of these expenditures, the city authorized its recruiting efforts to
include a $15 bounty per man in September 1861. Taber recommended also that
New Bedford fund the fortifications at Clark's Point if state or federal governments refused to pick up the tab.[7] All of these new costs reflected unanticipated
demands of war, highlighted by the city council's readiness to accept another
temporary loan of $100,000 as an advance on expected tax revenue. With a
combination of short-term loans, tax revenues of $155,622, and miscellaneous
receipts, the city's revenue in fiscal 1861 stood at nearly $342,000.[8]

The unprecedented civil war affected all levels of government and the in-
teractions among them. The city of New Bedford, the Commonwealth of
Massachusetts, and the US government all faced unusual costs and new admin-
istrative demands. New Bedford's Finance Committee oversaw and tabulated
the city's costs during the war. Unique expenses in 1861 included monies for
the Relief Fund ($7,533.70), Home and Coast Guard ($19,337.08), and Military
Expenditures ($5,352.07). New incidental expenditures rose that year to over
$9,000, including more than $2,000 in interest for the temporary loans. In
addition, nearly $20,000 was spent for home and coast defense. Over $4,600
was expended for military bounties and another $6,300 for payments to sol-
diers' families, all expected to be reimbursed as part of the state's massive military mobilization.[9] In an annual address in January 1862 that detailed the

Commonwealth's war costs, Governor John Andrew reported that the state's ordinary expenses amounted to almost $1.2 million. Military costs were nearly three times greater at $3.4 million, of which about $775,000 had been reimbursed by the US government. Andrew reminded his fellow citizens about their duty to provide "the men and the money required of us for the common defence."[10]

By early 1862, as the "Great Rebellion" showed no signs of abating, New Bedford's city officials began to make difficult fiscal decisions. Mayor Taber worked with the Board of Aldermen, the Common Council, and the School Committee to reduce salaries and cut costs. The School Committee, for example, reduced expenditures by about $10,000 from the previous year by not retaining some teachers and closing the Parker Street Primary School. City officers pocketed lower salaries. The City Clerk's salary dropped from $1,000 to $900 and the Clerk of the Common Council's from $200 to $150, in line with cuts between 10 and 20 percent in most departments. Only the fire department was spared in the budget reductions.[11] More frugality was demonstrated that summer when the city eliminated annual Fourth of July celebrations. Cost-cutting frugality continued when the Common Council rejected in July a bid to renovate the basement of City Hall for $4,200 and tabled an order to light the street lamps at night. Stating that "funds were low and would not hold out," the Fifth Ward's Howland opposed night-time street lighting, adding that he "could carry a lantern on dark nights, and thought we ought to save all we could."[12]

Although they cut funding and spending where possible, city leaders showed a willingness to contribute as needed for military needs. With a good measure of ambition and foresight, the city appropriated $7,500 for a general hospital that could be housed in the spacious City Alms House and accommodate three hundred sick and wounded soldiers. New Bedford made the offer to state and federal officials in the summer of 1862 when an influx of wounded soldiers returned home amid reports of poor medical treatment. Stories from the Fifth Massachusetts Battery were typical. Josiah Gardner and James Baldwin arrived home in New Bedford with alarming reports about their hospital stays. Gardner spoke of a New York hospital where physicians from Massachusetts were excellent, but where one nurse earning only two dollars per week was expected to care for thirty men. "She did not mean to do any more than earn her money," Gardner complained, adding that a soldier would only survive such poor medical care if he could fend for himself. Troubled by such accounts, New Bedford's leaders offered to provide a hospital so "our brave soldiers may be cared for by their own friends." The federal government did not accept the city's offer.[13]

New Bedford enjoyed greater success in selling a variety of war bonds and raising funds to support the war. The city's Finance Committee reported favorably in August 1862 of securing a loan to meet "expenditures made necessary by the war." All city-backed bonds were purchased by the New Bedford Institution for Savings with a total premium of $970.29. "It is believed that no municipal securities in our State, issued by any town or city out of Boston, have been disposed of on terms so favorable," the *Standard* reported. The total amount of the offer was $282,000. The commingling of public and private monies was seen in other endeavors. The Soldiers' Fund operated through the City Treasurer's office and received contributions ranging from $2 (from a "poor patriot") to $100 each from J. Howland and Latham Cross. The total amount in the fund stood at just under $8,000, and the committee continued to "thankfully receive any funds, however small."[14]

Wartime anxiety and fiscal uncertainty persisted into 1863 when incoming Mayor George Howland Jr. described the "general depression and gloom which overhang our land." The city had cut its budget by $21,000 for the fiscal year, to an appropriation of $159,000, but the mayor worried that increased taxes and "paralyzed" energies would make it difficult for citizens to pay their taxes. Howland reported that the city's budgets for streets, schools, and street lighting were slashed, but he noted that never before had the city collected such a high proportion of taxes—about 95 percent of all assessments. One city agency, the Overseers of the Poor, received a $2,000 funding jump, the mayor explained, because of a "constant . . . [and] increasing demand" for public charity."[15] In the 1863 fiscal year, bounties paid to volunteers constituted the largest single item in the city's budget, for whom the city council appropriated a staggering sum of $143,000.[16] The city's wartime frugality was highlighted again in July 1863 when New Bedford did not fund a public Fourth of July celebration. A self-appointed critic named "Legend" complained in a letter to the editor that the Fourth instead would feature a parade of six police officers, a few sober and inebriated pedestrians, and "unimportant persons from abroad, candy boys and other pedlars."[17]

Favoring scant budgets for patriotic pomp and parades, New Bedford's leaders focused on the more important endeavor of recruiting troops. Like other Northern communities, New Bedford's bounty system was designed to recruit soldiers and sailors and discourage the need for a military draft. By January 1863 the city had expended $141,690 for bounties and another $25,000 to persons dependent on support from military volunteers. The state was expected to reimburse these costs.[18] City Treasurer Congdon, who carefully documented the war's costs and city's contributions, explained to the mayor in 1863 about the process and problems of making these payments. As Congdon distributed thousands of dollars to "father, mother, wife, brother, sister, friend, savings bank &c. &c.," his office expended a "great amount of labor." In May 1863, Treasurer Congdon, Mayor Howland, and City Aldermen signed a tally that reflected bounties paid to over 700 men for two national calls for soldiers. They affirmed that 481 men had been paid for enlisting in nine-month regiments (total of $95,650), while another 244 were paid for volunteering in three-year regiments (just over $44,000).[19] Most local bounties came in the war's second year, and by mid-1863 New Bedford had disbursed over $161,000 in bounties and spent over $14,500 on advertising and other expenses. The city's total cost of mobilizing troops was over $176,000 by the middle of the war.[20]

The vital bounty expenditures and city's expenses were met by continued high rates of tax collection. Patriotic sentiment appeared high, as typically 95 percent or more of taxes were received by the city each year. Leaders still complained about a time lag in receiving state reimbursements and their loss of potential interest while the money sat in state coffers instead of the city's.[21] Local budget challenges help to explain the mayor's consternation over the state's refusal to pay for special police and military support in July 1863. Fearing a New York City–styled draft riot, city officials expended over $3,500 to maintain order, including $2,000 distributed to two military companies. Mayor Howland viewed these costs as an "advance to the State" that should be reimbursed. When New Bedford's pay rolls and bills were presented to the State House, Howland reported, "we were told by the Auditor that the troops were not called out in accordance with any law which renders their service an expense to the Commonwealth." Consequently, city authorities in New Bedford (and similarly in Boston) were responsible for the costs of their local militarization in July 1863. Mayor Howland concluded that, "There never was any understanding, either expressed or implied, that this city would pay the troops called out by the authorities." He urged that the issue be forwarded again to the state legislature for their consideration, adding to the bill another request of $770 to pay for cavalry horses.[22]

In summarizing the city's finances in January 1865, Mayor George Howland Jr. spoke positively a few months before the war ended. Thrilled with the reelection of President Abraham Lincoln and recent Union military victories, he was pleased also by the changes in the military quota laws in July 1864 that brought a credit of 1,188 naval enlistees to New Bedford, along with credit for other men who enlisted in 1863. This promising news complemented the "very satisfactory" financial status of the city, and the mayor was even optimistic that taxes might be reduced in the coming year. He was not afraid to address more contentious fiscal issues by complaining about the rising costs of serving the poor. War-related expenses included interest payments of almost $8,000 on loans and another $800 each on armory rentals. Finally, at the end of the war with victory in hand, city officials loosened up for the Fourth of July 1865 by committing more than $5,000 for its celebration, a remarkable sum for frugal public leaders like George Howland Jr.[23]

Public Schools in Wartime

Although Massachusetts had long been in the forefront of American public education, New Bedford's educational system remained unexceptional at the outset of the Civil War, apart from having racially integrated schools. When Abner J. Phipps arrived in 1861 as the city's first schools superintendent, he encountered an inadequate infrastructure and traditional notions of education inherited from the antebellum era.[24] Phipps provided a strong voice for a centralized school district and educational innovations while working with a school committee that placed primary focus on "reading, writing, and the elementary rules of arithmetic." School Board members occasionally tied public education to moral and political issues, and such sentiments became more pronounced as the nation inched toward war. In 1860 the School Committee suggested that students who gained a "love of our common country and the Union" would also acquire and an "unrelenting detestation of the fiend-hearted traitors at home."[25] Strong sentiments were also expressed for the qualities of the ideal teacher and the efficacy of moral instruction. Black students were welcome in the city's schools, including evening schools for adults, and the School Committee congratulated itself for educating "that portion of the population, who by misfortune or by birth in places where the light and blessedness of New England schools do not shine, have hitherto been unable to read or write."[26]

Debates over school funding during the war illustrate how the exigencies of war crowded out moral imperatives of education and altered notions of municipal governance. New Bedford's public schools faced significant cuts during the war. Education was an area where the city's tradition of enlightened governance conflicted with longstanding patterns of frugality. Before the war, the city's public schools expanded because of population growth, pressure by civic leaders, and state laws that supported mandatory public education. In the flush times of the late 1850s, New Bedford funded a dozen primary schools (for children aged four to nine), "intermedial" schools, grammar schools, and a high school. Between 1850 and 1856, public school annual appropriations more than doubled, from less than $23,000 to more than $49,000 (see Table 8-2). Still, New Bedford was possibly the largest city in the country without a schools

Table 8-2. New Bedford Municipal Expenditures, 1850–75

Year	Schools ($)	Poor ($)	Streets ($)	Paid Debt ($)	Police Dept. ($)	Fire Dept. ($)	Sewers ($)
1850	22,754.80	11,688.17	10,471.30	4,883.68	3,806.28	10,275.46	
1851	24,992.15	9,508.58	13,275.62	4,405.26	4,179.47	7,924.43	
1852	30,774.19	11,634.43	16,963.75	4,242.11	5,838.40	7,225.60	
1853	37,927.35	13,261.98	25,387.08	3,820.44	6,207.29	9,731.94	17,338.08
1854	40,347.29	18,216.62	26,608.87	6,782.70	7,788.64	9,239.67	15,982.92
1855	35,698.71	14,863.50	39,563.08	12,128.92	10,712.28	24,863.96	20,918.22
1856	49,939.34	15,899.40	41,237.58	14,605.13	9,949.77	18,213.44	11,761.65
1857	49,530.86	14,291.71	43,620.91	22,255.92	10,791.52	14,675.22	11,684.81
1858	47,924.26	19,540.76	59,203.39	19,906.56	14,301.43	16,488.91	14,455.24
1859	46,337.42	19,070.03	31,697.59	31,102.82	14,518.91	13,349.15	47.85
1860	45,339.60	20,431.74	37,944.41	12,901.15	6,702.58	13,904.49	
1861	43,590.09	24,161.98	38,805.06	30,616.00	14,501.57	19,291.18	1,888.40
1862	40,054.33	27,498.92	22,402.06	29,976.50	14,413.45	12,255.87	
1863	32,154.59	21,632.98	27,717.40	33,013.00	11,191.54	12,109.79	
1864	39,617.01	22,382.37	15,098.77	41,421.50	11,751.97	11,542.10	
1865	40,193.40	24,458.66	20,128.85	40,562.00	13,478.60	11,840.85	
1866	51,379.95	30,991.45	21,853.91	38,990.50	13,833.65	19,531.15	
1867	51,421.81	28,900.50	32,281.44	42,049.00	16,753.55	19,053.84	4,751.3 8
1868	56,598.94	30,074.47	29,879.14	43,341.50	16,776.39	20,485.17	1,399.96
1869	62,289.56	31,170.14	40,782.46	51,570.00	17,320.86	18,678.19	
1870	62,392.47	30,601.16	41,191.92	67,650.50	19,440.76	16,801.50	24,372.49
1871	62,862.05	33,259.91	88,569.63	63,639.00	18,495.12	19,927.01	10,552.00
1872	68,819.90	33,040.69	41,505.26	70,326.33	18,622.75	17,402.15	32,146.17
1873	69,940.18	38,924.48	47,206.18	72,995.00	18,897.00	19,710.47	24,058.50
1874	71,442.75	39,415.04	46,192.56	81,884.81	19,291.50	26,264.42	11,239.83
1875	77,715.09	41,321.52	68,029.69	85,026.00	19,302.75	21,082.72	5,386.86

Source: Finance Committee Reports, 1850–75, NBCD, reel 2.

superintendent, a deficiency remedied in 1861 with the appointment of Abner J. Phipps. In his first year, the progressive Phipps decried excessive corporal punishment and encouraged more high school graduates. After six months as superintendent, Phipps strongly called for greater funding, mainly to improve classrooms. "Our city has by some been called the 'City of Palaces,'" Phipps stated, but most public school classrooms remained in his words, "ill-ventilated, repulsive apartments."[27]

Superintendent Phipps's tenure coincided with the start of the war, and he accelerated reforms with energetic and professional leadership for the next four years. Phipps and School Committee members funded evening and adult schools aimed at adult mill workers in the city's northern reaches.[28] Education and literacy, it was hoped, would prevent people from "promenading the streets" or "visiting low places of entertainment." Besides reaching out to presumably white factory workers, the School Committee encouraged education among black house servants who had come from the "'Sunny South' where their educational privileges were rather limited."[29] Besides promoting better morals, northern public education was a valuable weapon in the Union cause, Phipps and colleagues argued. Public schools taught loyalty and submission to "rightful authority" while helping a "peace loving people" to train and mobilize for war. In their view, the "enlightened patriotism and invincible courage" of Massachusetts' citizen soldiers were inculcated through the state's strong system of public education, the "true nurseries of an enlightened democracy." By championing the efficacy and patriotism of public education, Phipps fought aggressively against further budget reductions even as the costs of war trumped home front needs.[30]

Despite lofty protestations by Phipps and the School Committee, municipal authorities cut the schools' budget during the war years. Beginning with appropriations of $43,590 in 1861, the budget was trimmed in 1862 to $40,000 and then sliced in 1863 to a wartime low of $32,154.59. Not only was this allocation $8,000 less than the previous year, but it was $3,000 less than what the board believed to be the absolute minimum needed for the upcoming school year. Officials opted to not repair buildings, to lower teachers' salaries, and to dismiss some teachers all together. In one classroom, the student-teacher ratio increased to sixty-five students per teacher. Furthermore, the school year was shortened by two weeks and teachers' compensation was reduced by a mandatory furlough. All salaries that exceeded $250 were cut by 5 percent, and the school board was now required to operate in the same fiscal year as other city departments. In response, the School Committee reminded fellow citizens in 1863 to recognize "the paramount importance of a liberal support of the public schools," singling out the city council for showing "a want of that liberality of spirit."[31] Despite Phipps's tireless work and advocacy, New Bedford's reduction in educational spending reflected wartime choices and revealed long-standing local debates over publicly funded education.[32]

Superintendent Phipps offered a unique perspective of the war's impact on New Bedford's home front. He wrote of extraordinary excitement during 1862 when New Bedford's "usually quiet community" was beset by frequent public meetings called together by ringing bells and martial music. During school time, students and citizens witnessed "the marching to and fro through our streets of military companies at all hours of the day, the enlistment of so many fathers and brothers, the frequent visits to the neighboring encampments." Although these public events underscored citizens' "love of country and of freedom, obedience to law, and devotion to the Union," these activities challenged the sound order he sought in public schools. Phipps continued to worry about overcrowded schools, persistent truancy by working children, and the complicity of parents in taking their children to other states that lacked compulsory school attendance laws. Without mentioning the Wamsutta Mills by name, Phipps complained about the managers of the "principal factory of our city" who disregarded state laws regarding children's school attendance. In his final report as superintendent before leaving to take a similar post in Lowell, Phipps devoted great attention to lax morals among parents and children.[33]

In a year-long interregnum without a superintendent, New Bedford's School Committee procured a 25 percent increase in annual appropriations to almost $40,000. Moralistic instruction continued through the war as each school day began with the principal or his designee reading scriptural passages and students were encouraged "to preserve and perfect a republican constitution and secure the blessings of liberty." School Committee members averred in 1864 that a primary lesson of the Civil War was the "paramount importance of a wise and universal system of public education" that ensured the restoration of the county and the destruction of slavery. "It is the mission of Massachusetts and the loyal North to quell the barbarism of the South," they reported, "not less by the spelling book and the grammar, than by bullets." The war also created unique educational lessons and settings, some posed by the absence of men. High school enrollments, for example, were two-thirds female, and ninety women, twice the number of men, attended New Bedford's evening schools.[34]

School officials joined others in expressing great relief as the war came to an end. Offering public thanks to God, the school board invoked continued aid" in maintaining the city's schools in the face of business depression, high taxes, and uncertainty. Help soon arrived in the form of a dynamic new superintendent infused with modern educational ideas. Assuming the superintendent's position on March 1, 1865, the Reverend Henry F. Harrington made a national name for himself and New Bedford's school system over the next two decades.[35] Promoting reform through what he called "flying visits" to the schools, Harrington criticized regimented exams, rote recitations, and excessive reliance on textbooks. Harrington believed that students should have more freedom to learn and to think, and he favored raising high school admissions standards. Furthermore, he ended formerly sex-segregated schools because they were "unnatural and unprofitable," and he addressed other gendered issues that may have grown out of wartime disruptions. In particular, Harrington and the School Committee criticized long-standing pay inequities between male and female teachers, and in 1865 the committee granted salary increases of 10 percent or more to female teachers while men's salaries remained unchanged. Committee members could not determine "any good reason why a woman for the same work, equally as well performed, should not have the same pay as a man." Similar efforts persisted into the late 1860s. Other progressive ideas were seen in Harrington's push to change from the year-round school year, with nine weeks of intermittent vacation, to one with an extended summer vacation.[36]

Arriving at the tail end of the Civil War, Superintendent Harrington and the School Committee explicitly connected public schools with civic events and the Union military victory. Harrington justified the participation of all three thousand school children in a massive Fourth of July parade in 1865 by stating that "there is something more to be learned by our youth than what is contained in ordinary school books." The Fourth of July celebrations showed everyone that the Declaration of Independence had become a "practical reality," he explained.[37] But there was a political calculus involved, also, as Harrington and the School Committee persisted in linking their funding requests to the successful outcome of the war. The annual appropriation for public schools rose from $40,193 in 1865, to over $51,000 in 1866, and to more than $57,000 in 1867. In 1866 female teachers received another catch-up salary boost of 12 to 15 percent, while men's salaries saw no increase. The superintendent called for a graduated salary scale to reward experienced teachers and to encourage the improvement of inexperienced ones.[38]

New Bedford's public schools continued to reflect some of the city's prewar patterns, however, such as the predominance of religious values and moral instruction. One example was the formation in 1865 of the "Howland Grammar School Association" through which students sought to combat profanity and vulgarity. City and school authorities thought highly of this organization and met with its members on the Fourth of July in the city's largest church to hear addresses by prominent citizens. The public school system also benefitted from the largesse of private benefactors when the School Committee was granted a bequest from the $2 million estate of Sylvia Ann Howland. She donated $100,000 for educational purposes to be divided equally between the schools and the New Bedford Free Public Library. Beginning in 1865, interest each year amounting to about $3,000 was to be spent for promoting "liberal education" for any purpose not covered by taxes. The Howland gift was another example of benevolent philanthropy by one of the city's leading Quaker families. Superintendent Harrington continued to fight the city's frugality by claiming that the North's common schools upheld republican institutions during the war, and his influence was felt when a new high school was dedicated in September 1876 at a cost of more than $215,000.[39] Under Harrington, the School Committee also reached out more effectively to families who lived or worked in the textile mills, an antebellum practice that became more pronounced during a postwar shift to manufacturing.[40]

Overseers of the Poor

Another municipal responsibility impacted directly by the Civil War was New Bedford's generous program of welfare administered by the Overseers of

New Bedford wharf scene, circa 1868. (Joseph G. Tirrell Collection. Courtesy of the Trustees of the New Bedford Free Public Library.)

the Poor. In the city and throughout the Commonwealth, Judith Giesberg explains, men's military enlistment could have "catastrophic effects on marginal families" because they lost breadwinners at a difficult time. Poor women who sought public relief often faced a bewildering set of rules and relief agencies and, Giesberg suggests, "the war became part of their everyday lives."[41] During the Civil War, New Bedford officials maintained their policy of aiding the poor as best they could. "It is truly said that it costs a great deal to support the poor," the Overseers reported, "but we see no way of reducing it but by pursuing a niggardly course, such as providing supplies of a poorer quality, and perhaps less in quantity." The Overseers preferred to continue their traditional and enlightened pattern of providing the worthy poor with ample assistance.[42]

Still, the Overseers struggled to aid the working and worthy poor between 1861 and 1865 as the city's economy slumped and unemployment jumped. Total expenditures in outdoor relief climbed from nearly $9,500 in 1860 to over $15,000 during the first year of the war. Thereafter, outdoor relief cost the city's taxpayers an average of more than $12,500 per year for the remainder of the Civil War. Per capita relief costs increased disproportionately because of wartime inflation, a problem that affected all city residents but harmed especially those with limited incomes. The Overseers complained that the costs of provisions, clothing, and fuel used by the almshouse increased in price over 30 percent in one year, adding $1,000 to an already strained budget. Between 1863 and 1864, the per capita costs of outdoor relief grew 67 percent. In New Bedford's almshouse, the average weekly costs paid by the city for each individual increased from $2.12 to $3.67 between 1864 and 1866.[43]

Patterns of poor relief reflected economic changes caused by war. For example, the Overseers reported that during 1861 the city provided aid to 1,937 persons from outside of Massachusetts, thus inflicting a "heavy tax" of nearly $5,500 on city residents, prompting some to question the city's policies and the Overseers' largesse.[44] Mayor Taber outlined the broader economic challenges that faced the city in January 1862 when he lamented that New Bedford's residents had "ceased in a great degree to be a producing people." During the first nine months of the war, requests made to the Overseers of the Poor had exceeded those of any previous year. Taber attributed this increase to the economic depression in the whaling industry and to the family heads who left the city after enlisting in military service. Taber observed that an "unusually large portion" of city residents were dependent on public charity. "Many are forced by necessity to make application, who would gladly work, could work be procured," he added. Some of the city's relief costs were offset, at least indirectly, by state and federal payments through military enlistment and bounties. The

Overseers of the Poor actually reduced their expenditures on outdoor relief in 1863 as men were drawn off by military opportunities.[45]

Rising relief costs, combined with a troubling economy, compelled many to question New Bedford's tradition of liberal charity payments. Following his reelection in 1864, Mayor George Howland Jr. spoke in January 1865 about poor relief laws and policies. Reminding the city council that the Overseers of the Poor were "not a Board of Charity," Howland explained that their "sole duty" was "to relieve the wants of the poor of our own city and those of other towns in the State." Howland remained sensitive to the plight of "worthy, industrious persons, generally females" who had to depend on the charity of friends or the city during times of bad weather, but he reiterated that relief appropriations were to serve only "the necessities of our own people." Clearly, the issue of poor relief had become an important political issue and policy question during the last two years of the Civil War. New Bedford's Overseers began to spend more money on residents of their own city, in line with the pronouncements of Mayor Howland and others. Table 8-3 summarizes the city's outdoor relief between 1861 and 1870.[46]

The Issue of Fresh Water and the City's Future

Challenged to meet New Bedford's needs during the war, city authorities sought solutions for both short- and long-term problems. Beginning in 1862, for example, for five years the city spent nothing on new sewer construction or maintenance. The issue of fresh water remained controversial and generated

Table 8-3. Outdoor Poor Relief in New Bedford, 1861–70

Year	Total Expense ($)	Per Capita Cost ($)	Total Aided	New Bedford Recipients	New Bedford as % of Total
1861	15,046.98	5.74	2,622	375	14.3
1862	14,874.79	4.69	3,169	565	17.8
1863	11,243.61	4.79	2,348	418	17.8
1864	13,011.12	7.11	1,830	354	19.3
1865	12,704.03	6.24	2,036	408	20.0
1866	16,361.73	8.69	1,883	522	27.7
1867	14,016.78	9.40	1,491	545	36.5
1868	13,100.58	8.03	1,632	530	32.5
1869	13,258.54	8.03	1,651	613	37.1
1870	12,214.80	7.16	1,707	663	38.8

Source: Annual Reports of the Overseers of the Poor, 1861–71, NBCD, reel 2.

debates between frugal fiscal conservatives and a more "progressive" element that looked ahead to a city filled with manufacturing enterprises. During the war's first year, Mayor Isaac Taber believed that the city could not afford a better system of water delivery. Taber died in September 1862, and he was succeeded by former mayor George Howland Jr., an opponent of a new municipal water system. Sounding old-fashioned and parsimonious, Howland contended that only a few people would pay for the private consumption of water and the extra costs of a new system were not justified. He doubted that local capitalists would develop new businesses even with fresh water freely available, and he favored delay through further investigations and a public referendum. Studies were followed by a public referendum in April 1864 in which a new water system was approved by a vote of 781 to 591. The following January, Mayor Howland stated that the city would put the act into effect when the city council determined.[47] New Bedford's ambitious and costly public works project would begin after the war's end propelled by a desire to lure large manufacturing enterprises that relied upon steam power.

New Bedford's foray into a water distribution system compared with other cities in the nineteenth century. Throughout the nation's urban areas, a new concept emerged of using public tax dollars for building a "safer, saner, and more sanitary urban environment," as Stanley Schultz has written. Boston opened their Cochituate Aqueduct in 1848 and within a decade it had nearly 90,000 connections. By 1860 Boston's average use of 97 gallons per capita was "without parallel in the civilized world."[48] Springfield, Massachusetts, shared similar experiences with New Bedford because city residents opposed high costs and additional taxes for a new water delivery system. Springfield's mayor in 1863 hired an outside consultant who recommended a $250,000 system of aqueducts, pipes, and pumping stations, an effort that drew support after the city endured a large fire in July 1864. The next year, Springfield authorities contracted with a small, nearly defunct private corporation to supply the city with water for the next ten years. A key difference between Springfield and New Bedford, however, was that Springfield had enjoyed wartime prosperity while the Whaling City's fortunes declined.[49]

For a wealthy city of its size (approximately twenty-two thousand residents) in 1860, New Bedford's water delivery system was deficient and outdated. City leaders showed their frugality by relying upon private wells and a few private water supply companies through mid-century, and these companies used crude and clumsy pumping plants and root-clogged wooden pipes. A local historian faulted these private enterprises for being more focused "upon the health of the investors' pocketbooks than . . . the physical well-being of their patrons." By the 1840s the city drew from public wells fed by underground springs along with a large reservoir in City Hall Square. These water sources were shown tragically inadequate during the great fire of April 1859. And, like other northern urban areas in the nineteenth century, New Bedford's population growth, geographical expansion, and business development overtook the city's natural springs and water sources. In the late 1850s, calls for more fresh water came from a younger group of capitalists who promoted growth through manufacturing and steam engines. They faced opposition from wealthy taxpayers, principally whaling families, who saw little need for an expensive municipal water system, new manufacturing, or higher taxes.[50]

Frederick S. Allen led the charge for fresh water beginning in March 1860. He called for a committee "to consider the practicability and expediency of introducing a permanent supply of fresh water into the city." A year later, another committee issued its alarm that New Bedford faced a water "crisis."[51] The 1861 report became a rallying point for proponents of fresh water who despaired the "stagnation and decay" of the whaling industry. The report portrayed New Bedford as a city with vacant houses, empty shops and stores, and citizens searching elsewhere for jobs. The solution was machinery, manufacturing, and the mechanical arts. "We have a beautiful city, handsomely located, a splendid harbor, good water communication, and ample railroad facilities," they noted. "Why not make it a Lowell or a Lawrence?" Water literally could bring economic life to New Bedford; without water, the city would "cease to prosper." The Wamsutta Mills alone needed one thousand barrels daily for their steam engines. Moreover, the wartime construction of water works could be done efficiently, if not cheaply, because of low labor costs and high unemployment. A fresh water system would bring to New Bedford improved sanitation, healthy distribution of a "wholesome beverage," efficient delivery of water to waiting ships, substantial enhancements in fire protection, and reduced fire insurance premiums. Proponents played as their trump card the argument that a water supply and steam power would promote manufacturing and "mechanical uses in all parts of the City."[52]

Progress was slowed not only by war but also by the mayoral transition from Taber to Howland, particularly since the latter bitterly opposed the project.[53] Howland's opposition included the influential Reverend William J. Potter, who offered a trenchant series of sermons entitled "A Pulpit View of the Business Interests of our City," delivered in two parts at the Unitarian Church on January 18 and 25, 1863. Mincing no words, Potter stated that New Bedford's monopoly on whaling was proof of failure, not success. Wartime was the right time to move in a new direction, Potter noted, as "everything is on trial—every institution, every department of government, and every branch of business." Fearful of a postwar recession, Potter wanted New Bedford to be prepared for peace when "we in this community ought to have our factories built, the machinery erected, the boilers fixed for the fires, the hammers set, the spindles in place—all ready to catch the first force of this returning tide and start into action." Continuing with an oceanic metaphor, Potter added, "Miss this wave, and I fear we are lost forever!" Speaking to New Bedford's "men of enterprise, men of capital, men of business judgment," Potter told them to save the city from ruin: "Do something; do it soon."[54]

Potter's sermons and agitation by others awakened many to the necessity of building a public water system. The Massachusetts General Court approved an act on April 18, 1863, for supplying New Bedford with fresh water, subject to a public referendum within one year. The act gave power to appointed commissioners to construct the works; to take lands, water, and water rights; to authorize the issue of bonds up to $500,000; to organize a department with management powers; to secure bylaws and ordinances as needed; and to establish water rates. The act itself plus reports from the various experts and committees were distributed to voters who approved the system in a referendum in April 1864. Actual construction was delayed by the war and some conservative opposition to the system's hefty price tag.[55] When a new committee convened in July 1865 and issued its report, opponents called the plans "positively reckless," pointing to estimated costs of nearly $480,000.[56] Skeptics favored a minority report that favored a less expensive natural system of water delivery without additional contraptions of pumping engines, pipes, and other mechanisms. The city council actually adopted the minority report on November 30, 1865, and two weeks later they authorized an appropriation of $100,000 to begin work.[57]

After years of debate and the fluctuations of war, "the great undertaking" as local historian Leonard Ellis described it, was not finished until late 1869. In the intervening years, water commissioners recommended a more extensive and expensive plan that required an engine and engine house, along with main and distribution lines. Sylvia Ann Howland's private bequests helped to offset construction costs by $200,000 in the late 1860s. When New Bedford's new water system became operational on November 25, 1869, William J. Rotch became the first subscriber for his home on Orchard Street. By December 1870 the city had issued $500,000 in bonds for the water works, by which time the city built seventeen miles of main distribution pipes. Two decades later, after the water works had cost the city more than $1.3 million, New Bedford owned sixty miles of water pipes serving a population of more than forty-one thousand people. By then, most locals agreed that the city's manufacturing growth was attributable to the introduction of a municipal water system. "The subsequent history of the city," Leonard Ellis wrote, "shows that its prosperity is largely due to its

View of County Street, New Bedford, circa 1867–77. (Stephen Adams, photographer. Courtesy of the Trustees of the New Bedford Free Public Library.)

abundant and cheap water supply."[58] City residents' experience with massive wartime spending, increased municipal debt, and a lagging whaling economy prodded them to embrace postwar public spending in ways not possible before the war.

War's End, Reimbursements, and Recovery

During and after the war, New Bedford and state authorities wrangled over reimbursable wartime expenses while they cheered the end of war and city tax collections that netted the largest return ever in 1866. Mayor John H. Perry was satisfied by the state's reimbursement of more than $15,000 for Home and Coast Guard expenses, and he hoped that another $20,000 was forthcoming for aid previously distributed to families of soldiers. Treasurer James B. Congdon estimated that the state's repayment practices had cost the city some $10,000 in labor costs and loss of interest, but the mayor claimed these were "cheerfully borne" because they demonstrated "increased devotedness to our soldiers and seamen." The mayor was not satisfied with the federal government, however, as Perry pressed national leaders to confront Great Britain over its support of Confederate raiders and to seek reimbursement for the losses of whaling merchants and ship owners. He estimated damages in the millions of dollars because New Bedford's whaling vessels had been "blotted out of existence by the torch of British pirates."[59]

Even two years after the Civil War, city leaders continued to administer disbursements to veterans and dependents that continued to cost money, time, and effort. Payments and reimbursements approached $20,000 in 1865, and a new state law passed in April 1866 compelled the city treasurer to disburse almost $10,000 to over two hundred beneficiaries without state reimbursement for a full year. Treasurer Congdon was peeved yet proud of this additional work, calling special attention to black families, one veteran and two widows, connected with Company C of the Fifty-Fourth Massachusetts Regiment and who benefited from these payments. He singled out Lewis Fleetwood, Joseph R. Campbell, and Abraham P. Torrence as members of the "gallant band which, led on by the noble Shaw, attacked the ramparts of Wagner. Two of them shared his grave."[60] Mayor Perry and his successors upheld the city's contributions to disabled veterans and their dependents, an important public declaration of gratitude, and the city's work in disbursing these funds was a source of civic pride.[61] "No town or city of the Commonwealth can," claimed Mayor Andrew G. Pierce, "in the matter of State aid advances, exhibit a more desirable record than New Bedford." For seven years running, monthly payments to local beneficiaries had totaled $155,000, a sum that reflected New Bedford's "contributions to the preservation and sustaining of our national government."[62]

Other fiscal impacts of the war were seen in the city's substantial funding for the Soldiers' and Sailors' Monument. Back in November 1865, city leaders made a special appropriation of $10,000, and additional funds of $1,800 were allocated in 1866. Altogether, New Bedford spent over $13,000 for the public monument, a high price compared with previous disbursements. As leaders looked back to the war, they also looked forward and drew lessons from wartime changes that included new accounting methods.[63] Perhaps as another outgrowth of wartime experiences, New Bedford authorities took new steps to improve citizens' health and living conditions. Prompted no doubt by cholera outbreaks the previous year, a Board of Health was established in 1867 and the city appointed its first health officer. The officer was granted broad powers to "receive and register complaints, to inspect dwellings, inclosures, work-shops and manufactories, to regulate the public health." Mayor Perry declared that the expense of these new efforts, about $2,000 per year, was "trifling" compared with the benefits. The turn toward public health can be viewed as another unanticipated consequence outcome of the Civil War as officials sought more effective municipal practices.[64]

Summary

In a city whose maritime economy suffered in the war years, leaders and citizens did their best to manage local governance in an effective, efficient manner. They embraced new accounting practices and coordinated with agents of the state and national governments to meet unprecedented military expenses. They proactively collected taxes, maintained detailed records, and managed to avoid huge deficits during the war by cutting costs in key areas. City leaders viewed their scrupulous oversight of budgetary matters as an additional wartime cost but also a contribution to the Union victory. Just months before the war's end, Mayor George Howland Jr. applauded all citizens who had rallied to "the support of their country and their country's cause." Howland's predecessor, Isaac Taber, who died while serving as mayor in September 1862, had urged city residents to work together. Taber hoped that once peace came, "we, or our children may look back with loyal satisfaction on the part we took in the struggle to preserve democratic institutions." New Bedford succeeded in fulfilling both mayors' hopes and the city's record of municipal governance stood as a testament to sound leadership.[65] The next chapter examines the broader context of economic development in postwar New Bedford. By the end of the nineteenth century, New Bedford would become more like Lowell than Nantucket, and textile and other manufacturing became the city's economic foundation. Industrialization rapidly transformed New Bedford and posed new challenges for city leaders and residents.

9

"The Great Hope for the Future": New Bedford in the Postbellum Era

Civic leaders looked both to the traditions of the past and an uncertain future during a transitional postwar period. Mayor Andrew G. Pierce, a Wamsutta Company official not raised amid whaling wealth, assumed office in early 1868. Sounding like many northern politicians, Pierce recalled the "untiring, self-sacrificing patriotism of the men, women, and children of our city" during the Civil War. Although he feared a coming recession because of the "unsatisfactory condition of business," he saw hopeful signs that included the city's funding of gas pipelines and the extensive and expensive water works that had cost about $500,000.[1] When Mayor George B. Richmond took office two years later he fondly recalled a not-too-distant "pleasant dream" when "the sea was regarded as our treasure-house." Like his contemporaries, however, Richmond looked ahead to manufacturing prosperity and compared New Bedford's climate and infrastructure with those of Fall River, Taunton, and Worcester. Richmond urged citizens to imagine a city where they could hear "the music of the spindle and shuttle, the cheering sound of the hammer and anvil, and the noise of countless artisans." "The great hope for the future," Mayor Richmond declared, "must rest upon the multiplication and growth of manufacturing enterprise."[2]

Even with ample evidence of modernizing manufacturing and urban progress, some residents clung to the past. For a decade or so after the war, a local observer suggested, New Bedford experienced a "transition state" in which a conservative group who favored the "older order of things" were opposed by "younger blood." Briefly, the old order held the upper hand, especially when in 1866 some forty whaling vessels brought home nearly $4 million in cargo thanks to very high prices. But, manufacturing and industrialism began to flourish and whaling losses and the economic downturn of the early 1870s compelled locals to place their capital where they could watch their investments. Local investors gradually paved the way for Wamsutta's expansion and that of other textile factories, along with banking institutions that grew substantially after the Civil War.[3]

Signs of continuing conservatism were displayed in leaders' attempts to police the city's moral order. For example, a December 1869 referendum led to strengthened prohibition laws and a divided city government. Mayor Richmond and the Aldermen were elected on a prohibition platform while the majority of the Common Council stood opposed. Following reelection the following year by a larger margin, Richmond proclaimed that drunkenness in the city had become very rare. The city marshall echoed these claims by reporting that every evening, "the streets are generally deserted by loungers and common night-walkers." Enforcement of prohibition laws in his view had "added to the average morality, decency, and happiness of the inhabitants," offering reassurance to those who sought stability and order in the community.[4]

City leaders also instituted new policies and agencies to maintain stability and public order. Education took on added significance in the emerging industrial environment. The Reverend Isaac H. Coe became the city's first truant officer in 1870, promising to function more as a "friend and adviser" than in a "police capacity." In his first year, Coe made two hundred personal visits to families and attended at least one school each day. He blamed increased truancy on industrialization and the growing numbers of working poor. Coe suggested that New Bedford follow Fall River's lead in establishing a Factory School for children of destitute and intemperate parents, a benevolent reform than might create a class of "practical workers."[5] An Evening School for adult learners continued to operate in the city's north end, followed by a second Evening School that opened in the city's south end in 1872. Nearly one hundred students enrolled in an evening drawing school for adults after its opening in February 1871. These programs demonstrated a more progressive school system, school Superintendent Harrington reported, that was evolving from "debris of the past" to a "structure yet to be reared."[6]

As an indication of larger economic changes underfoot in New Bedford, postwar mayors hailed from an emerging entrepreneurial class in place of the old guard of wealthy whaling merchants. When John H. Perry assumed office in 1865 as a coowner of the New England Gutta Percha Roofing Company, he had a diverse business career that had evolved away from whaling. After giving up an antebellum ship chandlery business, Perry turned to shoe and leather manufacturing and in 1847 he became a purveyor of coal, groceries, and provisions. George Wilson soon joined him in the John H. Perry & Company in a paint mill, coal, and trucking business. Perry also owned and refurbished the Parker House, bought coasting vessels, and built schooners. A longtime Whig, he was the only remnant of the Whig party elected to the Common Council in 1859 and again in 1861. In 1862 Perry served as president of the Common Council and was chosen an alderman for Ward Six in 1863, 1864, and 1866. Perry cast deciding votes on fresh water measure despite severe criticism, yet he must have been respected by many as he was elected mayor without opposition in 1865 and again in 1866.[7]

Subsequent city leaders illustrated a new political pattern of success for men from modest beginnings known for their morality and manufacturing backgrounds. Andrew G. Pierce, elected mayor in 1867, began his career as a clerk in the Wamsutta Mill in 1854 with "little of any means" after being educated in the city's public schools. He became the company's treasurer by 1855 and served for forty years. He joined with entrepreneur Edward L. Baker to inaugurate the New Bedford, Vineyard and Nantucket Steamboat Company, and Pierce also founded the New Bedford and Fairhaven Street Railway and was its first president. After the Civil War, Pierce's business leadership expanded into other textile companies. Originally a Democrat, Pierce aligned early on with the Republican Party and was considered respectable, intelligent, and honest. His stint as mayor represented the city's embrace of manufacturing at the war's end.[8] Pierce's successor, George B. Richmond, a five-time mayor after 1869, worked as a customhouse inspector from 1861 to 1874. Raised in a Quaker family and a Baptist in his later years, Richmond was a staunch temperance advocate who converted to the Republican Party before the Civil War and chaired the city's Republican Committee. Not known for wealth, Richmond's philanthropic endeavors encompassed the First Baptist Society, New Bedford Port Society, and the Young Men's Christian Association, serving as its president.[9] In the place of a ruling Quaker elite, these men represented a combination of moral leadership and manufacturing support.

Mayoral elections showed increased competition and political agitation moving into the 1870s. For example, George H. Dunbar, elected in late 1872 on an antiprohibition platform, promised to modernize the city's governance and improve its welfare system. He called for revising the city charter and ordinances, along with overhauling policies at the almshouse. Dunbar was perplexed by persistent poverty in New Bedford, asking how "in a city possessed of so much wealth, where labor is the rule and idleness the exception, [that] so much pauperism should exist[?]" He urged Overseers of the Poor to be cautious in granting outdoor relief because its only object was to "relieve suffering." Dunbar contended that new manufacturing business enterprises and economic development would come through "liberal" municipal governance that also adhered to a Jeffersonian view that the best government governs least. Local leaders continued to draw on private munificence that allowed "liberal" policies to persist. In 1876, for example, the New Bedford Orphan's Home gained a permanent fund of $60,000 from the estate of Sylvia Ann Howland.[10]

Historian Thomas McMullin has explored with insight the impacts of New Bedford's postbellum industrial development. Through the 1880s, the city's Overseers of the Poor continued the city's tradition of enlightened governance and benevolent paternalism through liberal disbursements of public aid. Although New Bedford was more generous to its poor than were other Massachusetts' communities before the mid-1880s, industrialization eventually led to "a more conservative and parsimonious welfare policy" in a city that ranked first or second in per capita relief expenditures of the largest cities in Massachusetts before 1880. By the 1890s the city ranked ninth of twelve cities. New relief officials and organizations prompted policy changes; for example, the recently established Charity Organization cut in half the number of people receiving outdoor relief in 1879. In the mid-1880s, the formerly elective body of ward-based Overseers gave way to the "conservative politics of centralization" and the establishment of a three-person board appointed by the mayor. Stingier public welfare policies and expenditures were tied to a massive influx of foreign-born immigrants. By 1900 New Bedford ranked ninth of the nation's 160 largest cities in percentage of foreign-born residents, and per capita reductions in public relief were paralleled by minimal support for the city's schools. By the late nineteenth century, McMullin summarizes, New Bedford's "sense of community that had supported more generous relief program and public education no longer existed."[11]

Whaling's Continuing Decline

A brief surge of optimism in the late 1860s led whaling merchants to dispatch formerly idle and newly outfitted whaling ships, but such hopes proved temporary. Maritime insurance rates climbed higher in the decade after the Civil War and the increased use of petroleum oil made whaling a precarious investment in the 1870s. Adding to whaling woes, New Bedford was devastated by disasters in the Arctic Ocean in 1871 and again in 1876. The dramatic 1871 events attracted national attention when over 1,200 sailors abandoned thirty-four ice-encrusted ships and were rescued by a flotilla of other vessels. No lives were lost in the saga, but property losses in New Bedford amounted to twenty ships and cargoes of $1 million dollars. Five years later, the Arctic fleet suffered when twenty ships were destroyed in ice and fifty men died. New Bedford losses included eleven vessels valued at $442,000, along with cargo estimated at $375,000. Some whaling firms would not give up, illustrated by the launch in September 1880 of the first steam-powered whaler, the *Mary & Helen*, that captured twenty-seven whales with a value of $100,000. New Bedford's whaling fleets continued to shrink rapidly through the end of the century (see Table 9-1), however, giving way to San Francisco as the nation's primary whaling port. "It must be conceded that the prosecution of the whale fishery has ceased to be of great importance to the community," commented New Bedford writer Leonard Bolles Ellis in 1892, "and there is no prospect for its future growth and development."[12]

Many factors caused the decline of whaling: a deteriorating labor market, low prices for whaling products, and the superior properties and lower costs of petroleum. The whaling labor force, a "sweated industry" in Elmo Paul Hohman's words, had become more foreign-born throughout the nineteenth century. As whaling masters cut labor costs by moving toward foreign-born (and presumably cheaper) workers, they also contributed to higher turnover, lower morale, and reduced efficiency. "After 1865," Hohman contended, "the dilution of the labor force by an ever-mounting percentage of ignorance, incompetence, and general inefficiency proceeded at a still swifter pace." By 1880, of the nearly four thousand hands associated with the New Bedford whaling fleet, about one-third consisted, in Hohman's words, of the "dregs of American-born men," one-third were Portuguese, and the final one-third comprised of a variety of "negroes, Kanaka, and scattered individuals from most of the ports of Europe and Asia." As whaling declined as an American-dominated enterprise, so did the percentage of native-born whalemen.[13]

The whaling industry's regression began before the Civil War even if some observers were blind to it. The discovery and refinement of petroleum, which supplanted whale and sperm oils as fuels and illuminants, provided a major blow. The Civil War diverted capitalists away from whaling, raised insurance premiums, and subjected the vulnerable New Bedford fleet to attacks by Confederate raiders such as the *Alabama* and *Shenandoah*. Economic historians have conjectured that whaling might have recovered in the late 1860s had not petroleum proven so plentiful. By the late 1800s American whaling faced growing competition from other entrants, principally Norwegian whalers who effectively used new technologies. New Bedford's capitalists made rational decisions to invest in cotton mills instead of whaling vessels because the longer, costlier voyages did not return adequate profits.[14] In line with regional and national trends, local New Bedford capitalists turned to industrialization through new investments in manufacturing, mining, and railroads, along with land and real estate speculation as the country expanded westward.[15]

Even as whaling's contraction played out on national and world stages, New Bedford retained its primacy in the manufacturing of whale oils. George Delano's Sons operated the world's largest grease oil refinery in the 1880s, when Stephen and James took over from their father in 1884. New Bedford was home also to the country's largest manufacturer of fish oil, first known as Hastings &

Table 9-1. United States and New Bedford Whaling Fleets, 1816–1905

	Tonnage			Number of Vessels		
Year	United States	New Bedford	New Bedford / United States (Ratio)	United States	New Bedford	New Bedford/ United States (Ratio)
1816–20	18,395	7,568	0.411		31	
1821–25	37,161	14,701	0.396		56	
1826–30	47,953	23,105	0.482		80	
1831–35	92,750	44,912	0.484		142	
1836–40	133,897	54,685	0.408		173	
1841–45	185,678	72,881	0.393	672	228	0.339
1846–50	208,347	82,035	0.394	656	252	0.384
1851–55	195,938	105,482	0.538	628	314	0.5
1856–60	195,692	108,551	0.555	628	320	0.51
1861–65	111,167	73,026	0.657	374	220	0.588
1866–70	73,224	58,331	0.797	312	180	0.577
1871–75	58,514	39,888	0.682	209	124	0.593
1876–80	46,517	39,217	0.843	178	129	0.725
1881–85	40,838	29,815	0.73	152	96	0.632
1886–90	31,364	18,492	0.59	113	59	0.522
1891–95	24,143	10,700	0.443	92	38	0.413
1896–1900	15,588	6,809	0.437	62	26	0.419
1901–5	10,462	6,810	0.651	40	23	0.575

Source: Lance E. Davis, Robert E. Gallman, and Karin Gleiter, *In Pursuit of Leviathan, Technology, Institutions, and Profits in American Whaling, 1816–1906* (Chicago and London: University of Chicago Press, 1997), 6.

Coopering on the wharf, circa 1868. (Joseph G. Tirrell Collection. Courtesy of the Trustees of the New Bedford Free Public Library.)

Company at the foot of Grinnell Street and later taken over by the firm of Swan & Finch of New York City in the mid-1880s. Another large refiner of sperm and whale oil, William A. Robinson & Company, had moved during the Civil War to a two-story factory at 50 South Water Street and employed up to twenty workers. George S. Homer and Sylvanus Thomas & Company merged in 1857 and survived an apparent bankruptcy in 1867. By the 1870s the company expanded its plant on one and one-half acres at Front, South, and Prospect Streets. Working with pits, vats, cisterns, kettles, strainers, and presses, nearly twenty workers annually produced several thousand barrels of oils. A few oil manufacturers transitioned to new lubricants, among them William F. Nye, who, by 1888, became the world's largest producer of oils for sewing machines, watches, and clocks. From his company's large operations on Fish Island, Nye distributed lubricants to major clock and watch companies in England and Switzerland, and his son, Joseph, patented several inventions that improved the refining and production processes.[16]

As a final coda to the city's whaling losses during the Civil War, the "Alabama Claims" persisted into the 1870s. Massachusetts Senator Charles Sumner, also Chair of the Senate Committee on Foreign Relations, had famously criticized Great Britain in April 1869 for aiding the Confederate States of America. Sumner argued that by providing the Confederates with munitions and vessels, Great Britain bore financial responsibility for prolonging the war. He estimated that the direct national loss to ships and cargoes was about $110 million, but the entire war had cost about $4 billion, of which Great Britain was responsible for half. The Treaty of Washington, signed in May 1871, outlined a process for adjudicating claims and the establishment of a special international tribunal, the first of its kind in the world. President Grant named Charles Francis Adams the chief American negotiator for meetings in Geneva that started in mid-December 1871. After lengthy delays and politicking, the tribunal narrowed American claims against three ships, the *Alabama*, the *Florida*, and the *Shenandoah*, with a final award of $15.5 million in gold to be paid within a year. Initial claims by Americans included nearly $6.5 million each against the *Alabama* and *Shenandoah*, and $3.6 million against the *Florida*. After the funds were transferred to the US treasury, the US government created a special court that eventually distributed about $6 million in direct damages, including tens of thousands of dollars to New Bedford whaling merchants.[17]

Wamsutta and Textile Manufacturing

Manufacturing grew rapidly as whaling languished. Despite slowdowns during the war, the Wamsutta Mills managed to keep afloat by importing

French-Canadian workers in 1864 and delaying the startup of Mill Number 3 until 1865. Because of pent-up demand, by the start of 1866 all machinery was operating with a total of 45,000 spindles and 1,100 looms, and company directors moved forward with plans for a fourth factory and increased Wamsutta's capitalization to $2 million in 1868. By 1875, when Mill Number 5 was constructed, the corporation had grown to a value of $2.5 million. In the early 1880s, Wamsutta consumed twenty thousand bales of cotton each year to produce twenty million yards of cloth, and its annual output of twelve thousand miles of shirting and sheeting would stretch halfway around the world. The Wamsutta Mills changed the face of New Bedford and its investors grew rich, even during the Civil War. Joseph Grinnell had calculated that between 1850 and 1863, total dividends were paid of nearly 150 per cent, and accounting data between 1850 and 1874 showed that twice-yearly dividends had averaged 6 percent each.[18]

In the aftermath of the Arctic whaling disaster of 1871, textile manufacturing looked even more attractive. Besides offering a humid climate that optimized textile processing, New Bedford had an excellent harbor for the delivery of coal that could power steam engines now fed by the city's extensive fresh water delivery system. Textile companies owned their own wharves to reduce transportation and wharfage fees. New Bedford's textile sector expanded beyond Wamsutta in the 1870s when a new company, the Potomska Mills, opened in 1872. Financed by local capitalists with a stake in the Wamsutta Mills, the Potomska company produced a coarser cloth that did not compete directly with Wamsutta's finer products. The first Potomska mill compared with the size of Wamsutta's largest factory, and Potomska Mill Number 2 opened six years later. This massive steam-powered complex included 108,000 spindles and 2,734 looms that provided work for 1,200 operatives. Like Wamsutta in the late 1840s, Potomska built company-owned housing rented to workers.[19]

Elements of a paternalistic old order and signs of a new one were displayed in the 1870s when longtime Wamsutta champion Thomas Bennett Jr. retired. The company cofounder and long-time superintendent received from company operatives a formal address and signed document that thanked him for "guidance and instruction" that helped workers to "become more skilled in our duties." Born in England, Ireland, and Francophone Canada, these workers demonstrated the distinct trend toward increased immigration and larger pool of more diverse factory workers.[20] A decade later, when textile industrialization took deeper root, Wamsutta had grown to over 2,500 workers, and the company claimed a weekly payroll of $15,000. By the time Mill Number 6 was constructed in 1882, Wamsutta's 2,600 employees worked over 200,000 spindles and 4,500 looms. The company's Corliss steam engines were larger than those displayed in 1876 at the nation's Centennial Exposition in Philadelphia. That industrial capitalism and mass-production had come of age in New Bedford was reflected in a contemporary anecdote. An English artist living in New Bedford claimed that British cotton textiles were superior to those made in the United States. To prove his point, he ordered a bolt of cloth from London and had it shipped to New Bedford. When the package was opened, the label read: "Made by Wamsutta Mills, New Bedford, Mass., U.S.A."[21]

Wamsutta's success after the war demonstrated the persistence of successful wealthy capitalists. Although Bennett retired in 1874, Joseph Grinnell continued as president until 1885 when he died at the age of ninety-six. Three directors came on board in 1868 who also enjoyed lengthy terms of service: George O. Crocker (served until 1887), William J. Rotch (served to 1893), and William W. Crapo (served until 1926, including a stint as president from 1889 to 1918). Crapo's recollections captured the economic transitions that he and others created. Born in 1830, Crapo recalled that in his early adult years he worked in a building near the harbor. "I could look down Center Street and see the ships discharging their cargoes or taking on board their outfits," he wrote. He listened to coopers tightening their casks of oil and watched caulkers driving oakum into ship's seams. After the Civil War, when Crapo emerged as one of the textile industry's leaders, his city harbored few coopers and caulkers. He wrote of walking through a "teeming" and "cosmopolitan city" where voices could be heard in French, Polish, Italian, Portuguese and Greek. The city's economy and social composition changed during Crapo's lifetime, much of it attributed to textile manufacturing directed by people like him.[22]

Manufacturing Growth and Growing Pains

In the first quarter-century after the Civil War, from 1865 to 1890, few cities in the country matched New Bedford's industrial growth and urbanization. In New Bedford between 1875 and 1885, the number of textile operatives jumped from 1,983 to 4,563, and by the latter year workers toiled for six separate textile corporations in New Bedford. Textile industrialization increased rapidly in the 1880s. The Grinnell Manufacturing Company, named after the founder of the Wamsutta Mills, was formed in 1882, as was the Acushnet Mills. In 1883 William D. Howland and other prominent citizens opened the first yarn mill in the city, which they duplicated in 1888, naming it the Howland Mills Corporation. In that same year, Horatio Hathaway and others created the Hathaway Manufacturing Corporation with twelve primary investors who had made or inherited money from whaling, among them Bourne, Hathaway, Howland, Mandell,

Wamsutta Mills and mill operatives, circa 1870–80. (Rotogravure Collection. Courtesy of the Trustees of the New Bedford Free Public Library.)

Rotch, Crapo, and Knowles. By 1890 New Bedford's national prominence as a manufacturing center was shown by ranking third among American cities in its number of spindles and fourth in looms. Altogether, more than 7,600 people worked in twenty mills.[23]

A local booster described the period between 1865 and 1890 as one in which a "great and stable manufacturing city" grew out of the "ruins of a structure built upon an uncertain foundation." By 1890 six factories outside of textiles employed more than one hundred workers, among them Hathaway, Soule, and Harrington's shoe factory (650); Pairpont Manufacturing Company (400); Mount Washington Glass Company (265); and the New Bedford Cordage Company (325). These companies, like the cotton textile firms, were locally owned and operated.[24] Other evidence of modern urban development arrived in 1881 when city residents first welcomed the telephone. Five years later, the Edison Illuminating Company built New Bedford's first electric plant. A new Board of Trade was established in 1884, and two years later a younger generation of business leaders took control and developed an active organization that claimed over 250 members in 1889. Sponsoring the city's first-ever "industrial fair" in the fall of 1887, board members were delighted by the "extent and variety" of manufacturing enterprises that abounded in New Bedford.[25]

During the last two decades of the nineteenth century, New Bedford emerged as one of the nation's top three textile centers. In the 1880s seven new textile manufacturing corporations were established, and in the following decade another seven mill companies commenced. Land in the city's north and south ends became sites of large factories. Cotton textile manufacturing pushed the city's population from about sixteen thousand when Wamsutta was founded in 1848 to about sixty thousand fifty years later. Celebrating New Bedford's semicentennial anniversary in 1897, US Speaker of the House Thomas B. Reed sent his best wishes to a "typical New England city" that had "shown itself capable of keeping up with a changing world." Within the next ten years, New Bedford ranked first in the county in the manufacture of fine cottons. A newspaper reported that the history of the textile industry "has been one continuous, unprecedented advance" until New Bedford housed twenty-five corporations operating fifty mills with more than two million total spindles. Some company's shares sold for more than three times their par value. As New Bedford's population climbed to over one hundred thousand by 1907, the city was described as a place where "mills have grown up like magic, many of them on made land, where ships were once moored." Instead of a forest of ship masts, New Bedford's urban landscape was dominated by factory chimneys that spewed smoke along the harbor and the Acushnet River (see Table 9-2).[26]

As much as the city's landscape changed to one of factories, smokestacks, and three-decker tenement housing, the business community remained a relatively small group of intermarried individuals and families, many from old whaling wealth. Of eighty-eight men who served as directors and officers of the

Table 9-2. New Bedford Cotton Textile Industry, Growth of Employment, 1855–1915

Year	Wage Earners/ Cotton Good Industry	Wage Earners/ All Mfg. and Mechanical
1855	500	
1865	520	
1875	1,983	
1885	4,563	8,745
1895	10,258	14,382
1905	14,545	17,855
1915	29,622	34,352

Source: Thomas A. McMullin, "Industrialization and Social Change in a Nineteenth-Century Port City: New Bedford, Massachusetts, 1865–1900," (PhD dissertation, University of Wisconsin-Madison, 1976), 23. McMullin's sources include Statistical Information, 1855, 1865; Census of Mass, 1875, 1885, 1895, 1905; Bureau of Statistics, Annual Report, 1915.

cotton textile mills between 1865 and 1896, seventy-eight (or 88.6 percent) lived in the city, and collectively, they held 389 director, trustee, and officer positions in the city's corporations and banks. The average mill director played a decision-making role in five other local corporations and banks. Nearly 60 percent of the resident textile directors were themselves involved or were sons of men involved in maritime or whaling endeavors. Established elites and leading local capitalists directed the transition from maritime to industrial capitalism and the shift from merchant partnerships to new corporations. One historian contends that "the city's tight, entrenched economic leadership instigated industrialization and was its main beneficiary." He suggests that their basic benevolence persisted into the postwar era, and the "socially responsive" Quaker and Unitarian leaders remained significant in New Bedford's private and public philanthropy through the 1880s.[27]

Local leaders who pushed industrialization could not foresee all consequences, however. The breakdown of an older and benevolent paternalism was seen in numerous and divisive strikes that characterized the city's postbellum industrial development. By one estimate, at least thirty-two strikes hit the city's mills between 1883 and 1893, many prompted by a growing reliance on fines to punish workers. The emergence of textile factories in New Bedford intensified social distance between classes, ethnic and racial groups, and natives and newcomers. New factory employees, mostly foreign-born and Catholic, had little in common with the native-born elite who were primarily Protestant. Industrialization after the Civil War brought more coercive labor practices, including lockouts, firings, and fines. Workers who did not acquiesce to the new order were dismissed. The city's first major strike occurred in 1867 at the Wamsutta Mills over the ten-hour workday. Active prostrike leadership included the city's leading black attorney, William Henry Johnson, an ex-slave, and Rachel Howland, a Quaker activist. For workers, the 1867 strike failed when no members of the strike committee were rehired and new operatives filled the factory by mid-March 1867. Some mill managers and owners were troubled by their workers' lack of "gratitude," especially that attributed to skilled operatives from the Lancashire region of England who proved to be the most active group in this and future strikes.[28]

A decade later New Bedford faced its next major strike during a national labor upheaval when nearly two thousand operatives signed a notice to leave their work at the Wamsutta Company. Ethnic divisions were illustrated by the French Canadian origins of twenty-six of thirty-two workers who refused to pledge. A local strike leader analyzed the aims of factory owners: "It is a favorite game of capitalists to set different nationalities among the help to opposing each other." The *New Bedford Daily Mercury* reported on February 2, 1877, that "the Scotch people do the calculating and the planning, the Irish exhort and animate their friends to rally for the right, and the English, with natural perseverance, say but little, but work in the front ranks and will be the last to relinquish their claims." African-American attorney William Henry Johnson was again an active proponent of the workers' cause, aided by Quaker leader Daniel Ricketson who chaired several strikers' meetings. Ricketson illustrated a lingering pattern of Quaker benevolence through his pro-workers stance. Ricketson sent letters to the *New Bedford Evening Standard* that complained of factory conditions and offered poetry "sympathetic to the operatives." Ricketson stood as one of the last links between traditional Quaker leaders and the city's textile workers.[29]

Mirroring national patterns, labor conflicts and new immigrants shaped the industrial transformation of New Bedford. Mill workers lived near factories on the city's previously unsettled northern and southern extremes. Historian Thomas McMullin notes that "the clustering of mill workers led to increasing ethnic and class segregation in New Bedford" in the postwar period.[30] New Bedford's central business district, home to wharves and counting houses during the heyday of whaling, remained relatively unchanged as the home of professionals, businesses, and a majority of the city's black community. New Bedford's spatial development contrasted with that of other industrializing cities of the time where factories were built in central business districts.[31] The city's native-born residents commented on the new arrivals. The Reverend William Potter of the First Unitarian Church spoke in 1892 about the arrival of foreign-born people, "a population without means except the capacity to labor." Potter described this process as creating "very different problems than those which were presented a generation ago." Like other American cities, New Bedford experienced a wave of anti-Catholic and anti-immigrant nativism in the 1890s, with an acute phase following the economic downturn of 1893.[32]

New Bedford's local boosters and leaders celebrated the city's semicentennial anniversary in 1897. Fifty years had passed since the city's incorporation, and three decades had elapsed since the Civil War ended. By shifting from whaling to manufacturing, one journalist suggested, New Bedford stood as "an epitome of the industrial progress of the times." But with "progress" came challenges. New manufacturing technology increased the reliance on unskilled labor, and ethnic tensions rose as the labor market was split by new arrivals. French-Canadian textile operatives encountered labor competition from new immigrants in the 1890s, particularly Portuguese, Germans, Russian Jews, and Poles.[33] More sobering news followed in 1898 during a bitter strike in the city that pitted the craft-oriented American Federation of Labor against the Socialist

Table 9-3. Percentage of Foreign Born Population, 1865–1910

Year	United States	Mass.	New Bedford
1865		21.0	14.0
1870	14.4	24.2	17.2
1875		25.4	23.0
1880	13.3	24.9	22.1
1885		27.1	30.7
1890	14.8	29.4	35.4
1895		30.6	41.1
1900	13.7	30.2	40.9
1910	14.7	31.5	44.1

Source: Thomas A. McMullin, "Industrialization and Social Change in a Nineteenth-Century Port City: New Bedford, Massachusetts, 1865–1900" (PhD dissertation, University of Wisconsin-Madison, 1976), 31.

Labor Party. Reporting from New Bedford, a *New York Evening Journal* correspondent wrote that "the New England mill operatives can compass a black despair and an amount of slow starvation not to be matched anywhere." In the age of yellow journalism, the *New York World* commissioned articles by a former slave and slave master that found mill workers' lives in New Bedford to be worse than those of slaves in an earlier era. These were jarring words and events for a city known as an antislavery bastion before the Civil War.[34]

Speaking before New Bedford's City Hall 1898 and reaching a national audience, socialist leader Daniel De Leon applauded striking workers for refusing to be "slaves." His rhetoric harkened back to antislavery orators like Frederick Douglass and Wendell Phillips but conveyed an antagonistic message to the white elites and capitalists of the city. Invited by the Socialist workingmen of New Bedford, De Leon spoke to everyone in the "class conscious revolutionary international organization of the working class" who preached the "gospel of labor." Offering didactic lessons in political economy about wages and the class struggle, De Leon praised workingmen over capitalists because "labor alone produced wealth." He defined wealth as the "accumulated past stealings of the capitalist," whom he compared with pickpockets. Corporate directors, De Leon claimed, were the country's "largest sponges" who bribed legislatures and judges. He attacked pure and simple unionism for not improving wages or working conditions and criticized AFL leader Samuel Gompers. In a rousing finish, De Leon encouraged New Bedford workers to "step out boldly upon the streets" in a massive parade while bearing banners that read, "We will fight you in this strike to the bitter end."[35] Such militant prolabor invectives would have been unthinkable fifty years earlier, although similar rhetoric had been directed against Southern slaveholders.

New Bedford could not outrun its past, and into the twentieth century local business leaders continued to dominate a declining textile industry. Moreover, by the 1920s New England textile factories were forced to compete with lower-cost operations in southern states. Michael W. Santos notes that by the 1920s a few families oversaw New Bedford's industrial and financial enterprises termed by one critic as an "interlocking directorate." Through inheritance and inter-marriage, leadership posts in textile mills and banks were passed to the next generation. Of twenty-seven businesses affiliated with the New Bedford Cotton Manufacturers Association, for example, only one was controlled by interests from outside the city. Similar to the whaling enterprise, mill leaders "ensconced themselves in inefficient and antiquated management structures" and exercised nepotistic control. Not unlike the ownership and operations of whaling firms in the mid-1800s, these manufacturing companies featured a closed system that protected a narrow clique of elites. Mills failed to modernize and persisted in producing large volumes of gray goods rather than fine-quality textiles. A shortage of investors, poor management, ethnic antagonism within the mills, and prolabor sentiment in the city led to a bitter six-month strike in 1928 after 10 percent wage cuts were first announced in April 1928. This event underscored the city's long-term economic malaise.[36]

In New Bedford's economic transition over several decades, the local African-American population was largely relegated to service sector employment as domestic help, and it continued to shrink in size as a percentage of the city's residents, paralleling the decline of the old order of Quaker elites. The city's black population never exceeded 1,700 people before 1900, when New Bedford had over 62,000 residents. The black percentage of the city's population peaked at 6.84 percent in 1870 (1,460 black residents out of 21,320), but then declined to under 3 percent of the total. An examination of the 1870 population census for New Bedford shows that of the black community, 37 percent (550) claimed Massachusetts birth, about 22 percent (319) were from Virginia, and about 9 percent (128) reported their births in Maryland.[37] At the same time in Worcester, Massachusetts, black residents there, many of them southern migrants, were excluded from manufacturing jobs and faced low and seasonal incomes through unskilled labor. Like New Bedford's black community, Worcester's African Americans "stagnated economically" into the 1890s. In New Bedford's postwar industrializing economy, native-born blacks were "squeezed out of jobs by immigrants," according to historian Lonnie G. Bunch. Similar patterns were seen in other northern cities such as Detroit and Cleveland.[38]

To counteract their collective economic decline, New Bedford's blacks could point to some individual success and together they maintained vital institutions such as churches and fraternal organizations. The city was home to at least four black attorneys in the 1880s, including the venerable William Henry Johnson who served on the Common Council in 1880 and 1881, and the younger Emmanuel Sullavou who sat on the Common Council in 1878 and was a member of the Board of Registrars in the 1890s. At least one licensed black pharmacist, Robert H. Carter, operated his own drugstore. In general, however, New Bedford's black residents were employed in menial service positions outside of the industrial labor force and mainly lived in the city's west end where they attended mostly segregated schools. Group cohesion was reinforced by several vital black churches, such as the Salem Baptist Church that celebrated its twenty-fifty anniversary in 1883. Residential and organizational racial segregation became the norm in New Bedford by the late 1880s, and a dozen separate "colored" churches and organizations included a Masonic Lodge, the Order of the Eastern Star, Grand United Order of Odd Fellows, and the all-black Robert Gould Shaw Post of the Grand Army of the Republic.[39]

Summary

Following the Civil War, New Bedford's officials and business leaders embraced an optimistic view of manufacturing as the city's economic salvation. Some city boosters pointed accurately to New Bedford's many advantages as a manufacturing center, among them ample capital, plentiful labor, a good public system of education, and a solid infrastructure of wharves, railroads, and communication lines. The introduction of a municipal fresh water system at a cost of a half million dollars seemed to be the final ingredient for New Bedford's anticipated prosperity through manufacturing. The accelerated shift toward textile manufacturing brought with it new problems that included labor strife, an influx of tens of thousands of immigrants, and, eventually, national notoriety for poor working conditions and workers' strikes. The New Bedford of 1900 epitomized to many the worst aspects of a manufacturing urban center. Problems included low and inconsistent wages, deleterious work environments, harmful air and water pollution, unhealthy living conditions, and growing conflict among native- and foreign-born residents. Local capitalists maintained close control of their holdings but failed to innovate, and New Bedford's textile industry largely collapsed by the 1920s. New Bedford hit hard times prior to the Great Depression, and many residents and their descendants struggled economically through the twentieth century.

10

"On the Altar of Our Common Country": Contested Commemorations of the Civil War

Long after the Civil War ended, New Bedford's citizens joined other Northerners in an outpouring of gratitude, self-congratulation, patriotism, and civic pride in celebrating the Union victory. Mayor John H. Perry's comments in 1866 were typical, as he noted with sadness the death of Abraham Lincoln a year earlier who had "providentially guided" the nation through its terrible trial. The mayor urged his audience to not forget the dead who had offered their lives "as a sacrifice for their country," a common theme for decades to come.[1] When New Bedford dedicated its Soldiers' and Sailors' Monument on the Fourth of July in 1866, Perry declared that the memorial had been "consecrated to the memory of our heroic brothers who offered their lives at the altar of our common country . . ." This monument, like others in the North, became a focal point and a sacred place for patriotic displays that commemorated dead soldiers and honored living veterans. Other postbellum events followed a similar course.[2] In the immediate aftermath of the Civil War, northern rituals upheld the myth of egalitarian wartime sacrifices in which all groups—white and black, native- and foreign-born, men and women—played their part in the national drama of the Civil War.[3]

In New Bedford and throughout the North, postbellum patriotic rituals sustained the memory of the war were led often by the Grand Army of the Republic (GAR) and its offshoots. Through Memorial Day celebrations, Fourth of July activities, and the quasi-militaristic rituals of the GAR posts, Union veterans and their families kept alive the meaning of the war through their own brand of patriotism. Both inclusive and exclusive, these celebrations separated veterans from civilians and also differentiated Americans by race, ethnicity, and gender.[4] After the Civil War, for example, New Bedford's African-American community participated in both integrated events and segregated ones that perpetuated a proud, patriotic version of *their* Civil War. Similarly, numerous Irish-born veterans joined William Logan Rodman GAR Post 1, and, beginning in the 1870s, organizations from the St. Lawrence Roman Catholic Church took a proud place in parades and public celebrations. By virtue of their demonstrated wartime loyalty to the United States, African Americans and Irish

Americans claimed a more visible place within New Bedford and the nation. This process was a gendered one, also, as much of the postwar rhetoric of the Civil War focused on masculine ideals of patriotism, bravery, and manhood. Women were typically acknowledged, if at all, as self-sacrificing wives, widows, and daughters of veterans.[5]

Notions of deliverance and rebirth became common themes in postwar celebrations, editorials, sermons, and commentaries. One prominent motif centered on the Civil War as an apocalyptic event that had cleansed and regenerated the nation by destroying slavery. Robert Bellah and others have explored American "civil religion," a belief system with its own prophets, martyrs, and "sacred events and sacred places, its own solemn rituals and symbols." The Civil War brought new themes into play, symbolized by the death and martyrdom of Abraham Lincoln.[6] In their historical quest for equality, African Americans embraced many tenets of American civil religion and created their own versions to press claims for full citizenship and fostered a use of history, memory, and myth that differed from that of white citizens.[7] New Bedford's African Americans added to efforts by their one-time neighbor Frederick Douglass who fought to "forge memory into action that could somehow save the legacy of the Civil War for blacks," as David Blight has written. Douglass created a "usable past" of enduring myths that could stand as "sacred values, ritualized in memory," using the language and themes of civil religion in preaching for black Americans to join the "high worship" of national inclusion. To borrow from historian John Bodnar's useful conception of memory, African Americans expressed a "vernacular" memory that competed for inclusion within the "official" public memory.[8]

Memory-making can be contentious and complex process. Eric Foner links public memory and historical amnesia by suggesting that "selective readings of the past, often institutionalized in rituals like veterans' reunions and publicly constructed monuments, help give citizens a shared sense of national identity." Michael Kammen commented that public memory "shapes a nation's ethos and sense of identity," a process that may explain why "memory is always selective and is so often contested."[9] Just as Northerners and Southerners, and whites and blacks, held differing views about the war's causes, they also debated the war's consequences and meanings. This battle was contested in the construction of public monuments, in diverse works of popular culture, and in blistering political debates. Today, the war's multiple meanings are seen in the names granted this conflict: some Southerners may still refer to the "War of Northern Aggression" or the "War Between the States," while most historians use the more neutral term, "the Civil War." A century and a half after the guns ceased firing, Americans continue to fight ideological battles over the causes, consequences, and meaning of the Civil War.[10]

This chapter examines efforts by New Bedford's white and black communities to shape local and national memories of the war. Americans' "memory work" through the late nineteenth century struggled against broader changes in New Bedford and the nation that undercut their claims. Such "memory work," explains John R. Gillis, is "like any other kind of physical and mental labor, embedded in complex class, gender and power relations that determine what is remembered (or forgotten), by whom, and for what end."[11] First, even as they faced further economic marginalization in the postwar era, black Americans in New Bedford and elsewhere underscored their public visibility as veterans in postbellum commemorations and parades. Second, the city's black veterans and community members supported an impoverished all-black post of the Grand Army of the Republic (named after Robert Gould Shaw), a group whose very segregation and poverty reflected the ambiguous victory of the Civil War. Finally, New Bedford's African Americans sustained a heroic local icon of the Civil War, Sergeant William Carney of the Fifty-Fourth Massachusetts, a modest warrior who upheld and symbolized blacks' claims for full equality and citizenship. By exploring the terrain of myth- and memory making, this chapter demonstrates the lingering ideological impacts of the Civil War on varied communities of civilians, veterans, blacks and whites who promoted specific interpretations to address contemporary needs.

Memorial Day and the Fourth of July Celebrations

Although Memorial Day did not become mandated by Massachusetts' state law until 1881, citizens of New Bedford were among the first in the nation to memorialize the war and its casualties as early as 1866. On May 30, 1866, the city hosted a parade through New Bedford that featured sixty-two African Americans organized into the "74th Unattached Company," a throwback to prewar black militias. After marching to leader Abram Conklin's home for refreshments, the group heard an address from the eminent local black attorney, William Henry Johnson, and then moved southward via County Street to the home of James B. Congdon. Although enfeebled by illness, Congdon—the former city treasurer, abolitionist, and local historian—offered "burning words of eloquence and encouragement . . . never [to] be forgotten by the members of the 74th unattached," that included veterans of the Fifty-Fourth Massachusetts. By drawing upon the city's most distinguished black and white citizens and claiming public space, the militia company legitimated blacks' status as citizens and military veterans.[12]

The 74th Unattached Company reappeared later that same summer for the official dedication of the cornerstone for the Soldiers' and Sailors' Monument. A crowd of five thousand gathered on the City Common to hear songs, prayers, speeches, and a public reading of the Declaration of Independence. Mayor John Perry reminded listeners to maintain the memory of the dead, while the Reverend Alonzo Quint prayed to the flag: "Flag of stars and the stripes, we bow in reverence before thee, thou symbol of a nation's majesty. To thee is our highest earthly allegiance." Quint employed themes of civil religion in explicitly addressing New Bedford's and the North's military service. "Our altar of liberty was the battle-field," he declared. "The offering of blood was the blood of our comrades." Quint also reminded his audience of New Bedford's antislavery heritage: "[P]eople of New Bedford, you who were the first to pronounce for the freedom of an oppressed race, pledge yourselves and your children forever to maintain liberty."[13] Quint drew together white and black citizens in suggesting that New Bedford's antebellum antislavery activism was fulfilled by the Civil War sacrifices of Union soldiers and sailors who helped to end slavery.

Black veterans participated fully in New Bedford's Memorial Day celebration two years later when local Post 1 of the GAR sponsored grave decorations of Union veterans. On May 30, 1868, nearly one hundred members of GAR Post 1 assembled under a line of flags to march through the city. At least twenty black veterans under the command of "Captain" Wesley Furlong joined the procession. The city's events conform with historian Barbara A. Gannon's insights about Memorial Day in which white and black veterans and GAR members interacted both in integrated and separate events, although parades were usually inclusive and multiracial.[14] After visiting the Rural, Oak Grove, and Catholic cemeteries, the cortege moved to the Soldiers' and Sailors' Monument where two thousand people assembled to speeches from favored orators James B. Congdon and the Reverend Alonzo Quint. Similar celebrations of Memorial Day continued into the 1870s. During the country's centennial observations in 1876, African-American veterans of New Bedford marched under the command of George T. Fisher in their own GAR group, Post 146. Sixteen black veterans in this GAR post participated in the day's events and were specifically honored by the main speakers. Although segregated into an all-black organization, the veterans were accorded respect.[15]

Patriotic events during the nation's centennial underscored civil religious themes and reminded people about the war that ended more than a decade earlier. In his "Memorial Address" before an audience of black and white GAR members and civilians from New Bedford, the Reverend B. P. Raymond made explicit use of themes of civil religion and apocalyptic imagery. He linked the soldiers of the Civil War with the heroes of the Revolution. He praised the "martyred Lincoln" and echoed Lincoln's Gettysburg Address by commenting on the "peculiar sanctity" of a soldier's grave as "holy ground." The debt to dead soldiers could never be repaid fully, Raymond noted, and he urged his audience to consecrate the dead and to worship the flag as a symbol of liberty and law. Following Raymond's speech, African Americans' Civil War experiences were brought front and center by Robert F. Nichols, past commander of GAR Post 13 in Providence, Rhode Island. He spoke vividly of the Fifty-Fourth Massachusetts Regiment and the assault on Fort Wagner. A local scribe highlighted Memorial Day events in 1876: "The ceremonies of this day had awakened recollections of many memorable events in the minds of members of the Grand Army of the Republic," suggesting that memory-making was an active, dynamic, and collective process played out in events like these.[16]

Subsequent celebrations illustrated ongoing tension between an inclusive, nonracial view of the war and a fragmented one of racial, ethnic, and regional differences. On July 4, 1867, for example, African-American men in the Schouler Guards, an all-black drill group under Wesley Furlong's leadership, put on an independent martial display of "military manoeuvres" on Market Street.[17] Another tension emerged between solemn events and those aimed at fun and frivolity. In 1868, for example, New Bedford's City Common hosted sack races, wheelbarrow races, hurdles, a sledgehammer throwing contest, and a greased pig chase.[18] These light and festive alternatives coexisted with the sober patriotism fostered by the GAR and black veterans. City officials in 1869 appropriated $2,500 for a day highlighted by a children's parade, a public picnic on Pope's Island, and fireworks in the evening. "The celebration was one long to be remembered as a very pleasant one," opined one local correspondent, ". . . with no long marches or meaningless parade, and as little as possible of hard work." The day also featured both integrated and segregated events including a major city parade with the all-black Schouler Guards who "looked well in their showy uniforms . . . and showed a good state of efficiency in drill."[19]

The trend toward commercialized, less patriotic, and more fun-oriented Fourths of July could be seen again in 1871 and public commemorations also took on a racial tenor. Some 175 men in the "Bungtown Invincibles" paraded in costumes and pulled a wagon that mocked a Mormon temple and featured characters who lampooned blacks. A "darkey on a horse" accompanied another comic figure who offered an "Oh! Ration" in insulting black dialect. This was the day's only "speech" printed verbatim in New Bedford's newspaper. Three years' later, African-American veterans were placed in the parade's Fourth Division, along with a satirical group, the Sir John Falstaff Lodge, and the recently organized New Bedford Division of the Ancient Order of Hibernians. Black Civil War veterans marched behind white veterans at a public event where commentators noted that "Irish societies were in gay regalia, and formed a prominent feature of the spectacle." African-American veterans' activities went unmentioned in the city's newspaper.[20]

New Bedford's postwar commemorations of the Civil War paralleled those of other northern communities. The city's ritualized events were highlighted by nationalistic oratory, well-organized parades, martial music, a profusion of flags, and colorful bunting. The Reverend William J. Potter, himself a war veteran, spoke for many when he delivered a "Soldiers' Memorial Sermon" before the Rodman GAR Post 1 on May 23, 1880. Like orators such as Frederick Douglass, Potter proclaimed that although the Civil War had been won years earlier, victory had not yet been attained. "Our army, the living & the dead, were seeking a country," Potter declared, "& they had glimpses of, & faith in, a *better* country than that which we had before the great struggle began." Unfulfilled promises remained. Potter argued that although the war ended slavery, it had not ended "gigantic evils" such as racial inequity, and he urged listeners to take up unfinished business and "carry it forward to completion."[21] By 1880, as David Blight has explained, memories of blacks' Civil War sacrifices in saving the Union were being eclipsed by sectional reconciliation and notions of white supremacy. Andre Fleche suggests, however, that black and white Union veterans "formulated a joint vision of the war at odds with more reconciliationist, segregationist, and racist trends in postwar society as a whole." Barbarba A. Gannon upholds this latter perspective, as well.[22]

The Grand Army of the Republic

The GAR sustained much of the postwar myth- and memory making in New Bedford and the nation. Founded in 1866, the GAR was an organization of honorably discharged veterans of the Union army and navy. New Bedford veterans led the way in establishing the state's first post, and by 1890 three GAR posts existed in the city, including one with an all-black membership. Although open to all veterans regardless of race or nationality, the GAR permitted *de facto* discrimination when local posts voted to accept or reject potential members. The GAR aided the transition to civilian life for the Union's citizen-soldiers. In their local posts, veterans could swap stories, relive the war, and share their military bonds with others who had known the rigors of war. Within the GAR posts, members engaged in "history-making" as they told their personal tales of the war and published commemorative stories of the battlefield. Founded upon the principles of fraternity, charity, and loyalty, the GAR functioned as fraternal lodge, charitable society, special interest group, and patriotic and political organization. Throughout the North, the GAR emerged as the preeminent fraternal association in the postbellum period.[23]

New Bedford's Union veterans quickly claimed opportunities to join and direct GAR efforts at city, state, and national levels. The Department of Massachusetts, the largest and the most efficiently administered state-level GAR unit, was organized in early May 1867. Within nine months it claimed eighty posts, including GAR Post 1 from New Bedford. At the Department Encampment in Boston in 1885, state Commander John D. Billings praised Massachusetts's men for their leadership in building a strong organization. Although in theory all GAR posts were comparable in status, the first local post was often a city's most prominent one, as was true with the Rodman GAR Post 1, named after the city's most famous casualty during the Civil War. New Bedford served as home to the first recognized memorial services held in the state on July 4, 1867 and was the site of the First Encampment of the Department of Massachusetts in 1867. The Department's first Commander, Major Austin S. Cushman, hailed from New Bedford, as well.[24]

A lawyer and former major, Cushman offered a succinct summary of the GAR's purpose. First, the organization was to preserve "those kind and fraternal feelings which have bound together the soldiers and sailors" during the Civil War. Second, the GAR was to offer material aid to those who needed assistance and to educate and care for orphans and widows of soldiers and sailors. Further, GAR members would help disabled veterans, whether hobbled by wounds, disease, old age or misfortune. Cushman explained that the GAR would defend veterans' rights so these would be appreciated and recognized by their community. Implicitly, Cushman laid out a "contractual" claim to military pensions, employment opportunities, and other rights. Finally, all GAR members pledged to maintain "an unswerving allegiance" to the United States, to the Constitution, and to defend "universal liberty, equal rights, and justice to all men."[25] Under Cushman's command, Post 1 of New Bedford served historically and symbolically as the premier GAR post in the Department of Massachusetts.

Through their local initiatives, New Bedford's Post 1 played a vital role in structuring patriotic rituals and beliefs that spread throughout the country after the war. The group's most significant act consisted of memorializing the war dead. As early as June 18, 1867, members of the post voted to assemble on the Fourth of July to visit the Soldiers' and Sailors' Monument in the New Bedford

Common. There, on the nation's birthday, the Reverend Alonzo Quint proclaimed, "We meet to remember" and addressed the ex-soldiers as saviors of
the nation. He addressed veterans as men who had "made history" and who
had been "baptized in a sacred cause." Quint also appreciated wartime contributions of civilian men who had contributed their money, time, labor, or their
own sons to the cause. Neither did Quint forget the "noble women who worked
and prayed and wept . . . who gave husbands, brothers, sons, and gave them
heroically." Quint explicitly connected the day's events with devotion to the
dead. Those who had given their lives for the country would never be forgotten,
he declared. "Never, while America is a nation, will your work pass from memory," he concluded.[26] Drawing the city's largest crowd ever of seven thousand
people, the GAR orchestrated a dramatic event and somber parade that shaped
memories of the Civil War.

Like other GAR posts around the country, New Bedford's Post 1 grew rapidly and joined the ranks of the country's most important fraternal organization. The first initiation of members took place on September 25, 1866; by
August 13, 1867, 121 men, all of them white, had joined the post. Through 1910,
a total of 525 veterans had become members, including numerous Irish-born
veterans. Comrades in this active organization recruited new members,
planned memorial celebrations, and printed promotional pamphlets such as
*New Bedford Soldiers' Monument, Ceremonies at the Laying of the Corner Stone
of the Soldiers' Monument, July 4, 1866* (1866).[27] An entertaining sign of the
growth of the Rodman Post 1 emerged about 1890, when members sold a souvenir booklet of *Old War Songs* that mixed patriotic appeals and commercial
endorsements. Lyrics contained references to "darkies" while other songs
pandered to sentimental notions of women's wartime sacrifices or venerated
the flag. This songbook commingled patriotism, racism, and simplistic sentiments of Civil War memorialization.[28]

Despite these racially tinged materials, the post's charity and relief records
demonstrate an interracial bond of veterans at least into the 1870s. Charity relief
constituted a major activity of all GAR posts, and members of Post 1 set aside
generous relief funds to "be held sacred for the aid of the needy." Only honorably discharged Union veterans and their wives, widows, or orphans were eligible for assistance. The private efforts of the GAR paralleled those of the city's
Overseers of the Poor, as one GAR comrade represented each of the city's six
wards. Committee members met weekly and could dole out emergency funds
of less than five dollars at any time. After a comrade's death, the Relief Committee could assume a burial cost of up to thirty dollars. Relief efforts constituted
a core activity of all GAR posts across the country, and New Bedford's efforts
demonstrated an interracial cooperation borne of shared sacrifices in the Civil

War. The ward-based relief system highlighted the ongoing community ties among former soldiers and sailors.[29]

The GAR's relief register illustrated the relative poverty of specific African-American veterans and their families in New Bedford. For example, Ella M. Gooding, the widow of James Gooding who died in a Confederate prison, collected eight dollars worth of groceries on January 24, 1870. Widow Caroline E. Jackson received aid on several occasion between 1870 and 1877. On February 7, 1870, Jackson obtained one half ton of coal, four dollars for shoes, and five dollars for provisions, and one year later she collected five dollars for groceries. On April 1, 1875, Jackson secured five dollars for food, and the GAR post granted her aid twice in February 1876, and again on January 2, 1877. Black Civil War veterans who applied for aid included Isaiah King who received a stipend for coal in February 1870, the same day that William Carney collected five dollars for food. Not all applications were granted, as Wesley Furlong's request was laid on the table at the Relief Committee meeting of January 24, 1870.[30] These sketchy records document the GAR's commitment to charity for Union veterans and families regardless of racial identity while also illustrating the palpable poverty of New Bedford's black veterans and their families.

Historian Donald Shaffer has argued that white veterans treated black comrades in the GAR as "second-class members," and notes that whites dominated leadership positions in state and national encampments. He suggests, furthermore, that black veterans held "opposite" memories of white veterans, illustrated by their choice of heroes and names for the GAR posts. More recently, Barbara Gannon's impressive work contends that the GAR was more racially egalitarian than most institutions and organizations of that era. Moreover, through their segregated GAR posts African-American veterans enjoyed leadership opportunities, public recognition, and often the respect of white comrades.[31] New Bedford was no different than other northern areas with a sizeable black population that maintained separate white and black GAR lodges. Although national encampments were racked by debates in 1887 and again in 1891 over racial proscriptions of southern GAR posts, northern leaders refused to accept an official southern-imposed color line. A committee that included three former national GAR commanders reported that during the war "we stood shoulder to shoulder as comrades tried. It is too late to divide now on the color line."[32] Despite the official repudiation of racial restrictions, however, segregation was the norm in northern GAR departments, including the GAR posts of New Bedford.

When black veterans joined GAR Post 146 they adopted the name of the martyred white leader of the Fifty-Fourth Massachusetts Regiment, Robert Gould Shaw. Presumably this name would help to associate New Bedford's black veterans with the battle of Fort Wagner where Shaw fell and was buried with his soldiers in a common grave. Chartered on December 4, 1871, GAR Post 146 maintained their camp through 1902 save for a brief period, although they suffered greatly from a lack of members and limited funds. At the Sixteenth Annual Department Encampment held in 1881, Post 146 briefly surrendered its charter because of insufficient members to fulfill basic functions and rituals. A short report touched on the post's challenges and highlights the interracial bond among GAR members: "This Post was composed of colored comrades and consequently had a small and limited membership, and against great odds they struggled manfully for an existence, but without avail. It is to be hoped that these comrades will not be lost to the Order and I think I express the wish of the mass of the comrades of the Department when I hope that the mother Post of the Department will take such as are worthy within her membership and thus illustrate the broad foundation stone on which our Order rests."[33] Reorganized under the leadership of Commander Harrison in April 1882, the post claimed eighteen members although the GAR's department inspector found it to be in "poor" condition. Writing in 1918, a local historian recalled the "now defunct" Robert Gould Shaw Post: "The colored veterans maintained their organization as long as there were enough veterans alive to keep the chapter, and now the few who are left are in other posts."[34]

Through the remainder of the nineteenth century, the post's meager relief fund stood as the most glaring indication of black veterans' impoverishment. Their plight contrasted dramatically with the relative affluence of the leading Rodman Post 1, as seen in Table 10-1. In 1891 Post 146 claimed its largest relief fund since 1885—$4.50. Between 1892 and 1900, the post reported no relief funds whatsoever. In the years between 1882 and 1900, the post disbursed a total of eighty dollars in relief, and maintained an average balance of $12.22 in its fund. In contrast, a new all-white post founded in 1889, the R. A. Peirce Post 190, claimed in 1900 a fund of $2,975.93, and made charity payments of over $200 per year between 1889 and 1900. While the new white Post 190 claimed property valued at more than $1,200 after its inception, the all-black post never claimed more than $100 in property, and usually claimed only fifty dollars, as it did between 1895 and 1900.[35]

Similar patterns were displayed by both black and white "ladies auxiliaries" of the GAR. The first Woman's Relief Corps (WRC) was organized in Massachusetts in 1879 to aid widows and orphans of "suffering comrades." WRC members viewed it their "sacred duty" to support Memorial Day celebrations by working closely with GAR posts to commemorate deceased veterans. On a national level, the WRC grew from its inception in 1883 to over 100,000 members by 1890, and women worked effectively to promote patriotic campaigns,

Table 10-1. Grand Army of the Republic Posts, New Bedford, Massachusetts, 1881–1900

Year	Post 1 (White)		Post 146 (Black)	
	Members	Relief Fund ($)	Members	Relief Fund ($)
1881	141	851.98	NA	
1882	155	NA	16	
1883	170	878.99	NA	
1884	214	722.51	NA	
1885	241	800.07	20	13.15
1886	263	934.00	19	
1887	283	868.75	21	2.55
1888	257	840.00	21	2.90
1889	281	565.76	20	3.90
1890	330	773.10	20	3.60
1891	335	507.82	16	4.50
1892	319	342.24	24	
1893	290	490.53	26	
1894	278	481.91	28	
1895	269	426.87	29	
1896	265	877.02	29	
1897	253	766.44	25	
1898	246	734.10	25	
1899	227	676.58	24	
1900	211	651.12	24	

Source: Proceedings of the Department of Massachusetts Encampments, GAR, 1881–1900.

foster flag worship, and ritualize Memorial Day. New Bedford's leading WRC, an auxiliary of the (white) Rodman post, was founded by twenty-five charter members in September 1885. Between 1885 and July 1893, the WRC expended over $2,000 in relief and presented substantial gifts of flags, cash, and, silver. The new R. A. Peirce GAR Post 190, comprised of white veterans, organized its own WRC on January 3, 1891, and within four years WRC 95 contributed $280 to the GAR post and donated more than $500 of items including an altar, United States flag, post flag, and state flag.[36]

Despite a fairly large membership, New Bedford's African-American WRC post lacked the resources and largesse of the two white women's auxiliaries. Instituted in February 1892 by thirty-one members, the Shaw WRC 148 tried to "assist as far as possible its Post and their needy comrades." They admitted, however, that they did not have the "facilities for doing the good that many have," speaking of their white counterparts. The total value of relief that year amounted to a paltry $48.50, an indication of the relative poverty of black citizens in New Bedford. In May 1893 black women raised funds to buy a new flag for the men of the Shaw GAR Post to carry on Memorial Day, along with providing refreshments and literary and musical entertainment. In 1895 the corps claimed forty members, headed by President Johanna Maddox, who had succeeded the group's two previous leaders, Mary A. Jackson and Harriet A. Chummack.[37] Similar to their brethren, African-American women of New Bedford sponsored poorly funded but proudly supported patriotic activities that paralleled white groups. The Shaw GAR Post's WRC highlighted the visibility of black veterans and their families in a city known for its support of antislavery before the war, but also reflected the reality of segregation in postwar America. Segregation permitted the black community to uphold its own patriotic discourses, events, organizations, and memory-making, but also showed that the Civil War had not transformed northern society and race relations.

Black Heroes and Commemorations of the War

Justly proud of their military service, African Americans in postwar New Bedford could call upon a full-fledged war hero as a symbol of their sacrifice, loyalty, and patriotism. Sergeant William H. Carney of the Fifty-Fourth Massachusetts earned fame and the Gilmore Medal for his heroism at Fort Wagner on July 18, 1863. This significant battle proved to many disbelievers that black soldiers could fight as manfully as white troops.[38] For his defense of the flag, Carney received the nation's highest military honor—the Congressional Medal

Grand Army of the Republic Post 190 veterans marching in parade, circa 1893. (Rotogravure Collection. Courtesy of the Trustees of the New Bedford Free Public Library.)

of Honor—nearly forty years after his act. Carney became an icon to the black community in New Bedford and to African Americans in Massachusetts. Lauded by white citizens as well, Carney served as an important figure in the perpetuation of mythic memories of the Civil War. For example, in January 1898, the *Boston Herald* headlined a story about Carney, "The Bravest Colored Soldier." Calling Carney a "grizzled hero," the reporter told of Carney's labors as a "hard-working letter carrier" in New Bedford, concluding that "the old hero is not as young as when he crawled bleeding into camp, with those immortal words, 'The old flag never touched the ground.'"[39]

After the war, William Carney fulfilled ceremonial roles in notable public functions. In 1870 New Bedford's African-American community named Carney chief marshal of a commemoration to honor passage of the Fifteenth Amendment that officially extended voting rights to black men. Beginning with an artillery salute in the city's western end where many of the city's blacks lived, Carney led a procession through the flag-bedecked streets of the city. Similar to antebellum events and militia parades, New Bedford drew blacks from Boston and southeastern New England for festivities that featured members of black churches and lodges. The all-black Schouler Guards offered a "very good appearance," noted one observer, "and are in better drill than ever before." Public events included addresses at City Hall, an oration at Liberty Hall by Dr. Ezra R. Johnson, and dancing at both City Hall and the Schouler Guards' armory.[40] The city's black residents emphasized through this public celebration their enduring quest for political equality, a right that had been earned by the participation of black men such as William Carney in the Union cause.

New Bedford's black citizens and white allies persisted in using public events to remind everyone of blacks' military service. On July 18, 1871, to commemorate passage of the Fifteenth Amendment, General William Cogswell addressed themes of civil religion and Civil War while emphasizing the interracial Union sacrifices. Emancipation, in his view, was "an event greater than the war itself" because it began a "new era for America." Besides duly praising the "sainted martyr" Abraham Lincoln and Governor John Andrew, Cogswell commended the anonymous "sainted heroes of the battlefield" who served the "sacred cause." Black soldiers, in particular, "defend[ed] a country and a flag which now for the first time had become their country and their flag," he concluded. Cogswell explicitly connected Sergeant Carney and Fort Wagner with the broader significance of the Civil War and, after quoting Carney's famous words, he added, "Brave words, brave deeds, brave men." Cogswell concluded, "see to it, no matter at what cost or sacrifice that your children are educated and brought up in the faith of a living God; and let the old flag, the emblem of your liberties, never touch the ground."[41]

William Carney again acted as chief marshal in August 1887 for the "Grand Reunion of Colored Veterans" at Boston's Tremont Hall. Like smaller and more local celebrations, the Grand Reunion exemplified the African-American push for equality by using civil religious themes and memories of the Civil War. Conventioneers sang the black national anthem, "We Are Rising as a People," along with the "Star-Spangled Banner" and "Battle Hymn of the Republic." Colonel N. P. Hallowell spoke about discriminatory pay during wartime for African-American soldiers to remind his contemporary audience of what black soldiers endured. Carney headed an afternoon parade joined by a special escort. "Rapturously received" at an evening session, Carney urged fellow veterans to be "useful citizens so that the republic may be proud of them." He encouraged everyone to "stand firm and see that the results of the war were preserved," invoking the name of Robert Gould Shaw. The evening closed with the audience signing "America," followed by "Taps" and "Lights Out," underscoring the use of military symbolism and rituals.[42]

Carney's prominence stretched beyond New Bedford and into the twentieth century. For example, the National Christian Congress Association tried to raise $1,200 to build a "Carney Memorial Hall" in Alexandria, Virginia, to honor "one of the Greatest heroes of the Civil War." A flyer featured a photograph of Carney clutching his Congressional Medal of Honor with the caption: "Keep the Flag Flying." This building was apparently never built, however.[43] Carney attended integrated events in Boston that mixed white former officers with select rank-and-file veterans, such as the annual reunion in 1901 of the Association of Officers of the 54th Regiment. Only two black men were invited to this fete: William Carney and Booker T. Washington.[44] Even as late as 1908, Carney was still asked about his wartime exploits of forty-five years earlier. In a letter to the New Bedford Sunday Standard, Carney restated his famous declaration at Fort Wagner, noting that part of his saying had been worked into a song, "The Old Flag Never Touched the Ground," and that he had met people from as far away as California familiar with his famous words. Carney died in 1908 while working as a messenger to the Massachusetts Secretary of State. In his honor, the governor ordered State House flags lowered to half-staff for part of one day, making Carney only the second African American to be so honored in Massachusetts.[45]

Despite Carney's war record and postwar reputation, his plight as a poor black veteran illustrated the limited economic success gained by African Americans after the Civil War. Carney needed financial assistance in the early 1870s from the white GAR post in New Bedford, plus he obtained a meager pension from the federal government after the war. He had acquired fame but not economic security. His work as a postal carrier and later messenger could be seen

as honorific employments that brought income to a living Civil War hero. Carney was the only black veteran in New Bedford elected to the otherwise all-
white Rodman GAR Post 1 in New Bedford, which he apparently joined in 1892.
It is not clear if he turned his back on the Robert Gould Shaw Post, still func-
tioning when he joined the Rodman GAR Post. Perhaps his election to the city's
premier GAR post was an offer he simply could not refuse. Or, Carney may
have objected to an abrupt increase in the membership fee assessed members
of the Shaw Post, as it jumped from $1.00 to $3.50 for the only time in the
post's history.[46]

Dedication of the "Shaw Monument," Memorial Day 1897

For veterans of the Fifty-Fourth Massachusetts and African Americans generally, the most significant of all postbellum patriotic celebrations was the dedication of Boston's monument to Robert Gould Shaw and the regiment. The
memorial encapsulated the romanticized meanings of the Civil War, civil religion, and the postbellum black quest for inclusion and full equality. Citizens
from Boston, New Bedford, and elsewhere in New England met on Memorial
Day in 1897 to dedicate the handsome sculpture created by Augustus St.
Gaudens.[47] The Massachusetts Department of the GAR issued "Circular No. 1"
in April 1897 that invited all survivors of the state's black military units to the
Monument's dedication. The *Boston Globe* of May 30, 1897, featured an article
entitled, "Color Bearer at Fort Wagner," in which William Carney recounted
the events at Fort Wagner. He emphasized that Fort Wagner did not end struggles by black troops. "While the government refused to pay us equally," Carney
explained, "we continued to fight for the freedom of the enslaved, and for the
restoration of our country. We did this, not only at Wagner, but also in the
battles on James Island, Honey Hill and Boykins mill."[48] Known for his quiet
modesty, Carney stirred positive memories of black valor and sacrifice with his
strong statement.

The exercises at the Shaw Monument—and the Memorial itself—represent
the conjunction of history, myth, memory, and American civil religion. Kirk
Savage has pointed out that "this monument to a local white hero is the closest
the country came to erecting a national tribute to the black soldier and the
black cause." David Blight places this monument in the context of sectional
reconciliation and an emergent nationalism and emphasizes its uniqueness in
representing emancipation and "manly, selfless devotion."[49] Black and white
luminaries blessed the day's events, ranging from Governor Roger Wolcott, to
Boston's Mayor Josiah Quincy, to Harvard's William James and Tuskegee's

Booker T. Washington. Speaking for the Committee of Subscribers, Colonel Henry Lee declared the monument would "commemorate that great event . . . by which the title of colored men as citizen soldiers was fixed beyond recall." Governor Wolcott reminded his audience of Fort Wagner where, on its "blood-stained earthworks, a race was called into sudden manhood." Boston's Mayor Quincy recalled the regiment's triumphal march through the city's streets almost to the day in May 1863, declaring that Fort Wagner had proven that the African-American soldier "could fight and die for his country, like the white man . . ." Quincy noted, moreover, the burial of Shaw and his men in a "common trench," a "fitting sepulchre of white and black, of officer and private."[50]

For African Americans, Booker T. Washington provided the most memorable oration and his place at the dedication symbolized the prominence of African-American soldiers in the Civil War. His address was replete with themes and images of civil religion and blacks' patriotism. On what he called a "sacred and memorable day," Washington explicitly appealed to the past to call for social progress. Washington struck a discordant political note in claiming that the "fruit of Fort Wagner and all that this monument stands for will not be realized" until all black men could have equal opportunities with whites. "Until that time comes," Washington intoned, "this monument will stand for effort, not victory complete. What these heroic souls of the 54th Regiment began, we must complete." Black soldiers' sacrifices were not in vain, Washington declaimed, for Southern blacks were lifting themselves up, and that the "greatest monument" was still being built in the South—the struggles and sacrifices of African Americans.[51]

In a rousing conclusion, Washington contended that lessons of the war could be put to contemporary use. Just as blacks and whites had fought side by side and died together at Fort Wagner, they could continue to cooperate in the "battle of industry, in the struggle for good government, in the lifting up of the lowest to the fullest opportunities." Emphasizing that interracial cooperation shown in the Civil War could shape civilian efforts thirty-five years later, Washington linked civil religion, the ideology of self-help, and an optimistic belief in progress. Washington invoked New Bedford's hero by concluding that under "God's guidance, . . . that old flag, that emblem of progress and security which brave Sergeant Carney never permitted to fall upon the ground, will still be borne aloft by Southern soldier and Northern soldier . . ." Washington related later that when he referred to Carney, present on the dais clutching the flag, the veteran "rose as if by instinct with the flag in his hands." Washington recalled that "in dramatic effect I have never seen nor experienced anything that equaled the impression made on the audience when Sergeant Carney arose. For a good many minutes the audience seemed to entirely lose control of itself, and patriotic feeling was at a high pitch." A living hero and symbol, Sergeant William H. Carney stood as a striking and potent reminder of what the war had wrought.[52]

After the speeches and the unveiling of the monument, African-American veterans were feted at Faneuil Hall. Bad poetry and earnest patriotism remained the order of the day. One photograph's caption read: "The National and State Ensigns were borne by Color Sergeants Carney and Wilkins, who were the standard bearers of the regiment. It was Sergt. Carney who carried the flag on the ramparts at Wagner and did not let it touch the ground." The *Boston Globe* reported that "grateful people" paid honor to Shaw and "his dusky braves." "Another Memorial Day has come and gone," the reporter continued, "but the memory of yesterday will remain peculiarly sacred to all those who witnessed the parade and the unveiling of the Shaw memorial, and to those who heard the intense words of patriotism that were spoken in Music Hall." Indeed, it was a "great day for the colored race through the country, . . . and the day will remain sacred for all time to the colored race as a day of vindication."[53]

For nearly a century the "Shaw Memorial" would be the last significant public Civil War monument that featured and feted black soldiers. Historian David Blight has offered perceptive analyses of the "Great Reunion" at Gettysburg in 1913 and other events that eroded an "emancipationist" view of the Civil War in favor of a "reconciliationist" perspective tinged with white racism. In the latter decades of the nineteenth century, white Americans from North and South sustained a Civil War mythology that denied the centrality of slavery, race, and competing sectional issues as causes of the war. As black veterans went largely unnoticed at the Gettysburg gathering, African-American newspapers lambasted the "Peace Jubilee" at a time when racial injustice ruled the nation. W. Calvin Chase, the editor of the *Washington Bee*, declared that the whites-only reunion event was "an insane and servile acknowledgment that the most precious results of the war are a prodigious, unmitigated failure." In short, national reconciliation was built upon the perpetuation of a racist order that excluded blacks from full equality and denied them a place of honor in the nation's collective memory.[54]

Summary

Like other people and communities throughout the North, black and white residents of New Bedford cheered the end of a bloody and expensive war. Relieved after four years of trying times, they celebrated the Union victory, mourned Lincoln's death, and praised the end to slavery. Initially, black veterans participated fully in public events and New Bedford's veterans proudly persisted in maintaining a segregated GAR post. Yet, their postwar experiences suggest ongoing challenges in keeping alive inclusive memories and meanings of the war. A minor but telling illustration of the racialized politics among veterans and citizens was displayed in April 1897, just a month before the Shaw Memorial's dedication in Boston. The black commander of Shaw GAR Post 146, Isaiah King, met with white comrades at New Bedford's John H. Clifford Camp of the Sons of Volunteers. Previously, the camp approved a recommendation to add a minstrel show for their anniversary celebration, but with King in attendance, the Minstrel Committee asked for further time and later voted to reconsider the event. King's presence as a black veteran may have derailed plans for the minstrel celebration and the integrated gathering featured cigars, speeches, and a rousing chorus of "America."[55] This would be a small victory among veterans, because for black Americans generally the struggle to maintain the memory of their wartime exploits was challenged and eclipsed by "reconciliationist" sentiments at the turn of the twentieth century. As memories of black contributions to the war faded in the collective minds of whites, African Americans faced a host of changes in the city's economic, social, and political environments that further marginalized them.

Epilogue

A century ago, New Bedford dedicated its iconic sculpture of "The Whaleman," by Bela Pratt. Placed in front of the New Bedford Free Public Library in 1912, the piece is an example of public art that looked back to the golden age of whaling. As Kingston William Heath has noted astutely, when the sculpture was dedicated whaling was all but dead as an industry and nearly 100 percent of the city's mill workers were of "foreign extraction." Although sculptor Bela Pratt had sought a "real boatsteerer" and was encouraged to use an African-American or Cape Verdean harpooner for a model, he opted to create a "Captain Ahab" type with distinctly Anglo-American features. This image of the white harpooner belied the new industrial order and the remarkable ethnic and racial variety of the whaling labor force, Heath argues. Through this sculpture, New Bedford's "power elite" told "their" story of the past that has become mainly the "official" history of the city. Heath concludes that the real history of the city is "everywhere in New Bedford except in the history books and public art."[1]

Many of New Bedford's local boosters and writers have glorified the city's history to emphasize a narrative of growth, prosperity, and modernization, often from the perspective of business and political leaders. One example is that of Leonard Bolles Ellis who published a detailed history of the city in 1892. He described New Bedford as a receptive community for "the introduction of modern ideas into the city government; modern methods of transportation; improved construction of streets; modern facilities of lighting; and many other improvements that go to constitute a progressive American city." A "modern day" resident in the early 1890s, Ellis suggested, "is in all respects to be congratulated on the bright prospects of his home." But these "bright prospects" were not equally distributed, and the city's textile economy peaked less than two decades later. Writing in the 1940s, Henry Beetle Hough penned a corporate history of the Wamsutta Mills that included his recollections of the city during World War One. Gazing at New Bedford from across the Acushnet River, Hough described factories' tall chimneys pouring "columns of smoke" into the sky while at night operatives worked around the clock and thousands of windows "glowed in the darkness." Marveling at "the beauty of the panorama," Hough lamented that "nothing of the sort was ever to be seen along the Acushnet River again."[2] In the aftermath of the war, New Bedford's textile mills would go into eclipse in the 1920s, punctuated by one of the country's most riveting strikes in 1928.[3]

New Bedford's economy did not recover for decades. Scallop fishing, cranberry harvesting, and factory outlets were few signs of success through the 1970s. After a federal highway project obliterated some of the city's historic downtown area in the 1960s, a local architecture preservation group, WHALE, fought to preserve the waterfront's historical buildings. One sign of a turnaround came in the 1980s when the nineteenth-century African-American blacksmith, Lewis Temple, received public recognition. Although a state legislative committee rejected a plan to rename a bridge after Temple, local citizens explored ways to commemorate the black inventor from the heyday of whaling. The Temple Memorial Committee, a partnership of public officials and private residents, commissioned African-American sculptor Jim Toatley to create a permanent image of Temple to be placed opposite Bela Pratt's monumental piece of 1912. In July 1987, a public ceremony unveiled the bronze statue of Lewis Temple. Mayor John K. Bullard told the crowd, "We are removing injustice and honoring a man who should have been honored 130 years ago." Historian Sidney Kaplan, who was most responsible for bringing Temple to scholars' attention a century after the blacksmith's death, believed that New Bedford was "setting history right" by supporting a public sculpture of the toggle-iron harpoon inventor.[4]

The Lewis Temple commemoration illustrates a grassroots effort to overcome historical amnesia about black participation in the city's history and the whaling industry. As Paul A. Schackel has noted, "Transforming the public memory of any sacred place does not come without persistence, hard work, and compromise."[5] This process parallels work by African Americans to keep alive the stories and memories of their military service and sacrifices in the Civil War. This ongoing struggle is finding success in New Bedford and in the nation. During the 1980s, William Carney's descendant Carl J. Cruz publicized his ancestor's exploits, helping to fuel additional attention generated by release of the movie, *Glory*, in 1989. The federal government soon took a lead role in promoting new memorials to African Americans in the Civil War, and the National Park Service helped to organize the centennial rededication of the Shaw Monument in Boston on May 31, 1997. George M. Fredrickson, then president of the Organization of American Historians, suggested that the event focused on black soldiers instead of their white commander. "To me," wrote Fredrickson, "this signified the growth in Civil War historiography, *and to some extent in public memory*, of a realization that blacks were active participants in the process of emancipation rather than passive beneficiaries of white humanitarianism." During the rededication ceremonies, Carl Cruz stood and displayed Carney's Congressional Medal of Honor. "The atmosphere was electrifying," Fredrickson commented, just like it had been one hundred years earlier when Booker T. Washington saw Carney rise while clutching the American flag.[6]

Thanks mainly to the efforts of Carl Cruz and other residents of New Bedford, the city continues to salute and sustain the memory of its African-American Civil War veterans. Public monuments and displays are located throughout the city, and a "Fifty-Fourth Memorial Plaza," dedicated in 1999, graces the city's downtown and promotes heritage tourism. The National Park Service dedicated the New Bedford Whaling National Historical Park in 1998 and has been crucial in maintaining downtown development centered on historical tourism. Visitors are invited to visit what was once "the richest city in the world" and to "walk in the footsteps of Herman Melville and Frederick Douglass," as one brochure explains. New Bedford's celebrations in 2005 featured colorful banners that paired Douglass and Melville as the city touted its interracial heritage and literary significance. The Nathan and Polly Johnson House on Seventh Street, now a national historic landmark, houses the New Bedford Historical Society that informs people today about African Americans in the nineteenth century. Popular tours include "Passages to Freedom: New Bedford and the Underground Railroad." The venerable New Bedford Whaling Museum has offered for decades scholarly resources and popular museum exhibits that explore the worlds of maritime and whaling history. Its exhibits have touched on the lives and significance of Paul Cuffe, Lewis Temple, Frederick Douglass, William H. Carney, and others. City visitors are encouraged to travel the "Black Heritage Trail."[7]

Through private and public partnerships and collaboration among city, state, and federal agencies, New Bedford is showcasing its inclusive and rich heritage. The "memory work" lives on as the Whaling City tries to profit from its history of 150 years ago. In 2011 New Bedford was named one of a "Dozen Distinctive Destinations," an award program of the National Trust for Historic Preservation. New Bedford joins a select list of cities and towns that offer an "authentic visitor experience by combining dynamic downtowns, cultural diversity, attractive architecture, cultural landscapes and a strong commitment to historic preservation, sustainability and revitalization." Residents have joined together to protect their town's "character." For the local group WHALE, this award was the culmination of nearly fifty years of hard work.

Today, residents and tourists walk the cobblestone streets amid period gas lamps and authentic buildings from the nineteenth century.[8]

The world of historical scholarship has also witnessed a more complete understanding of African Americans in the Civil War and in New Bedford's history.[9] Most recently, historian Barbara A. Gannon examined interracial memory-making and comradeship among Civil War veterans. Entitling her study *The Won Cause*, Gannon demonstrates how veterans kept alive a meaning of the Civil War at odds with the pro-Southern "Lost Cause" and its white-washed version of American history. Most Americans and many historians through the twentieth century "remembered" the Civil War as having nothing to do with slaves or slavery while "forgetting" military service by nearly 200,000 black men. Gannon draws upon David Blight whose pioneering work concluded that "the problems of 'race' and "reunion' were trapped in a tragic mutual dependence." At the turn of the twentieth century, white Northerners and Southerners reconciled at the expense of African Americans who were increasingly segregated and disenfranchised. The service and sacrifices of blacks in the Civil War disappeared from public memory and were excluded in history books. While Gannon does not specifically address New Bedford or its white and black GAR members, her detailed and sweeping account is a convincing one.[10]

Writing after Barack Obama's election to the presidency in 2008, Gannon concludes that "the Won Cause finally won." She suggests that the modern United States, sustained by a strong belief in freedom, is a "living legacy of the black and white comrades of the Grand Army of the Republic."[11] This optimistic view has been upheld in recent scholarship, popular culture, and public memory.[12] Certainly this is true in New Bedford where African Americans are lauded for their roles as soldiers during the Civil War. The success of "memory work" is reflected in a song composed by Young Ambassadors associated with the New Bedford Whaling National Historical Park. Merging hip-hop music and art, the group aims to connect local history with "kids of today." In honor of the Civil War's sesquicentennial, the Youth Ambassadors composed and performed a song, "54," about the Fifty-Fourth Massachusetts. With a typical rap beat, the song begins with dialog excerpted from the movie *Glory* and segues into a rhyming narrative about blacks' enlistment in the Civil War. Repeated refrains include, "We do what we gotta do," and "Freedom at last, freedom at last." Toward the end of the song, a new voice represents Sergeant William H. Carney who sings, "Can't forget my family," "gotta date with destiny," "I am inspired," and "the old flag never touched the ground, boys."[13] Today, in music, in art, in public commemoration, and in historical scholarship, the contributions of New Bedford's black soldiers in the Civil War are not forgotten.

Notes

Introduction

1. *Centennial Celebration, Proceedings in Connection with the Celebration at New Bedford, September 14, 1864, of the Two Hundredth Anniversary of the Incorporation of the Town of Dartmouth* (New Bedford: E. Anthony & Sons, Printers, 1865) (hereafter cited as *Centennial Celebration*).

2. "Address of His Honor George Howland, Jr., Mayor of New Bedford," *Centennial Celebration*, 61–67.

3. "Address of William W. Crapo," *Centennial Celebration*, 69–103.

4. The terms *Civil War cities* and *city biography* are used by J. Matthew Gallman in his insightful review essay, "Urban History and the American Civil War," *Journal of Urban History* 32, no. 4 (May 2006): 631–42; quotes on pp. 632, 635. Much of the following discussion is framed by Gallman's perspective, just as this book has been influenced by his major works in this area: *Mastering Wartime: A Social History of Philadelphia during the Civil War* (New York: Cambridge University Press, 1990; reprint ed., Philadelphia: University of Pennsylvania Press, 2000); *The North Fights the Civil War: The Home Front* (Chicago: Ivan R. Dee, 1994); and *Northerners at War: Reflections on the Civil War Home Front* (Kent, OH: Kent State University Press, 2010). Peter J. Parish's essays have been helpful in shaping this study; see in particular "Conflict and Consent," in Peter J. Parish, *The North and the Nation in the Era of the Civil War*, ed. Adam I. P. Smith and Susan-Mary Grant (New York: Fordham University Press, 2003), 149–70.

5. Parish also notes that the "Study of the home front—and especially of civilian morale, popular commitment, and the means of promoting them—can shed light on other issues, quite apart from how and why the North won the Civil War." Parish, "Conflict and Consent," 164.

6. Maris A. Vinovskis, "Have Social Historians Lost the Civil War? Some Preliminary Demographic Speculations," in *Toward a Social History of the American Civil War: Exploratory Essays*, ed. Maris A. Vinovskis (New York: Cambridge University Press 1990), 1–30.

7. Michael H. Frisch, *Town into City: Springfield, Massachusetts, and the Meaning of Community, 1840–1880* (Cambridge, MA: Harvard University Press, 1972). Vinovskis mentioned four books that addressed his concerns: Randall C. Jimerson, *The Private Civil War: Popular Thought During the Sectional Conflict* (Baton Rouge: Louisiana University Press, 1988); Reid Mitchell, *Civil War Soldiers: Their Expectations and Their Experiences* (New York: Viking Penguin, 1988); Philip Shaw Paludan, *"A People's Contest": The Union and the Civil War, 1861–1865* (New York: Harper & Row, 1988); and James I. Robertson, Soldiers Blue and Gray (Columbia: University of South Carolina Press, 1988). Mitchell subsequently published *The Vacant Chair: The Northern Soldier Leaves Home* (New York: Oxford University Press, 1993). Other studies of Northern cities include Ernest A. McKay, *The Civil War and New York City* (Syracuse, NY: Syracuse University Press, 1990); Donald K. Spann, *Gotham at War: New York City, 1860–1865* (Wilmington, DE: Scholarly Resources, 2002); Thomas H. O'Connor, *Civil War Boston: Home Front & Battlefield* (Boston: Northeastern University Press, 1997); Theodore J. Karamanski, *Rally*

"Round the Flag": Chicago and the Civil War (Chicago: Nelson-Hall, 1993); and Russell L. Johnson, *Warriors into Workers: The Civil War and the Formation of Urban-Industrial Society in a Northern City* (New York: Fordham University Press, 2003). The gendered dimensions of the war first received serious scrutiny by Catherine Clinton and Nina Silber, eds., *Divided Houses: Gender and the Civil War* (New York: Oxford University Press, 1993), and more recently in Catherine Clinton and Nina Silber, eds. *Battle Scars: Gender and Sexuality in the American Civil War* (New York: Oxford University Press, 2006). See also two fine collections of essays edited by Paul A. Cimbala and Randall M. Miller, *An Uncommon Time: The Civil War and the Northern Home Front* (New York: Fordham University Press, 2002) and *Union Soldiers and the Northern Home Front: Wartime Experiences, Postwar Adjustments* (New York: Fordham University Press, 2002). Probably the best overview at a "grass roots" level is David Williams, *A People's History of The Civil War: Struggles for the Meaning of Freedom* (New York: Free Press, 2005).

8. Using methods and evidence associated with the practice of social history, this book explores the lives of ordinary and mostly anonymous Americans drawn from all ranks of society by relying upon standard sources such as newspapers, censuses, and city directories. To better examine New Bedford's business community, and the transition from whaling to manufacturing, this book incorporates R. G. Dun credit reports, a source housed at Harvard University's Baker Library. To shed light on political leaders and city authorities, city documents have been scoured to investigate municipal governance. Ranging from published mayoral addresses to committee reports to itemized budgets, these sources round out coverage in local newspapers and information located in letters and journals of New Bedford residents. To investigate patterns of social welfare among black residents and military veterans, this book draws on detailed local records from the Overseers of the Poor and federal military pension files, rich sources that provide unexpected nuggets of personal and family history. Some pioneering works of the "new social history" made great strides in quantitative methods but also neglected the Civil War. See Stephan Thernstrom, *Poverty and Progress: Social Mobility in a Nineteenth Century City* (Cambridge, MA: Harvard University Press, 1964; repr., New York, 1978), and the massive efforts led by Theodore Hershberg, ed., *Philadelphia, Work, Space, Family, and Group Experience in the Nineteenth Century: Essays Toward an Interdisciplinary History of the City* (New York: Oxford University Press, 1981).

9. See Reid Mitchell, chapter 3, "From Volunteer to Soldier, The Psychology of Service," in *Civil War Soldiers*, 56–89, and Reid Mitchell, "The Northern Soldier and His Community," in Vinovskis, *Social History*, 78–92. Detailed analysis of separate communities upholds these findings; see Thomas R. Kemp, "Community and War: The Civil War Experience of Two New Hampshire Towns," in Vinovskis, *Social History*, 31–77.

10. Thomas Bender, *Community and Social Change in America* (New Brunswick, NJ: Rutgers University Press 1978), 7. Another important work in understanding "community" is that of Benedict Anderson who contended that a nation was a socially constructed community, imagined by people with shared group characteristics and loyalties. See Benedict Anderson, *Imagined Communities: Reflections on the Origin and Spread of Nationalism* (London and New York: Verso Press, 2006; orig. pub. 1983).

11. The shared community origins of regimental enlistees is corroborated by James McPherson: "Companies and even whole regiments often consisted of recruits from a single township, city, or county. Companies from neighboring towns combined to form a regiment . . . Sometimes brothers, cousins, or fathers and sons belonged to the same company or regiment. Localities and ethnic groups retained a strong sense of identity with 'their' regiments." James McPherson, *Battle Cry of Freedom: The Civil War Era* (New York: Oxford University Press, 1988; 2003), 326. Philip Shaw Paludan also explored these issues in his survey of the North in *"A People's Contest."*

12. Historians of African Americans in the Civil War era are indebted to the work of Ira Berlin and colleagues who compiled rich documents and offered great insights in several edited volumes. They were among the first historians to emphasize that blacks fought a "different war." "Because [African Americans] struggled to end inequality as well as to save the Union," Berlin and his associates wrote, "they faced enemies on two fronts, battling against the blue as well as the gray to achieve freedom and equality." See Ira Berlin, Joseph P. Reidy, and Leslie S. Rowland, eds. *The Black Military Experience. Series 2, Freedom: A Documentary History of Emancipation, 1861–1867* (New York and Cambridge: Cambridge University Press, 1982), 18. The same point is made in a more recent and succinct account, Ira Berlin, Joseph P. Reidy, and Leslie S. Rowland, eds., *Freedom's Soldiers: The Black Military Experience in the Civil War* (New York: Cambridge University Press, 1998), 26. For readers interested in the important topic of black Union sailors, see Steven J. Ramold, *Slaves, Sailors, Citizens: African Americans in the Union Navy* (De Kalb: Northern Illinois Press, 2002); Michael J. Bennett, *Union Jacks: Yankee Sailors in the Civil War* (Chapel Hill: University of North Carolina Press, 2003); and the online index and database of "Black Sailors," part of the National Park System's Civil War Soldiers and Sailors System overseen by Joseph P. Reidy at http://www.itd.nps.gov/cwss/sailors_index.html.

13. O'Connor gauged the war's effects on four groups: business leaders, Irish Catholics, African Americans, and women. O'Connor explained that, "Each of these groups appeared to have clear physical attributes, distinctive social characteristics, a fairly well-defined and recognizable living space in the city, and coherent values and beliefs that ordered their personal and professional lives." Thomas H. O'Connor, *Civil War Boston: Home Front and Battlefield* (Boston: Northeastern University Press, 1997), xv.

14. Kathryn Grover, *The Fugitive's Gibraltar: Escaping Slaves and Abolitionism in New Bedford Massachusetts* (Amherst: University of Massachusetts Press, 2001).

15. Lance E. Davis, Robert E. Gallman, and Karin Gleiter, *In Pursuit of Leviathan: Technology, Institutions, and Profits in American Whaling, 1816–1906* (Chicago and London: University of Chicago Press, 1997). Recent work by the economic historian Eric Hilt extends these analysis; see Eric Hilt, "Investment and Diversification in the American Whaling Industry," *Journal of Economic History* 67, no. 2 (June 2007): 292–314. An accessible and comprehensive overview of whaling is offered by Eric Jay Dolin, *Leviathan: The History of Whaling in America* (New York: W. W. Norton & Company, 2007). Whaling has been the focus of innovative social and women's historians; standouts include Margaret S. Creighton, *Rites & Passages, The Experience of American Whaling, 1830–1870* (Cambridge: Cambridge University Press, 1995), and Lisa Norling, *Captain Ahab Had a Wife: New England Women and the Whalefishery, 1720–1870* (Chapel Hill: University of North Carolina Press, 2000). Older works that contextualize New Bedford and whaling include John R. Bockstoce, *Whales, Ice, & Men: The History of Whaling in the Western Arctic* (Seattle and London: University of Washington Press, 1995); Everett S. Allen, *Children of the Light: The Rise and Fall of New Bedford Whaling and the Death of the Arctic Fleet* (Boston: Little, Brown, and Co., 1973; reprint ed., Illinois: Parnassus Press, 1983); Elmo Paul Hohman, *The American Whaleman: A Study of Life and Labor in the Whaling Industry* (New York: Longmans, Green, and Co., 1928); Alexander Starbuck, *A History of the American Whale Fishery from Its Earliest Inception to the Year 1876*, originally part 4 of the *Report of the US Commission on Fish and Fisheries* (Washington, DC, 1878; New York: Argosy-Antiquarian Ltd., 1964).

16. Grover, *Fugitive's Gibraltar*, 1, 6–10. Other accounts of New Bedford's history include: Daniel Ricketson, *The History of New Bedford, Bristol County, Massachusetts: Including a History of the Old Township of Dartmouth and the Present Townships of Westport, Dartmouth, and Fairhaven, From Their Settlement to the Present Time* (New Bedford, MA: Published by the author, 1858); Leonard Bolles Ellis, *History of New Bedford*

and Its Vicinity, 1602–1892 (Syracuse, NY: D. Mason & Co., Publishers, 1892); Zephaniah W. Pease and George W. Hough, *New Bedford, Massachusetts: Its History, Industries, Institutions, and Attractions,* ed. William L. Sayer (New Bedford, 1889); Zephaniah W. Pease, ed., *History of New Bedford* (New York: The Lewis Historical Company, 1918); Judith A. Boss and Joseph D. Thomas, *New Bedford A Pictorial History* (Norfolk, VA: The Donning Company, Publishers, 1983); Christopher McDonald, *The Military History of New Bedford: Images of America* (Charleston, SC: Arcadia Publishing, 2001); Anthony Sammarco and Paul Buchanan, *New Bedford, Images of America* (Charleston, SC: Arcadia Publishing, 1997; reissued 2003).

17. James Oliver Horton and Lois E. Horton, *In Hope of Liberty: Culture, Community and Protest Among Northern Free Blacks, 1700–1860* (New York: Oxford University Press, 1997), xi. Initial research on New Bedford's black community was inspired by James Oliver Horton and Lois E. Horton, *Black Bostonians: Family Life and Community Struggle in the Antebellum North,* rev. ed. (Teaneck, NJ: Holmes & Meier Publishers, 2000; orig. pub. 1979); Leonard P. Curry, *The Free Black in Urban America 1800–1850: The Shadow of the Dream* (Chicago: University of Chicago Press, 1981), and Hershberg, *Philadelphia, Work, Space, Family, and Group Experience in the Nineteenth Century.* See also James Oliver Horton, *Free People of Color: Inside the African American Community* (Washington and London: Smithsonian Institution Press, 1993).

18. Frederick Douglass wrote about his inability to find employment as a caulker in New Bedford because white workers threatened to walk off the job if he were hired. See *Frederick Douglass, Life and Times of Frederick Douglass, Written by Himself* (rev. ed., 1892; reprint, New York: Collier Books, 1962), 208–13. Historian W. Jeffrey Bolster's pioneering work emphasized that black seafarers could earn equal wages with white men of the same rank, work on "substantially integrated" ship decks, and share a sense of camaraderie and egalitarianism that countered heavy racist proscriptions in the larger American society. See W. Jeffrey Bolster, *Black Jacks: African-American Seamen in the Age of Sail* (Cambridge, MA: Harvard University Press, 1998), along with his path-breaking article, "'To Feel like a Man': Black Seamen in the Northern States, 1800–1860," *Journal of American History* 76 (March 1990): 1173–99. Martha Putney's work is also helpful, see her *Black Sailors: Afro-American Seamen and Whalemen Prior to the Civil War* (Greenwood, CT: Greenwood Publishing Group, 1987). For a negative assessment of blacks' opportunities in whaling, see James B. Farr, *Black Odyssey: The Seafaring Traditions of Afro-Americans* (New York: Peter Lang, 1989), 77–104.

19. The work of Michael Frisch and J. Matthew Gallman has been particularly helpful. Frisch devoted several chapters to the Civil War in his study of Springfield, Massachusetts, painting a detailed portrait of a community's urban growth during the "boom years" of the war. Gallman's investigation of Philadelphia offers many parallels with this study of New Bedford. He examined military recruitment, civic celebrations, voluntarism, public order, and business and economic changes wrought by war. In addition, Gallman was one of the first social historians to make use of R. G. Dun credit reports. See Frisch, *Town Into City,* and Gallman, *Mastering Wartime.* One of the most insightful accounts of military mobilization in a Northern community is provided by Russell L. Johnson. In his detailed analysis of Dubuque, Iowa, Johnson contends that voluntarism early in the war gave way to "coercion" in 1862, a "controlled market" in 1863, and a "free market" in 1864–1865. See Johnson, *Warriors into Workers,* 58–100.

20. The depth and breadth of historians' work devoted to ordinary combatants is seen in to two collections: Aaron Sharon-Dean, ed., *The View From the Ground: Experiences of Civil War Soldiers* (Lexington: University Press of Kentucky, 2007), and Michael Barton and Larry M. Logue, *The Civil War Soldier: A Historical Reader* (New York: New York University Press, 2002).

21. Readers interested in a comprehensive and contextualized account of death can turn to Drew Gilpin Faust, *This Republic of Suffering: Death and the American Civil War* (New York: Knopf, 2008).

22. "The vehicles of home influence were many," Linderman explained, "letters, army chaplains, visiting relatives, hometown newspaper correspondents, relief workers, hospital volunteers—even strangers." Gerald F. Linderman, *Embattled Courage: The Experience of Combat in the American Civil War* (New York: Free Press, 1987), 93.

23. James Henry Gooding, *On the Altar of Freedom: A Black Soldier's Civil War Letters from the Front*, ed. Virginia Matzke Adams; Foreword by James M. McPherson (Amherst: University of Massachusetts Press, 1991). For their insights, see McPherson's foreword, xi–xiv, and Adams's introduction, xv–xxxvii. A succinct account of the pay issue is provided by Donald Yacovone, "The Fifty-Fourth Massachusetts Regiment, The Pay Crisis, and the 'Lincoln Despotism,'" in Martin Blatt, Thomas J. Brown, and Donald Yacovone, eds., *Hope and Glory: Essays on the Legacy of the Fifty-Fourth Massachusetts Regiment* (Amherst: University of Massachusetts Press, 2001), 35–51.

24. Important works include Noah Andre Trudeau, *Like Men of War: Black Troops in the Civil War* (Boston: Little, Brown, & Company, 1998); John David Smith, *Black Soldiers in Blue: African American Troops in the Civil War* (Chapel Hill: University of North Carolina Press, 2002); Donald Yacovone, ed., *A Voice of Thunder: A Black Soldier's Civil War* (Urbana and Chicago: University of Illinois Press, 1997); Edwin S. Redkey, ed. *A Grand Army of Black Men: Letters from African-American Soldiers in the Union Army, 1861–1865* (New York: Cambridge University Press, 1992); Joseph T. Glatthaar, *Forged in Battle: The Civil War Alliance of Black Soldiers and White Officers* (New York: Free Press, 1990); Wilbert L. Jenkins, *Climbing Up to Glory: A Short History of African Americans During the Civil War and Reconstruction* (Wilmington, DE: Scholarly Resources, 2002); Robert Ewell Greene, *Swamp Angels: A Biographical Study of the 54th Massachusetts Regiment, True Facts about the Black Defenders of the Civil War* (Madison, FL: BoMark/Greene Publishing Group, 1990); Dudley Taylor Cornish, *The Sable Arm: Black Troops in the Union Army, 1861–1865* (Lawrence: University Press of Kansas, 1987; 1956).

25. Michael B. Katz, *Poverty and Policy in American History* (St. Louis: Academic Press, 1983), 14.

26. Theda Skocpol, *Protecting Soldiers and Mothers: The Politics of Social Provision in the United States, 1870s–1920s* (Cambridge, MA: Harvard University Press, 1992), and Patrick Kelly, *Creating A National Home: Building the Veterans' Welfare State: 1860–1900* (Cambridge, MA: Harvard University Press, 1997).

27. Donald R. Shaffer, *After the Glory: The Struggles of Black Civil War Veterans* (Lawrence: University Press of Kansas, 2004); also see Barbara A. Gannon, *The Won Cause: Black and White Comradeship in the Grand Army of the Republic* (Chapel Hill: University of North Carolina Press, 2011). Other works that explore Civil War veterans include Larry M. Logue and Michael Barton, eds., *The Civil War Veteran: A Historical Reader* (New York: New York University Press, 2007); Eric T. Dean, *Shook Over Hell: Post-Traumatic Stress, Vietnam, and the Civil War* (Cambridge, MA: Harvard University Press, 1997).

28. Recent works on Confederate raiders include James Tertius deKay, *The Rebel Raiders: The Astonishing History of the Confederacy's Secret Navy* (New York: Ballantine Books, 2002) and Tom Chaffin, *Sea of Gray: The Around-the-World Odyssey of the Confederate Raider Shenandoah* (New York: Hill and Wang, 2006).

29. Several studies examine this transformation, most recently an innovative work on New Bedford's architectural landscape by Kingston William Heath, *The Patina of Place: The Cultural Weathering of a New England Industrial Landscape* (Knoxville: University of Tennessee Press, 2001). The work of Thomas McMullin is invaluable for understanding postbellum New Bedford; see McMullin, "Industrialization and Social

Change in a Nineteenth-Century Port City: New Bedford, Massachusetts, 1865–1900"
(PhD dissertation, University of Wisconsin-Madison, 1976); "Industrialization and the
Transformation of Public Education in New Bedford, 1865–1900," *Historical Journal of
Massachusetts* 15 (June 1987): 106–23; "Lost Alternative: The Urban Industrial Utopia of
William D. Howland" *New England Quarterly* 55 (1982): 25–38; and "Overseeing the
Poor: Industrialization and Public Relief in New Bedford, 1865–1900" *Social Science
Review* 65 (December 1991): 548–63.

30. David Blight, *Race and Reunion, the Civil War in American Memory* (Cambridge,
MA, and London: Harvard University Press, 2001). David Thelen points out that "Making a memory underscores a shared identity among people, and these memories serve
contemporary needs in building traditions, legends, myths, rituals, and more formalized
cultural expressions of collective memory." David Thelen, "Memory and American History," *Journal of American History* 75 (March 1989): 1117–29. Teresa Thomas has contended that social class and context shaped postwar memories of war veterans; see Teresa
A. Thomas, "For Union, Not for Glory: Memory and the Civil War Volunteers of Lancaster, Massachusetts," *Civil War History* 40, no. 1 (1994): 25–47. Also see the excellent
collection of essays in Alice Fahs and Joan Waugh, eds. *The Memory of the Civil War in
American Culture* (Chapel Hill: University of North Carolina Press, 2004); see especially
David Blight, "Decoration Days, The Origins of Memorial Day in North and South,"
94–129, and Stuart McConnell, "Epilogue: The Geography of Memory," 258–66. The
topic of Civil War memorialization has been made accessible for teachers and college
students in Thomas J. Brown, *The Public Art of Civil War Commemoration: A Brief History with Documents* (Boston and New York: Bedford St. Martin's, 2004).

31. Douglass created a "usable past" of enduring myths that would stand as "sacred
values, ritualized in memory," using the language and themes of civil religion in preaching for black Americans to join the "high worship" of national inclusion. See David W.
Blight, "'For Something Beyond the Battlefield': Frederick Douglass and the Struggle
for the Memory of the Civil War," *Journal of American History* 75 (March 1989): 1156–78.
This essay and others were reprinted in *Beyond the Battlefield: Race, Memory, and the
American Civil War* (Amherst: University of Massachusetts Press, 2002). An excellent
study of African-American commemorations is Mitch Kachun, *Festivals of Freedom:
Memory and Meaning in African American Emancipation Celebrations, 1808–1915*
(Amherst: University of Massachusetts Press, 2003).

1. "A Burning and Shining Light": Prosperity and Enlightened Governance in Antebellum New Bedford

1. Charles Francis Adams quoted in Zephaniah W. Pease, ed., *History of New Bedford* (New York: Lewis Historical Publishing Company, 1918), 354; Herman Melville,
Moby-Dick (New York: Oxford University Press, 1988), ed. Tony Tanner, 34.

2. Nathaniel Parker Willis's travel accounts and letters were published in the *Home
Journal*, in *Hurrygraphs* (New York, 1851), and excerpted in Pease, *History*, 381–82.

3. Hartford (Connecticut) *Courant*, September 3, 1855, located in Connecticut Miscellaneous Newspapers, SHSW microfilm; William Schouler, *A History of Massachusetts
in the Civil War, vol. 2, Towns and Cities* (Boston: Published by the Author, 1871), 141.

4. Henry Beetle Hough, *Wamsutta of New Bedford, 1846–1946: A Story of New
England Enterprise* (New Bedford: Wamsutta Mills, 1946), 20–21.

5. *Harper's New Monthly Magazine* 21 (June 1860): 6–8; possibly written by D. H.
Strother.

6. *The New Bedford Directory, Containing the City Register and a General Directory
of the Citizens* (New Bedford: Charles Taber & Co., B. Lindsey, Printer, 1859) (hereafter
cited as *1859 City Directory*).

7. Melville, *Moby-Dick*, 33–34.

8. "New Bedford, Massachusetts," *National Magazine* (September 1845): 330–40, excerpted in William W. Crapo, *Centennial in New Bedford, Historical Address by Hon. William W. Crapo Delivered on the occasion of the Celebration in New Bedford of the Fourth of July 1876* (New Bedford, 1876), 99–100, 96.

9. Among numerous studies of the whale fishery in the nineteenth century, still an excellent starting point is Elmo P. Hohman's *The American Whaleman* (New York: Longmans, Green and Company, 1928). The most sophisticated overview of whaling and New Bedford's whaling agents is provided by Lance E. Davis, Robert E. Gallman, and Karin Gleiter, *In Pursuit of Leviathan: Technology, Institutions, Productivity, and Profits in American Whaling, 1816–1906* (Chicago: University of Chicago Press, 1997). A readable overview of whaling is provided by Eric Jay Dolin, *Leviathan: The History of Whaling in America* (New York: W. W. Norton and Company, 2007). Several nineteenth-century government reports contain valuable details and data; see A. Howard Clark, "History and Present Condition of the Fishery," and James Templeman Brown, "The Whalemen, Vessels, Apparatus and Methods of the Fishery," in part 15, The Whale-Fishery, The Fisheries and Fishery Industries of the United States, section 5, vol. 2, Senate Misc. Documents, 47th Congress, 1st sess., misc. document 124, part 6 (1881–82), Washington, GPO, 1887.

10. Lance E. Davis, Robert E. Gallman, and Teresa D. Hutchins, "Productivity in American Whaling: The New Bedford Fleet in the Nineteenth Century," *Working Paper No. 2477, National Bureau of Economic Research*, 1987; Davis et al., "The Structure of the Capital Stock in Economic Growth and Decline, The New Bedford Whaling Fleet in the Nineteenth Century," in Peter Kilby, ed., Quantity & Quiddity, *Essays in U.S. Economic History* (Middletown, CT: Wesleyan University Press, 1977), 336–98; and Teresa D. Hutchins, "The American Whale Fishery, 1815–1900: An Economic Analysis," PhD dissertation, University of North Carolina, Chapel Hill, 1988). Other works that focus on New Bedford's whaling business include David Moment, "The Business of Whaling in America in the 1850s," *Business History Review* 31 (Autumn 1957): 261–91; Michael Maran, "The Decline of American Whaling," (PhD dissertation, University of Pennsylvania, 1974); and Joseph L. McDevitt, *The House of Rotch: Whaling Merchants of Massachusetts, 1734–1828* (New York: Garland Publishing Company, 1986).

11. This section is drawn from Davis et al., *In Pursuit of Leviathan*; R. G. Dun reports; and Martin Joseph Butler, "J. & W. R. Wing of New Bedford: A Study of the Impact of a Declining Industry upon an American Whaling Agency" (PhD dissertation, Pennsylvania State University, 1973). Pease lists a number of whaling entrepreneurs on pp. 28–29, including Jonathan Bourne, on p. 28.

12. Davis, *Leviathan*, chap. 10, 381–422; Howland information on p. 399; other material on pp. 411–13.

13. Although W. Jeffrey Bolster does not discuss whaling per se, his arguments are applicable to New Bedford's labor market, as paternalism practiced by Quaker whaling merchants diminished over time. See his pioneering article, W. Jeffrey Bolster, "'To Feel like a Man': Black Seamen in the Northern States, 1800–1860," *Journal of American History* 76 (March 1990): 1173–99, and his more comprehensive *Black Jacks, African-American Seamen in the Age of Sail* (Cambridge, MA: Harvard University Press, 1998).

14. The Outfitters Association of New Bedford first met on March 7, 1859, and continued to meet through 1873. See "New Bedford Outfitters," *Old Dartmouth Historical Society Sketches, no. 44* (New Bedford, n.d.): 23–27. Writing in *Harper's New Monthly Magazine*, a correspondent reported that sharks were "keen-scented" and could tell the success of the voyage and each man's lay. The sharks surrounded returning whalemen, "hugging him about the neck, lover-like, whispering jolly good jokes into his ears, cramming bundles of cigars into his pockets, and, unseen by master or mate, slyly pressing

to his lips the mouth of an uncorked pocket-flask." See Strother, "New Bedford," *Harper's* (June 1860): 16–17.

15. Lisa Norling argued that local whaling agents turned their paternalism away from crew members as the increasingly foreign-born crews became more diverse and less experienced. See "Contrary Dependencies, Whaling Agents and Whalemen's Families, 1830–1870," *The Log of Mystic Seaport* 42 (Spring 1990): 3–12, and her more comprehensive account, *Captain Ahab Had a Wife, New England Women and the Whalefishery, 1720–1870* (Chapel Hill: University of North Carolina Press, 2000).

16. One of the most active ship building enterprises, located in Padanaram, was headed by Alonzo Matthews and John Mashow. The firm enjoyed great success from 1845 until 1858 when the firm constructed fourteen barks, one brig, nineteen schooners, and one sloop, all together an average of three ships per year. L. A. Littlefield, "Traditions of Padanaram," *Old Dartmouth Historical Sketches*, no. 2 (1903): 8–11. Information about New Bedford's ship building in 1848 is in *Hunt's Merchant's Magazine* (June 1848): 647.

17. From "New Bedford, Massachusetts," *National Magazine* (September 1845): 330–40, excerpted in Crapo, *Centennial* (1876), appendix 20, 96–111.

18. See *Statistical Information . . . for Year Ending June 1, 1855,* Industry of Massachusetts, New Bedford, 87–91; Boston: Office of Secretary of State.

19. Pease, *History*, 75–77. Zephaniah W. Pease and George W. Hough devote a full chapter to "The Manufacture of Oil," in Pease and Hough, *New Bedford, Massachusetts: Its History, Industries, Institutions, and Attractions,* ed. by William L. Sayer (New Bedford, 1889), 73–193 (hereafter cited as Pease and Hough *History* (1889)). Besides Samuel Leonard, other oil manufacturers active in the 1850s included Nehemiah Leonard, Sanford A. & Howland, Milliken Brothers of Boston, George T. Baker, Cornelius Grinnell, Joseph Ricketson, the Hastings, and S. Thomas & Co.; see ibid., 175–76.

20. Pease and Hough, *History* (1889), 184–85.

21. Davis et al., chap. 9, "Product Markets," in *Leviathan*, 342–80; quote on p. 515.

22. *New Bedford and Old Dartmouth*, 208–9.

23. The *New Bedford Republican Standard* posted a notice of auction sale for Samuel Leonard's Candle Works on October 17, 1861. Samuel Leonard & Son and Samuel Leonard Jr., information in Massachusetts, vol. 17, pp. 43, 57, 198, 208; Charles Leonard information in Massachusetts, vol. 17, pp. 182, 250, 208; R. G. Dun & Co. Collection, Baker Library Historical Collections, Harvard Business School.

24. Pease and Hough, *History* (1889), 103, 169–70.

25. New Bedford Cordage Company in Massachusetts, vol. 17, p. 41; William J. Rotch information in Massachusetts, vol. 17, pp. 34, 176; R. G. Dun & Co. Collection, Baker Library Historical Collections, Harvard Business School.

26. Analysis is based on 1855 state census information: *Statistical Information . . . Industry of Massachusetts . . . Year Ending June 1, 1855* (Boston: Office of the Secretary of State, 1855), 87–91.

27. In 1855 Wamsutta's estimated textile production over the previous year stood at $350,000, a figure more than one-half of the value of all other manufacturing businesses not tied to whaling.

28. Ibid.

29. Only males with occupations are included in these figures; see *1859 New Bedford City Directory*. For an informative explanation of using city directories, see Peter R. Knights, *The Plain People of Boston, 1830–1860: A Study in City Growth* (New York, 1971), appendix A, "Using City Directories in Ante-Bellum Urban Historical Research," 127–39. Knights explains sampling bias among directories, noting the "distinct economic bias in directory inclusion" with an approximate cutoff in Boston of $1,000 in assessed real

and personal property. Knights notes similar problems with "racial, economic, areal, and other biases." Quotes on pp. 134, 137.

30. Nathaniel Parker Willis quoted in Pease, *History*, 381–82.

31. Hough, *Wamsutta*, 9, 13, 17, 20. Caroline Ware emphasized the conservative and calculating efforts in the establishment of the Wamsutta Mill; see Caroline Ware, *The Early New England Cotton Manufacture, A Study in Industrial Beginnings* (1928; reprint, New York: Johnson Reprint Corporation, 1966), 107–8. Also see an economic analysis of textile factories touches upon New Bedford's development, Paul F. McGouldrick, *New England Textiles in the Nineteenth Century, Profits and Investment* (Cambridge, MA: Harvard University Press, 1968). Thomas A. McMullin, "Industrialization and Social Change in a Nineteenth-Century Port City: New Bedford, Massachusetts, 1865–1900" (PhD dissertation, University of Wisconsin-Madison, 1976), 14; Pease, ed., *Diary of Samuel Rodman*, 272, 274; Hough, *Wamsutta of New Bedford*, 9, 13. Henry H. Crapo, "The Story of Cotton, and Its Manufacture into Cloth in New Bedford," Paper read at Meeting of the Old Dartmouth Historical Society, November 1937. *Old Dartmouth Historical Sketches No. 67* (n.d.). Thomas Bennett Jr. recalled opposition from business leaders and working people who predicted that the Wamsutta Mills company was "doomed to failure from the start." See "Memorial and Paper of Thomas Bennett, Jr.," Thomas Bennett Jr. Papers, ODHS, 1–2, quoted in McMullin, "Industrialization and Social Change," 16.

32. Hough, *Wamsutta*, 7–17. Also see a succinct overview of Wamsutta's history in Ellis, *History* (1892), 454–61. Also see Stockholders' Statement, June 2, 1847, and Statement of Dividends, 1849–1880; Bennett Papers, ODHS Manuscripts, Mss. Collection 9, subgroup 4, series D, folder 1.

33. Initially, shares sold for $100 each with plans to raise $300,000. Besides Joseph Grinnell's stake of over $12,000, other investors included Gideon Howland and his daughter and partner, Sylvia Ann Howland, whose worth was estimated at $700,000. Abraham Barker, a Quaker merchant with a fortune of $150,000, bought twenty-five shares, as did Joseph C. Delano, worth about the same as Barker. David R. Greene, described as a cabinetmaker turned oil broker with an estate of $200,000, procured fifty shares. Pardon Tillinghast, a "shrewd and industrious" merchant worth $100,000, bought twenty shares. Jonathan Bourne Jr. also bought twenty shares; Ward Parker bought fifty; Thomas Mandell obtained fifty shares from his estate estimated at $350,000. Small stock holdings were parceled out among many with an attitude to "help the thing along." Hough, *Wamsutta*, 19.

34. Ellis, *History* (1892), 456.

35. At the first meeting of stockholders on June 9, 1847, Joseph Grinnell was elected chairman and Thomas Bennett Jr. was named secretary. Of the company's first set of directors, all five would serve at least through 1870 when Thomas Mandell became the first to step down. Lengthy terms of service endured beyond the Civil War; for example, Pardon Tillinghast, David R. Greene, and Joseph C. Delano continued as directors until 1871, 1876, and 1877, respectively, while Joseph Grinnell persisted until 1885. No new directors would be named again until 1868, when George O. Crocker, William J. Rotch, and William W. Crapo were added to the board. Directors between 1847 and 1946 are listed on page 72 in Hough, *Wamsutta*, 21–22.

36. Hough, *Wamsutta*, 25–27.

37. Ibid., 27, 30–32. Also see Bennett Papers, ODHS Manuscripts, Mss. Collection 9, subgroup 4, series D, folder 2, for a Statement of Dividends and 1860 estimate and actual costs of building the Number 3 Mill.

38. See box 21, folder Letters from E. L. Baker, New Bedford, 1851–55; Greenleaf and Hubbard Collection. Baker Library, Harvard Business School. Mss: 761 1850–1860 G814.

39. See Massachusetts, vol. 17, pp. 134, 172, 178, R. G. Dun & Co. Collection, Baker Library Historical Collections, Harvard Business School.

40. See box 21, folder, Letters from Thomas Bennett and A. G. Peirce, New Bedford, 1855–59; Greenleaf and Hubbard Collection. Baker Library, Harvard Business School. Mss: 761 1850–1860 G814.

41. Thomas Bennett Jr. was not entered into the Dun reports until after the Civil War with a salary of $8,000 and a modest estate of $15,000. Andrew G. Peirce began as a clerk at Wamsutta in 1854 and had "little of any means of his own," although he was deemed intelligent, respectable, and honest. For Grinnell, see Massachusetts, vol. 17, pp. 216, 244; for Baker, see Massachusetts, vol. 17, pp. 129, 326, 228; for Peirce, see Massachusetts, vol. 17, p. 131; for Bennett, see Massachusetts, vol. 17, p. 75; R. G. Dun & Co. Collection, Baker Library Historical Collections, Harvard Business School.,

42. Pease and Hough, History (1889), 149–50; Hough, Wamsutta, 35–37. Boston Pilot, October 13, 1860.

43. Hough, Wamsutta, 21–22, 25–27.

44. Of the large body of literature on Irish immigration and Irish communities in Massachusetts and New England, the following published works are most helpful: Kerby A. Miller, Emigrants and Exiles, Ireland and the Irish Exodus to North America (New York: Oxford University Press, 1985); Oscar Handlin, Boston's Immigrants, A Study in Acculturation, rev. and enlarged ed. (Cambridge, MA: Belknap Press of Harvard University Press, 1991); Stephan Thernstrom, Poverty and Progress: Social Mobility in a Nineteenth-Century City (Cambridge, MA: Harvard University Press, 1964; reprint ed., New York, 1978); Brian C. Mitchell, The Paddy Camps: The Irish of Lowell, 1821–1861 (Urbana: University of Illinois Press, 1988); Thomas Dublin, Women at Work, The Transformation of Work and Community in Lowell, Massachusetts, 1826–1860 (New York: Columbia University Press, 1981); Hasia R. Diner, Erin's Daughters in America, Irish Immigrant Women in the Nineteenth Century (Baltimore: Johns Hopkins University Press, 1983).

45. Francis DeWitt, Abstract of the Census of the Commonwealth of Massachusetts, Taken With Reference to Facts Existing on the First Day of June, 1855. With Remarks on the Same. (Boston, 1857), 10, 102. DeWitt, Abstract of the Census [1855], Table 3, 10; Table 3, 102, 234.

46. In 1855 New Bedford was the seventh most populous city in Massachusetts, but it ranked near the bottom of the state's urban areas in its percentage of foreign-born residents, about 15 percent, as 2,875 foreign-born individuals lived in a city of 20,389 people. Population of the United States in 1860; Compiled from the Original Returns of the Eighth Census, Under the Direction of the Secretary of the Interior, By Joseph C. G. Kennedy, Superintendent of Census. (Washington, DC, 1864), xxii, xxxi.

47. Caroline F. Ware, Early New England Cotton Manufacture, 3, 8, 107–11, 117, 199, 203, 209, 228, 232. In Women at Work, Thomas Dublin demonstrated that the Irish community in Lowell grew with textile production after 1845. Irish immigrants faced increased ethnic segregation and isolation, along with discrimination in housing and wages, necessitating the employment of women and children to sustain their households. See Dublin, Women at Work, 140–43, 146–47, 153–56, 160, especially chapter 10, "Housing and Families of Women Operatives," 165–82.

48. Samuel Eliot Morison, The Maritime History of Massachusetts, 1783–1860 (Boston and New York: Houghton Mifflin, 1921; repr., Scituate, MA: Converpage, 2008), 316–19. Frederick Tolles emphasized that the leading New Light Quakers in New Bedford were quite wealthy; in fact, at least eight of them were "among the richest men in the state" of Massachusetts; see Frederick B. Tolles, "The New-Light Quakers of Lynn and New Bedford," New England Quarterly 32 (September 1959): 291–319, 292n3.

49. With a total value of real and personal value of $22.5 million, the "whaling depot" was home to Isaac Howland Jr. & Co. ($900,000); John A. Parker ($816,500); James Arnold ($504,500); Edward Mott Robinson ($465,000); Sylvia Ann Howland ($311,900); William R. Rodman ($378,000); and Edward C. Jones ($224,000). *The New York Times*, August 23, 1853. Davis et al. draw on tax lists from 1855 that include John Avery Parker ($631,700); James Arnold ($544,500); Edward Mott Robinson ($464,600); William Rodman's estate ($462,400); and Sylvia Ann Howland ($342,600). Davis et al., *Leviathan*, 107.

50. Davis, *Leviathan*, chap. 10, "Agents, Captains, and Owners," 381–422; Howland information on p. 399; other material on pp. 411–13.

51. *1859 City Directory*, 37–45. Wealth estimates come from Massachusetts, vol. 17, R. G. Dun & Co. Collection, Baker Library Historical Collections, Harvard Business School.

52. This analysis depends on a database derived from the *1859 City Directory*. Davis et al. noted the presence of business cliques, which they term "discrete family groupings," among leading capitalists; see Davis et al., *Leviathan*, 404; also, chapter 10, "Agents, Captains, and Owners," provides detail about leading capitalists and makes effective use of R. G. Dun credit reports; see 381–482.

53. Peter Temin, "The Industrialization of New England, 1830–1880," in Peter Temin, ed., *Engines of Enterprise: An Economic History of New England* (Cambridge, MA: Harvard University Press, 2000), 145–52; also see Naomi R. Lamoreaux, *Insider Lending: Banks, Personal Connections and Economic Development in Industrial New England* (Cambridge: Cambridge University Press, 1994).

54. For these banks, see *1859 City Directory*, 38–39; Pease and Hough (1889), 233–40; Ellis, *History* (1892), 509–15. Also see Henry H. Crapo, "Banks of Old Dartmouth," reprinted in Pease, *History* (1918), 233–50.

55. *1859 City Directory*, 39–40; Pease and Hough, *History* (1889), 245–48; Ellis, *History* (1892), 516–19; Henry H. Crapo, "Banks of Old Dartmouth," 249–50.

56. Population figures are summarized in many places, including Pease, *History of New Bedford* (1918), 151. Once postbellum textile manufacturing began to grow, the city swelled to over 40,000 people in 1890, more than 62,000 in 1900, and over 96,000 in 1910. By 1915 the state census indicated that New Bedford was home to 109,678 residents.

57. Pease, *History* (1918), 83–189.

58. Ellis, *History* (1892), 302–4; "When Congressman Lincoln spoke he 'enchained' his New Bedford audience," *New Bedford Standard-Times*, September 14, 1980.

59. Grover, *Fugitive's Gibraltar*, 284. Grover's insights about the city's political leaders include an assertion that these abolitionists may have been less eager to accept blacks as social equals, perhaps with "a lingering and almost unconscious belief in the prevailing racial order of things." See Grover, *Fugitive's Gibraltar*, 284–85.

60. See excellent biographical sketch of George Howland Jr. in Ellis, *History*, 2:52–53, and supplementary business information in Massachusetts, vol. 17, pp. 47, 187, R. G. Dun Collection, Baker Library Historical Collections, Harvard Business School

61. "New Bedford Massachusetts," *National Magazine* (September 1845): 330–40, excerpted in Crapo, *Centennial*, (1876), appendix 20, 96–111.

62. *The New Bedford Port Society, A Brief History* (New Bedford, MA: Reynolds-DeWalt Printing, Inc., 1979), 3–4; Zephaniah W. Pease, *Historical Address, One Hundredth Anniversary of the New Bedford Port Society, be held on Sunday, May 18th, at 7:30 P.M., at the Seamen's Bethel, Johnny Cake Hill, New Bedford, Mass.* (New Bedford, MA: New Bedford Port Society and George Reynolds, Printer; reprinted from the *New Bedford Morning Mercury*; 1930).

63. Curtis Dahl, "Who Was Father Mapple?," in *The Seaman's Bethel, and it's chaplains—in fiction and facts* (New Bedford, MA: New Bedford Port Society and Reynolds-DeWalt Printing, Inc., 1979), 13–19.

64. Pease, *One Hundredth Anniversary*, n.p.

65. *Thirty-Seventh Annual Report of the Board of Managers of the New Bedford Port Society, for the Moral Improvement of Seamen*, . . . (New Bedford: Fessenden & Baker, Printers, 1867); Pease, *One Hundredth Anniversary*, n.p.

66. Quoted material from George H. Tripp, "New Bedford Libraries—Then and Now," reprinted from the *New Bedford Standard-Times*, 1934; NBFPL, Special Collections. Also see *Proceedings on the Occasion of Laying the Corner-Stone of the Library Edifice, for the Free Public Library of the City of New Bedford, August 28, 1856* (New Bedford, E. Anthony, Printer to the City, 1856). An extended history of the New Bedford Free Public Library is contained in Crapo, *Centennial*, appendix 22, 114–30; Eleventh Annual Report of the Trustees of the Free Public Library Dated January 3, 1863; NBCD, reel 2, NBFPL.

67. Thomas A. McMullin notes that the Overseers demonstrated the "persistence of older values and institutions." See Thomas A. McMullin, "Overseeing the Poor: Industrialization and Poor Relief in New Bedford, 1865–1900," *Social Science Review* 65 (December 1991): 548–63; Sixth Annual Report of the New Bedford Benevolent Society, dated November 30, 1845, New Bedford Benevolent Society, Records, 1829–93, Massachusetts Historical Society (hereafter cited as MHS).

68. D[aniel] R[icketson], "Charity," New Bedford Mercury, January 29, 1840, in New Bedford Benevolent Society, Records, 1829–93; MHS.

69. See *1859 City Directory*, 49–51; Zephaniah Pease, ed., *History of New Bedford* (New York, 1918), 189–90. Michael Katz has emphasized the continuing ties between public and private relief efforts; see particularly Katz, *Shadow of the Poorhouse*, ix–xi, 11, 46; and Katz, *Poverty and Policy*, 239–41. McMullin makes the connection between the overseers system and generous payments; see McMullin, "Overseeing the Poor," 552.

70. Report of the Overseers of the Poor, For the Year Ending February 29, 1860, New Bedford City Documents (hereafter cited as NBCD), reel 2.

71. Report of the Overseers of the Poor, for the Year Ending February 29, 1860, NBCD, reel 2.

72. "New Bedford, Massachusetts," *National Magazine* (September 1845), 330–40, excerpted in Crapo, *Centennial* (1876), appendix 20, 96–111.

73. *1859 City Directory*, 46. See also "New Bedford Churches," typescript list, NBFPL Special Collections. More detailed histories of each church are found in Ellis (1892), Pease and Hough (1889), and previous versions of *History of New Bedford Churches* (1854 and 1869).

74. Grover, *Fugitive's Gibraltar*, 103–4. *1859 City Directory* refers to two meetings of Friends and dates the separation to 1847; see p. 46.

75. Ricketson, *History*, 41–42.

76. *1859 City Directory*, 18–19.

77. The New Bedford Port Society, *The New Bedford Port Society, A Brief History* (New Bedford, MA: Reynolds-DeWalt Printing, Inc., 1979), 3. This concept of a "divided" city can be traced back to Zephaniah Pease, ed., *Diary of Samuel Rodman*, 37–38, as noted by Grover, *Fugitive's Gibraltar*, 28–29. Pease addressed similar dynamics in *Historical Address, One Hundredth Anniversary of the New Bedford Port Society, be held on Sunday, May 18th, at 7:30 P.M., at the Seamen's Bethel, Johnny Cake Hill, New Bedford, Mass.* (New Bedford, MA: New Bedford Port Society and George Reynolds, Printer; reprinted from the *New Bedford Morning Mercury*; 1930), 1.

78. Ellis, *History* (1892), 709–10; City Marshal's Reports for 1858 and 1859, NBCD, reel 2. Helpful secondary accounts include Erik H. Monkkonen, *Police in Urban American, 1860–1920* (New York: Cambridge University Press, 2004); David Grimsted, *American Mobbing, 1828–1861: Toward Civil War* (New York: Oxford University Press, 2003);

Thomas P. Slaughter, *Bloody Dawn: The Christiana Riot and Racial Violence in the Antebellum North* (New York: Oxford University Press, 1994).

79. Grover details several of these cases in Grover, *Fugitive's Gibraltar*, 274–75. Grover also provides an insightful account of the "Ark riots" of 1826 and 1829; see pp. 106–12.

80. Grover, *Fugitive's Gibraltar*, 274–75. Ellis, *History*, 307–8. Also see Pease, *History* (1918), 192–93.

81. Ellis, *History*, 309–11.

82. Ibid., 305–7; Grover, *Fugitive's Gibraltar*, 232; Potter, *First Congregational Society of New Bedford*, 69.

83. Ellis provides extensive details about the fire's progress and destruction, including the names of property owners and their losses. Ellis, *History*, 311–14. Also see "The Great Fire at New Bedford," *New York Times*, August 27, 1859, reprinted from the *New Bedford Standard*.

2. "The Nearest Approach to Freedom and Equality": African Americans in Antebellum New Bedford

1. Frederick Douglass, *Life and Times of Frederick Douglass, Written by Himself* (rev. ed., 1892; repr., New York, 1962), 205, 208.

2. Narratives connected with New Bedford included Henry "Box" Brown, Leonard Black, William Grimes, Harriet Jacobs, John S. Jacobs, Thomas H. Jones, Edmund Kelley, George Teamoh, and John W. Thompson. Kathryn Grover, *The Fugitive's Gibraltar: Escaping Slaves and Abolitionism in New Bedford Massachusetts* (Amherst: University of Massachusetts Press, 2001), 6. Also see Kathryn Grover, *Behind the Mansions: The Political, Economic, and Social Life of a New Bedford Neighborhood* (2006), available online from the New Bedford Whaling National Historic Park as *Whaling, Integration, and Abolitionism in a New Bedford Neighborhood, 1800–1865,* http://www.nps.gov/nebe/historyculture/places.htm.

3. Ricketson, *The History of New Bedford* (New Bedford, 1858), 252.

4. James Oliver Horton and Lois E. Horton, *Black Bostonians, Family Life and Community Struggle in the Antebellum North* (New York: Holmes & Meier Publishers, 1979); quoted in James Oliver Horton and Lois E. Horton, *In Hope of Liberty: Culture, Community and Protest Among Northern Free Blacks, 1700–1860* (New York: Oxford University Press, 1997), xi. See also Leon F. Litwack's pioneering survey, *North of Slavery: The Negro in the Free States, 1790–1860* (Chicago: University of Chicago Press, 1961); David M. Katzman, *Before the Ghetto: Black Detroit in the Nineteenth Century* (Urbana: University of Illinois Press, 1973); Leonard P. Curry, *The Free Black in Urban America 1800–1850, The Shadow of the Dream* (Chicago: University of Chicago Press, 1981); Gary B. Nash, *Forging Freedom: The Formation of Philadelphia's Black Community, 1720–1840* (Cambridge, MA: Harvard University Press, 1988); George A. Levesque, *Black Boston: African American Life and Culture in Urban America, 1750–1860* (New York and London: Routledge, 1994). An insightful recent work focuses on Worcester's black community that numbered 272 in 1860, about 1 percent of the city's total population of 25,000. See Janette Thomas Greenwood, *First Fruits of Freedom: The Migration of Former Slaves and Their Search for Equality in Worcester, Massachusetts, 1862–1900* (Chapel Hill: University of North Carolina Press), 2009.

5. Patrick Rael, *Black Identity & Black Protest in the Antebellum North* (Chapel Hill and London: University of North Carolina Press, 2002), 285.

6. Grover, *Fugitive's Gibraltar*, 56, 297n45.

7. Leonard P. Curry compiled comparative data for fifteen cities in 1850, including nine northern ones, with their percentage of black population: Albany (1.69 percent);

Boston (1.46 percent) Brooklyn (2.5 percent); Buffalo (1.6 percent); Cincinnati (2.8 percent); New York City (2.68 percent); Philadelphia (8.85 percent); Pittsburgh (4.2 percent); and Providence (3.61 percent). Curry, *Free Black*, Table A-2 in appendix A, 246. For New Bedford's white and free black populations in 1850, see *Seventh Census of the United States, 1850* (Washington, DC, 1853), Table 2, 50; for Massachusetts, see ibid., Table 1, ix; for proportion of blacks to total population, see ibid., Table 5, 53.

8. Grover, *Fugitive's Gibraltar*, 1 and *passim*.

9. Ward lines for 1859 that correspond to the 1860 Census are described in *The New Bedford Directory, Containing the City Register and a General Directory of the Citizens* (New Bedford 1859), 26.

10. Grover, *Fugitive's Gibraltar*, 272–74.

11. Ibid., 67–68, 72–73, 75–77, 84–85, 92.

12. Grover suggests that more black mariners may have signed on for voyages in the aftermath of the Fugitive Slave Law of 1850 prompting an increase in the number and percentage of "no proofs" on crew lists. Grover, *Fugitives' Gibraltar*, 56–58.

13. Paul Cuffe and his descendants offer the best evidence on these patterns. Writing in 1858, Daniel Ricketson called Cuffe "a man of great worth" who proved that black men could achieve much despite "many great disadvantages" faced by African Americans. See Ricketson, *History*, 252–64. Also see Martha S. Putney, *Black Sailors: Afro-American Merchant Seamen and Whalemen Prior to the Civil War* (Greenwood, CT: Greenwood Press, 1987); Rodney Carlisle, "Black-Owned Shipping Before Marcus Garvey," *American Neptune* 35 (July 1975): 197–206. Carlisle quotes at length from Alexander Crummell's positive recollections of New Bedford in the early 1840s. "It is now some twenty years since I visited that important seaport [of New Bedford]," wrote Crummell in 1862, ". . . and I retain still a vivid remembrance of the signs of industry and thrift among [black residents], of the evidences of their unusual wealth, and of their large interest in shipping. . . . Among those I remember well some youthful descendants of Paul Cuffee." Quoted in ibid., 201.

14. W. Jeffrey Bolster, "'To Feel like a Man': Black Seamen in the Northern States, 1800–1860," *Journal of American History* 76 (March 1990): 1173–99.

15. [D. H. Strother], "New Bedford," *Harper's New Monthly Magazine* 21 (June 1860): 8–9.

16. James B. Congdon, "Impact Questionnaire [1863]," prepared for the New England Friends' Freedmens' Aid Society, in James B. Congdon Papers, Special Collections, NBFPL. I wish to thank Paul Cyr, Curator of Special Collections, for providing me with a transcript of Congdon's answers.

17. Hohman emphasized the increasingly exploitative aspects of the whaling enterprise as owners and agents became increasingly differentiated from workers as the "older conditions of simplicity and intimacy were displaced by specialization of function, intricacies of structure, and problems of organization." Hohman suggests that greedy outfitters favored "green hands" over experienced mariners because the former could be paid less and exploited more easily. See Elmo P. Hohman, *The American Whaleman* (New York: Longmans & Green, 1928), 70–71, 224, 277–78. More recent work by Lance Davis et al. confirm this view of declining crew quality before the Civil War. "The evidence, both quantitative and qualitative, conclusively demonstrates that, by a traditional definition, the quality of whaling crews deteriorated over at least two decades preceding the Civil War. Qualitative sources suggest that the decline was the result of a conscious decision by agents, aimed at reducing labor turnover and thus increasing profits." See Lance E. Davis, Robert E. Gallman, and Karin Gleiter, *In Pursuit of Leviathan, Technology, Institutions, and Profits in American Whaling, 1816–1906* (Chicago and London: University of Chicago Press, 1997), 195.

18. Putney, *Black Sailors*, 15. According to Putney's figures, nineteen black boatsteerers sailed out of New Bedford between 1841 and 1850, while only six did so in the following decade, suggesting a decline in opportunities for skilled black whalemen. Putney notes that of 3,189 identifiable black men who sailed out of New Bedford between 1803 and 1860, at least 643 of them made repeat voyages. See pp. 152, 45–46.

19. 1860 Census database for Wards 2, 3, 4.

20. Ibid.

21. Data from the 1855 state census shows that 65.8 percent of New Bedford's skilled workers of color were from southern states. The city's labor market for skilled trades workers may have followed the pattern of seamen in which native-born blacks were largely excluded in the 1850s. Grover, *Fugitive's Gibraltar*, 268–69. As for skilled black workers who toiled at unskilled pursuits, Grover mentions several New Bedford men: butcher William Ferguson who became a laborer and city crier; blacksmith John Taseo sold bread on the streets; caulker Frederick Douglass did a variety of unskilled jobs. She writes: "In statistical terms these evidences of occupational discrimination do not surface. Yet it may be true that on the whole it was hard for a family of color to make ends meet in New Bedford no matter what sorts of jobs its breadwinners occupied." See Grover, *Fugitive's Gibraltar*, 269.

22. George Teamoh's autobiography and photograph are excerpted in Grover, *Fugitive's Gibraltar*, 234–37.

23. Grover, *Fugitive's Gibraltar*, 266. Based on her extensive research, Grover concludes: "The percentage of the black workforce that worked in unskilled jobs was 71.2 in 1836, 63.9 in 1845, 68.6 in 1850, 70.2 in 1855 (perhaps reflecting an infusion of fugitive slaves), and 54.4 in 1856." See ibid., 330–31n13. She adapted the occupational classification of Peter Knights, *The Plain People of Boston, 1830–1860: A Study in City Growth* (New York: Oxford University Press, 1971), 149–56, appendix E. Grover also points to Leonard Curry's comprehensive work, *Free Blacks in Urban America*, 260–62, Tables B-1, B-2, B-9. The Hortons provide a solid survey of antebellum northern black occupations *In Hope of Liberty*, 110–24, and also in their examination of *Black Bostonians*.

24. New Bedford's *Whaleman's Shipping List* of May 31, 1853 reported that the whaler *Ohio* captured twenty-one bowhead whales with only eight harpoons, all toggle-irons. Another local blacksmith, James Durfee, made some thirteen thousand toggle-irons between 1848 and 1868. Sidney Kaplan, "Lewis Temple and the Hunting of the Whale," *New England Quarterly* 26, no. 1 (March 1853): 78–88. Also see Emil F. Guba, "Lewis Temple and Contemporaries, New Bedford Blacksmith, Inventor of the Toggle Iron Headed Harpoon," typescript unpublished manuscript, "Lewis Temple Folder," NBFPL. Guba asserts that Temple and Frederick Douglass were "friendly contemporaries, and they worshipped in the church on William St., today the Frederick Douglass African M. E. Church, Zion." Thomas G. Lytle, *Harpoons and Other Whale Craft* (New Bedford: Old Dartmouth Historical Society, 1984) illustrates the Temple story. Megan Secatore, "City paying a debt to inventor," *New Bedford Standard-Times*, July 5, 1987. Lisa Borders, "Statue is tribute to inventor—and sculptor," *New Bedford Standard-Times*, July 6, 1987. Also: John H. Ackerman, "Temple changed whalers' fortunes," *Chowder* (*New Bedford Standard-Times* magazine), February 6, 1983; Robert C. Hayden Jr., *Eight Black Inventors*, has a chapter on Temple; Jane Waters, *New Bedford's Black Heritage Trail* (1976), 20–23.

25. Kaplan, "Lewis Temple," 80–86.

26. Today, the city of New Bedford honors Temple with a sculpture in front of the New Bedford Free Public Library. Receipt located in "Lewis Temple Folder," NBFPL; Kaplan, "Lewis Temple," 86–88; Guba, "Lewis Temple."

27. Grover discounts the arrival of Irish immigrants as a factor in shaping the labor force; Grover, *Fugitive's Gibraltar*, 267–68.

28. This paragraph and succeeding materials are based on analysis of the 1860 Census database.

29. 1860 census sample for Wards 2, 3, 4.

30. Among these skilled black men, the wealthiest was Bela C. Perry, who claimed $2,000 in real estate and $5,000 in personal property, followed by William Berry ($2,000 and $2,000); Joseph M. Scott ($1,000 and $200); and James Vassals ($1,000 in real estate). Per capita figures for the group of black men is skewed heavily by the inclusion here of soap manufacturer Zenos Whitmore, a mulatto man of sixty-one years of age credited with over $9,000 in real estate and $6,000 in personal property.

31. All married women were subject to prevailing laws of coverture that denied them rights of property ownership. Eighty-three black women, or 96.5 percent of this sample, owned nothing.

32. Curry, *Free Blacks*.

33. See Kusmer's chapter, "Almost Equal: Black Cleveland before 1870," which shows some economic opportunities for black citizens; Kenneth Kusmer, *A Ghetto Takes Shape: Black Cleveland, 1870–1930* (Urbana: University of Illinois Press, 1976).

34. See especially, Theodore Hershberg, Alan N. Burstein, Eugene P. Ericksen, Stephanie W. Greenberg, and William L. Yancey, "A Tale of Three Cities: Blacks, Immigrants, and Opportunity in Philadelphia, 1850–1880, 1930, 1970," and Theodore Hershberg, "Free Blacks in Antebellum Philadelphia: A Study of Ex-Slaves, Freeborn and Socioeconomic Decline," in *Philadelphia, Work, Space, Family, and Group Experience in the Nineteenth Century: Essays Toward an Interdisciplinary History of the City*, ed. Hershberg (New York: Oxford University Press, 1981).

35. Clyde Griffen and Sally Griffen, *Natives and Newcomers: The Ordering of Opportunity in Mid–Nineteenth-Century Poughkeepsie* (Cambridge: Cambridge University Press, 1978). In her study of blacks in Boston, Elizabeth Pleck contended that "Southern" blacks were "insulated" from some of the worst effects of poverty because of their religion, kin structures, and "strong drive for material success." Elizabeth H. Pleck, *Black Migration and Poverty, Boston, 1865–1900* (New York: Academic Press, 1979).

36. Douglass, *Life and Times of Frederick Douglass*, 245.

37. Frederick Cooper, "Elevating the Race: The Social Thought of Black Leaders, 1827–50," *American Quarterly* 24 (December 1972): 604–25; reprinted in Patrick Rael, ed. *African-American Activism before the Civil War, The Freedom Struggle in the Antebellum North* (London: Routledge, 2008), chap. 3; James B. Stewart, *Holy Warriors, The Abolitionists and American Slavery* (New York: Hill and Wang, 1976), 134–35.

38. Seeking a "wider sphere of usefulness," Douglass later "cut loose from the church" in protest of Christian churches' ties with slavery. See William S. McFeely, *Frederick Douglass* (New York: W. W. Norton, 1991), 81–85. McFeely relies upon William L. Andrews, "Frederick Douglass, Preacher," *American Literature* 54 (December 1982): 592–97.

39. See *History of the New Bedford Churches* (1854), 68–69; Jesse Fillmore Kelley and Adam Mackie, *History of the Churches of New Bedford, To which are added Notices of Various Other Moral and Religious Organizations. Together with short memoirs of Rev. Messrs. Wheelock Craig, John Girdwood, Timothy Stowe, Daniel Webb, and Rev. Messrs. Henniss and Tallon, of St. Mary's Church.* (New Bedford, 1869), 118; Leonard B. Ellis, History of New Bedford (Syracuse, NY: Mason, 1892), 595–96; Charles Cook, *A Brief Account of the African Christian Church in New Bedford, Being the First of the Christian Denomination in the United States Formed by People of Colour* (New Bedford: Benjamin T. Congdon, Printer, 1834), 3, 4–7, 9–10. See also Paul Cyr, "The Black Community in New Bedford, Massachusetts," (unpublished ms., 1988), 7–8; Robert J. Barcellos, "Black

congregations have rich history," *New Bedford Sunday Standard-Times*, February 22, 1987.

40. Cook, *Brief Account*, 10–12; *History of New Bedford Churches* (1854), 68–69; Kelley and Mackie, *Churches of New Bedford*, 118.

41. For the founders of the Second Baptist Church, see *History of New Bedford Churches* (1854), 66–67. In their 1869 account, Kelley and Mackie update the story: "We understand that the church is without a settled pastor at the present time. The church now reports a membership of about 120. The Sunday School, under the charge of Mr. J. D. Hayden, numbers 50. . . . The society, although not in as prosperous condition as formerly, is free from debt, and make some progress towards regaining its former position." See Kelley and Mackie, *New Bedford Churches*, 68–69.

42. The (white) First Baptist Church of New Bedford professed that its school had an average attendance of 156 students taught by 42 teachers who could draw upon 600 volumes in the library. In contrast, the all-black Second Baptist Sabbath School averaged 60 students in attendance, 10 teachers, and no library. The First Baptist school raised over $171 for the Foreign and Home Mission while the all-black Sabbath School donated nothing. *Minutes of the Twenty-Second Anniversary of the Taunton Baptist Association, held with the First Baptist Church in New-Bedford, on Wednesday and Thursday, Sept. 9 and 10, 1857* (New Bedford, 1857), 4, 6, 17, 20–24.

43. Kelley and Mackie, *New Bedford Churches*, 70–71; see also Ellis, *History of New Bedford*, 564. William Jackson, a navy veteran, was appointed Chaplain of the Fifty-Fifth Massachusetts Colored Infantry on July 14, 1863. Upon returning to New Bedford in January 1864 with a medical discharge, Jackson resumed his pastorate of the Salem Baptist Church. By 1869 Jackson's church stood as "one of the most flourishing among the colored churches in the city; it numbers upwards of 200 members, and is entirely free from debt," according to Kelley and Mackie, *New Bedford Churches*, 71. The Salem and Second Baptist Churches reconciled in April 1895 when they incorporated as the Union Baptist Church and their cooperation led to a new church building dedicated in 1900. See "Installation of Pastor Today Marks New Milestone in Union Baptist Church History," *New Bedford Standard-Times*, June 15, 1952. Information on the Reverend Jackson is found in Keith Wilson, *Campfires of Freedom: The Camp Life of Soldiers During the Civil War* (Kent, OH: Kent State University Press, 2002).

44. See Records of the Salem Baptist Church, Old Dartmouth Historical Society Collections; "Acts of Incorporation for New Bedford Churches," microfilm, Special Collections, NBFPL; Kelley and Mackie, *New Bedford Churches*, 71; and Ellis, *History of New Bedford*, 564.

45. *Report of the Nineteenth Anniversary of the American Baptist Missionary Convention, held in the Meeting-House of the First Baptist Church, Newburgh, N. Y., Friday, August 19, 1859* (New Bedford, 1859), 14–17. For information on women's groups and convention meetings, see *Report of the Twenty-Fifth Anniversary of the American Baptist Missionary Convention, Held in the Meeting House of the First Colored Baptist Church, Alexandria, Va., From Friday, August 18th, to Sunday, August 27th, 1865* (New Bedford, 1865), 31–33.

46. For local church efforts, see *History of New Bedford Churches* (1854); Kelly and Mackie, *Churches of New Bedford*, 99–100; Barcellos, "Black congregations," *New Bedford Standard-Times*, February 22, 1987. On the national level, black Methodists created the AME denomination in April 1816, and soon the national movement created regional associations, including one in New England. For a concise history of black Methodism, see C. Eric Lincoln and Lawrence H. Mamiya, *The Black Church in the African-American Experience* (Durham, NC: Duke University Press, 1990), chap. 3, "The Black Methodists: The Institutionalization of Black Religious Independence," 47–75. Bishop Daniel A. Payne wrote a history of his denomination, *History of the African Methodist Episcopal*

Church (Nashville, TN, 1891; repr., New York: Ayer Company, 1969). For more recent accounts, see Howard D. Gregg, *History of the African Methodist Episcopal Church* (Nashville, TN: The African Methodist Episcopal Church, 1980), and Clarence E. Walker, *A Rock in a Weary Land: The African Methodist Episcopal Church During the Civil War and Reconstruction* (Baton Rouge: Louisiana State University Press, 1982).

47. Payne quoted in *Minutes of the New England Annual Conference, of the African Methodist Episcopal Church, held in the City of New Bedford, Mass. from June 10th to the 21st, 1852.* (New Bedford, 1852), 407, 13–14. New Bedford membership information in ibid., 7–12. Extant records of the New England AME Annual Conference found at the New Bedford Free Public Library cover the years of 1852, 1854, 1858, 1859, 1860, 1861, 1862, 1866, and 1868, all of them printed in New Bedford. The Conference met in New Bedford several times after the initial meeting, including convocations in 1853 and 1862. See *Minutes of the New England Annual Conference, of the African Methodist Episcopal Church, Held in the City of Providence, R. I., from June 17th to the 26th, 1854* (New Bedford, 1854); *Minutes of the Sixth Annual Conference of the New England District of the African Methodist Episcopal Church, in America, held in Bethel Church, Newport, R. I. From June 4th to June 9th, 1858* (New Bedford, 1858); *Minutes of the New England Annual Conference of the African Methodist Episcopal Church in America, held in Bethel Church, Centre Street, Boston, From June 3d to June 13th, 1859* (New Bedford, 1859); *Minutes of the New England Annual Conference of the African Methodist Episcopal Church in America, held in Bethel Church, Sperry Street, New Haven, Conn., From June 29th to July 9th, 1860* (New Bedford, 1860); *Minutes of the New England Annual Conference of the African Methodist Episcopal Church in America, held in Bethel Church, Meeting Street, Providence, R. I., From June 13th to June 20th, 1861* (New Bedford, 1861); *Minutes of the New England Annual Conference of the African Methodist Episcopal Church in America, Held in Bethel Church, Kempton Street, New Bedford, Mass., From May 31st to June 9th, 1862* (New Bedford, 1862); *Minutes of the New England Annual Conference of the African Methodist Episcopal Church in America, Held in Kempton Street, New Bedford, Mass., From June 15th to June 21st, 1866* (New Bedford, 1866); *Minutes of the New England Annual Conference of the African Methodist Episcopal Church in America, Held in Bethel Church, Spruce Street, Newport, R. I., From July 1st to July 7th [1868]* (New Bedford, 1868).

48. New Bedford's AME donations in 1860 were nearly double the amount provided by second-place Boston, and New Bedford's black women donated more money for traveling preachers than other women's groups. In the realm of religious education, the Bethel Church held the largest number of students (seventy-five), teachers (ten), and library volumes. See *Minutes of the New England Annual Conference . . . 1860*, 14. Membership information for 1860s is drawn from extant records of the New England Annual Conference of the African Methodist Episcopal Church; see above for full citations.

49. Kelley and Mackie, *Churches of New Bedford*, 100; Robert Barcellos, "Bethel AME Church marks 130th anniversary," *New Bedford Sunday Standard-Times*, October 29, 1972.

50. For names of the founding members of the AMEZ church in New Bedford, see *History of New Bedford Churches* (1854), n.p., and Kelley and Mackie, *History of New Bedford Churches*, 101. For an overview of this denomination, see William J. Walls, *The African Methodist Episcopal Zion Church: Reality of the Black Church* (Charlotte, NC: A. M. E. Zion Publishing House, 1974).

51. Resolutions dated January 23, 1859, located in "Acts of Incorporation of New Bedford Churches," microfilm, NBFPL. See Robert Barcellos, "Black congregations," *New Bedford Sunday Standard-Times*, February 22, 1987.

52. Grover, *Fugitive's Gibraltar*, 121–24. For information about the Quakers from the 1820s through the 1850s, see Ricketson, *History*, 41–42, 86–87, 229–30, 334; *History of the New Bedford Churches* (New Bedford, 1854), 73–74; Kelley and Mackie, *New Bedford*

Churches); Mary Jane Howland Taber, "Friends Here and Hereaway," *Old Dartmouth Historical Society Sketches, No. 8* (New Bedford, n.d.), 16. For an earlier period, see Alice Sue Friday, "The Quaker Origins of New Bedford, 1765–1815" (PhD dissertation, Boston University, 1991).

53. Grover, *Fugitive's Gibraltar*, 132–35.

54. Earl F. Mulderink III, "'The Whole Town Is Ringing with It': Slave Kidnapping Charges against Nathan Johnson of New Bedford, Massachusetts, 1839," *New England Quarterly* 61, no. 3 (September 1988): 341–57.

55. Samuel Rodman, for example, recorded in his diary on December 30, 1839, that he had attended an antislavery event where the audience contained a "considerable portion" of "colored people." Zephaniah W. Pease, ed., *The Diary of Samuel Rodman, A New Bedford Chronicle of Thirty-Seven Years, 1821–1859* (New Bedford: Reynolds Printing Company, 1928), 200. For Liberty Hall, see William L. Potter, *First Congregational Society in New Bedford, Massachusetts: Its History as Illustrative of Ecclesiastical Evolution* (New Bedford: Printed for the Society, 1889), 69; Pease, *History*, 150.

56. Frederick Douglass to William Lloyd Garrison, *Liberator*, November 18, 1842.

57. Diary of Charles W. Morgan, October 1 and October 4, 1850, quoted in *New Bedford and Old Dartmouth: A Bicentennial Exhibition of the Old Dartmouth Historical Society at the Whaling Museum in New Bedford, December 4, 1975—April 18, 1976* (New Bedford: Old Dartmouth Historical Society, 1975), 139.

58. Ricketson, *History*, 253.

59. As Grover explains, the letter was first published in the Boston *Chronotype* (n.d.) and reprinted as "A City of Refuge," *New Bedford Republican Standard*, November 1, 1850. Grover, *Fugitive's Gibraltar*, 221, 223–26.

60. Grover, *Fugitive's Gibraltar*, 255–56.

61. Pease, ed., *Diary of Samuel Rodman*, 330.

62. Ricketson, *History*, 23–24, 252–53, 342–45.

63. Grover, *Fugitive's Gibraltar*, 247–48.

64. J. R. Kerr-Ritchie, "Rehearsal for War: Black Militias in the Atlantic World," Chapter 6 in *Rites of August First, Emancipation Day in the Black Atlantic World* (Baton Rouge: Louisiana State University Press, 2007), 164–92. This chapter was published previously under the same title in *Slavery and Abolition* 26, no. 1 (April 2005): 1–33. Grover addresses the black militias on 247–48.

65. Grover, *Fugitive's Gibraltar*, 230–31. See also Mitchell Alan Kachun, *Festivals of Freedom: Memory and Meaning in African American Emancipation Celebrations, 1808–1915* (Amherst: University of Massachusetts Press, 2003); William H. Wiggins, *O Freedom! Afro-American Emancipation Celebration* (Knoxville: University of Tennessee Press, 1987); William B. Gravely, "The Dialectic of Double-Consciousness in Black American Freedom Celebrations, 1808–1863," *Journal of Negro History* 67, no. 4 (Winter 1982): 302–17.

66. Howard H. Bell, ed., *Minutes of the Proceedings of the National Negro Conventions, 1830–1865* (New York: Ayer Company, 1969) and Bell, ed., *A Survey of the Negro Convention Movement, 1830–1861* (New York: Ayer Company, 1970). See also "Introduction to the Black State Conventions," in Philip S. Foner and George E. Walker, *Proceedings of the Black State Conventions, 1840–1865*, vol. 1, *New York, Pennsylvania, Indiana, Michigan, Ohio* (Philadelphia, PA: Temple University Press, 1979), xi–xx.

67. New Bedford's convention leaders included Vice-Presidents Solomon Peneton, William Berry, and Anthony T. Jordain, along with Secretaries Bela C. Perry and Anthony T. Jordain, Jr. "Convention of the Colored Citizens of Massachusetts, August 1, 1858," in Philip S. Foner and George E. Walker, *Proceedings of the Black State Conventions, 1840–1865. Vol. 2, New Jersey, Connecticut, Maryland, Illinois, Massachusetts,*

California, New England, Kansas, Louisiana, Virginia, Missouri, South Carolina (Philadelphia, PA: Temple University Press, 1980).

68. Foner and Walker, *Proceedings,* 2:96–107.

69. Mitch Kachun, "From Forgotten Founder to Indispensable Icon, Crispus Attucks, Black Citizenship, and Collective Memory, 1770–1865," *Journal of the Early Republic* 29 (Summer 2009): 249–86.

70. Foner and Walker, *Proceedings,* 2:99–100.

71. As an indication of the solicitous treatment of blacks by New Bedford's residents and elected officials, the convention's final resolution thanked the city's men and women for their "courtesy and hospitality so generously extended to us during our Convention sojourn in their beautiful Garden City." Foner and Walker, *Proceedings,* 2:100–5.

72. Grover, *Fugitive's Gibraltar,* 261–62; *Boston Pilot,* August 11, 1860.

73. Kathryn Grover provides a detailed overview of the public battle in the 1840s over the New Bedford Lyceum's segregated policies that drew in such noted speakers as Wendell Phillips, Charles Sumner, and Ralph Waldo Emerson. "Aired extensively in local, state, and antislavery newspapers, the Lyceum issue crowned the controversy over segregation in New Bedford and sullied the town's reputation as a haven of racial tolerance," Grover wrote. Grover, *Fugitive's Gibraltar,* 176–80.

74. *New York Times,* April 12, 1861.

75. Joseph Ricketson to Deborah Weston, April 11, 1861, BPL, Rare Books, Ms. A.9.2. vol. 30, no. 62.

3. "Suppression of an Unholy Rebellion": Wartime Mobilization on the Home Front

1. William Schouler, *A History of Massachusetts in the Civil War, vol. 1,* Civil and Military History of Massachusetts in the Rebellion (Boston: E. P. Dutton & Co., Publishers, 1868), 44, 2–4, 12–16, 20–21.

2. Howland to Capt. James Stewart of January 18, 1861; Matthew Howland letter book, Baker Library Historical Collections, Harvard Business School.

3. John H. Clifford's records include "an unpublished chapter of war history," a memorandum prepared circa 1894 by Stephen H. Phillips, who had been subordinate to John H. Clifford, senior counsel for Massachusetts. See Edwin Stanton to John H. Clifford, February 11, 1861; Clifford Papers, MHS.

4. *New Bedford Daily Evening Standard* (hereafter cited as *NBDES*), April 12, 1861; *NBDES,* April 13, 1861. Also see *NBDES* for April 15–19, 1861. A full roster of the New Bedford City Guards was printed in the *NBDES,* April 19, 1861.

5. *NBDES,* April 18, 1861; Schouler, 1:66–67.

6. See *NBDES,* 18 April 1861 and April 25, 1861. Also, see Report of the Committee on Home and Coast Guard Dated January 3, 1862, New Bedford City Documents (hereafter cited as NBCD), reel 2, New Bedford Free Public Library Special Collections. For a very succinct chronology of New Bedford during the war, see "New Bedford Responds to the Civil War," in William Schouler, *A History of Massachusetts in the Civil War, vol. 2, Towns and Cities* (Boston: Published by the Author, 1871). Zephaniah Pease, *History of New Bedford* (1918) offers a chapter on "The Civil War Period," 195–202, as does Leonard Bolles Ellis, *History of New Bedford* (1892).

7. Ellis, *History* (1892), chap. 11, 158–72.

8. Kathryn Grover, *The Fugitive's Gibraltar: Escaping Slaves and Abolitionism in New Bedford Massachusetts* (Amherst: University of Massachusetts Press, 2001), 10, 102–4, 124.

9. Joseph Ricketson to Deborah Weston, April 28, 1861, Weston Papers, BPL, Rare Books, Ms. A.9.2 vol. 30, no. 65. Davenport Diary, ODHS, Mss. Collection 64, series D, box 13, subseries. Also see Schouler, 1:565.

10. George W. Nason, *History and Complete Roster of the Massachusetts Regiments, Minute Men of '61 who responded to the First Call of President Abraham Lincoln, April 15, 1861, to defend the Flag and Constitution of the United States, Together with Photographs and Biographical Sketches of Minute Men of Massachusetts* (Boston: Smith & McCance, 1910). See especially A. S. Cushman's summary, "Company L, Third Massachusetts Regiment, Minute Men of '61 (New Bedford Guards)," 28–29. Clifford's speech is quoted in Schouler, 1:66–67.

11. Other officers from New Bedford included Surgeon Alexander R. Holmes, Assistant Surgeon Johnson Clark, Adjutant Austin S. Cushman, Sergeant Major Alberto C. Maggi, and Quarter Master Sergeant Frederick S. Gifford. Nason, *Minute Men of '61*, 13–15; Cushman, "Company L," 29; Ellis, *History*, 319.

12. Nason, *Minute Men of '61*, 327; Horton's "The Vanguard Volunteers," 331.

13. Address of Isaac C. Taber, Mayor, January 6, 1862; NBCD, reel 2; Schouler, 2:144.

14. James W. Geary, *We Need Men: The Union Draft in the Civil War* (DeKalb: Northern Illinois University Press, 1991), 46–47. See Report by Treasurer James B. Congdon in letter dated July 30, 1865, to Hon. Tappan Wentworth, Chair, Joint Special Committee upon the subject of Taxation and the Finances. Congdon Papers, NBFPL, folder 17. See also summary of war's costs in Zephaniah W. Pease and George W. Hough, *New Bedford, Massachusetts: Its History, Industries, Institutions, and Attractions*, ed. by William L. Sayer (New Bedford, 1889), 23–25.

15. Emily J. Harris, "Sons and Soldiers: Deerfield, Massachusetts and the Civil War," *Civil War History* 30 (June 1984): 157–71. For a detailed study of recruitment and bounties, see Eugene Converse Murdock, *Patriotism Limited, 1862–1865: The Civil War Draft and the Bounty System* (Kent, OH: Kent State University Press, 1967).

16. Address of George Howland Jr., Mayor, January 5, 1863, NBCD, reel 2. For an explanation of the state's generous aid to families of volunteers, see Schouler, 1:186, 316–18.

17. New Bedford, Mass., Treasurer, Account of Bounties Paid to Enlistees in Massachusetts Regiments, New Bedford, 1862–63; BPL, Rare Books, Ms. Am. 2383 (1–2).

18. Geary, *We Need Men*, xiii.

19. Michael H. Frisch, *Town into City: Springfield, Massachusetts, and the Meaning of Community, 1840–1880* (Cambridge, MA: Harvard University Press, 1972), quote on p. 60; see pp. 60–71 for detailed account.

20. Register showing Debits and Credits for Enrollment Districts, First District, New Bedford, Massachusetts, Entry 177, RG 110; National Archives. The totals are not consistent. The ledger records a total of 7,956, while my calculations are 8,763. More information specific to New Bedford is found in the Register of Quotas and Enlistments Credited to Towns, 1864–65, Entry 805, p. 418. According to these records, New Bedford gained a credit of 1,276 men for naval enlistments in August 1864, while only 28 men were drafted in August and September 1864. Someone added figures in pencil that appear to be the city's "surplus" of 1,104 men.

21. Hatch reported in May 1864 that "The Board of Enrollment still continues the examination of those who when drafted (July 1863) were absent at sea, but are now returning home. Conscripts of draft of May 1864 are daily reporting and being examined. Of the number reported thus far, about one half have been held to service." Trimonthly Reports of Business and General Transactions of District Provost Marshal Offices, 1863–65, First District, Massachusetts; Entry 63, RG 110, Records of the Provost Marshal General, NA.

22. Frisch notes that Springfield and the state of Massachusetts paralleled national averages in which about 25 to 30 percent were held to service and only about 10 percent were drafted. In the Massachusetts Tenth District, which included Springfield, 3,395 names produced 89 conscripts, 53 substitutes, and 689 commutees, a total of 831 men

held to service. Frisch, *Town Into City*, 265n25. His figures align with Murdock, *Patriotism Limited*, 13.

23. Captain W. R. Pease to A. D. Hatch, September 15, 1863, Letters Received, 1863–65, entry 849, RG 110. Also see Assistant Provost Marshal General A. M. Clark to A. D. Hatch, September 19, 1863, Letters and Telegraphs Sent (by the Deputy Provost Marshal of Massachusetts), July 1863 to May 1867, entry 790, RG 110; F. M Clark, Major of 5th Mass. Artillery and Acting Assistant Provost Marshal General, to A. D. Hatch, August 25, 1863, entry 790, RG 110.

24. Details included their list number, name, rank, company, regiment, date and place of desertion, and remarks. Descriptive List of Deserters Received from Washington, DC, 1861–64, First District, 1 bound volume (no. 9), entry 861, RG 110. Adjutant General Schouler argued that most deserters within the state were not men from Massachusetts because "they came from other States, stimulated to enlist by the offer of large bounties, and intending to desert as soon as they receive the money." See Schouler, 1:474–75.

25. Descriptive Book of Arrested Deserters (August 1863 to May 1865), First District. entry 862, RG 110.

26. Register of Disbursements made by Officers of the Provost Marshal General's Office, 1862–1865, 1 volume; shows total for First District, New Bedford, entry 99, RG 110.

27. Register of Accounts with Companies and Individual Employees for Employment, Equipment, and Supplies (no. 28); entry 820, RG 110.

28. Register of Persons Employed and Property Hired (no. 29), 1 bound volume, entry 821, RG 110. In box 9, entry 852 lists weekly pay accounts for the office between December 9, 1863 and February 1864. The PMG's Office also contracted with individuals on an as-needed basis as shown in a 44-page ledger of disbursements to a wide range of individuals and businesses. Register of Accounts of Companies and Individuals for Equipment, Supplies, Employment, 1863–64 (1 vol., no. 7), entry 863, RG 110.

29. Report of the City Marshal for 1862, dated December 31, 1862, from NBCD, reel 2.

30. Board members (Provost Marshal A. D. Hatch, Surgeon Fenton Hooper, and Commissioner Nathan Hinckley) initially divided the district into eighteen subdistricts, each headed by one enrolling officer. Each of New Bedford's three subdistricts were comprised of two combined wards. Meeting minutes and an accounting ledger were maintained by Cornelius Howland Jr., Clerk and Deputy Provost Marshal. Soon New Bedford was further subdivided with Ward 1 becoming Subdistrict 15 headed by Horatio A. Kempton; Ward 2 became Subdistrict 16 headed by James R. Ricketson; Wards 3 and 4 became Subdistrict 17 under David B. Wilcox; and Wards 5 and 6 became Subdistrict 18 under Gilbert R. Thornton. Proceedings of the Board of Enrollments, May 1863 to June 1865, First District, New Bedford, entry 853, RG 110. Information is from volume 1: May 20, 1863, to May 28, 1864. (Volume 2 covers May 31, 1864 to June 15, 1865.)

31. Letters and Telegraphs Received, 1863–65; entry 849, RG 110. For Hatch's letter of July 13, 1863 to PMG Fry, see entry 848: Letters Sent by 1st District Provost Marshal from New Bedford, 1863–65, RG 110.

32. The more important accounts of these racially charged riots in New York City are Barnet Schecter, *The Devil's Own Work: The Civil War Draft Riots and the Fight to Reconstruct America* (New York: Walker & Company, 2006); Iver Bernstein, *The New York City Draft Riots: Their Significance for American Society and Politics in the Age of the Civil War* (New York: Oxford University Press, 1990); Iver Bernstein, "The Volcano Under the City: The Significance of Draft Rioting in New York City and State, July 1863," in Harold Holzer, ed., *State of the Union: New York and the Civil War* (New York: Fordham University Press, 2002), 17–33; Adrian Cook, *The Armies of the Streets: The New York City Draft Riots of 1863* (Lexington: University of Kentucky Press, 1974); Ernest A.

McKay, *The Civil War and New York City* (Syracuse, NY: Syracuse University Press, 1990).

33. Letters and Telegraphs Received, 1863–65; entry 849, RG 110. See A. D. Hatch to Provost Marshal General Fry, September 10, 1863, Trimonthly Reports, First District, Massachusetts, entry 63, Records of the Provost Marshal General's Bureau, RG 110. Daily figures for total examinations, exemptions, commutations, passes, and substitutions are located in Proceedings of the Board of Enrollments, May 1863 to June 1865, volume 1, First District, Massachusetts, entry 853, RG 110, NA.

34. William Schouler details the "disgraceful and cruel riot" in New York and also describes the scene in Boston where an estimated 4,000 to 5,000 "rioters assume[d] a menacing, hostile attitude" and were dispersed with force after several rioters were killed. Schouler, 1:475–80. For Boston, see Thomas H. O'Connor, Civil War Boston: Home Front and Battlefield (Boston: Northeastern University Press, 1997), and William Hanna, "The Boston Draft Riot," *Civil War History* 36 (September 1990): 262–73.

35. Report of the Mayor, George Howland Jr., January 5, 1864, NBCD, reel 2.

36. Trimonthly Report of District Provost Marshal Hatch to Provost Marshal General Fry, July 31, 1863, in Trimonthly Reports of Business and General Transactions of District Provost Marshal General Offices, 1863–65, First District, Massachusetts, entry 63, RG 110, NA.

37. Joseph Ricketson to "Dear Geo. Lieut. Guerrier," July 17, 1863, typescript transcription in Curriculum Project, ODHS, taken from the Ricketson Collection. Ricketson wrote a nearly identical letter to Deborah Weston, July 19, 1863, Weston Papers, Special Collections, BPL. In the latter missive, Ricketson wrote: "As the water poured upon the head flows over the whole body, so has the spirit of Rowdyism reached even unto the godly Quaker City." Ricketson made it clear that none of his family had borne arms during the panic.

38. Ricketson to Guerrier, ODHS.

39. James B. Congdon, "The Society of Friends and the War against Treason, by James B. Congdon, written in May 1864," handwritten manuscript, in folder 51, Congdon Papers, Special Collections, NBFPL.

40. Descriptive Books of Drafted Men and Substitutes, 1863–64, First District, New Bedford, Massachusetts, 2 volumes, entry 855, RG 110, NA. The first volume provides information on the draft of July and August 1863, listing the community of residence for each man. New Bedford begins with entry 2349, Thomas O. Brien, continuing through entry 2762, thus yielding at total of 413 men drafted from New Bedford in July 1863. Also see the Register of Drafted Men, First District, Massachusetts, entry 808, RG 110, NA.

41. Proceedings of the Board of Enrollments, May 1863 to June 1865, First District, New Bedford, entry 853, RG 110; Trimonthly Reports of Business and General Transactions of District Provost Marshal Offices, 1863–65, First District, New Bedford, Massachusetts, entry 63, RG 110.

42. The only reference to New Bedford in the entire volume is related to credits on September 1, 1864. No numbers are listed for Wards 1 or 2, while Wards 3 and 4 were given credit for three substitutes, and Wards 5 and 6 were credited with five substitutes. Register of Quotas and Enlistments Credited to Towns, 1864–1865, entry 805, RG 110 (1 bound volume, with alphabetical index). The Descriptive Books of Drafted Men and Substitutes, 1863–64, First District, reflect the low numbers of men drafted from New Bedford. According to volume 2, for May and June 1864, New Bedford had no entries, while towns like Fall River and Dartmouth had numerous entries. The index to volume 2 does not mention New Bedford at all. For state figures of the 1863 summer conscription, see Schouler, 1:481. For more details about the operations of New Bedford's PMG, see Letters Received, 1863–65, First District, Massachusetts, entry 849, RG 110; Register of Companies and Individuals for Employment, Supplies and Equipment, First District,

Massachusetts, entry 863, RG 110; Medical Register of Examinations of Drafted Men, 1864–65, First District, entry 856, and Medical Register of Examinations of Recruits, Substitutes, and Enrolled Men, 1864–65, First District, Massachusetts, entry 858, RG 110.

43. *New Bedford Mercury* dispatches of July 24 and July 27 reprinted in *New York Times* on July 27, 1863, and July 29, 1863, respectively.

44. Records of the Provost Marshal General provide the names and homes of nine "substitute deserters" and their homes: John Riley and William Johnson (Ireland); Anderson Howard, James Wright, and John Rice (New Brunswick); Daniel Williams and Charles W. White (Canada); James Greene (New York); James Wilson (unknown). See Register of Quotas and Enlistments Credited to Towns, 1864–65, entry 805, RG 110 for official report of substitute deserters of July 26, 1863.

45. "The Draft in New England," *New Bedford Mercury*, August 1, 1863, reprinted in *New York Times*, July 29, 1863, and August 2, 1863. Through August 10, the Board had examined nearly 1,300 men; an average of 72 percent (or 922) were exempted and 28 percent (or 364) passed. Of those exempted, 555 individuals were exempted because of disease and 367 because of other causes. Some 121 men were passed without furnishing substitutes or commutation, 50 were commuted, and 193 furnished substitutes. See *New York Times*, August 7, 1863, and August 14, 1863.

46. William J. Potter, "The Voice of the Draft," sermon delivered July 26, 1863, and reprinted by the New Bedford Mercury Press, n.d. (August 1863). See article, "A Drafted Clergyman, He Determines to Shoulder the Musket," *New York Times*, August 12, 1863. Original sermon is in W. J. Potter Papers, NBFPL, Special Collections, sermon 115. For a solid biographical sketch of William James Potter, see article by Richard Kellaway at the Unitarian Universalist Association web site, http://tinyurl.com/william-potter.

47. For similar sermons and ideas among other Northern Protestant clergymen, see Peter J. Parish: "From Necessary Evil to National Blessing: The Northern Protestant Clergy Interpret the Civil War," in *An Uncommon Time: The Civil War and the Northern Home Front*, ed. Paul Cimbala and Randall Miller (New York: Fordham University Press, 2002), 61–89, and "The Just War," in Peter J. Parish, *The North and the Nation in the Era of the Civil War*, ed. Adam I. P. Smith and Susan-Mary Grant (New York: Fordham University Press, 2003), 171–99.

48. New Bedford Recruiting Committee, 1863–1864, ODHS, Manuscripts, Mss. Collection 77, subgroup 1, series F, box 12, subseries 27.

49. Governor Andrew wrote to John H. Clifford on July 11, 1864 about his delight at gaining naval credits and recommended Clifford's name to Secretary Stanton, in part because the naval rendezvous were located in Boston and New Bedford. Despite complications based on a basic unit of three-year service, the entire state ended up with a surplus of 13,083 soldiers and sailors. New Bedford's portion of 1,188 credited sailors allowed the city to forego the draft. See Schouler, 1:551–56, 561–63, 567.

50. Address of George Howland Jr., Mayor, January 2, 1865, NBCD, reel 2.

51. *NBDES*, April 18 and 19, 1861.

52. Report of the Committee on Home and Coast Guard Dated January 3, 1862, NBCD, reel 2. Also, Ellis, *History*, 320–21.

53. Schouler, 1:34; Mayor Isaac C. Taber to John H. Clifford, April 26, 1861, in John H. Clifford Papers, MHS; Joseph C. Delano to J. M. Forbes of April 25, 1861, folder 9, Joseph Delano Papers, Baker Library, Harvard University.

54. Joseph Ricketson to Deborah Weston, April 28, 1861, Weston Papers, BPL, Rare Books, Ms. A.9.2 vol. 30, no. 65. Davenport Diary, ODHS, Mss. Collection 64, series D, box 13, subseries 4.

55. *NBDES*, April 25, 1861; *NBDES*, May 2, 1861; Report of the Committee on Home and Coast Guard Dated January 3, 1862, NBCD, reel 2; Address of Mayor Isaac C. Taber, January 6, 1862, NBCD, reel 2; and Ellis, *History*, 320.

56. Roster and Journal of Company C, Home and Coast Guard, May 1861, in Special Collections of the NBFPL.

57. Lydia G. Davenport Diary, ODHS Manuscripts, Mss. Collection 64, series D, box 13, subseries 4.

58. Hathaway's journal and Burt's comments are located in the Roster and Journal of Company C, Home and Coast Guard, May 1861, in Special Collections of the NBFPL. Ricketson's song was and arranged for the piano by William F. Hathaway, and its lyrics included an antislavery refrain at the end:

And here's to Howe, to Sergeant Howe,
Of Company C, Company C,
For he knows how, for he knows how
Company C, Company C,
To put us through in right good style
Squad Two of Company C,
Open rank or single file,
Squad Two of Company C. . . .
And always let your watchwords be
Company C, Company C, Union is strength, let all be free.

59. *NBDES*, July 3, 1861.

60. Entries of July 4, 1861 and July 22, 1861, Lydia G. Davenport Diary; Old Dartmouth Historical Society, Manuscripts, Mss. Collection 64, series D, box 13, subseries 4.

61. *NBDES*, July 11, 1861.

62. *NBDES*, July 18, 1861. Two articles were written by an "A. M., Jr.," whose identity remains unknown.

63. Roster and Journal of Company C, Home and Coast Guard, May 1861, in Special Collections, NBFPL.

64. A ledger for Home and Coast Defence explained expenditures in the first year of war:

Paid to families of NB City Guards: $1,360.50
Clothing, Provisions, other materials: 1,347.84
Total: $2,708.34
Appropriations: $16,500.00
Fairhaven contribution: $2,266.01
Articles sold: $8.00
Total: $18,774.01
Paid for labor, materials: $13,617.10
Military pay rolls: $3,521.75
To navy beneficiaries: $664.50
Total: $17,803.35
Credit balance: $970.66

Report of the Committee on Home and Coast Guard Dated January 3, 1862, NBCD, reel 2. Bourne's quote is mentioned in the Minute Book of the Home Protective Guard, Company C, ODHS Manuscripts, Mss. Collection 77, subgroup 1, series F, box 10, subseries 17. This latter source also includes a handwritten "Constitution and By-Laws of the New Bedford City Guards" for 1861 that explains that its members had to be eighteen years or older and approved by a two-thirds vote of members. Fees included five dollars for annual dues along with a system of fines for tardiness, absences, and other problems.

65. *NBDES*, October 3, 1861, October 10, 1861, October 17, 1861, October 31, 1861, April 12, 1862.

66. Despite a Congressional appropriation of $56,000 in February 1846 for the erection of stone fort at the Clark's Point site, final plans were not completed until the end of December 1848. The intervening war against Mexico slowed planning despite the noteworthy contributions of Robert E. Lee, a captain in the Corps of Engineers. Ten years passed until sixty acres of land was purchased on Clark's Point at a cost of $78,000, and construction commenced in 1860 with a wharf, railroad spur, and a foundation. Christopher McDonald, *The Military History of New Bedford, Images of America* (Charleston, SC: Arcadia Publishing, 2001). This book's first chapter is devoted to the Civil War and features photographs, maps, and diagrams of Clark's Point fort; see especially pp. 15–21.

67. Schouler, 1:397–99, 419–22; *NBDES*, February 26, 1863; NBDES, February 27, 1863. Colonel Alberto Maggi became a notable military figure in New Bedford and accompanied Major Wool and Governor and Andrew in their visit. Governor Andrew applauded Maggi's military conduct. Maggi graduated at the head of 216 students at a military school in Turin and served seven years under Garibaldi. His "undoubted" patriotism was shown when he enlisted as a private upon hearing of Fort Sumter's surrender. A short time later, the *Standard* printed a letter from officers and staff of the Thirty-Third Massachusetts who expressed "sincere regret" that Maggi would resign because of lingering "honorable wounds" from service in Italy. See *NBDES* April 15, 1863.

68. Schouler, 1:419–24, 486–488, 410–522; *NBDES*, April 6, 1863. Some twenty-eight men had been recruited by April 15, 1863; see *NBDES* April 15, 1863.

69. In computing a ratio of enlisted soldiers to civilians, Massachusetts offered one soldier to every 17.06 people, Rhode Island one soldier to every 11.10 persons, and Maine ranked last with a 1 to 20.24 ratio. *NBDES*, April 20, 1863.

70. Governor John Andrew to Captain W. W. McKim, April 22, 1863; see "Consolidated Correspondence File, 1794–1915," under subject, "New Bedford," entry 225 of RG 92, Office of the Quartermaster General (box 724), National Archives. I wish to thank Michael Musick for his suggestion to examine these records.

71. In 1871 the War Department officially halted construction at the Clark's Point fort after finishing only two of the planned three tiers. Later, the fort became a public park, and was taken over by the federal government and renamed Fort Rodman on July 26, 1898. As a side note, Lieutenant Martyn Robert later became famous because of what he learned in wartime New Bedford. After attending meetings in the city that lacked rules or protocols, Robert formulated guidelines for parliamentary law published in 1876 as *Pocket Manual of Rules of Order for Deliberate Assemblies*. This work was published in 1915 as *Robert's Rules of Order Revised*. McDonald, *Military History of New Bedford,* and also Jack Stephenson, "Skeleton of old fort sits and waits," *New Bedford Sunday Standard-Times,* April 17, 1988.

72. Captain Allen's comments, and those posted subsequently by Captains Alphonse Kilbourn and Caleb E. Niebuhr, are found in entry for New Bedford, Massachusetts, June 1863–May 1865; Returns from US Military Posts, 1800–1916; RG 94, National Archives; NARS Microfilm 617, roll 837. See *NBDES*, August 7, 1863.

73. Under Special Order No. 1087 of September 8, 1864, the numbered companies were organized into the Third Regiment Volunteers Heavy Artillery and acquired new letter designations; the 6th Company was reconstituted as Company B. See entry for Third Regiment Massachusetts Volunteer Heavy Artillery, *Massachusetts Soldiers, Sailors, and Marines in the Civil War*, Compiled and Published by the Adjutant General (Norwood, MA, 1931–35), 5:770–71; Company B roster is on pp. 782–88 (hereafter cited as *MSSCW*).

74. For Fourth Unattached Company (Ninety Days), see *MSSCW*, 5:181; the Captain's name is listed as "Alpheus J. Hillbourn," while my notes from RG 94 have his

name as "Alphonse Kilbourn." For the First Battalion Massachusetts Volunteer Heavy Artillery, see *MSSCW*, 4:80–81; roster of Company B is on pp. 92–100.

75. Report of the City Marshal for 1858, dated December 20, 1858; NBCD, reel 2. Additional information is found in Ellis, *History*, 709–11, and an undated manuscript, "New Bedford Police Department," n.d. NBFPL, file 6, folder 39. Ellis includes a list of city marshals and captains of night watch, noting that the first chief of police was named in 1876; see 711.

76. Report of the City Marshal for 1858, dated December 20, 1858; Report of City Marshal for 1859, dated December 31, 1859; NBCD, reel 2.

77. "New Bedford Police Department," undated manuscript, NBFPL, file 6, folder 39. Report of the City Marshal for 1860; NBCD, reel 2.

78. Report of the City Marshal for 1862, dated December 31, 1862, from NBCD, reel 2.

79. Report of the City Marshal for Year ending December 31, 1861; Report of the City Marshal For 1862, dated December 31, 1862; NBCD, reel 2.

80. Report of City Marshal for 1863, NBCD, reel 2. The Night Watch functioned much the same during war as it had prior to 1861. Evening duties begin with roll call at 9 p.m. with one officer of the watch, two sergeants, and twenty-four men who policed twelve sections or beats. The captain of the watch submitted a written report to the mayor every morning. Report of the City Marshal for 1864; NBCD, reel 2.

81. Marshal Brownell made an unusual statement that is not explained or corroborated in any other source. He suggested that a secret police force had infiltrated the city. Some arrests and prosecutions came "from a source hitherto unknown to this Commonwealth; namely, through the secret agents of the State Constable and his Deputies, who have entered our city in disguise, and have themselves induced the citizens to violate the laws that they might procure an opportunity to prefer charges against them before the Court." Report of the City Marshal for 1865; NBCD, reel 2.

82. Reports of the City Marshal from 1859 to 1868 were used to compile these figures. Note: In grouping crimes by type, the following classification was employed: *Alcohol-Related Crimes:* Drunkenness, Common Drunkard, Sales of Liquor, Liquor Nuisance; *Assault Crimes:* Assault and Battery, Assault with Knife, Assault with Intent to Kill/Felonious Assault, Assault with Intent to Rob/Robbery, Assault with Stone/Slung Shot, Assault with Dangerous Weapon, Assault on Officer, Obstructing Officer, Carrying Dangerous Weapons, Attempt to Kill by Poison, Threats/Dangerous Weapon, Throwing Stones; *Theft & Property Crimes:* Larceny, Burglary, Embezzlement, Forgery, Counterfeining [*sic*], Receiving Stolen Goods, Passing Counterfeit Money, Obtaining Goods False Pretense, Breaking and Entering, Stealing a Ride; *Disorderly Crimes:* Idle and Disorderly, Vagrants/Vagabonds, Malicious Mischief, Common Nuisance, Common Seller, Disorderly Conduct, Disturbing Meeting/Peace, Truancy, Disobedient Children, Perjury, Profanity, Riots, Violation of City Ordinance, Violation of Sunday Law, Defacing Public Buildings; *Sexual and Vice Crimes:* Disorderly Houses, Lewd and Lascivious/Indecent Exposure, Bastardy, Rape, Fornication/Adultery, Polygamy, Sodomy, Night Walking, Gambling; *Miscellany:* Murder, Contempt of Court, Perjury/Inciting Witness, Violation of Dog Law, Seining, Fast Driving, Selling Fireworks, No License, Rescuing Cow/Cattle at Large, Unlawful Use of Property, Arson, Incendiaries, Peddling without License, Firing Squib, Trespass, Breaking Glass, Kidnapping, Enticing Away Female, Attempt at Abortion, Violation Billiards, Attempt to Rescue Prisoner, Cruelty to Animals, Escape from Work House.

83. Reports of City Marshal, 1861 to 1871, NBCD, reel 2.

84. Paludan noted that arrests peaked in 1862. In Massachusetts, women comprised about 20 percent of jail inmates in 1860, but by 1864, about 60 percent of inmates in county jails were women, Paludan reported. Phillip Shaw Paludan, *"A People's Contest" The Union and Civil War, 1861–1865* (New York: Harper & Row, 1988), 184. Recent work

by Judith Giesberg suggests that rising crime rates reflected the incarceration of transient poor people, including women, who sought public relief in a confusing system. For example, Boston's watch house took in more female lodgers between 1861 and 1863, but arrests for drunkenness were about the same in 1862 and 1863. Judith Giesberg, *Army at Home, Women and the Civil War on the Northern Home Front* (Chapel Hill: University of North Carolina Press, 2009), 49–59.

85. Some individuals, such as G. S. Hustin of Nantucket, sought "conscientious objector" status during the war, claiming: "I want to be a Christian; but I cannot be unless I live up to Christ's teachings." By the end of 1863, the War Department outlined a policy for conscientious objector status for persons in "religious societies whose creed prohibits them to serve in the Army" and who could prove that they "consciously opposed to bearing arms, and to paying the commutation money for exemption from draft." For Hustin's case, see A. D. Hatch to PMG James B. Fry, August 14, 1863, Letters Sent by 1st District Provost Marshal from New Bedford, 1863–65, entry 848, RG 110. Circular Letter by order of the Provost Marshal General US dated December 17, 1863, Letters and Telegraphs Sent, 1863, vol. 1, entry 790, RG 110. A. D. Hatch to PMG James B. Fry, August 14, 1863, Letters Sent by 1st District Provost Marshal from New Bedford, 1863–65, entry 848, RG 110.

86. Joseph Ricketson to Deborah Weston, n.d. [1862], Boston Public Library, Rare Books, Ms. A.9.2. vol. 31, no. 4.

4. "Citizen-Soldiers of Massachusetts": New Bedford's Volunteers in the Civil War

1. Frank W. Loring to Mr. Rodman, June 5, 1863, excerpted in Thomas Wentworth Higgingson, "William Logan Rodman," in Higginson, Harvard Memorial Biographies, vol. 1 (Cambridge, MA: Sever and Francis, 1867): 59–71; letter on pp. 69–70.

2. Higginson, "Rodman," 59–61. The only son of Benjamin and Susan (Morgan) Rodman, William was born in 1822 to a prominent Quaker whaling family and educated at the New Bedford Friends Academy and matriculated at Harvard University in 1838. Graduating in 1842, Rodman became a whaling oil merchant, sailed to California in 1849, and spent almost two years traveling in India and Europe before returning home. Through the 1850s, Rodman lived a gentleman's life as one of New Bedford's wealthy Quaker leaders. He was president of the New Bedford Horticultural Society, a trustee of the Friends' Academy and the Five Cent Savings Bank, and elected as a conservative Republican to the Common Council in 1852 and to the State Legislature in 1862. For two decades after his Harvard graduation, according to Higginson, Rodman "studied no profession, developed no marked ambition," and was probably satisfied with the "pleasant surroundings to which he was born." When war came, the single forty-year-old Rodman "had enjoyed almost too much repose, and whose mind almost too much leisure," according to Higginson. Higginson, "Rodman," 59. Rodman's leadership positions in local organizations are listed in *The New Bedford Directory, Containing the City Register and a General Directory of the Citizens* (New Bedford: Abraham Taber and Brother, 1859), 35, 48.

3. See Report by Treasurer James B. Congdon in letter dated July 30, 1865, to Hon. Tappan Wentworth, Chair, Joint Special Committee upon the subject of Taxation and the Finances. Congdon Papers, NBFPL, folder 17. See also summary of war's costs in Zephaniah W. Pease and George W. Hough, *New Bedford, Massachusetts: Its History, Industries, Institutions, and Attractions*, ed. William L. Sayer (New Bedford: Board of Trade, Mercury Publishing Company, 1889), 23–25. See below for "New Bedford Roll of Honor."

4. Rodman's journal entries of November 7, 1860, April 15, 1861, April 16, 1861, May 24, 1861 extracted in Higginson, "Rodman," 61–62. For the probable source of these

excerpts, and for additional information from May 5, 1861, and May 24, 1861, see "Extracts from the Journal of William Logan Rodman," James Bunker Congdon Papers, NBFPL Special Collections.

5. Higginson, "Rodman," 62–63. Additional comments for entries of September 25, 1861 and December 20, 1861, located in "Extracts," Congdon Papers, NBFPL Special Collections.

6. Higginson, "Rodman," 63–64. Quaker leader George Howland Jr. similarly relinquished Quaker leadership while serving as New Bedford's wartime mayor. He served on the governing board of the Providence Friends' School between 1847 and his death in 1891 except for the years of 1862, 1863, and 1864. According to a biographer, Howland "withdrew temporarily, during the years just mentioned, because the views he held concerning the civil war were not in accord with the commonly accepted beliefs of the Society of Friends." Curiously, the pamphlet's sketch is authored by William Logan Rodman Gifford, *George Howland Junior* (New Bedford: E. Anthony & Sons, 1892), 24–25, 36–37.

7. More men died in the second assault in mid-June, and Port Hudson finally fell to Union forces on July 9. *MSSCW*, 4:1–3, 33–37; *RMV*, 2:794–810.

8. See letters and diary excerpts of September 5, 1862, February 23, 1863, and April 18, 1863 in Higginson, "Rodman," 63–66. In an unpublished diary extract of February 24, 1863, Rodman extolled his military life: "I feel as young as ever. . . . I never was better in my life. Life in the open air & sleeping in a tent are just suited to my call. I have hardly had an ache or a pain . . . of any kind whatever since I entered the service." "Extracts," Congdon Papers, NBFPL Special Collections.

9. See especially diary entries of January 16, 1863, February 4, 1863, March 9, 1863, April 18, 1863, April 17, 1863 excerpted in Higginson, "Rodman," 64–67. Higginson reprinted Emory's letter to Benjamin Rodman, June 3, 1863, on p. 71 that eulogizes Rodman's leadership and his unit as "one of the best" in military service.

10. Joseph Ricketson to Deborah Weston, July 19, 1863, Boston Public Library, Rare Books, Ms. A.9.2 vol. 31 no. 73.

11. At least eleven of the three dozen New Bedford men suffered wounds, and six died in battle or because of wounds. Sixteen of the men survived the war, three of them prisoners of war who were exchanged or paroled before the war's end. Eight men were discharged for disability, while five others were promoted in rank and moved to other units. Of the twenty-six men who enlisted as privates, at least twelve were promoted during the war. Leonard B. Ellis, *History of New Bedford and Its Vicinity, 1602–1892* (Syracuse, NY: D. Mason & Co., 1892), 333–39.

12. James McPherson, *Battle Cry of Freedom: The Civil War Era* (New York: Oxford University Press, 1988; 2003), 323, 326.

13. Although New Bedford remained as the First District's center of conscription and recruitment, the city met its quota through the additional naval enrollments. Congdon to Wentworth, July 30, 1865; Congdon Papers, NBFPL, folder 17. The "Army and Navy Register" was compiled through a "canvass of the city," city records, files of the *New Bedford Standard*, the *New Bedford Mercury*, the *Boston Almanac* for 1862 and 1863, and other sources. The list was complete up to January 1, 1865, providing the latest rank and regiment and the "deaths that have occurred, so far as they could be ascertained." See *1859 New Bedford Directory*, "Introductory" dated January 31, 1865. The Register is printed as an appendix on pp. 155–74.

14. James McPherson, *Ordeal by Fire: The Civil War and Reconstruction*, 2nd ed. (New York: McGraw-Hill, 1992), 355–57.

15. James Geary, *We Need Men: The Union Draft in the Civil War* (DeKalb: Northern Illinois University Press, 1991), 170–77. In his appendix, 175–77, Geary discusses methodology and use of RG 110. While he considered using Hershberg's occupational classifica-

tion from *Historical Methods Newsletter* 9 (1976): 59–98, he adapted a version used by McPherson in *Ordeal by Fire*, 359.

16. W. J. Rorabaugh, "Who Fought for the North in the Civil War? Concord, Massachusetts, Enlistments," in *Journal of American History* 73, no. 3 (December 1986): 695–701; see p. 699, especially Table 2, p. 698. He adapted an occupational classification used by Michael B. Katz, *People of Hamilton, Canada West: Family and Class in a Mid–Nineteenth Century City* (Cambridge, MA: Harvard University Press, 1975), 697n3.

17. Robertson uses five categories: skilled workers; laborers; farmers; a grouping of professionals, white-collar workers and students; and no listed occupation. Robertson combines skilled workers (the largest group of soldiers at 33 percent of the total) with the professional class (professionals, white-collar workers, and students) to conclude that 63 percent of enlistees were in these classes, and the remaining 37 percent were laborers or had no occupation listed. Robertson used the occupational grouping followed by McPherson in *For Cause and Comrade* on p. 182. Although McPherson grouped farm laborers with farmers, Robertson grouped farm laborers with "urban laborers because of the growing difficulty for even farmers' sons to become farm owners. In addition, the low, seasonal wages of farm laborers led many laborers to migrate between urban and rural employment." In using a two-classes model, Robertson places skilled workers in the upper class by following Stuart Blumin's *The Emergence of the Middle Class: Social Experience in the American City, 1760–1900* (New York: Cambridge University Press, 1989), 24n17. See John Robertson, "Re-enlistment Patterns of Civil War Soldiers," *Journal of Interdisciplinary History* 32, no. 1 (Summer 2001): 15–35.

18. All together, 1,007 entries were located for men with New Bedford residences among sampled units. Among the infantry units surveyed, one was for three months' service, four for nine months', one for one year, and five for three years' service, including Company C of the Fifty-Fourth Massachusetts Colored Infantry. The Third Massachusetts Cavalry served for three years, and two artillery units sampled initially were mustered in for three-year terms. In addition to name, rank, residence, age, and occupation, each individual's military service is briefly noted, including commissions, mustering in and out dates, transfers to other units, and notes of death, desertion, or discharge. Fifty-one men were listed twice, as they served in more than one unit, and one man, Walter D. Keith, was listed three times in the sample. Units with substantial New Bedford enlistments not in this sample include the Twenty-Eighth MVI (Taber Guards); Fifty-Eighth MVI, Co. E; Second Massachusetts Cavalry; Fifteenth Unattached Company (100 Days). See *Massachusetts Soldiers, Sailors, and Marines in the Civil War*, compiled and published by the Adjutant General, 9 vols. (Norwood, MA: Norwood Press, 1931–35) (hereafter cited as *MSSCW*).

19. I largely followed Rorabaugh's occupational categories: 1) merchants, professionals; 2) small shopkeepers, clerks; 3) skilled workers; 4) semiskilled and unskilled workers; 4) agricultural; 5) no occupation; 6) students. I added the category of "maritime" and made some changes to categorization of skilled, semi-, and unskilled workers using James and Lois Horton's methodology in *Black Bostonians*. I adhered to McPherson's scheme in placing farm laborers with farmers (not like Robertson who included them with laborers).

20. Sorted by decadal ages, 189 (nearly 19 percent) were in their teens; 501 (almost 50 percent) were between the ages of twenty and twenty-nine; 227 men (22.5 percent of the sample) were in their thirties; and 88 men (less than 9 percent) were forty years or older.

21. Reid Mitchell surveys his own and classic works by Bell Irvin Wiley, Joseph T. Glatthaar, Gerald F. Linderman, James I. Robertson, Earl J. Hess, James McPherson, Stuart McConnell, among others in Mitchell, "'Not the General But the Soldier,' The Study of Civil War Soldiers" in *Writing the Civil War: The Quest to Understand*, ed. James M. McPherson and William J. Cooper Jr. (Columbia: University of South Caro-

lina Press, 1998), 81–95; quotes on pp. 81–82. Reid Mitchell's work stands the test of time; see *Civil War Soldiers: Their Expectations and Their Experiences* (New York: Viking, 1988) and *The Vacant Chair: The Northern Soldier Leaves Home* (New York: Oxford University Press, 1993).

22. Mitchell suggests there is no "better book on combat" during the Civil War than Earl J. Hess, *The Union Soldier in Battle: Enduring the Ordeal of Combat* (Lawrence: University Press of Kansas, 1997); Mitchell's comments in "Not the General," 93–94. Also see Aaron Sheehan-Dean, ed., *The View from the Ground: Experiences of Civil War Soldiers* (Lexington: University Press of Kentucky, 2007); Michael Barton and Larry M. Logue, *The Civil War Soldier: A Historical Reader* (New York: New York University Press, 2002); Chandra Manning, *What This Cruel War Was Over: Soldiers, Slavery, and the Civil War* (New York: Vintage, 2008).

23. John Robertson, "Re-enlistment Patterns," 31–32. Robertson found most satisfactory the work by W. J. Rorabaugh, "Who Fought for the North," and Teresa A. Thomas, "For Union, Not for Glory: Memory and the Civil War Volunteers of Lancaster, Massachusetts," *Civil War History* 90, no. 1 (1994): 25–47.

24. At least forty-two (59 percent) of the New Bedford men enlisted again in one or more military units, headed by eight who signed up for nine months in the Third Massachusetts Volunteer Infantry and eight in a three-years' regiment, the Eighteenth Massachusetts. The latter group was led by six skilled workers, a baker, and merchant Timothy Ingraham who had served as captain of the New Bedford City Guards. *MSSCW*, 1:148 for summary; see pp. 149, 162–65 for Company L roster. See William Schouler, *A History of Massachusetts in the Civil War.* Vol.1, *Civil and Military History of Massachusetts in the Rebellion* (Boston: E. P. Dutton & Co., Publishers, 1868), 108. For detailed histories of military units, also see Frederick H. Dyer, A Compendium of the War of the Rebellion (Part 3), available at http://www.civilwararchive.com/regim.htm and cited subsequently as *Dyer's Compendium.* Other accounts include Ellis, *History of New Bedford* (1892), 317–20, 196. Information from *MSSCW* is more complete and was used in place of material located in *Record of the Massachusetts Volunteers, 1861–1865, Published by the Adjutant-General Under a Resolve of the General Court* (Boston: Wright & Potter, Printers to the State, 1868) (hereafter cited as *RMV*). This latter source provides name, age, bounty paid, residence or place credited to, date of muster in, and termination date and cause. Volume 1 covers short-term infantry enlistments up to nine months, along with artillery and cavalry units in longer terms. Volume 2 provides rosters of long-term infantry units, along with enlistments in the Regular Army, Veteran Reserve Corps, and other organizations. The *RMV* provides a useful "recapitulation" of the unit's service that includes a table related to death (killed in action, died of wounds and disease), desertion, transfer, missing, and unaccounted. Also, tables offer summaries of the number of honorable and dishonorable discharges, promotions, and disabilities. The Third Massachusetts is detailed in *RMV*, 1:2–8. The most detailed source for additional information is *The War of the Rebellion: A Compilation of the Official Records of the Union and Confederate Armies*, often abbreviated *Official Records* or *OR*, which is available and searchable online at Cornell University's "Making of America" site, http://cdl.library.cornell.edu/moa.

25. Significant combat came with Second Bull Run on August 30, 1862. At Fredericksburg in mid-December 1862, the Eighteenth Massachusetts took part in the assault on Mary's Heights, losing 134 officers and men. Following winter camp, as part of the Fifth Corps, the Eighteenth engaged at Chancellorsville and Gettysburg but without severe losses. When winter rolled around in 1863–64, the regiment was "much reduced in numbers," but still 139 men reenlisted for three years, and they would participate in the opening battle of the Wilderness, followed by engagements at Spotsylvania, Cold Harbor, and Petersburg. New Bedford men were distributed in Companies A (32 men),

F (10), and H (8). For initial recruiting problems at federal, but not state levels, see
Schouler, 1:130–32.

26. Schouler, 1:108. Schouler computed 30,736 officers and enlisted men, plus other
units such as the Union Coast Guard and 7,658 naval enlistees to come up with a total
of 42,294 enlisted in 1861; Schouler, 1:196.

27. Heavy losses followed when the regiment joined the Army of the Potomac near
Cold Harbor, and later they were ravaged by yellow fever in the fall of 1864 and winter
of 1865. Survivors were finally discharged and paid off on July 5, 1865. Ellis, *History*
(1892), 322–23; *MSSCW*, 2:719–20, 737–42; *RMV*, 2:419–41.

28. Of eleven captains among New Bedford's soldiers, only one was a skilled worker,
the rest were merchants or professionals. Both colonels from New Bedford were merchants, as was one of two majors. Occupations were distributed across a wide range with
10 percent of the sample featuring seamen (108) and laborers (106), respectively. Other
occupations with twenty or more men included clerk (94), carpenter (65), farmer (63),
teamer or teamster (50), painter (39), blacksmith (30), weaver (30), and merchant. The
patterns basically corroborate Robertson's findings that "soldiers from urban and
higher-class backgrounds seemed to have more opportunities outside the army than
those from rural and lower-class backgrounds." See Robertson, "Re-enlistment Patterns," 23–24, 35; Thomas, "For Union, Not for Glory," 26–28.

29. Eppendorf was replaced by former First Lieutenant George D. Allen. Ellis, *History*
(1892), 323–25; *MSSCW*, 5:397–98, 399–411; *RMV*, 1:420–25. The *New Bedford Standard*
of October 24, 1861 printed a roster of men in the battery.

30. "From the beginning to the end of the Rebellion," Schouler wrote, "the Governor, the city and town authorities, and the people of the Commonwealth, were opposed
to a draft, and labored to avoid it." Election results and excerpts from Clifford's address
on in Schouler, 1:250, 284; state expenditures for 1861 are covered on 285–86; Lincoln's
call in July and status of war on 339–40; Lincoln's call of August and Andrew's comments on 347–56.

31. Arriving near Washington, DC, in mid-August 1862, the regiment mostly performed patrol duty followed by winter camp when Maggi resigned because of ill health.
MSSCW, 3:536–37, 577–81; *RMV*, 2:696, 711–12.

32. Ellis, *History* (1892), 345–46; *MSSCW*, 4:387–88; *RMV*, 1:303–18; *Dyer's Compendium*, Part 3.

33. Ellis, *History* (1892), 339–41; *MSSCW*, 1:166, 181–92; *RMV*, 1:168–82; *Dyer's Compendium*, Part 3.

34. Schouler, 1:368–70.

35. New Bedford Bounties lists more than one hundred men who each received a
bounty of $250 to enlist in Company A of the 41st Regiment. Organized as the Forty-
First Massachusetts Infantry Regiment in the late summer and early fall of 1862, the unit
was folded into the Third Massachusetts Cavalry led by Colonel Thomas E. Chickering.
Most of the unit mustered out on May 20, 1865. *MSSCW*, 6:329–31, 333–38; *RMV*, 1:705–
39. *New Bedford Standard* has a roster of Company A in issue of March 10, 1864. The
unit's organization is a little confusing. Company A, headed by Captain John F. Vinal,
arrived in Baton Rouge, Louisiana, on December 17, 1862, where the men engaged
mainly in garrison and picket duty. While serving at Port Hudson, Louisiana, on June
17, 1863 the unit was organized as the Third Regiment Massachusetts Volunteer Cavalry,
but it would also operate as an infantry unit in 1864 when it joined the Army of the
Shenandoah. By mid-April 1864, the men of the Forty-First had confiscated sufficient
horses to be called the "Forty-first Mounted Infantry." In mid-February 1865 the unit
was remounted as a cavalry until the Confederates surrendered. *MSSCW*, 6:329–31; Ellis,
History (1892), 341–45.

36. Adjutant General Schouler reported that 33,000 men were recruited in Massachusetts during the final five months of 1862. By the end of 1862, Massachusetts had raised nearly 70,000 soldiers and over 13,618 sailors, and about 60,000 men were engaged in war at start of 1863. See Schouler, 1:378, 384, 390.

37. Rodman's positive attitude was reinforced on the eve of his death when he met with Colonel Nelson who commanded an all-black regiment of Louisiana soldiers. Rodman summarized: "The general impression was that they were a fine lot of men, and will fight," supported by Colonel Nelson's strong opinion that his "niggers" would lead the assault at Port Hudson and take its colors. "If they fight well, and Port Hudson falls," Rodman commented, "the great question of 'Will the blacks fight?' will be solved forever." In other letters, Rodman expressed his belief that the "vile system" of slavery would end with the war, and that the "grand experiment" of black military service would create "splendid results" for African Americans and the entire country. Diary entries of February 24, 1863, May 8, 1863, May 26, 1863 in Higginson, "Rodman," 65–68. Unpublished diary extracts contain specific information about New Bedford and unflattering mention of James Grace; see February 24, 1863, March 2, 1863, March 25, 1863, "Extracts," Congdon Papers, NBFPL Special Collections.

38. Schouler wrote that 1862 was an "anxious" year. By the end of December 1862, Massachusetts had in active service fifty-three infantry regiments; one regiment and three unattached companies of cavalry; twelve companies of light artillery; two companies of sharpshooters; and three companies of heavy artillery. See Schouler, 1:378, 384, 390. Ellis, *History* (1892), 346–48; *MSSCW*, 4:656–57, 670–74; *RMV*, 2:846–66. See also the excellent regimental history by officer Luis F. Emilio, *History of the Fifty-Fourth Regiment of Massachusetts Volunteer Infantry, 1863–1865* (Boston: Boston Book Company, 1891).

39. John A. P. Allen of New Bedford was granted command of one of the three battalions and the regiment was dispersed around the nation's capital as a garrison force until they were mustered out on September 18, 1865. After the Sixth Regiment was dispatched to defend the nation's capital, New Bedford was garrisoned by unattached companies of infantry such as the Fourth Company under Captain Alphonse Kilbourn at Clark's Point in May 1864. They were subsequently reinforced in August 1864 by Company B of the First Battalion Heavy Artillery Massachusetts Volunteers under Captain Caleb E. Niebuhr. Ellis, *History* (1892), 351–52; *MSSCW*, 5:770–71, 782–88; *RMV*, 1:554–84.

40. About 16 percent of the unit's men deserted. Of the six New Bedford seamen listed as deserters, three left military service in the New Bedford area and the other three deserted at Fort Totton near Washington, DC. *RMV*, 1:584, "Recapitulation." John Robertson suggests that urban mobility and anonymity may have created greater opportunities to skedaddle, as he found it harder to trace urban soldiers than rural ones. I suggest that a maritime background may have led to higher chances of desertion because of sailors' mobility. Robertson, "Re-enlistment Patterns," 27.

41. Some of the best efforts to examine individual soldiers have focused on African-American enlistees traced through military pension records and census data. See Richard M. Reid, *Freedom for Themselves: North Carolina's Black Soldiers in the Civil War Era* (Chapel Hill: University of North Carolina Press, 2008) and Donald R. Shaffer, *After the Glory, The Struggles of Black Civil War Veterans* (Lawrence: University Press of Kansas, 2004).

42. The 1860 population census provides household and family information that is not found in either *MSSCW* nor *RMV* records. The one thousand entries from *MSSCW* rosters were sorted alphabetically and then compared with alphabetical ward-based indexes of the 1860 population census prepared at the New Bedford Free Public Library. Every effort was made to use all information (name, age, occupation, marital status) to correctly link records.

43. The sample also tilts toward native-born residents. Of the 317 individuals, 233 (or 73.5 percent) were born in Massachusetts, followed by smaller numbers of those born in Rhode Island (23 or 7 percent), New York (10 or 3 percent), and other New England states (13 or 4 percent). The total of foreign-born enlistees stood at 34, led by Ireland (21 or 6.7 percent), followed by England (7), Germany (3), and Scotland (1), Canada (1), and Nova Scotia (1).

44. For an explanation of the methodology used for Table 4-3 refer to notes 17 and 19 above.

45. Ten of the sixteen merchants (62.5 percent) owned no real estate, while six men owned property ranging from $1,300 to $10,000. Of the occupational groups with six of more members in the sample, merchants had the highest percentage of married men, probably reinforced by their older ages, as well. One-half (eight) of the merchants headed their own household, six were "other," and two were sons. A small-time merchant, James W. Grace, became the chief recruiting agent and later captain of the Fifty-Fourth Massachusetts Colored Infantry. In 1860, before the war, Grace was twenty-nine, married to Mary, and they had one child and $800 in personal property.

46. Eleven of the carpenters were single, including the most prosperous one, twenty-four-year-old Samuel J. Rodman. All carpenters were white and native-born, one born in New York, two in Rhode Island, the remainder (eighteen or 86 percent) in Massachusetts.

47. This group had a wide range of ages with four younger than twenty, fifteen in their twenties, eleven between the ages of thirty-five and thirty-nine, and three forty or over. Among the laborers were five black men, all single: eighteen-year-old John Blackburn, nineteen-year-old Charles H. Harrison, twenty-one-year-old Lewis A. Fleetwood, twenty-two-year-old Cornelius Henson, and the elder of the group, Robert Lawrence, aged twenty-eight.

48. Marital status and age were clearly linked among this group, as the average age of the twenty-one married men was thirty-six, and the average age of the twenty-three single men was twenty-three. Individual men were allocated to one of three categories: "heads," "sons," or "other." For a very helpful analysis of family status as a determinant of military enlistment, see Russell Johnson, *Warriors into Workers: The Civil War and the Formation of the Urban-Industrial Society in a Northern City* (New York: Fordham University Press, 2003). Emily J. Harris uses "sons" to describe townsmen, not filial connections, in her important article, "Sons and Soldiers: Deerfield, Massachusetts and the Civil War," *Civil War History* 30 (June 1984): 157–71. "Soldiers" refers to non-native combatants who were paid bounties or hired as substitutes to meet Deerfield's military obligations.

49. One-fifth of the "sons" worked as clerks, while a smaller numbers worked as seamen (thirteen), laborers (eleven), carpenters (ten), and farmers or farm laborers (seven). Rorabaugh noted that three-quarters of Union soldiers were under thirty and one-quarter under twenty years of age; see Rorabaugh, "Who Fought," 695.

50. The vast majority of married military enlistees owned no real estate. Among married soldiers, only five had wives with known occupations listed in the 1860 census: two weavers (one Irish, the other English), one tailoress, one dressmaker, and one who worked out. Married men had an average of 2.2 children per family, although twenty-two had no children. None of the families with six or more children owned any real estate, and only one, merchant Timothy Ingraham, claimed personal property of $1,500.

51. Historians begin with Ella Lonn's long-standing contention that immigrants, principally the Irish, were over-represented in Union forces. Maris Vinovskis supports "recent work [that] suggests that foreign-born men were represented at a rate equal to, or less than that of native-born men." Thomas Kemp, who studied the New Hampshire towns of Claremont and Newport, concluded that "in both towns the Irish-born partici-

pated at a lower rate than their proportion within the two communities." W. J. Rora-baugh discovered that the Irish were less likely to enlist than native-born men in Concord, Massachusetts. See Maris Vinovskis, "Have Social Historians Lost the Civil War? Some Preliminary Demographic Speculations," in Maris A. Vinovskis, ed., *Toward a Social History of the American Civil War, Exploratory Essays* (New York: Cambridge University Press, 1990), 16–17. See Thomas R. Kemp, "Community and War: The Civil War Experience of Two New Hampshire Towns," in ibid., 67. See Rorabaugh, "Who Fought?" and Ella Lonn, *Foreigners in the Union Army and Navy* (Baton Rouge: Louisi-ana State University Press, 1951).

52. A useful analysis of black and Irish identities in the Civil War era is Christian G. Samito, *Becoming American Under Fire: Irish Americans, African Americans, and the Poli-tics of Citizenship During the Civil War Era* (Ithaca, NY: Cornell University Press, 2009). An important work that examines the evolution of a "racial" African-American identity versus an "ethnic" identity for Irish Americans is Richard Williams, *Hierarchical Struc-tures and Social Value: The Creation of Black and Irish Identities in the United States* (New York: Cambridge University Press, 1990). Building upon the work of George Fredrickson who explored white racism and racial ideologies, and of labor historians who have explored the notion of republicanism, David Roediger posits the creation of "*Herrenvolk* republicanism" that linked together all whites, including immigrant Irish. By acquiring the status of "whiteness," immigrant Irish gained superiority over all blacks in the racial-ized conceptions of equality in the nineteenth century. David Roediger, *The Wages of Whiteness: Race and the Making of the American Working Class*, rev. and exp. ed. (Lon-don and New York: Verso, 2007). Historian Dale Knobel argues that the Irish, over time, "passed" for "white," an identity that shaped their place in American society. After the Civil War, there emerged two primary "racial images": the Anglo-Saxons (which now included the Irish), and everyone else—blacks and immigrants from southern and east-ern Europe. Dale T. Knobel, *Paddy and the Republic: Ethnicity and Nationality in Ante-bellum America* (Middletown, CT: Wesleyan University Press, 1986), 103, 181–83.

53. William L. Burton discusses the respective origins of the Ninth Regiment and the Twenty-eighth Massachusetts Regiments; see William L. Burton, *Melting Pot Soldiers, The Union's Ethnic Regiments*, 2nd ed. (New York: Fordham University Press, 1998). The Ninth's military service was chronicled by one of its members, Daniel George MacNa-mara, *The History of the Ninth Regiment, Massachusetts Volunteer Infantry, Second Bri-gade, First Division, Fifth Army Corps, Army of the Potomac, June, 1861–June, 1864* (Boston: E. B. Stillings and Company, 1899). Welsh highlighted the racial animosity of many Irish Union volunteers by noting that "The feeling against nigars [*sic*] is intensely strong in this army." Lawrence Frederick Kohl and Margaret Cosse Richard, eds., *Irish Green and Union Blue: The Civil War Letters of Peter Welsh, Color Sergeant, 28th Regiment Massachusetts Volunteers* (New York: Fordham University Press, 1986), "Introduction," 1–14, and 62–63.

54. Similar to the African-American press, this Irish Catholic newspaper proclaimed the link between military service, citizenship, and anticipated assimilation. In discussing issues ranging from abolitionism to recognition of African nations, the *Boston Pilot* expressed a distinctly racialized world-view. Stridently Democratic and anti-black before the Civil War, *Pilot* editor and owner Patrick Donahoe supported the Union cause while promoting Irish enlistment. Francis Robert Walsh, "The *Boston Pilot*: A Newspaper for the Irish Immigrant, 1829–1908," (PhD dissertation, Boston University, 1968), and "The *Boston Pilot* Reports the Civil War," *Historical Journal of Massachusetts* 9, no. 2 (June 1981): 5–16. For a typical editorial about the Irish contribution to the Union cause and the death of nativism, see *Boston Pilot*, July 6, 1861. At the war's end, an editorial in July 1865, entitled "Heroes of the War," proclaimed that Irish soldiers had saved the country

and the Constitution and accelerated the process of assimilation; see *Boston Pilot*, July 15, 1865.

55. *Boston Pilot*, August 23, 1862; September 27, 1862. See Burton, *Melting Pot Soldiers*, 112–19.

56. A variety of sources were used to discover and verify the birthplace for Irish-born men who enlisted from or in New Bedford during the Civil War. For example, records of the William Logan Rodman Post Number 1, Grand Army of the Republic, contained the names of forty-one Irish-born men who had joined the post before 1890. These names were compared with individual service records compiled in *Massachusetts Soldiers and Sailors in the Civil War* (*MSSCW*) to determine place of enlistment and military service. Another effort was made to identify all New Bedford enlistees in the Twenty-Eighth Massachusetts Infantry. Finally, a database of all men of Irish descent between the ages of 12 and 40 enumerated in the 1860 federal population census for New Bedford—a total of 646 individuals—was compared to the *MSSCW*. The names, ages, and occupations of 43 individuals matched, and their regimental affiliations were used to seek their military pension records.

57. Burton, *Melting Pot Soldiers*, 131–35, provides an overview of the regiment's history. The *New Bedford Daily Evening Standard* printed Meagher's letter on September 16, 1861, followed by notices relating to the recruitment of Irish men in the issues dated September 27, October 17, October 23, October 25, and October 29, 1862. Company B of the Twenty-Eighth Massachusetts was one of three companies organized in the city during 1861, and comprised of volunteers who enlisted for three years, according to William Schouler, *History of Massachusetts in the Civil War*, vol. 2, repr. in William W. Crapo, *Centennial in New Bedford . . .*, appendix 23, (New Bedford, 1864), 130–34. The payment of a $100 state bounty at the end of service was promised in advertisements for the regiment; see, for example, *Boston Pilot*, October 5, 1861.

58. More than 1,800 men served in the regiment, of whom 161 were killed in action and 203 died of wounds or disease. *Boston Pilot*, October 5, 1861; Burton, *Melting Pot Soldiers*, 131–34.

59. Their diverse military service was seen in affiliations of the Irish veterans who later joined the New Bedford's premier Grand Army of the Republic Post, William Logan Rodman Post Number One. Of forty-one Irish-born members who had joined that post by 1890, slightly more than half of them, twenty-two, had served in the state's army units, three had been in the US Navy, and the remaining sixteen men served in units outside Massachusetts. Membership rosters of the William Logan Rodman Post Number One, Grand Army of the Republic, Special Collections, NBFPL.

60. No scholar has done more to enhance our understanding of Civil War mortality than Drew Gilpin Faust, most recently in *This Republic of Suffering: Death and the American Civil War* (New York: Knopf, 2008). Briefer versions include "The Civil War Soldier and the Art of Dying," *Journal of Southern History* 67, no. 1 (February 2001): 3–55, reprinted in Michael Barton and Larry M. Logue, *The Civil War Soldier: A Historical Reader* (New York: New York University Press, 2002), 485–511.

61. Congdon's explanations in Folder 11 of the Congdon Papers, NBFPL. See State Aid Treasurer's Report, City Document no. 4, dated January 1, 1867. The city council accepted the "Roll of Honor" in May 1869, and Leonard Ellis printed it verbatim in his *History of New Bedford* (1892), part 2, Biographical, appendix, 126–37. One man, Thomas Almy, was listed as both soldier and sailor; for this analysis, he was counted only once as a navy enlistee, and thus the database has 256 separate entries, not 257.

62. About 82 percent of desertions took place within two weeks of each of the six deadliest battles, according to Robertson. Also, urban soldiers died at rate of 140 percent above rural soldiers, and deserted at an 87 percent higher rate. Upper-class soldiers (farmers, white-collar workers, and skilled workers) "suffered death in combat 35 per-

cent more often and deserted 68 percent more often than lower-class laborers and men listing no occupation." Robertson, "Re-enlistment Patterns," 25–26.

63. Of more than fifty dead soldiers with ranks listed, nineteen had been corporals, fourteen sergeants, three quartermaster sergeants, three first sergeants, two second lieutenants, two first lieutenants, two captains, and one lieutenant colonel, William Logan Rodman of the Thirty-Eighth Massachusetts, killed at Port Hudson. Thirty-four seamen died during the war, along with three acting master's mates, an acting ensign, a first class boy, a cook, and a steward. New Bedford Roll of Honor.

64. The largest number, seventeen, were interred in the Oak Grove Cemetery, while another thirteen were buried in the Rural Cemetery. A few were buried in Fairhaven or other locations. Only three of the Roll of Honor designees were buried in the local Catholic Cemetery. See New Bedford Roll of Honor.

65. Joseph Ricketson to Deborah Weston, July 19, 1863, Boston Public Library, Rare Books, Ms. A.9.2 vol. 31, no. 73. Thomas R. Rodman to "My Dear Uncle" [Benjamin Rodman], June 7, 1863, printed in Higginson, "Rodman," 68–69. *NBDES*, December 25, 1862, and December 30, 1862.

66. Joseph Ricketson to Deborah Weston, July 19, 1863, Boston Public Library, Rare Books, Ms. A.9.2 vol. 31, no. 73.

67. Ezra had served in the Twentieth Massachusetts, and William in the Tenth Heavy Artillery. *NBDES*, October 20, 1864.

68. Colonel Albert C. Maggi was born in Italy where he served as a military officer under Garibaldi and had seen duty in South America, as well. He enlisted in spring 1861 in New Bedford and worked his way up the ranks in the Third Massachusetts from sergeant-major to acting brigade-major. Later, he was named the lieutenant-colonel of the Twenty-First and then the Thirty-Third Regiments. Although Governor Andrew wrote that Maggi spoke good English and could command foreign troops. Maggi was not promoted and left the service after resigning his colonelcy on April 1, 1863. Another local man who acquired some attention was Timothy Ingraham, who had commanded the New Bedford City Guards. Enlisting as an officer of the Thirty-Eighth Massachusetts, Ingraham was deemed a "trustworthy, and reliable man, conscientious, and sure fire" by Governor Andrew; he later was appointed provost-marshal in Washington, DC, and brevetted brigadier-general on October 2, 1865. Andrew to Secretary of War, n.d., excerpted in Schouler, 1:386–88.

5. "Boys, I Only Did My Duty": New Bedford's Black Soldiers in the Fifty-Fourth Massachusetts

1. *New Bedford Daily Evening Standard* (hereafter cited as *NBDES*), April 25, 1861. Also covered in Corporal James Henry Gooding, *On the Altar of Freedom, A Black Soldier's Civil War Letters from the Front*, ed. Virginia Matzke Adams (Amherst: University of Massachusetts Press, 1991), xix.

2. Similarly, in May 1861, Boston's black citizens led by Robert Morris petitioned the state for the legal right to form military companies and to have the word "white" stricken from militia laws. Such petitions and legislation failed at the state level. See William Schouler, *A History of Massachusetts in the Civil War, Volume 1, Civil and Military History of Massachusetts in the Rebellion* (Boston: E. P. Dutton & Co., Publishers, 1868), 175–80, 392. For a discussion of black militians in the war, see J. R. Kerr-Ritchie, *Rites of August First, Emancipation Day in the Black Atlantic World* (Baton Rouge: Louisiana State University Press, 2007), 185–92. Mitch Kachun provides ample evidence of a growing militancy and militia formation among Massachusetts' black communities, particularly in Boston, during the 1850s and into the war years; see Mitch Kachun, "From

Forgotten Founder to Indispensable Icon, Crispus Attucks, Black Citizenship, and Collective Memory, 1770–1865," *Journal of the Early Republic* 29 (Summer 2009): 249–86.

3. All wartime issues of *Douglass' Monthly* contained strident editorials calling for black enlistments. In February 1863, for example, Douglass blasted the federal government's failure to enlist African Americans as "a marvel of folly and imbecility." See especially *Douglass' Monthly*, May 1861, September 1861, December 1861, February 1863. David Blight's work on Frederick Douglass has been most helpful; see especially David W. Blight, *Frederick Douglass' Civil War: Keeping Faith in Jubilee* (Baton Rouge: Louisiana State University Press, 1989), and David W. Blight, "'For Something Beyond the Battlefield': Frederick Douglass and the Struggle for the Memory of the Civil War," *Journal of American History* 75 (March 1989): 1156–78; and David W. Blight, *Beyond the Battlefield: Race, Memory, and The American Civil War* (Amherst and Boston: University of Massachusetts Press, 2002).

4. Luis F. Emilio, A Brave Black Regiment: History of the Fifty-fourth Regiment of Massachusetts Volunteer Infantry, 1863–1865, 2nd ed., rev. (Boston, 1894; New York: Johnson Reprint Corp., 1968), 10.

5. Among the first scholarly works to emphasize the "different war" fought by black soldiers was Ira Berlin, Joseph P. Reidy, and Leslie S. Rowland, eds., *Freedom, A Documentary History of Emancipation, 1861–1867, series 2,* The Black Military Experience (New York: Cambridge University Press, 1982). Also see their succinct version, Ira Berlin, Joseph P. Reidy, and Leslie S. Rowland, eds., *Freedom's Soldiers: The Black Military Experience in the Civil War* (New York: Cambridge University Press, 1998), and Ira Berlin et al., "The Black Military Experience, 1861–1867," in *Slaves No More: Three Essays on Emancipation and the Civil War*, ed. Ira Berlin (Cambridge: Cambridge University Press, 1992), 187–233. Books that focus on the Fifty-Fourth Massachusetts include Martin H. Blatt, Thomas J. Brown, and Donald Yacovone, eds., *Hope & Glory: Essays on the Legacy of the Fifty-fourth Massachusetts Regiment* (Amherst: University of Massachusetts Press in association with Massachusetts Historical Society, 2001); Russell Duncan, *Where Death and Glory Meet: Colonel Robert Gould Shaw and the 54th Massachusetts Infantry* (Athens: University of Georgia Press, 1999); Peter Burchard, *One Gallant Rush: Robert Gould Shaw and His Brave Black Regiment* (New York: St. Martin's Press, 1965); Robert Ewell Greene, *Swamp Angels, A Biographical Study of the 54th Massachusetts Regiment, True Facts about the Black Defenders of the Civil War* (n.p., Bomark/Greene Publishing Group, 1990). The best general accounts of the black experience in the Civil War build from Benjamin Quarles, *The Negro in the Civil War* (Boston: Little, Brown, and Company, 1953) and Dudley Taylor Cornish, *The Sable Arm, Black Troops in the Union Army, 1861–1865* (Lawrence: University of Kansas Press, 1956; repr., 1987). See Joseph T. Glatthaar, *Forged in Battle: The Civil War Alliance of Black Soldiers and White Officers* (New York: Free Press, 1990; repr., Baton Rouge: Louisiana State University Press, 2000); Howard C. Westwood, *Black Troops, White Commanders, and Freedmen During the Civil War* (Carbondale: Southern Illinois University Press, 1992). Noah Andre Trudeau, *Like Men of War: Black Troops in the Civil War, 1862–1865* (New York: Little, Brown and Company, 1998); Hondon B. Hargrove, *Black Union Soldiers in the Civil War* (Jefferson, NC: McFarland and Company, 1988); John David Smith, ed., *Black Soldiers in Blue: African American Troops in the Civil War Era* (Chapel Hill: University of North Carolina Press, 2002); Keith P. Wilson, *Campfires of Freedom: The Camp Life of Black Soldiers During the Civil War* (Kent, OH, and London: Kent State University Press, 2002); Richard M. Reid, *Freedom for Themselves: North Carolina's Black Soldiers in the Civil War Era* (Chapel Hill: University of North Carolina Press, 2008). Many internet sites now provide excellent materials; see Written in Glory, Letters from the Soldiers and Officers of the 54th Massachusetts, http://54th-mass.org/, and sites by the National Park Service

including: The Civil War: 150 Years, http://www.nps.gov/features/waso/cw150th/, and the Civil War Soldiers and Sailors System, http://www.itd.nps.gov/cwss/.

6. *Douglass' Monthly*, August 1861; for meeting of October 9, 1861, see *Douglass' Monthly*, November 1861.

7. *NBDES*, September 12, 1861; November 7, 1861; March 13, 1862; March 20, 1862.

8. *Douglass' Monthly*, September 1862.

9. *NBDES*, December 31, 1862. Reporting on Emancipation Day, the *Standard* reported that "The colored people appear to be in high enjoyment to-day, which is natural," describing an integrated event in Liberty Hall under the direction of Reverend Kelley. Looking forward to 1863, the *Standard* wrote, "We trust that this year is to witness the end of slavery and the end of the rebellion." *NBDES*, January 1, 1863.

10. *NBDES*, January 22, 1863. Andrew's order quoted in Emilio, *Brave Black Regiment*, 2. For background on Governor Andrew's efforts in establishing black regiments, see Henry Greenleaf Pearson, *The Life of John A. Andrew, Governor of Massachusetts, 1861–1865* (Boston and New York: Houghton, Mifflin and Company, 1904), 2:63–121; Cornish, *The Sable Arm*, 105–6; Glatthaar, *Forged in Battle*, 37–38, 135–36. Schouler pays much attention to Andrew's efforts to raise black regiments; see 1:392, 407–10.

11. Emilio describes a variety of leaders who created a "line of recruiting posts" in the North, among them George E. Stephens, A. M. Green, Charles L. Remond, William Wells Brown, Martin R. Delany, John Rock, George T. Downing, plus religious leaders such as the Reverends William Jackson, J. B. Smith, Henry H. Garnett, and J. W. Loqueer. Emilio, *Brave Black Regiment*, 3–12; also Schouler, 1:407, 410. J. Matthew Gallman emphasizes that the most successful recruiting pitch was the "core message" of upholding blacks' "manhood"; see J. Matthew Gallman, "In Your Hands That Musket Means Liberty, African American Soldiers and the Battle of Olustee," in Joan Waugh and Gary W. Gallagher, eds., *Wars Within a War: Controversy and Conflict over the American Civil War* (Chapel Hill: University of North Carolina Press, 2009), 87–108. Thomas O'Connor writes that "many blacks were bitterly determined to stay out of the war entirely" because of the threat of unequal pay and their inability to serve as officers. Still, he estimates that about 40 percent of military-aged black men from Boston enlisted in the Fifty-Fourth. Thomas H. O'Connor, *Civil War Boston, Home Front and Battlefield* (Boston: Northeastern University Press, 1997), 129–30.

12. Emilio, *Brave Black Regiment*, 17–18. Andrew to Congdon, February 9, 1863, in Soldiers' Fund Committee Records, Special Collections, New Bedford Free Public Library (hereafter cited as NBFPL). See also Gooding, *Altar*, xviii.

13. Emilio, *Brave Black Regiment*, 9–10. William Logan Rodman, the most prominent white officer from New Bedford killed in the war, was not confident about Grace's leadership when he addressed "negro soldier raising" in a letter of March 2, 1863. "I wish well to the enterprise," Rodman wrote, "[but] I hardly think Grace is just the man for Captain, but with the right man, one who is very decided, prompt, active and knows his business, I see no reason why a first rate company may not be raised in our town." A few weeks later he wrote about "whether darkies will or will not fight. Why we all unite in hoping they will, and thus save thousands of white lives, and give employment to a great number of them. Try the experiment fully, & then form an opinion. . . . If the blacks wont fight, why then they will be like a great many white men. If they will, then we have material for an army which may whip the world." Letters by William Logan Rodman, March 2, 1863 and March 25, 1863, extracted and transcribed by James B. Congdon, Congdon Papers, NBFPL.

14. Initial recruits included Alexander Johnson, George Lee, Lewis F. Fleetwood, James H. Buchanan, John Wilmot, James Adams, and James Filker. Grace's first public notice, published in the *New Bedford Mercury*, promised the same pay, rations, and family support as that granted to white soldiers. See Gooding, *Altar*, jacket and 96.

15. An array of white and black speakers offered encouragement, including Colonel Alberto Maggi, the Reverend L. C. Lock, and Reverend Charles L. Remond. *NBDES*, February 12, 1863; February 16, 1863; February 19, 1863.

16. *NBDES* February 21, 1863; *NBDES*, February 26, 1863.

17. Congdon tallied 189 eligible black men on the city's rolls, of whom 20 were in the service (presumably in the Union navy) and another 37 were abroad (presumably in maritime employment). Congdon correspondence located in Records of the Soldiers' Fund Committee, 1861–63, Special Collections, NBFPL. J. Ricketson to D. Weston, February 27, 163; Weston Papers, Special Collections, NBFPL; Carney's account in Leonard B. Ellis, *History of New Bedford* (Syracuse, NY, 1892), 346–47.

18. James B. Congdon informed Governor Andrew that nearly all of New Bedford's black enlistees had signed up without any promised bounty, "excepting, perhaps, the trifling prospect of Ten dollars," and he explained that the city council did not want to violate state laws. James B. Congdon to Governor John A. Andrew, March 16, 1863 (copy), in James B. Congdon Papers, Special Collections, NBFPL.

19. Emilio, *Brave Black Regiment*, 10; Gooding, *Altar*, xxx.

20. *NBDES*, March 26, 1863.

21. One of the enlistees, Richard Nelson, forty-four years old, was rejected from military service for medical reasons after going to camp in Readville. He returned to New Bedford where he lived into his mid-nineties and requested a military pension in 1912 at the age of ninety-four. Richard C. Nelson pension file, Invalid application no. 1,402,704; Civil War Pension Files, Records of the Adjutant General's Office, Record Group 15, NA.

22. John W. Blackburn was counted twice, apparently. Like Richard Nelson, he was discharged at Readville for medical reasons on May 28, 1863, but he apparently reenlisted in Company C in August 1863 and served through the war until mustered out with the regiment. Given their same names, nearly approximate ages (18 and 20, respectively), and the same occupation of laborer, it seems safe to assume that the "John Blackburn" listed twice in the regimental roster was the same individual, thus reducing the New Bedford contribution to Company C to a total of thirty-two men. See Roster in Emilio, *Brave Black Regiment*, 349.

23. *Douglass' Monthly*, March 1863, followed by his editorial, "Why Should a Colored Man Enlist?" in April 1863. For one discussion of African American "manhood," see Jim Cullen, "'I's a Man Now': Gender and African American Men" in *Divided Houses: Gender and the Civil War*, ed. Catherine Clinton and Nina Silber (New York: Oxford University Press, 1992), 75–91. Donald R. Shaffer also draws upon "manhood" as a key explanation of blacks' motivations during the war; see Donald R. Shaffer, *After the Glory: The Struggles of Black Civil War Veterans* (Lawrence: University Press of Kansas, 2004).

24. For Hunter's letter to Andrew, see *NBDES*, May 15, 1863. For Thomas Wentworth Higginson's experiences with black troops in Florida, see *NBDES*, March 26, 1863, and his published account, *Army Life in a Black Regiment*.

25. Noah Andre Trudeau pointed out the difficulty in finding firsthand accounts from the black rank and file because the majority of African-American soldiers were illiterate. Helpful accounts include Edwin Redkey's published and unpublished work, along with wartime issues of *The Christian Recorder*. See Trudeau, *Like Men of War*, xv–xvi; Edwin S. Redkey, ed., *A Grand Army of Black Men: Letters from African-American Soldiers in the Union Army, 1861–1865* (Cambridge: Cambridge University Press, 1992).

26. See Adams's introduction for biographical information on James Henry Gooding, *Altar*, xv–xxxvii.

27. James Henry Gooding to *New Bedford Mercury*, March 3, 1863, Gooding, *Altar*, 3–4 (hereafter cited as JHG, date of letter, date of publication, *Altar*, page number).

Gooding adopted the "broad" view of black enlistment propounded by Frederick Douglass and analyzed perceptively by J. Matthew Gallman, "In Your Hands," 99–100.

28. JHG, letter dated March 6, 1863, published on March 7, 1863, *Altar*, 5; JHG letter dated March 15, 1863, published on March 18, 1863, *Altar*, 5–6. JHG, letter dated March 21, 1863, published on March 24, 1863, *Altar*, 7–8; JHG, letter dated April 11, 1863, published on April 13, 1863, *Altar*, 12. Frederick Douglass's son, Lewis, corroborated Gooding when he wrote home from camp that "The young men from Boston and New Bedford receive many little niceties from their friends which keeps them in cheerful spirits." Lewis Douglass to Amelia, April 8, 1863, Douglass Papers, reel 32, Library of Congress. The *Boston Traveller* reported on March 4, 1863, that Lieutenant Grace commanded fifty-one enlisted men from New Bedford; see The Civil War Records of the Fifty-Fourth Massachusetts Volunteer Infantry, vol. 1, January 26, 1863–October 18, 1863, Massachusetts Historical Society (hereafter cited as Fifty-Fourth Records, MHS).

29. Official Order of the Governor, March 3, 1863, Order Book for Company C (Companies A–F), Descriptive Books, 54th Massachusetts Regiment (Colored), Entry 114, Records of the Adjutant General's Office, Record Group 94, NA. See also JHG, letter dated March 30, 1863, published on March 31, 1863, *Altar*, 8; JHG, letter dated April 3, 1863, published on April 6, 1863, *Altar*, 10.

30. JHG, letter dated April 11, 1863, published on April 13, 1863, *Altar*, 11.

31. Edwin S. Redkey, "Black Chaplains in the Union Army," *Civil War History* 32, no. 4 (1987): 331–50; see 332, 335. See Gooding, *Altar*, 8–9n8, and 11–12n11, for a useful explanation of the Jackson-Grimes conflict. Other explanations are provided by Shaffer, *After the Glory*, 63; Wilson, *Campfires of Freedom*, 111–24; Kathryn Grover, *The Fugitive's Gibraltar, Escaping Slaves and Abolitionism in New Bedford Massachusetts* (Amherst: University of Massachusetts Press, 2001), 239, 254–55.

32. Tensions emerged at Readville where civilians were introduced to military life at Camp Meigs. Black and Irish enlistees grappled on occasion, as described by Charles Douglass, one of Frederick Douglass's sons, who fought with an Irish soldier at Readville in July 1863. In a letter to his father, Douglass reported that the angry Irish man "stepped in front of me with his fist doubled up in my face and said ain't McClellan a good Gen. you black nigger. I dont care if you have got the uniform on." After battling the man for some time, a white police officer came over and arrested the white combatant. Douglass explained that he "felt as though I could whip a dozen [I]rish. . . . I'm all right for I have got my mind made to shoot the first Irishman that strikes me[.] [T]hey may talk but keep their paws to themselves." Charles R. Douglass to Frederick Douglass, July 6, 1863, Douglass Papers, Library of Congress.

33. Emilio, *Brave Black Regiment*, 23–24; JHG, letter dated May 4, 1863, published on May 6, 1863, *Altar*, 16–17.

34. JHG, letter dated May 24, 1863, published on May 26, 1863, Gooding, *Altar*, 24.

35. Andrew's words were later inscribed on the Shaw Memorial in Boston; see Emilio, *Brave Black Regiment*, 25–27, 30.

36. Emilio, *Brave Black Regiment*, 24–25, 28–30; Andrew's speech on 25–30. Gooding provided a detailed synopsis, too: JHG, letter dated May 18, 1863, published May 20, 1863, *Altar*, 21–23.

37. JHG, letter dated May 24, 1863, published on May 26, 1863, *Altar*, 24. Opposition to blacks' enlistments was pronounced in the pages of the *Boston Pilot*, an Irish Catholic newspaper, that declared: "The blacks will neither bring up the rear with decency, nor lead at the front with honor. They are not yet fit to lead for such a great nation as this." This excerpt was contained and countered in a commemorative pamphlet about the black regiment, *Souvenir of the 54th*, in Fifty-Fourth Records, vol. 1, MHS. In Boston, the Irish hostility to blacks is noted by Thomas H. O'Connor, Civil War Boston 137–38.

The competing claims of citizenship by Irish-Americans and African-Americans in the war has been explored by Christian G. Samito, *Becoming American Under Fire: Irish Americans, African Americans, and the Politics of Citizenship* (Ithaca, NY: Cornell University Press, 2009). Luis Emilio, who participated in the Boston procession, reported: "All along the route the sidewalks, windows, and balconies were thronged with spectators, and the appearance of the regiment caused repeated cheers and waving of flags and handkerchiefs. The national colors were displayed everywhere. . . . Only hearty greetings were encountered; not an insulting word was heard, or an unkind remark made." Newspaper quoted in Emilio, *Brave Black Regiment*, 31–33. Adjutant General William Schouler described the march as "one of the most splendid ovations ever seen in Boston"; Schouler, 1:409.

38. Emilio, *Brave Black Regiment*, 47–48. Writing with sarcasm, Gooding suggested that antiblack newspapers would find good things to say if black troops died, for it would be a cheaper way of "'getting rid of them, than [by] expending money to send them to President Lincoln's Paradise in Central America, or to colonize them at Timbuctoo or Sahara." JHG, letter dated June 14, 1863, published on June 30, 1863, *Altar,* 29–30; also see JHG, letter dated June 22, 1863, published on July 8, 1863, *Altar,* 30–32.

39. *NBDES*, June 8, 1863.

40. See Emilio, *Brave Black Regiment*, 51–66; Adams provides a concise background to the assault on Fort Wagner in Gooding, *Altar,* 34–36. Trudeau explains the difference between "battery" and "fort" and offers an excellent synopsis of strategies, troop movements, and the attack on Fort Wagner. See Trudeau, *Like Men of War*, chap. 3, 63–90.

41. "J.W.G.'s" letter dated July 4, 1863, *NBDES*, July 20, 1863.

42. Terry quoted in Emilio, *Brave Black Regiment*, 63. JHG, letter dated July 20, 1863, published on August 1, 1863, *Altar,* 36–38. Luis Emilio corroborated this outpouring of soldierly enthusiasm by white troops; see Emilio, *Brave Black Regiment*, 67.

43. JHG, letter dated July 20, 1863, published on August 1, 1863, *Altar,* 36–38. For a concise overview of the assault on Fort Wagner, see Emilio, *Brave Black Regiment*, 67–78.

44. Emilio, *Brave Black Regiment*, 78–85; JHG, letter dated July 20, 1863, published on August 1, 1863, *Altar,* 36–38.

45. Casualties noted in Emilio, *Brave Black Regiment*, 88–91; Hallowell to Brigadier General Seymour, November 7, 1863, reprinted in full in ibid., 88–91. Hallowell's report is located in *Official Records of the War of the Rebellion*, Series 1, vol. 28, part 1, 362–63. Joseph Glatthaar describes the assault and explains its significance in *Forged in Battle*, chapter 7, "Proving Their Valor," 121–42.

46. *NBDES*, March 24, 1863.

47. Fleetwood provided an affidavit for Carney's Congressional Medal of Honor application in a deposition dated January 15, 1900. Other corroborating testimony came from affidavits of John W. M. Appleton, former Captain, Company A, Fifty-Fourth Massachusetts Volunteers, and Charles H. Harrison and Lewis H. Douglass, both black veterans of the same regiment. "The Negro in the Military Service of the United States, 1607–1889," National Archives and Record Service Microfilm, roll M929, record group 94, Records of the Adjutant General's Office, National Archives (hereafter cited as NARS Microfilm M929).

48. Andrew to Stanton, NARS Microfilm M929.

49. Emilio mentioned first that the national flag was planted at the parapet and "gallantly maintained by the brave Sergt. William H. Carney of Company C." Also, Emilio reported that "Sergeant Carney had bravely brought this flag from Wagner's parapet, at the cost of two grievous wounds." Emilio, *Brave Black Regiment*, 81, 85, frontispiece.

50. Carney responded by letter to an inquiry about his life and related that he had been born in 1840 in Norfolk, Virginia, to former slave parents. As a child, Carney claimed that he had attended a "secret school" run by a minister in Norfolk, and at the

age of fifteen he "embraced the gospel" while "engaged in the coasting trade with [his] father" who eventually escaped to Massachusetts. After moving himself to New Bedford, William Carney "formed connection" with the Reverend William Jackson's church and planned to become a minister until he had the opportunity to enlist in the Fifty-Fourth Massachusetts. Carney to the editor, *The Liberator*, November 6, 1863, reprinted in Herbert Aptheker, ed., *A Documentary History of the Negro in America* (New York: Citadel Press, 1951), 484–85. See also an interview with Carney's descendant, Carl J. Cruz, "Sergeant William H. Carney, Civil War Hero" in "It Wasn't in Her Lifetime, But It Was Handed Down," *Four Black Oral Histories of Massachusetts*, ed. Eleanor Wachs (Boston: Office of the Massachusetts Secretary of State, 1989), 12–13.

51. Grace recalled the attack in a letter sent home. As they advanced toward the Confederate battery, Grace reported, "Our men fell like grass before a sickle." When Colonel Shaw fell at the parapet, the colors were "caught up by Sergeant Carney, of Co. C, who was very badly wounded. He carried them, creeping on his knees, holding up the flag and advancing toward the Fort, until he fell into the ditch." *NBDES*, July 28, 1863. A succinct and colorful account is Brian C. Pohanka, "Fort Wagner and the 54th Massachusetts Volunteer Infantry," *America's Civil War Magazine*, http://tinyurl.com/fortwag nerand54th. The most comprehensive account is Stephen R. Wise, *Gate of Hell: Campaign for Charleston Harbor, 1863* (Columbia: University of South Carolina Press, 1994).

52. Fort Wagner casualties discharged before the war's end included William Carney; George Delevan, a forty-one-year-old married laborer; and Lewis A. Fleetwood, a single laborer of twenty-one. At least three men returned to full service after recuperating and served for the full duration of the war: David Fletcher, a twenty-year-old hostler when he enlisted; Sergeant William H. W. Gray, a married seaman in his late thirties; and Samuel Leighton, a married laborer in his early forties. Cornelius Henson presented a special case, for he was taken prisoner at Fort Wagner and later served as part of a prisoner exchange on March 4, 1865. Henson was discharged from the Union army at Boston on July 8, 1865, about five weeks before the surviving soldiers of the Fifty-Fourth mustered out. Emilio, *Brave Black Regiment*, "Roster of the Fifty-fourth," Company C, 349–53.

53. JHG, letter of August 3, 1863, published August 16, 1863, *Altar*, 45. Second quote is from JHG, letter of September 5, 1863, published September 15, 1863, *Altar*, 55.

54. On August 24, 1863, the Fifty-Fourth Massachusetts joined the Second South Carolina and the Third U.S.C.T. to form the Fourth Brigade. Emilio, *Brave Black Regiment*, 125–27; Emilio quoted on 123; Gilmore on 127. JHG, letter of September 9, 1863, published on September 21, 1863, *Altar*, 56–58.

55. *NBDES*, August 14, 1863; *NBDES*, September 16, 1863.

56. *NBDES*, August 14, 1863.

57. *NBDES*, March 5, 1863; *NBDES*, October 30, 1863; *NBDES*, May 5, 1864.

58. See William H. W. Gray pension file; Invalid application number 225,736, certificate number 145, 514; Widow application number 362,027; Minor application number 500,756; RG 15, NA. William H. W. Gray was, at the time of enlistment, a seaman in his later thirties, who was later wounded at Fort Wagner. While the regiment was laying siege to Charleston, Gray organized a black Masonic lodge on Morris Island, according to Luis Emilio. See Emilio, *Brave Black Regiment*, 129. In unpublished letters, Luis Emilio corroborated the stories about Martha Gray. In a letter of April 22, 1864, Emilio wrote: "I refer to Mrs. Gray wife of 1st Sergt. Gray of our regt. from New Bedford. She is a nurse (or rather matron) in the hospitals at Beaufort & came here to see her husband. She is nearly white & has very lady like manners." On April 24, he wrote that "Mrs. Gray has now gone from the island." The Civil War Records of the Fifty-Fourth Massachusetts Volunteer Infantry, vol. 2, October 13, 1863–July 31, 1864, Massachusetts Histori-

cal Society, compiled by Luis Emilio (hereafter cited as Fifty-Fourth Regiment Papers, 1863–1901, vol. 2). For a general overview black women during the war, see Ella Forbes, *African American Women During the Civil War* (New York and London: Garland Publishing, 1998).

59. Emilio letter of January 2, 1864 in Fifty-Fourth Regiment Papers, 1863–1901, vol. 2, MHS.

60. JHG, letter of January 2, 1864, published January 14, 1864, *Altar*, 96–101.

61. *NBDES*, December 31, 1863 and *NBDES* January 7, 1864.

62. Nineteenth-century African-American historians subsequently highlighted Carney's bravery. In George Washington Williams' account, *A History of the Negro Troops in the War of the Rebellion, 1861–1865; Preceded by a Review of the Military Services of Negroes in Ancient and Modern Times* (New York: Harper & Brothers, 1887), Carney's bravery is recalled with poetry on p. 200, and a laudatory report about Carney from Colonel Littlefield is detailed; Littlefield to Col. A. G. Brown Jr. extracted from Williams' *History of the Negro Race in America*, vol. 2, 330–31, in NARS Microfilm M929. Joseph T. Wilson, who enlisted in Company C of the Fifty-Fourth Massachusetts Regiment in New Bedford, later wrote *The Black Phalanx; A History of the Negro Soldiers of the United States in the Wars of 1775–1812, 1861–65* (Hartford, CT: American Publishing Company, 1890), in which he included an illustration of Carney on page 181.

63. Emilio, *Brave Black Regiment*, 109; JHG, letter of August 9, 1863, published on August 21, 1863, *Altar*, 48–49; JHG, letter dated August 30, 1863, published on September 15, 1863, *Altar*, 54.

64. Congdon to Andrew, August 20, 1863, in Gooding, *Altar*, 120–21. Congdon wrote to Andrew on December 14, 1863 and forwarded a letter from James Henry Gooding who wrote from Morris Island on November 29, 1863; see Gooding, *Altar*, 121–22. Andrew responded to Congdon in letter dated December 20, 1863; see ibid., 122–24. Schouler devotes much attention to Governor Andrew's campaign for equal pay; see 1:416, 487–88, 549.

65. JHG to President Lincoln, September 28, 1863, in Gooding, *Altar*, 118–20. Gooding's letter also located in Aptheker, ed., *A Documentary History of the Negro*, 483–84. See also Trudeau, *Like Men of War*, 91–93, 155, 252–55.

66. JHG, letter dated November 21, 1863, published December 4, 1863, *Altar*, 83; JHG, letter dated February 2, 1864, published February 15, 1864, *Altar*, 110–11.

67. Emilio's letters, unnamed Boston newspaper, and letter from Andrew to Lincoln, in Fifty-Fourth Regiment Papers, 1863–1901, vol. 2, MHS.

68. Luis Emilio wrote that some soldiers had been slaves, but "they took the oath as freemen, by God's higher law, if not by their country's. . . . That they were compelled to take this or any oath at the last was an insult crowning the injury." Emilio, *Brave Black Regiment*, 220–21. Hallowell to Andrew, September 19, 1864, entry 114, Descriptive books, 54th Massachusetts Regiment (Colored), Records of the Adjutant General's Office, Record Group 94, NA.

69. Under a banner headline, "Paid Off," the *Liberator* estimated that perhaps $145,000 had been sent back to Massachusetts by all of its black soldiers. Luis Emilio wrote: "It required $170,000 to pay the Fifty-fourth. Over $53,000 was sent home by Adams' Express; and the sum ultimately forwarded reached $100,000." Emilio, *Brave Black Regiment*, 228; Accounts from Fifty-Fourth Regiment Papers, 1863–1901, vol. 3, MHS.

70. In a letter written in late-November 1863, Gooding described a poignant Thanksgiving celebration and religious service, followed by sports and games. White officers treated their men to cakes, fruits, and breads, and placed a $13 prize (one month's pay) atop a greased pole. "So you see the boys are all alive and full of fun," Gooding wrote with reassurance, "they don't intend to be lonesome or discouraged whether Uncle Sam

pays them or not; in fact the day was kept up by the 54th with more spirit than by any other regiment on the island." JHG, letter dated November 28, 1863, published December 15, 1863, *Altar*, 85–87.

71. *Liberator*, March 18, 1864, published as "Epilogue," in Gooding, *Altar*, 115.

72. Gallman, "In Your Hands."

73. Emilio, *Brave Black Regiment*, 276–88, 314, 318–21; see also *The Liberator*, September 15, 1865.

74. Emilio, *Brave Black Regiment*, 324–25.

75. More work is needed on free blacks who served in the Union navy. Michael Bennett suggests that black Union sailors fought a "different type of war"; Michael J. Bennett, Union Jacks, Yankee Sailors in the Civil War (Chapel Hill: University of North Carolina Press, 2004), see especially chapter 7, "Frictions: Shipboard Relations between White and Contraband Union Sailors," 155–81. Joseph P. Reidy, "Black Jack: African American Sailors in the Civil War Navy," in William B. Cogar, ed., *New Interpretations in Naval History: Selected Papers from the Twelfth Naval History Symposium* (Annapolis Naval Institute Press, 1997). Steven J. Ramold, *Slaves, Sailors, Citizens: African Americans in the Union Navy* (DeKalb: Northern Illinois University Press, 2002). The online database maintained by Joseph P. Reidy pulled up nearly fifty black sailors who enlisted from their "home" of New Bedford, out of a total of 434 from Massachusetts. See http://www.itd.nps.gov/cwss/sailors_index.html. Also see David Valuska, *The African American in the Union Navy, 1861–1865* (New York: Garland, 1993). In Valuska's dissertation, appendixes listed seventy-six black seaman who enlisted in or originated in New Bedford between 1861 and 1865; of these, I located eight military pension records. See David Valuska, "The Negro in the Union Navy: 1861–1865," (PhD dissertation, Lehigh University, 1973), appendixes.

76. JHG, letter dated February 8, 1864, published February 22, 1864, *Altar*, 113.

6. "Worthy Recipients": New Bedford's Black Veterans and the Web of Social Welfare

1. Entries for Fanny L. Wright, August 23, 1864; January 4, 1865; January 19, 1865; January 27, 1865; February 10, 1865; February 17, 1865; New Bedford Overseers of the Poor Records, 1864–66, Special Collections, NBFPL (hereafter cited as NBOR).

2. Thomas A. McMullin, "Overseeing the Poor: Industrialization and Poor Relief in New Bedford, 1865–1900," *Social Science Review* 65 (December 1991): 548–63.

3. William Schouler, *A History of Massachusetts in the Civil War. Vol. 1*, Civil and Military History of Massachusetts in the Rebellion (Boston: E. P. Dutton & Co., Publishers, 1868), 488. The best collection of documents relevant to the pay issue is Ira Berlin, Joseph P. Reidy, and Leslie S. Rowland, *Freedom: A Documentary History of Emancipation, 1861–1867; Series 2, The Black Military Experience* (New York: Cambridge University Press, 1982), chapter 7, "Fighting on Two Fronts: The Struggle for Equal Pay," 362–406.

4. Michael B. Katz, *Poverty and Policy in American History* (New York: Academic Press, 1983), 14.

5. For nineteenth-century poor relief in general, see Paul Boyer, *Urban Masses and Moral Order in American, 1820–1920* (Cambridge, MA: Harvard University Press, 1978); Michael B. Katz, *In the Shadow of the Poorhouse: A Social History of Welfare in America*, rev. ed. (New York: Basic Books, 1996); Walter I. Trattner, *From Poor Law to Welfare State: A History of Social Welfare in America*, 6th ed. (New York: Simon and Schuster, 1999); Robert W. Kelso, *The History of Public Poor Relief in Massachusetts, 1620–1920* (Boston, 1922; repr., Montclair, NJ: Patterson Smith, 1969); Robert H. Bremner, *The Public Good: Philanthropy and Welfare in the Civil War Era* (New York: Knopf, 1980).

For an insightful study of local welfare policies during the Civil War, see Glenn C. Alt-schuler and Jan M. Saltzgaber, "The Limits of Responsibility: Social Welfare and Local Government in Seneca County, New York, 1860–1875," *Journal of Social History* 22 (Spring 1988): 515–37.

6. William Henry Glasson, *History of Military Pension Legislation in the United States* (New York: Columbia University Press, 1900), 9, 73–78; Commissioner Barrett is quoted on pp. 77–78.

7. The Overseers of the Poor maintained a detailed chronological accounting of all aid doled out between 1864 and 1866. During a one-year period between March 1, 1864, and March 1, 1865, 170 African Americans obtained assistance, about 9 percent of the group's total population in the city as of 1860. Until January 5, 1865, black recipients were designated by "c" or "cold" for "colored," but a new hand entered information after that date and paid less strict attention to the racial designation. To build case histories for these 170 recipients, other information was used and included household address, spouse's name, and children's names.

8. Edward A. Miller Jr., *The Black Civil War Soldiers of Illinois: The Story of the Twenty-Ninth U.S. Colored Infantry* (Columbia: University of South Carolina Press, 1998), 205–6.

9. Theda Skocpol further summarizes the "contractual" nature of the pension system: "Legitimate Civil War pensions were idealized as that which was justly due to the righteous core of a generation of men (and survivors of dead men)—a group that ought to be generously and constantly repaid by the nation for their sacrifices. Politicians spoke of a 'contract' between the national government and the Union's defenders in the Civil War, arguing that in return for their valiant service the former soldiers and those tied to them deserved all the public provision necessary to live honorable and decent lives free from want." Theda Skocpol, *Protecting Soldiers and Mothers: The Politics of Social Provision in the United States, 1870s–1920s* (Cambridge, MA: Harvard University Press, 1992), 149.

10. Miles Carter Jr. rose to the rank of Quarter Master Sergeant after enlisting in Company E of the all-black Fifth Massachusetts Cavalry. He died in New York City in May 1885 in his mid-thirties, and four years later his mother, Elizabeth Carter, contended that her son's death from pneumonia was linked to "lung trouble contracted in the army." In a letter to the Pension Bureau Commissioner of May 4, 1901, Mrs. Carter outlined her poverty and the costly process of appealing for pension payments: "I am 80 years of age lost my home and in feeble health and unable to earn a penny have no income or by the little State aid I receive. Have house rent to pay and am if any body was in need of a pension. Any evidence I can give that I have not already given I will try to give[.] No lawyer or Justice of Peace or any official will keep swearing in statements for me for nothing. And I have not a penny at this time to call my own." Carter gained support from Congressman William Greene who intervened beginning in April 1901, but a pension examiner denied the appeals because the soldier's death was not connected to or caused by his military service. Elizabeth Carter never received pension benefits. Miles Carter Jr., pension file, Mother application number 476,766; RG 15, NA.

11. Schouler, 1:316–81, 402.

12. Richard M. Reid, "Government Policy, Prejudice, and the Experience of Black Civil War Soldiers and Their Families," *Journal of Family History* 27, no. 4 (October 2002): 374–98, quote on 377. Also see Richard Reid, *Freedom for Themselves: North Carolina's Black Soldiers in the Civil War Era* (Chapel Hill: University of North Carolina Press, 2008). Philip Shaw Paludan outlines some of the economic fallout of the war in Philip Shaw Paludan, "What Did the Winners Win? The Social and Economic History of the North during the Civil War," in James McPherson and William J. Cooper Jr.,

Writing the Civil War: The Quest to Understand (Columbia: University of South Carolina Press, 1998), 174–200.

13. *New York Tribune* of January 23, 1864, is quoted in an unnamed Boston paper in Luis Emilio's records. The Civil War Records of the Fifty-Fourth Massachusetts Volunteer Infantry, vol. 2, October 13, 1863–July 31, 1864, Massachusetts Historical Society. Compiled by Luis Emilio. (Fifty-Fourth Regiment Papers, 1863–1901). Andrew to Charles Sumner, May 10, 1864, in Schouler, 1:549.

14. In the one-year period between 1863 and 1864, the per capita costs of outdoor relief jumped 67 percent. At the city's almshouse between 1864 and 1866 the average weekly costs paid by the city for each individual in that institution increased from $2.12 to $3.67, an increase of nearly 60 percent. Annual Reports of the Overseers of the Poor, 1860–70, NBCD, reel 2.

15. Address of Isaac C. Taber, Mayor, January 6, 1862; New Bedford City Documents (hereafter cited as NBCD), reel 2.

16. See "Impact Questionnaire," James B. Congdon Papers, Special Collections, NBFPL.

17. Fanny Wright, entries dated August 23, 1864, January 4, 1865, January 19, 1865, January 27, 1865, February 10, 1865, and February 17, 1865; NBOR. For a concise biography of John L. Wright, see Robert Ewell Greene, *Swamp Angels: A Biographical Study of the 54th Massachusetts Regiment, True Facts about the Black Defenders of the Civil War* (R. E. Greene Publisher, 1990), 300–1.

18. Henrietta Williams, September 12, 1864, NBOR. The Overseer noted that her husband was in the Fifty-Fourth Regiment, and that she had been born in North Carolina and arrived in Massachusetts in 1849. Wharton A. Williams was a Sergeant in Company C; see Greene, *Swamp Angels*, 292.

19. Nancy Douglass, September 20, 1864 and January 21, 1865, NBOR. Emery Phelps had enlisted in Company C in New Bedford on February 12, 1863, attaining the rank of Corporal, and was discharged on September 20, 1865; see Greene, *Swamp Angels*, 208–9.

20. Margaret Harrison, January 25, 1865, NBOR. John Harrison and Charles H. Harrison enlisted together on February 14, 1863, and both survived through the war until their discharge on August 20, 1865. See Luis F. Emilio, A Brave Black Regiment: History of the Fifty-fourth Regiment of Massachusetts Volunteer Infantry, 1863–1865 2nd ed. (Boston, 1891; repr., New York: Arno Press, 1968), 351.

21. Elizabeth Lawrence, January 28, 1865, NBOR. See Greene, *Swamp Angels*, 167. Emilio's Roster notes that at the time of enlistment, Robert Lawrence was a single laborer, aged twenty-eight, who signed up for Company C in New Bedford. He was discharged with the regiment at war's end on August 20, 1865. See Emilio, *Brave Black Regiment*, 352.

22. Delevan's story included details about his birth in Virginia, move to Massachusetts in 1855, his wife, Margaret, and their home at 236 Middle Street, where they had resided since 1859. George Delevan, September 10, 1864, NBOR. See Greene, *Swamp Angels*, 82.

23. Eliza Williams, March 3, 1864, NBOR.

24. Catherine Hill, March 3, April 16, May 11, August 31, September 24, October 18, November 22, December 6, and December 22, 1864; and January 10, January 23, February 6, and February 20, 1865, NBOR.

25. John Tolivar, March 5 and March 25, 1864, NBOR.

26. Harriet Brown, March 26, September 12, October 28, and December 16, 1864, and January 27, 1865, NBOR.

27. Writing more than a century ago, William Glasson noted that the "the history of Civil War pension legislation [was] one of continuing liberality on the part of Congress"; see Glasson, *Pension Legislation*, 9. Several prominent sociologists have examined

the Civil War pension system to examine the origins of social welfare policy, most nota-
bly Skocpol, *Protecting Soldiers and Mothers*, chapter 2, "Public Aid for the Worthy
Many: The Expansion of Benefits for Veterans of the Civil War," 102–152. See also Ann
Shola Orloff and Theda Skocpol, "Why Not Equal Protection? Explaining the Politics
of Public Social Spending in Britain, 1900–1911, and the United States, 1880s–1920,"
American Sociological Review 49 (December 1984): 726–50, and Ann Shola Orloff, "The
Political Origins of America's Belated Welfare State" in *The Politics of Social Policy in the
United States,* ed. Margaret Weir, Theda Skocpol, and Ann Orloff (Princeton: Princeton
University Press, 1988), 37–80. Heywood T. Sanders argues that expansion of the pension
system was central to the political strategies of the Republican Party after the Civil War;
Heywood T. Sanders, "Paying for the 'Bloody Shirt': The Politics of Civil War Pensions"
in *Political Benefits, Empirical Studies of American Public Programs,* ed. Barry S. Rund-
quist (Lexington, MA, 1980), 137–59.

28. In 1866 over 126,000 pensioners were on the national rolls at an annual expenditure of nearly $13.5 million. Two new pension acts in 1866 increased payments and
expanded the support of widows with large families, followed by legislation of 1868 that
extended application deadlines for five years. By 1871 the federal government spent more
than $25 million per year on pension benefits, which averaged $8.92 per month for an
invalid army veteran, $12.65 for widows and dependents, $9.10 for navy invalids, and
$15.40 for navy widows. For all pension recipients, the average payment was just one
cent under $11 per month. During the 1870s some effort was made to codify and system-
atize the pension laws, culminating in the Arrears Act of 1879, legislation termed by
Glasson as "a new era in the history of pension legislation." This legislation provided
full payments for all new and existing pension claims paid retroactively to the date of
death or discharge. This act led to an explosion of claims filed with the Pension Bureau.
Recipient's individual arrears payments could be substantial, amounting to a rough
average of $1,000. Between 1879 and 1890, numerous laws increased the rate of pension
payments for specific disabilities, leading to the enactment of the Dependent Pension
Bill of 1890, which Glasson called the "most important pension law ever enacted." The
1890 act became a "limited service pension bill," because any ex-soldier who had served
ninety days and could no longer perform manual labor might be entitled to monthly
payments of $12. In just one year, over 650,000 new pension claims were filed with the
Pension Bureau. By 1893 the pension rolls claimed 966,012 Union pensioners who
received total benefits of nearly $160 million per year. These disbursements constituted
42 percent of all federal expenditures for 1893. See Glasson, *Pension Legislation,* 78–79,
81–84, 87, 95, 102, 105, 118; Sanders, "Paying for the 'Bloody Shirt,'" 141–43; Skocpol,
Protecting Soldiers, 110, 117–18, 128–30. For a concise summary of how the pension laws
affected widows of Union veterans, see Amy E. Holmes, "'Such is the Price We Pay':
American Widows and the Civil War Pension System" in *Toward a Social History of the
American Civil War, Exploratory Essays,* ed. Maris A. Vinovskis, (New York: Cambridge
University Press, 1990), 172–73.

29. Vinovskis calculated that the average pension recipient received $122 annually (in
current dollars) in 1866, a figure that climbed to $139 per year in 1900. This latter figure
was "substantial" when the average annual earnings of all American employees was $375
in 1900. See Vinovskis, "Have Social Historians Lost the Civil War?, Some Preliminary
Demographic Speculations," in Vinovskis, ed., *Social History,* 1–30. Donald Shaffer
offers an authoritative account, *After the Glory: The Struggles of Black Civil War Veterans*
(Lawrence: University Press of Kansas, 2004). Also see Donald R. Shaffer, "'I Do Not
Suppose That Uncle Sam Looks at the Skin': African Americans and the Pension System,
1865–1934," *Civil War History* 46 (2000): 132–35; and Donald R. Shaffer and Elizabeth A.
Regosin, eds., *Voices of Emancipation: Understanding Slavery, the Civil War, and Recon-*

struction through the U.S. Pension Bureau Files (New York: New York University Press, 2008).

30. Skocpol, *Protecting Soldiers*, 108–10.

31. Shaffer, *After the Glory*, "Social Welfare," chap. 5, 119–42; quotes on pp. 122, 129, 133.

32. For representative works that use military pension files, see Joseph T. Glatthaar, *Forged in Battle: The Civil War Alliance of Black Soldiers and White Officers* (New York: The Free Press, 1990); Elizabeth Pleck, *Black Migration and Poverty: Boston 1865–1900* (New York, 1979); James Oliver Horton and Lois E. Horton, *Black Bostonians: Family Life and Community Struggle in the Antebellum North* (New York: Holmes & Meier, 1979).

33. Thomas Bender, *Community and Social Change in America* (New Brunswick, NJ: Rutgers University Press, 1978). See Patrick J. Kelly, *Creating a National Home, Building the Veterans' Welfare State, 1860–1900* (Cambridge, MA, and London: Harvard University Press, 1997).

34. Of the black men who enlisted in Company C of the Fifty-Fourth Massachusetts Colored Infantry and were considered from New Bedford, pension records of twenty-five of the contingent were located in the National Archives. Of this number, seventeen applied for veterans' pensions, with varying degrees of success, while eight other applications came from widows, dependent parents, or dependent children.

35. Joseph L. Hall pension file, Mother application number 171,917; certificate number 176,765; Civil War Pension Files, Records of the Adjutant General's Office, Record Group 15, National Archives (hereafter each pension file will be cited once and as RG 15, NA). Pension files are indexed alphabetically by the name of the soldier in the "General Pension Index"; a separate index sorts by military unit. Unless otherwise noted, all quoted material from the pension files has been transcribed verbatim, and original spellings have been retained throughout. I appreciate early advice from Joseph T. Glatthaar about how to best access individual pension records at the National Archives. In addition to original records available through the National Archives, the National Park Service has created an online database of Civil War Soldiers and Sailors at http://www.itd.nps.gov/cwss/ along with a site to celebrate the war's sesquicentennial at http://www.nps.gov/civilwar/.

36. Lucy and her three children had been sold by one J. Mathew Wright of Washington, DC, in February 1847. Gideon Welles apparently purchased the family in September 1849 with terms that promised their eventual freedom. Welles sped up the process by issuing his own emancipation proclamation on May 3, 1853, presumably to provide the family with greater security when Lucy Hall moved to New Bedford. Witnesses included Welles's son, Edgar, and a friend, Greenesbury W. Offley, who would later offer additional supporting information for Lucy Turner's pension claim. Joseph Hall pension file.

37. As part of her application, Lucy Turner submitted records from New Bedford's Overseers of the Poor that demonstrated payments averaging $24 per year in 1874 and 1875, with dramatic jumps to over $140 in 1876. For a focused evaluation of black women's applications for military pensions, see Michelle A. Krowl, "'Her Just Dues,' Civil War Pensions of African American Women in Virginia" in *Negotiating Boundaries of Southern Womanhood, Dealing with the Powers That Be*, ed. Janet L. Coryell, Thomas H. Appleton Jr., Anastatia Sims, and Sandra Gioia Treadway (Columbia and London: University of Missouri Press, 2000), 48–70.

38. Discharged from the Fifth Massachusetts Cavalry in October 1865, King first filed for a pension in October 1891, alleging injuries to his spine, head, neck, and shoulders after being thrown from his horse. The War Department found no specific records to uphold King's claims, forcing him to wait thirteen years until granting a pension in 1904. King wrote a number of letters in his own hand to make plaintive pleas for a military

pension. Original spelling is retained here. Isaiah King pension file, Invalid application number 1,060,718; certificate number 1,086,126; XC number 2,515,815; RG 15, NA.

39. Grace's letter about the Fort Wagner assault was published in *NBDES,* August 14, 1863. Lewis Fleetwood pension file, Invalid application number 48,481; certificate number 32,590; RG 15, NA. James W. Grace wrote to Joseph H. Barrett of the Pension Office on August 25, 1864. Robert Ewell Greene incorrectly writes that Fleetwood was discharged on July 7, 1865. See Greene, *Swamp Angels,* 99.

40. George Delevan pension file, Invalid application number 55,304; certificate number 73,732; RG 15, NA.

41. The aging widow continued her battle by enlisting the support of New Bedford's city physician, Dr. John Mackie, who acknowledged that George Delevan's death could have been related to his war wound. Furthermore, he attested, the black veteran had been a "man of good habits, regular and temperate." George Delevan pension file.

42. Carney first received an invalid pension in December 1864 and his widow was sent her last check in January 1916. Carney offered graphic details about his wounds, as he explained in May 1875: "I fell in the Rifel Pit and received a breast wound from which I have suffered much, while in the Pit I was struck with a Rifel ball, which severed the bones in my left Hip, the ball remaining inside of me." After being taken to the rear, "I was struck by a pease of a shell on the Head from which injury I have nearly lost the sight of my right eye." Original spelling retained these quotes. William H. Carney pension file, Invalid application number 56,619; certificate number 35,944; Widow application number 911,068; widow's certificate number 690,230; RG 15, NA.

43. Carney appreciated an arrears payment in March 1888 of more than $500, when his monthly payments increased to $10 and then rose in 1891 to $12 per month. William H. Carney pension file.

44. Cornelius Henson pension file, Invalid application number 313,080; certificate number 256,106; Widow application number 284,814; certificate number 203,956; RG 15, NA.

45. Ibid.

46. Arrears were computed as follows. Cornelius Henson's pension of $4 per month, to be paid from his discharge on July 9, 1865, through his death on September 28, 1880, amounted to $728. In addition, Mary Henson was to be paid $8 per month in arrears from July 28, 1881, until January 16, 1884, amounting to probably $240. Arrears then totaled approximately $968, in line with amounts paid to other veterans.

47. As Corporal James Gooding's widow, she first filed in March 1864 and began receiving $8 per month in May and received checks until her death in 1903. James Gooding pension file, Widow application number 49,290; certificate number 21,553; RG 15, NA

48. Joseph Campbell was killed at Fort Wagner, and his widow, Amelia, then a twenty-six-year-old mother of one child, first filed for a widow's pension on July 25, 1865. She married her husband in New Bedford in April 1862, and their son was born two weeks after the soldier left New Bedford for camp. George Delevan joined others in corroborating her application, and he offered a graphic account of Joseph Campbell's death at Fort Wagner: "I saw him for the last time not more than a second before the first volley was fired at us while the Regiment was advancing in the attack on Fort Wagner on the 18th day of July 1863 just about sundown. I heard his voice when the first volley was fired[.] I recognized it, He cried 'Oh my leg[,] I'm wounded, I am dead[.]' I am satisfied that he was killed at that time."

Amelia Campbell delayed filing a widow's pension claim until the war's end, possibly hoping that her husband was alive as a prisoner of war. She died in December 1866 without pension benefits, but her orphaned son obtained a minor's pension of $8 per month payment until his sixteenth birthday, plus arrears amounting to $360 to be paid to his uncle and guardian, Henry Johnson. Joseph Campbell pension file; Widow application number 103,250; certificate number 87,834; Minor application number 140,455; certificate number 93,190; RG 15, NA. Abraham (or "Abram") Torrence pension file; Widow application number 105,030; RG 15, NA.

49. Wright's widow, Caroline, had been married earlier to William Jackson who died in Texas during the Civil War. As a military widow, she received an $8 monthly pension paid regularly until 1879 when she married John Wright. Her widow's pension resumed in January 1905 after Wright's death. John L. Wright pension file, Invalid application number 422,195; law J., certificate number 482,457; Widow application number 817,910; law J., certificate number 600,177; record includes remark: "See W[idow's]. Cer'f. 71,325, W.S. Jackson F 5 Mass. Cav." RG 15, NA.

50. John Wright's prewar life in slavery was fleshed out in his pension file. In 1905 Caroline Wright deposed that "My said husband was first married while he lived in the south as a slave to woman named Sarah Thistres [?] before the war. He run away from Slavery before the war, and left his wife in the South. His masters name was Swon, and he went by that name while he was a slave. After he run away from slavery he came north and took the name of John L. Wright. His slave wife came north after the war and was married to a man named Valentine. . . . in slavery. She did not die until long after he was married to me." One of John Wright's former slave children, Nancy Webb, offered her account of the family's history in 1905. Living in New Bedford as the wife of Hezekiah Webb, the fifty-six-year-old Webb worked as a laundress and related her family history: "I am the daughter [of] Stethy Swons and Sarah Wiggins Swons. My father and mother were slaves in Virginia when I was born. I am informed that he run away to the north two or three years before the war broke out. He left my mother and three children in Virginia. He came through Philadelphia, Pa on his way north and then to New Bedford Mass. where he . . . [?] made his home. He changed his name to John L. Wright after he came here. He was married to Fanny Wilkins after he came here and he lived with her until she died." "After my father run away from Slavery," Webb continued, "my mother remained in Va. at Keep Creek Va until after the close of the war. Then she went to Newark N.J." Webb testified that she had moved to New Bedford in search of her father.

51. Furlong deposed that Craig had been healthy upon enlistment in 1863 but in the late 1880s he "appear[ed] very lame indeed, and was apparently suffering much." Craig's widow, Julia, successfully applied for a widow's benefit in June 1902, collected arrears of $288, and accepted pension benefits through her death on April 30, 1906. Noah Craig pension file, Invalid application number 553,254; certificate number 448,898; Widow application number 727,691; law O., certificate number 534,787; RG 15, NA. Wesley Furlong pension file, Invalid application number 631,717; certificate number 403,370; RG 15, NA. At the time of his death in February 1918, Furlong was receiving a monthly pension payment of $30. Curiously, Furlong kept hidden his slave origins, for as late as March 1907 he claimed to have been born in New Bedford. In June 1910, however, Furlong deposed that he was born "in slavery," his first such admission. Furlong deposed that "I was born in Martinsburg, Buckley County Virginia, May 25, 1835. I was born in slavery, my father and mother were sold to a slave trader in New Orleans, and I have never seen them since. I ran away and came north [and] later joined the army. After the war I found a brother married and settled in Gettysburgh [sic] Pennsylvania. He had the family bible from which I copied the date of my birth as given above. He and his wife have since died, and the family bible has been lost, and all account of the children, or remnants of the family lost. I have no relatives living now, outside of wife and children. I have always celebrated this as my birthday since I found it in the old family bible."

52. At the time of his death in 1927, the eighty-two-year-old Harrison collected $72 per month in pension payments. After the war, Harrison sought work as a mason, a

skilled trade that allowed him to support his wife, Marie, and their one daughter, Ada, born in 1892. Harrison married again in 1910 to a woman thirty years his junior who did not remain long in the marriage or in New Bedford. Ada ministered to her father's care in his later years and claimed that his military pension was the family's sole income. Charles H. Harrison pension file, Invalid application number 638,503; law J., certificate number 705,959; RG 15, NA.

53. The level of intimate knowledge in pension files was illustrated when Phelps said of Johnson: "I have seen him go to Stool 6 or 8 times a day very often." When he died at eighty-three, Johnson's family was reimbursed for unpaid medical and funeral expenses amounting to nearly $450, an unusual grant that probably reflected Johnson's fame as a veteran of the Fifty-Fourth. Johnson's youngest daughter explained that her father "leads a very quiet life, most all time [he] sits in chair out in kitchen. He goes to Post a time or two a week. That is his life." Alexander Johnson pension file, Invalid application number 693,409; law J., certificate number 515,081; RG 15, NA.

54. Phelps lived until 1912, and his widow, Abby, collected a widow's pension until 1938, when she died at the age of ninety-four. Emery Phelps pension file, Invalid application number 1,013,317; law J.O.; certificate number 878,016; Widow application number 994,340; law A., certificate number 751,894; XC 2,686,035; RG 15, NA. Emory Phelps is described as a "North Carolina migrant" in *First Fruits of Freedom: The Migration of Former Slaves and Their Search for Equality in Worcester, Massachusetts, 1862–1900, Janette Thomas Greenwood* (Chapel Hill: University of North Carolina Press, 2009), 145. Greenwood devotes several pages to postwar veterans in Worcester; see 143–47.

55. One of Harrison Lee's comrades, Watson Cooper, also lived in New Bedford after the Civil War, applying first for a pension in 1890. Cooper died of consumption late in April 1891 before any pension was paid to him, forcing his widow, Ella, to seek her own benefits. She proved up to the task, battling the bureaucracy for two years until she claimed a widow's pension and an additional $2 per month for each of her two children. Her appeals were supported by both Harrison Lee and Charles Harrison, and she collected pension payments through her death in early 1934 at the age of eighty-five. Watson Cooper pension file, Invalid application number 920,316, law J., certificate number 1,120,425; Widow application number 514,908, law J., certificate number 359,077; RG 15, NA. Charles Dixon's case reflected problems posed by the healing of wartime wounds. Discharged after his head was pierced by a minie ball at Honey Hill in November 1864, Dixon collected a full disability pension until the wound healed in 1867 and he was dropped to a three-fourths disability payment. Subsequent appeals were not successful. Charles Dixon pension file (his surname is spelled "Dixson" in some records), Invalid application number 80,742; certificate number 60,999; RG 15, NA.

56. After examining Lee in September 1881, Dr. Mackie reported that Lee "never was wounded in leg, but at some time during the war had a piece of wood fall upon him." Although some military records stated that Harrison Lee was "sick in hospital" for four months beginning in July 1863, and during later stints, too, these documents did not detail Lee's wounds or disabilities. Harrison Lee pension file, Invalid application number 403,344; law J., certificate number 503,928; RG 15, NA.

57. Lee's poverty and illiteracy also impaired his pension application: "I have been poor and could not employ doctors. I have doctored my self and got along the best I could. . . . I have lived in a shanty by myself since the war closed." The special examiner's favorable report was overruled by a supervisor, unfortunately, but changes in the legal standing of pension claimants in 1890 brought a change of fortune for Harrison Lee when he obtained a $4 monthly pension. The Pension Bureau doubled Lee's payments to $8 in 1904, a figure raised to $10 per month in February 1905. Harrison Lee pension file, Invalid application number 403,344; law J., certificate number 503,928; RG 15, NA.

58. In 1895 Jackson received a $6 per month pension benefit. Jackson was issued a windfall of over $300 in January 1901, but he had died two months previously. William Jackson pension file, Invalid application number 756,842; law J., certificate number 888,288; RG 15, NA.

59. James E. Fuller pension file, application number 33,274; certificate number 26,375; RG 15, NA. The online database of African-American Sailors in the Union Navy lists 49 men who claimed New Bedford as their home, 175 for Boston, and 434 total for Massachusetts. These records provide an excellent starting place for further study of Northern blacks in the Union Navy, but they need corroboration. For example, the New Bedford list has duplicate entries for men who probably enlisted more than once, and not all New Bedford naval enlistees are located in the online database. For example, my research found pension files for several men with New Bedford connections that are not corroborated by the online list: Nathaniel Borden, John Handy, Thornton Smith, and Lodrick Turner.

60. Nathaniel Borden pension file, Invalid application number 24,467, certificate number 25,489; RG 15, NA.

61. After his discharge in September 1864, Lee lived in Boston, possibly as a barber, and later in New York City, working as a laborer. When asked in 1912 to list his occupation, Lee wrote: "have none—to[o] old." He lived until 1926 and collected a military pension of $50 per month. Luke R. Lee pension file; Invalid application number 1,405,720; certificate number 1,170,146; CR number 2,459,857; RG 15, NA.

62. The Pension Bureau granted the elder Handy a dependent father's pension in March 1898, but it was issued two weeks after Caleb Handy died so he never collected. Joshua Handy pension file, Father's application number 8,563; certificate number 12,483; RG 15, NA.

63. Michelle Krowl notes that women applicants did not always receive support from other community members. For example, Sophia Shears was forced to testify to her own "respectability," as did her daughter, in the face of complaints from other African Americans. See Krowl, "Her Just Dues," 52.

64. Elizabeth Sisco, who called Sarah Townsend a "most intimate friend," recollected that Missouri drove away her husband. Frederick H. Pierce pension file, Widow's Pension application number 668,184; RG 15, NA.

65. She also collected arrears in August 1899 that amounted to about $160. Frederick H. Pierce pension file, Widow's Pension application number 668,184; RG 15, NA.

66. Reid, "Government Policy," 390. Also see Shaffer and Regosin, *Voices of Emancipation.*

67. Martha Gray's role as "mother of the regiment" is mentioned in chapter 5. Applying first for a military pension in 1876, William Gray complained of persistent problems caused by a gunshot wound. He was granted a one-half disability payment of $4 per month, increased three years later to full payments of $8 per month. The Grays received a windfall when the Pension Bureau issued arrears dating back to his original discharge, amounting to nearly $675. In July 1881 Martha declared that her husband's recent death had left her in "very bad condishon." She wrote of being "completely destitute," of eating only rice and potatoes, of having lost $2,000 worth of property when her family was "burnt out," presumably by marauding whites. William H. W. Gray pension file; Invalid application number 225,736, certificate number 145, 514; Widow application number 362,027; Minor application number 500,756; RG 15, NA.

7. "Business Is Extremely Dull": Whaling and Manufacturing in Wartime New Bedford

1. Leonard Bolles Ellis, *History of New Bedford* (Syracuse, NY: Mason, 1892), 374.

2. Reverend William J. Potter, "A Pulpit View of the Business Interests of our City," sermons delivered at the Unitarian Church, January 18, 1863, and January 25, 1863. Also located in Potter Papers, NBFPL, sermons 98 and 99. Matthew Howland to Capt. Edward B. Phinney, 8 January 1862; Matthew Howland Letter Book, 1858–1879, Baker Library Historical Collections, Harvard Business School. Mss: 252 1858–79 H864.

3. Phillip Shaw Paludan, "What Did the Winners Win? The Social and Economic History of the North during the Civil War" in *Writing the Civil War: The Quest to Understand*, ed. James McPherson and William J. Cooper Jr. (Columbia: University of South Carolina Press, 1998), 174–200, quotes on 175, 186. See the works of J. Matthew Gallman, especially his *Mastering Wartime: A Social History of Philadelphia during the Civil War* (Cambridge: Cambridge University Press, 1990); J. Matthew Gallman and Stanley Engerman, "The Civil War Economy: A Modern View" in *Northerners at War: Reflections on the Civil War Home Front*, ed. Gallman (Kent, OH: Kent State University Press, 2010), 87–119; and J. Matthew Gallman, "Entrepreneurial Experiences in the Civil War: Evidence from Philadelphia" in *American Economic Development in Historical Perspective*, ed. Thomas Weiss and Donald Schaefer (Stanford, CA: Stanford University Press, 1994), 205–22. For Peter Temin's analysis, see chapter 3, "The Industrialization of New England, 1830–1880" in *Engines of Enterprise: An Economic History of New England*, ed. Peter Temin (Cambridge, MA: Harvard University Press, 2000), 109–52; quote on 3. A succinct overview of the war's economic impact is offered in Patrick K. O'Brien, *The Economic Effects of the American Civil War* (Atlantic Highlands, NJ: Humanities Press International, 1988). O'Brien writes on page 53: "Apart from woolens and watches, it seems difficult to find any industry-wide examples of accelerated growth from 1860–5. Nearly all statistical data point the other way and in the industralised states of Massachusetts and New York, the real value of manufactured output declined by large margins." For a dated but detailed study of Boston, see Raymond H. Robinson, *The Boston Economy during the Civil War* (New York and London: Garland Publishing, 1988), reprint of PhD thesis, Harvard University, 1957.

4. Temin, "Industrialization," covers Massachusetts' whaling on 125–26.

5. Lance E. Davis, Robert E. Gallman, and Karin Gleiter, *In Pursuit of Leviathan, Technology, Institutions, and Profits in American Whaling, 1816–1906* (Chicago and London: University of Chicago Press, 1997); see especially 41, 120, 170–72, 233, 442, and 513.

6. The best overview is found in "The Stone Whalers," *Dictionary of Naval Fighting Ships*, vol. 5, (1970), N-Q, 427–41. For general histories of the Union navy during the war, see Michael J. Bennett, *Union Jacks: Yankee Sailors in the Civil War* (Chapel Hill: University of North Carolina Press, 2004), and William M. Fowler Jr., *Under Two Flags: The American Navy in the Civil War* (New York: W. W. Norton, 1990). Also see Eric Jay Dolin, *Leviathan: The History of Whaling in America* (New York: W. W. Norton, 2007), 309–34.

7. "Stone Whalers," 430.

8. Zephaniah W. Pease ed., *History of New Bedford* (New York: The Lewis Historical Publishing Company, 1918), 50–52. Moulton offered his recollections in December 1904, according to notes located in the Charles Walter Agard papers, folder 31, ODHS. See also "Stone Fleet," ODHS Notebooks Number 4, that includes Editors of Time-Life Books, *The Civil War, The Blockade, Runners and Raiders* (Alexandria, VA: Time-Life Books, n.d.), 26–27.

9. Willis quoted in Pease, *History* (1918), 54; for details on Willis's log and reminiscences, see 53–56.

10. "The Great Stone Fleet," *New York Times*, November 22, 1861; next article published on December 4, 1861, was extracted from the *New Bedford Mercury* and reported sixteen ships carrying some 5,221 tons of stone. Another account reprinted locally was

found in the *Journal of Commerce* that detailed plans to sink an "immense number of old whaling vessels," with an expectation that southern harbors "will be hermetically closed against commerce, and a great war fleet will be detached from the dull blockading service and put to livelier business." *NBDES*, 27 November 1861.

11. The R. G. Dun credit reports for Rodney French include comments that he "talks politics too much" and "engages a g[oo]d deal in politics." French was barely making a living in 1856, and reportedly "owes everybody" in 1858 when he was described as a "ranting politician." See Massachusetts, vol. 17, pp. 46 and 179, R. G. Dun & Co. Collection, Baker Library Historical Collections, Harvard Business School. The anecdote about "Commodore French" is in "Stone Whalers," 428.

12. *NBDES*, December 5, 1861. For the Second Stone Fleet, see especially "Stone Whalers," 432–33.

13. "Stone Whalers," 433–35; "The Sunken Fleet," *New York Times*, December 26, 1861. The same issue had another article, "The Stone Fleet," with a first-hand account of Captain J. D. Childs of the bark *Cossack* that sailed from New Bedford on November 20, 1861. Mary Malloy, "The Old Sailor's Lament: Recontextualizing Melville's Reflections on the Sinking of 'The Stone Fleet,'" *New England Quarterly* 64, no. 4 (December 1991): 633–42.

14. *NBDES*, December 12, 1861. The protracted siege of Charleston is captured best in Stephen R. Wise, *Gate of Hell: Campaign for Charleston Harbor, 1863* (Columbia: University of South Carolina Press, 1994). Union authorities backpedaled on blockade plans because of objections from both Great Britain and France who complained of possible interruptions to commerce with the South. Secretary of State William H. Seward reassured them that the blockades were temporary and it was "not likely that any others will be used for that purpose." See "Stone Whalers," 437.

15. *NBDES*, January 16, 1862; *NBDES* February 14, 1862. Rodney French rode his fame as far as he could. He was scheduled to speak at the Free Will Baptist Society in Taunton in mid-March 1862 at their annual fair with an address about "some of the incidents of his recent voyage to Port Royal with the 'stone fleet.'" See *NBDES*, March 8, 1862.

16. *NBDES*, April 18, 1861.

17. Martin Joseph Butler, "J. & W. R. Wing of New Bedford, A Study of the Impact of a Declining Industry upon an American Whaling Agency" (PhD dissertation, Pennsylvania State University, 1973), 88–90.

18. *NBDES*, November 1, 1862; *NBDES*, November 4, 1862.

19. *NBDES*, December 12, 1862. New Bedford residents learned about the *Alabama*'s destructive swath through published accounts and private letters, such as those of Edward Maffitt Anderson to his father in mid-November 1862. The younger Maffit described the *Alabama*'s capture of the bark *Ocmulgee* of Martha's Vineyard, followed by separate attacks on the barks *Ocean Rover*, *Alert*, and *Elisha Dunbar* of New Bedford. Edward Maffitt Anderson to father, Edward Clifford Anderson, November 18, 1862, William Stanley Hoole Papers, William Stanley Hoole Special Collections Library, The University of Alabama. See the excellent web site, "C.S.S. Alabama Digital Collection, W. S. Hoole Special Collections Library, The University of Alabama," located at http://www.lib.ua.edu/libraries/hoole/digital/cssala/ander.htm. Other sites include http://www.history.navy.mil/branches/org12-1.htm (US Navy) and http://www.css-alabama.com (CSS *Alabama* Association).

20. James Tertius deKay, *The Rebel Raiders, The Astonishing History of the Confederacy's Secret Navy* (New York: Ballantine Books, 2002), 99–100, 114–15, 134–35, 143, 154, 185–86, 188. The exciting defeat of the *Alabama* by the *Kearsage* is covered on pp. 196–201, 205.

21. After the war an English friend asked Semmes if he had hated the North, and Semmes replied: "I believe the Yankee, puritanical race of New England to be, taken all in all, the most unamiable and corrupt race that the sun shines upon." He called them "cowards . . . treacherous and fanatical," and remained unrepentant until his death in 1877. See deKay, *Rebel Raider*, 247. Adding to New Englanders' anger and anxiety, Massachusetts Governor Andrew received a copy of a letter captured at Chancellorsville claiming that CSA President Jefferson Davis spoke of having the *Alabama* attack Boston. Adjutant General William Schouler believed the letter was genuine and that the Confederates might order Semmes and his "pirates [to] make a dash upon Boston or Portland." William Schouler, *A History of Massachusetts in the Civil War*, vol. 1, *Civil and Military History of Massachusetts in the Rebellion* (Boston: E. P. Dutton & Co., Publishers, 1868), 423.

22. The *Oreto's* escape illustrated the ineptitude of the Union's blockading squadron. Built in Liverpool, the *Oreto* was described as a wooden steamer of great speed, carrying eight guns and measuring 750 tons under the command of John Newland Maffit, formerly a lieutenant in the US Navy. *NBDES*, January 29, 1863.

23. The *Lafayette* had sailed from New Bedford on May 20, 1862, and when captured it had processed 500 barrels of sperm oil. Owned by I. H. Bartlett & Sons, the ship and outfits were valued at $20,000, with insurance coverage of nearly $16,000. The new vessel *Kate Cory* had sailed on June 26, 1862, with a value of $12,000 and insurance coverage in New Bedford for $8,700. From Fairhaven, the schooner *Kingfisher* was destroyed, also. After leaving home on July 30, 1861, the ship had been reported at Ascension Island with 220 barrels of sperm oil and 10 barrels of whale oil, having sent home 50 barrels of sperm. Valued at $7,200, this ship of 120 tons was insured in New Bedford for $4,700, and its catching at $1,400. *NBDES*, May 28, 1863. For more on the *Oneida*, see editorial and account by its shipmaster, Jesse F. Porter, *NBDES*, June 1, 1863.

24. Quoted in John R. Bockstoce, *Whales, Ice, & Men: The History of Whaling in the Western Arctic*, Second ed. (Seattle: University of Washington Press, 1995; 1986), 106; see also pp. 104–8 for a detailed account of the secretive purchasing and fitting out of *Shenandoah*. See also D. Alan Harris and Anne B. Harris, *The Voyage of the CSS Shenandoah: A Memorable Cruise* (Tuscaloosa: University of Alabama Press, 2005), and Tom Chaffin, *Sea of Gray: The Around-the-World Odyssey of the Confederate Raider Shenandoah* (New York: Hill and Wang, 2006).

25. The Wings had one ship, the *Brunswick*, destroyed by the *Shenandoah*. See Butler, "J. & W. R. Wing," 90–96.

26. John R. Bockstoce, "Civil War in Bering Strait: The Cruise of CSS *Shenandoah*," in *Whales, Ice, & Men*, 103–28; Waddell anecdote, 120.

27. Bockstoce, *Whales, Ice, & Men*, 124; also see, for example, *New Bedford Republican Standard* (weekly), August 3, 1865.

28. Ellis includes a list of twenty-five New Bedford whalers destroyed between 1862 and 1865, along with 2,742 barrels of sperm and 4,150 barrels of whale oil. Ellis, *History* (1892), 351, 423–24. A list of the destroyed whalers is presented similarly in Crapo, *Centennial*, appendix 21, 112–13. *Whaleman's Shipping List* quoted in *New Bedford and Old Dartmouth*, 114; photograph caption on 117.

29. *NBDES*, August 8, 1861; *NBDES*, September 5, 1861; *NBDES*, January 1, 1863; NBDES, June 4, 1862.

30. Of New Bedford's thirty-nine ships withdrawn from whaling that year, twenty-five were transferred to the merchant service, eleven were wrecked, condemned or captured by rebel cruisers, and three were transferred in whaling to other ports. *NBDES*, October 23, 1862; *NBDES*, January 1, 1863.

31. Ellis, *History*, 423–25, 351. Also see Elmo Paul Hohman, *The American Whaleman: A Study in Life and Labor in the Whaling Industry* (New York: Longmans, Green, and

Co., 1928), chapter 13, "Civil War, Petroleum, and the Arctic," 289–301; Teresa Dunn Hutchins, "The American Whale Fishery, 1815–1900: An Economic Analysis" (PhD dissertation, University of North Carolina at Chapel Hill, 1988); Dolin, Leviathan; Miscellaneous Statistics of the United States . . . in 1860, 8th Census, 1860; see section on "The Whale Fishery," 542–49; Whalemen's Shipping List quoted on 547–48.

32. The average annual tonnage of United States and New Bedford whaling fleets in five-year intervals is provided by Lance E. Davis, Robert E. Gallman, and Teresa D. Hutchins, "The Structure of the Capital Stock in Economic Growth and Decline: The New Bedford Whaling Fleet in the Nineteenth Century," in Quantity & Quiddity, Essays in U.S. Economic History, ed. Peter Kilby (Middletown, CT: Wesleyan University Press, 1987), 343. Also see Hutchins, "American Whale Fishery," 64–65, 185–86. New Bedford's "great diminution in the valuation" was explained by William Schouler as "the effect of the war upon the whaling interest." William Schouler, A History of Massachusetts in the Civil War, vol. 2, Towns and Cities (Boston: Published by the Author, 1871), 141.

33. Mark R. Wilson, The Business of Civil War: Military Mobilization and the State, 1861–1865 (Baltimore: The Johns Hopkins University Press, 2006); see especially appendix, "Note on the Value of a Dollar in the Civil War Era," 227–29. McCusker used a commodity price index pegged at 100 in 1860 to compute a value of 196 in 1865; John J. McCusker, How Much is That In Real Money? A Historical Commodity Price Index for Use as a Deflator of Money Values in the Economy of the United States, 2nd ed. (Worcester, MA: American Antiquarian Society, 2001). See also the excellent web site, "Measuring Worth," http://www.measuringworth.com/index.php.

34. Beginning in 1844, many of New Bedford's businesses were reviewed by agents of an emergent credit reporting agency later known as R. G. Dun & Company. While the reportage varied, typically a business or individual was described with notes about their occupation, estimated net worth, value of personal and real property, and general business prospects. Dun & Company records are significant for their volume, scope, and detail, but they are not always inclusive. Larger and more successful businesses were evaluated because they were deemed more likely to apply for credit or engage in transactions beyond the local community. See James D. Norris, R. G. Dun & Co., 1841–1900, The Development of Credit-Reporting in the Nineteenth Century (Westport, CT: Greenwood Press, 1978); James H. Madison, "The Evolution of Commercial Credit Reporting Agencies in Nineteenth-Century America," The Business History Review 48, no. 2 (Summer 1974): 164–86; and Travis Blackman, ed., A Chronicle of Credit Reporting: The Story of Dun & Broadstreet (Murray Hill, NJ: Dun & Broadstreet, 1985); James H. Madison, "The Credit Reports of R. G. Dun & Co. as Historical Sources," in Historical Methods Newsletter 8, no. 4 (September 1975), 128–31.

35. My main aim in using R. G. Dun records was to analyze all relevant businesses that began in the antebellum era and were still in operation in 1861 when the war started. Their credit reports were followed into the 1870s or until they went out of business before 1870. Research centered on whaling owners, agents, and outfitters, banks, insurance companies, merchants, and companies engaged in oil processing, shipping, and trade. Small businesses, such as grocers, tailors, blacksmiths, and druggists, were not surveyed. Table 7-2 shows the largest forty-three whaling-related businesses that were in operation when war commenced in 1861 and survived the war years. The second column refers to any obvious business diversification by the firm. Duration refers to the number of years the firms were traced from their first entry through the mid-1870s or until they went out of business before 1870. The credit rating refers to the highest rating awarded to the firm by a R. G. Dun credit report, and these ratings could fluctuate depending on the firm's value and success. The peak value is the highest value ascribed to the firm by a Dun reporter during the entire period along with the year that value was reported.

These figures were estimated in current dollars and reflected well-informed if subjective evaluations by Dun reporters, who were typically local correspondents. Mainly, I was interested in showing whether the firms relative value increased or decreased through the Civil War years. Because Dun credit reports were prepared by local correspondents, the estimates offer insight even if they lack precision or corroboration. Beginning at the first chronological entry in volume 17, New Bedford entries followed through p. 275 when new businesses commenced after the Civil War. R. G. Dun & Co. Collection, Baker Library Historical Collections, Harvard Business School.. For imaginative use of Dun records by historians, see J. Matthew Gallman, "Entrepreneurial Experiences in the Civil War: Evidence from Philadelphia" in *American Economic Development in Historical Perspective*, ed. Thomas Weiss and Donald Schaefer (Stanford, CA: Stanford University Press, 1994), 205–22; Rowena Olegario, *A Culture of Credit: Embedding Trust and Transparency in American Business* (Cambridge, MA: Harvard University Press, 2006); and Davis, Gallman, and Gleiter, In Pursuit of Leviathan). Research on Boston during the Civil War found that at least 311 individuals joined the ranks of those with at least $100,000 in wealth in 1865; see Robinson, *Boston Economy*, 356 and appendixes 7 and 8.

36. Sylvanus Thomas & Company, Massachusetts, vol. 17, 157 and 1, R. G. Dun & Co. Collection, Baker Library Historical Collections, Harvard Business School. From other sources, we learn more about Sylvanus Thomas. The *1859 City Directory* listed Thomas as living on the 200 block of Purchase Street with candle works below South Street and a counting room at Front and Union Streets. See *1859 City Directory*, 165. The *New Bedford Standard* contained several mentions of Thomas during the 1860s, including notice of receiving an oil contract from the Lighthouse Board (March 31, 1864), purchasing the estate of William R. Rotch (October 6, 1864), pursuing building projects (July 13, 1865), and dying as an "enterprising merchant" (November 22, 1866).

37. As one example, the outfitting firm of Wood & Nye, established in 1850, had an estimated peak value of $175,0000 in 1858 and survived the war intact, although Nye died in 1865 and Wood carried on with an estimated worth of $75,000 in 1865. He would be an agent for at least two ships in 1871 when he was seventy-five years old. Wood & Nye, Massachusetts, vol. 17, 102; R. G. Dun & Co. Collection, Baker Library Historical Collections, Harvard Business School. As another example, Hathaway & Luce, first established in 1844 by two former sea captains, Matthew Luce and William H. Hathaway Jr. also survived the war. Hathaway carried on after Luce's death in 1852, faced whaling losses in 1860 and 1861, but was worth about $150,000 when he retired in 1866. Hathaway & Luce, Massachusetts, vol. 17, R. G. Dun & Co. Collection, Baker Library Historical Collections, Harvard Business School. Other whaling or outfitting firms that were reported to have diminished values in the Civil War years were John R. Thornton; Samuel W. Rodman; James H. Howland; Pope & Morgan; Cornelius Howland; B. Franklin Howard; Weston Howland; Russell Maxfield; and Paul Ewer.

38. J. S. and F. S. Hathaway, Massachusetts, vol. 17, 38 and 2, R. G. Dun & Co. Collection, Baker Historical Library Collections, Harvard Business School.

39. Jonathan Bourne Jr., Massachusetts, vol. 17, 50 and 241, R. G. Dun & Co. Collection, Baker Historical Library Collections, Harvard Business School.

40. Butler, "J. & W. R. Wing," 126 and 12, and chapter 6, "Riding the Crest of the Wave," 83–102.

41. Butler, "J. & W. R. Wing," 85–87, 97–98.

42. After the war, John Wing became senior partner in 1865, Joseph slowly disengaged from whaling, and their clerk, Hiram W. Wentworth, became a partner (with a 3/18th interest) in 1867 and eventually claimed an equal partnership. Butler, "J. & W. R. Wing," 98–102, 126. The Wings' investments in textile factories, railroads, mining, and area real estate are detailed by Butler, 121–26.

43. Davis et al., *Leviathan*, 38–41, 170–71, 233, 401–4, 513–15. Despite the Quaker schism of the 1820s, leading families continued to follow marriage and business patterns. Davis et al. describe several "discrete family groupings" among the wealthy elites. For example, the Rotches and Rodmans intermarried and added James Arnold and Charles W. Morgan. The Howlands married Allens, a Bartlett, Bournes, a Durfee, a Delano, a Kempton, a Peirce, a Parker, Robinson, Russells, Shearmans, a Sherman, Tabers, a Wings, Woods, and various Howlands. The authors concluded that "There seem to be no links between certain groups (the Rotches and the Howlands); in other cases the links, while few and chiefly indirect (the Howlands and the Parkers), do exist." Quoted on 404.

44. Price fluctuations were common in whaling, but the Civil War added to economic uncertainty. For representative rumors and reports of whale and sperm oil prices, see *NBDES*, March 4, 1862; *NBDES*, March 8, 1862. The best contemporary source for whaling prices is *The Whalemen's Shipping List and Merchants' Transcript*, published weekly in New Bedford between 1843 and 1914 and now available online through the National Maritime Digital Library at http://www.nmdl.org/.

45. See Davis et al., *Leviathan*, 423–58; quotes from *The Whalemen's Shipping List* on 428.

46. Robinson, *Boston Economy*, 45.

47. Wamsutta Mills, Massachusetts, vol. 17, 134, 172, 178, R. G. Dun & Co. Collection, Baker Historical Library Collections, Harvard Business School. New Bedford Cordage Company, Massachusetts, vol. 17, 41, R. G. Dun & Co. Collection, Baker Historical Library Collections, Harvard Business School. Also see New Bedford Cordage Company Records, 1842–1959, Old Dartmouth Historical Society, Manuscripts, MSS Collection 1, series D, (Production Records, 1846–1953), subseries 1, vol. 1—Time and wage book, 1846–64, and folder 1—Table for computing wages, 1865.

48. Thomas O'Connor, Thomas H. O'Connor, *Civil War Boston, Home Front and Battlefield* (Boston: Northeastern University Press, 1997), 161; Temin, *Engines of Enterprise*, 124–25. Phillip Shaw Paludan, "A People's Contest," in *The Union and Civil War, 1861–1865* (New York: Harper & Row Publishers, 1988), 147.

49. New Bedford Union Shoe Company, Massachusetts, vol. 17, 104, 160, 173, R. G. Dun & Co. Collection, Baker Historical Library Collections, Harvard Business School.

50. Two years' later, however, mismanagement led directors to "settle up" and the business began "winding up" later in 1868. New Bedford Shoe Company, Massachusetts, vol. 17, 195, R. G. Dun & Co. Collection, Baker Historical Library Collections, Harvard Business School.

51. Pease, *History* (1918), 84, 350, 211. See also Zephaniah W. Pease and George W. Hough, *New Bedford, Massachusetts: Its History, Industries, Institutions, and Attractions*, ed. by William L. Sayer (New Bedford, 188), 211–12, who note that the Snell & Simpson Biscuit Co. succeeded Snell's operation. The *New Bedford Standard* contained several references to Snell's bakery and his receipt of army contracts; see issues of February 12, 1863; November 24, 1864 (fire); and March 9, 1865 ("Snell's Bakery running day and night"). The *1859 City Directory* lists David Snell as co-owner (with Charles D. Capen) of Capen & Snell, makers of "Fancy and Ship Bread," with a workplace at 51 and 53 S. Water Street.

52. *NBDES*, February 19, 1863. The Dun reporter noted that Snell diversified into real estate, but was also a "fast man" who kept a number of horses. David A. Snell, Massachusetts, vol. 17, 234, R. G. Dun & Co. Collection, Baker Historical Library Collections, Harvard Business School. For example, shipbread baker Henry Sanders bought out Tillson Denham in 1860 but was out of the bakery business by November 1864. Henry Sanders; Massachusetts, vol. 17, 9, R. G. Dun & Co. Collection, Baker Historical Library Collections, Harvard Business School.

53. Morse Twist & Drill Machine Company, Massachusetts, vol. 17, 5, R. G. Dun & Co. Collection, Baker Historical Library Collections, Harvard Business School.

54. New Bedford Copper Works, Massachusetts, vol. 17, 195 and 201, R. G. Dun & Co. Collection, Baker Historical Library Collections, Harvard Business School.

55. Manufacturing statistics are found in 1855 and 1865 state manufacturing censuses. Paludan, *People's Contest*, 167. Temin notes that women workers declined in some industries such as boot and shoe manufacturing; see Temin, *Engines of Enterprise*, 125, 142. Also see Mary H. Blewett, *Men, Women, and Work: Class, Gender, and Protest in the New England Shoe Industry, 1780–1910* (Urbana: University of Illinois Press, 1988).

56. The *1859 City Directory* listed eight firms as oil and candle manufacturers: W. A. Robinson & Co.; A. S. Howland; Fisher & Baker; James G. Howland; Edmund Rodman; Hastings & Co.; E. C. Milliken & Co.; Samuel Leonard & Son. Charles Leonard operated a candleworks and maintained a counting room on No. 7 Merrill's Wharf; *1859 City Directory*, 121; Charles Leonard, Massachusetts, vol. 17, 182, 250, 208, R. G. Dun & Co. Collection, Baker Historical Library Collections, Harvard Business School.

57. Samuel Leonard & Son, Massachusetts, vol. 17, 43, 57, 198, 208, R. G. Dun & Co. Collection, Baker Historical Library Collections, Harvard Business School. For a summary of oil prices, see Ellis, *History* (1892), 390.

58. See Davis et al., *Leviathan*, chapter 8, "Productivity," for an excellent analysis of products, and their prices, that competed with whale oil, 297–341. Quotes in Davis et al., *Leviathan*, 363.

59. William J. Potter, "A Pulpit View of the Business Interests of our City." Potter Papers, NBFPL, sermons 98 and 99.

60. In early June 1862, reports from the *Oil City Register* showed production on the "celebrated Oil Creek" where nearly five hundred wells had been drilled and one million barrels of oil shipped. At $1 a barrel, the total value of oil shipped and on hand was nearly $1.1 million. NBDES, June 2, 1862; NBDES, June 4, 1862. Before the war, kerosene challenged the superior properties of whale oil as an illuminant, particularly after 1856 when a safer lamp was developed. By 1858 in New Bedford, kerosene was distilled in a factory on South Street overseen by Abraham Howland and other wealthy investors; Ellis, *History*, 422–23.

61. Brian Black, Petrolia, *The Landscape of America's First Oil Boom* (Baltimore, MD: Johns Hopkins University Press, 2000), 20–21; Davis et al., *Leviathan*, 358–60. The authors write that Weston Howland "came close to committing industrial treason when he opened the first New Bedford petroleum-refining plant"; 403. Reports for New Bedford Coal Oil Company, Massachusetts, vol. 17, 191, 208, 249; Reports for W. & I. Howland, Massachusetts, vol. 17, 17 and 251; R. G. Dun & Co. Collection, Baker Library Historical Collections, Harvard Business School. See entries for New Bedford Coal Oil Company, 191, 208, 249; W. & I. Howland, 17, 251; Abraham H. Howland, 48; Massachusetts, vol. 17, R. G. Dun & Co. Collection, Baker Historical Library Collections, Harvard Business School.

62. O'Connor, *Boston*, 161; Paludan, *People's Contest*, 147; Henry Beetle Hough, Wamsutta of New Bedford, 1846–1946, A Story of New England Enterprise (New Bedford, MA: Wamsutta Mills, 1946), 25–35; quotes on p. 35.

63. Company documents point to the limited supply of cotton, and bales were sometimes weighted with extraneous materials. A shipment to the Wamsutta Mills in January 1863 contained nearly fifty pounds of clay, reported the local newspaper, and other companies found iron, bricks, and sand as extraneous weight in their cotton shipments. Superintendent Bennett addressed the labor problem prompted by male operatives leaving for military service and "large bounties" by recruiting French Canadian workers. Hough, *Wamsutta*, 35–38; Typescript "From Mem. and paper of Thos. Bennett, Jr," Ben-

nett Papers, ODHS Manuscripts, Mss. Collection 9, subgroup 4, series E, folder 1; *NBDES*, February 19, 1863.

64. Hough wrote that in place of fantastic but risky whaling returns, the Wamsutta Mills created a "reliable, 6-per-cent kind of business, which returned dividends, satisfactory but still conservative, year in and year out, to a considerable number of people." Hough, *Wamsutta*, 35–38; quotes on pp. 37–38.

65. For Grinnell, see Massachusetts, vol. 17, 216, 244, R. G. Dun & Co. Collection, Baker Library Historical Collections, Harvard Business School. For Baker, see Massachusetts, vol. 17, 129, 326, 228; R. G. Dun & Co. Collection, Baker Library Historical Collections, Harvard Business School.

66. Wartime inflation was shown in the construction costs for a new mill. Estimated to cost $34,766 in August 1860, the actual costs climbed to more than $65,000 by May 1864. See Bennett Papers, ODHS Manuscripts, Mss. Collection 9, subgroup 4, series D, folder 2, Statement of Dividends, 1849–1880. Loose sheet has cost estimates for Mill Number 3. See Massachusetts, vol. 17, 172 and 178; R. G. Dun & Co. Collection, Baker Library Historical Collections, Harvard Business School.

67. James W. Geary, We Need Men, *The Union Draft in the Civil War* (DeKalb: Northern Illinois University Press, 1991), 186; also see James McPherson, *Battle Cry of Freedom* (New York: Oxford University Press, 1987), 437–50. Letter from Major G. N. Mendell, of New Bedford, to Brevet Major General M. C. Meigs, dated September 14, 1865; "Consolidated Correspondence File, 1794–1915" under subject, "New Bedford;" entry 225 of RG 92, Office of the Quartermaster General (box 724). *NBDES*, October 30, 1863.

8. "The Position of Our City Has Materially Changed": Public Costs and Municipal Governance during the Civil War

1. Zephaniah W. Pease, *History of New Bedford* (New York: Higginson Publishing Company, 1918), offers a chapter on "The Civil War Period," 195–202; quotes on are 195 and 201.

2. Address of Mayor Isaac C. Taber, January 6, 1862; New Bedford City Documents, NBFPL (hereafter cited as "NBCD"), reel 2.

3. Emily J. Harris, "Sons and Soldiers: Deerfield, Massachusetts and the Civil War," Civil War History 30 (June 1984): 157–71; Michael Frisch detailed similar increases in municipal debt in Springfield, Massachusetts; see Michael C. Frisch, *Town Into City: Springfield, Massachusetts and the Meaning of Community, 1840–1880* (Cambridge, MA: Harvard University Press, 1972).

4. See annual reports of the Committee for Finance, 1850–1875, NBCD, reel 2. Leonard B. Ellis, History of New Bedford, and Its Vicinity, 1620–1892 (Syracuse, NY: D. Mason & Company, 1892), provides a table of city figures from 1848–91, 390.

5. City finance records prior to 1863 show that New Bedford's municipal needs provided income for hundreds of people and businesses that went beyond salaried city officials. Skilled workers were paid for painting, making coffins, and crafting iron work, while unskilled men and some women were paid to clean buildings, cart wood, stable horses, and flag streets. Within the school district during 1859–60, over 120 individuals were paid a total of $1,780 for "cleaning, whitewashing, sweeping, making fires, &c." Evidence of whites' paternalistic employment practices are seen in the payments made to black individuals such as city messenger Lloyd Brooks, janitor Abraham Conklin who earned $107.49, and sweeper Louisa Dorster who received $2 for similar work. Report of the Committee on Finance for Year ending March 1, 1860; NBCD, NBFPL, reel 2. Also see Report of the Committee on Finance for Year ending March 1, 1863, for comparison of methods.

6. *NBDES*, July 25, 1861.

7. Address of Isaac C. Taber, Mayor, January 6, 1862, NBCD, reel 2.

8. Report of the Committee on Finance for Year Ending March 1, 1862; NBCD, reel 2.

9. Incidental expenses in 1861 included for repairing guns for the Home and Coast Guard ($113.67), paying interest on temporary loans ($2,281.84), hiring extra clerks by Mayor Taber ($300), and repairing the flag at City Hall ($41.63). Some well-connected individuals drew from city coffers. In 1860 a payment $550 was made to John H. Clifford for "professional services" and James B. Congdon received $100 for "indexing town documents" in addition to his yearly salary of $1,450 as City Treasurer and Collector. See Reports of the Committee on Finance for 1861 and 1862, respectively.

10. *NBDES*, January 3, 1862. Andrew's address is covered also in William Schouler, *A History of Massachusetts in the Civil War, vol. 1, Civil and Military History of Massachusetts in the Rebellion* (Boston: E. P. Dutton & Co. Publishers, 1868), 285–86.

11. *NBDES*, February 28, 1862.

12. *NBDES*, July 5, 1862.

13. *NBDES*, July 14, 1862. Also see "New Bedford responds to Civil War," excerpt from Schouler, *A History of Massachusetts in the Civil War*, 2:142. Also see Congdon Papers, NBFPL, folder 17. William Schouler details contemporary concerns about the treatment of wounded and dead soldiers that led to the formation of the Massachusetts Soldiers' Relief Association; see Schouler, 1:294–300.

14. *NBDES*, August 28, 1862; postponed draft reported in *NBDES*, September 16, 1862.

15. Address of George Howland Jr., Mayor, January 5, 1863; NBCD; reel 2.

16. Report of Committee on Finance for Fiscal Year Ending March 1, 1863; NBCD, reel 2.

17. The lack of a public event was illustrated in a commercial notice that read: "In the entire absence tomorrow of all public celebration of the National Independence, nothing could be more timely than the proposed excursion to Newport" with promises of an enjoyable day at a reasonable cost. *NBDES*, July 3, 1863.

18. Address of George Howland Jr., Mayor, January 5, 1863, NBCD, reel 2. See James W. Geary, *We Need Men: The Union Draft in the Civil War* (DeKalb: Northern Illinois Press, 1991) for an explanation of the bounty system.

19. See Mass., Treasurer, Account of Bounties Paid to Enlistees in Massachusetts Regiments, New Bedford, 1862–63; Boston Public Library, Rare Books, Ms. Am. 2383 (1–2). In addition to a ledger, the file includes letters and other supporting documents.

20. Bounty figures are in ibid., vol. 1. Other costs of war in Report by Treasurer James B. Congdon in letter dated July 30, 1865, to Hon. Tappan Wentworth, Chair, Joint Special Committee upon the subject of Taxation and the Finances. Congdon Papers, NBFPL, folder 17.

21. Howland explained that the city had paid dependent families of soldiers about $41,000 since January 1, 1863, but the state would not reimburse New Bedford until December 1, 1864, when the city's tax was due to the state. Like other cities, New Bedford would not receive any interest on that sum for the entire period. Address of George Howland Jr., Mayor, January 4, 1864; NBCD, reel 2.

22. Address of George Howland Jr., Mayor, January 4, 1864; NBCD, reel 2. Report of the Committee on Finance for the Fiscal Year ending March 1, 1864. NBCD, reel 2. See also NBDES, July 3, 1863, for complaints about the city's stinginess in not funding the Fourth of July. James Congdon's account suggests that of $3,452.58 of "Riot Expenses," the state refunded just over $2,063, leaving a balance of nearly $1,400 that the city presumably covered. Report by Treasurer James B. Congdon in letter dated July 30, 1865, to

Hon. Tappan Wentworth, Chair, Joint Special Committee upon the subject of Taxation and the Finances. Congdon Papers, NBFPL, folder 17.

23. Address of George Howland Jr., Mayor, January 2, 1865; NBCD, reel 2; Report of the Committee on Finance for Year ending March 1, 1865; NBCD, reel 2; Report of the Committee on Finance for Year ending March 1, 1866; NBCD, reel 2.

24. The school system expanded in the 1840s in response to enrollment pressures, especially after the city gained its charter in 1847. Marilyn Lynds, "The History of the New Bedford High School, part 1, Early New Bedford to 1899," unpublished manuscript prepared with Carroll Chase for the New Bedford Office of Historic Preservation; Special Collections, NBFPL, 15–17; for new schools, see Ellis, *History* (1892), 613–14. Helpful accounts of Massachusetts public schools include Carl Kaestle, *Pillars of the Republic: Common Schools and American Society, 1780–1860* (New York: Hill and Wang, 1983); Stanley K. Schultz, *The Culture Factory: Boston Public Schools, 1789–1860* (New York: Oxford University Press, 1973); and David Tyack, *The One Best System: A History of American Urban Education* (Cambridge, MA: Harvard University Press, 1974).

25. Report of the Board of the School Committee for 1859; Report of the School Committee for 1860; NBCD, reel 2.

26. Enrollment at the Adult School averaged twenty-eight men and forty-one women, schooled separately on alternate evenings. Report of the School Committee for 1860; NBCD, reel 2.

27. A historical overview of New Bedford's public schools is in Ellis, *History* (1892), 608–19. For school appropriations between 1822 and 1866, see "Sketch of the Public Schools of New Bedford," an appendix to the Report of the School Committee for 1866; NBCD, reel 2. Also see Lynds, "New Bedford High School," Special Collections, NBFPL. Superintendent Phipps provided two semiannual reports, the first on June 24, 1861, the other dated December 23, 1861, as an appendix to the Report of the School Committee for 1861; NBCD, reel 2.

28. Public evening schools were first authorized in 1847, and opened in New Bedford in December 1848. Enrollments that first year were significant: 127 males and 154 females. Ellis, *History* (1892), 615–16.

29. Report of the School Committee for 1861; NBCD, reel 2.

30. Report of the School Committee for 1862; Report of the School Committee for 1863; NBCD, reel 2.

31. For example, repairs to the Bush Street School House were estimated at $2,500, but the council budgeted only $1,400. Superintendent Phipps acknowledged the success of the Evening Schools that included twenty African-American men, "several of whom were contrabands, who were very constant in their attendance, and made gratifying proficiency in learning to read and spell." He estimated that seventy women attended the evening schools last year, with an average age of more than twenty-three. Of the male students, twenty of them were over thirty years of age. Report of the School Committee for 1862; NBCD, reel 2; Report of the School Committee for 1863; Superintendent's Annual Report for 1863; NBCD, reel 2.

32. Ellis summarizes the cost of New Bedford's public schools between 1848 and 1891 and addresses class-based debates over public education. Ellis, *History* (1892), 610, 619. Also see Lynds, "New Bedford High School," 9–15.

33. Superintendent's Annual Report; Report of the School Committee for 1862; NBCD, reel 2; Superintendent's Annual Report; Report of the School Committee for 1863; NBCD, reel 2.

34. "Rules of the School Committee, and Regulations of the Public Schools of the City of New Bedford," Report of the School Committee for 1864; NBCD, reel 2.

35. Known for his "keen observations and a facile pen," Harrington exerted great influence until his death in 1887. At the nation's Centennial Exposition in Philadelphia

in 1876, New Bedford's and Boston's school systems showcased Massachusetts' progress in the field of public education. In 1878 the New Bedford school manual was found by a commission of the French government to be one of the ten best in the United States. Through the early 1890s, New Bedford ranked near the top of all Massachusetts' cities in educational expenditures per resident between the ages of five and fifteen. Ellis, *History* (1892), 614–15; Thomas A. McMullin, "Industrialization and the Transformation of Public Education in New Bedford, 1865–1900," *Historical Journal of Massachusetts* 15, no. 2 (June 1987): 106–23.

36. Report of the School Committee for 1865; Superintendent's Report; NBCD. reel 2. In 1867, male teachers' salaries were raised by 25 percent, and the School Committee expressed outrage that female teachers were paid "a little less than one third as much" as male teachers. They suggested that "the compensation of our female teachers is but little if any more than that paid uneducated labor. We believe that justice to them requires that their salaries should be increased, . . . not for simple justice to them alone, but because it would bring to the work better minds, more efficient workers, and thus elevate not only our public schools, but the whole country." Report of the School Committee for 1867; NBCD, reel 2; see also Lynds, "New Bedford High School," 20–21.

37. Report of the School Committee for 1865; Superintendent's Report; NBCD, reel 2.

38. The School Committee's Report of 1866 included a table showing teachers' salaries in New Bedford compared with other Massachusetts communities. In 1869 the School Committee declared that poorly paid teachers would only lead to inferior instruction. Report of the School Committee for 1866; Superintendent's Report [for 1866]; Report of the School Committee for 1867; Report of the School Committee for 1869; NBCD, reel 2.

39. Report of the School Committee for 1867; NBCD, reel 2. Information about the Sylvia Ann Howland bequest and funding in the 1870s is in Lynds, "New Bedford High School," 19–26, and Ellis, *History* (1892), 617.

40. After Wamsutta Mills workers went on strike in March 1867 with demands for better schools, New Bedford opened an evening school near the mills. In 1871 the School Board opened a mill school, like those in Fall River, that operated year-round and allowed students between the ages of ten and fourteen to attend for thirteen consecutive weeks. Mill officials became more cooperative after being reassured that the company had no financial responsibility for the school. See McMullin, "Industrialization and the Transformation of Public Education," 1–4.

41. Judith Giesberg, *Army at Home, Women and the Civil War on the Northern Home Front* (Chapel Hill: University of North Carolina Press, 2009), 16, 46.

42. Report of the Overseers of the Poor, 1861–62, for Year ending February 28, 1862, and Report of the Overseers of the Poor, for Year ending February 28, 1863, NBCD, reel 2.

43. Annual Reports of the Overseers of the Poor, 1860–70, NBCD, reel 2.

44. Annual Reports of the Overseers of the Poor, 1862, 1863, 1864, NBCD, reel 2.

45. Address of Isaac C. Taber, Mayor, January 6, 1862; NBCD, reel 2.

46. Address of George Howland Jr., Mayor, 2, 1865, NBCD, reel 2.

47. Address of Mayor Isaac C. Taber, January 6, 1862; NBCD; reel 2; Address of George Howland Jr., Mayor, January 5, 1863; NBCD, reel 2; Report of the Committee on Finance for the Fiscal Year ending March 1, 1864; NBCD, reel 2. Report of the Committee on Finance for Year ending March 1, 1865; NBCD, reel 2; Address of George Howland Jr., Mayor, January 2, 1865; NBCD, reel 2.

48. Schultz provides an excellent context for New Bedford in chapter 7, "Promoting Public Works," 153–81; see Stanley K. Schultz, *Constructing Urban Culture: American Cities and City Planning, 1800–1920* (Philadelphia: Temple University Press, 1989).

49. Frisch, *Town Into City,* 102–7; quotes on pp. 106 and 107.

50. R. C. P. Coggeshall, "The Development of New Bedford Water Supplies," *Old Dartmouth Historical Society Sketches, Number 42* (New Bedford, 1915): 3, 8–9; see also Ellis, *History* (1892), 371–74; Pease, *History* (1918), 203–4, 278–79.

51. The Joint Committee was established in July 1860 with representatives of the Mayor, Aldermen, and Common Council. Funded by an appropriation of $300, Captain Charles H. Bigelow, then in charge of construction at the Clark's Point fort, was hired to make the first surveys and measurements. He was assisted by George A. Briggs, the city surveyor, and William F. Durfee. Their encouraging first report was released in December 1860. The 1861 report marshaled an array of scientific and engineering evidence to support their claims. Bigelow and colleagues favored a water system that drew from the Acushnet River with a holding reservoir near the Ansel White Mill dam. They proposed aqueducts that connected with a pumping and distribution system throughout New Bedford, but the plans carried a shocking price tag of more than $430,000. Although Bigelow died shortly after making this report, his ideas would be largely implemented in the late 1860s once funding was secured. Coggeshall, "Development," 9–10; Ellis, *History* (1892), 371.

52. Report of the Joint Special Committee of the City Council of New Bedford on the Introduction of Fresh Water, dated December 21, 1861; NBCD, reel 2.

53. Although Howland claimed that very few if any residents would subscribe to public distribution of water, he changed his mind after his private water well was tested in 1864 and found to be deficient and overloaded with chlorine. His aggressive opposition stopped and he promptly applied for residential service when fresh water was piped to Sixth Street. Coggeshall, "Development," 10–12.

54. The Reverend William J. Potter, "A Pulpit View of the Business Interests of our City," reprinted sermons delivered at the Unitarian Church, January 18, 1863, and January 25, 1863. Sermons were combined and reprinted in 1863. Also located in Potter Papers, NBFPL, sermons 98 and 99.

55. In their report of December 1863, the Joint Special Committee explained cost estimates and comparative data from the cities of Boston and Hartford. Making a persuasive case for fresh water, committee members were rewarded when the referendum passed on April 14, 1864. Ellis, *History* (1892), 372; Coggeshall, "Development," 11–12; and Report of the Joint Special Committee of the City Council on the Introduction of Fresh Water, with the Act of the Legislature authorizing the same; The Report of Professor George I. Chace on the Valley of the Acushnet River, with an Analysis of the Water; and the Report, Plan, and Estimates of George A. Briggs, City Surveyor. Dated December 29, 1863; NBCD, reel 2; see p. 37 for summary conclusions about advantages of fresh water. Cost estimates are found on 34–37.

56. On July 20, 1865, a Joint Committee was appointed to pursue the water works, and they hired William J. McAlpine, a nationally known engineer, with assistance from Professor George I. Chace and City Surveyor George H. Briggs. Their report, issued in October 1865, provided detailed analyses of water samples and McAlpine's plans for a permanent water supply from the Acushnet River. Coggeshall, "Development," 12–13; Report of the Joint Special Committee of the City Council of New Bedford, on the Introduction of Fresh Water, with the Report of Wm. J. McAlpine, Civil Engineer, the Analysis of Prof. Chace (1865); NBCD, reel 2.

57. Four members submitted a minority report: Joseph Knowles, Matthew Howland (Mayor George Howland's brother), Charles H. Gifford, and David B. Kempton. See "Minority Report" appended to Report, ibid. Also, Coggeshall, "Development," 13–14; Ellis, *History* (1892), 372–73.

58. Ellis, *History* (1892), 373. Coggeshall, "Development," 14–19; quote on p. 19. Annual rates were set at $5 for one house, one family, and first faucet. Manufacturing

establishments were charged fifteen cents per 1,000 gallons if less than 15,000 gallons were used per day. Furthermore, the city was to pay $12,000 per year for "unlimited" use of water. See "An Ordinance establishing the Water Rates of the New Bedford Water Works," effective January 1, 1870; City Ordinances, NBCD, reel 2.

59. Address of John H. Perry, Mayor, January 1, 1866; NBCD; reel 2.

60. In 1866, the City Tax Collector collected 97 percent of taxes of the largest amount ever apportioned—$340,382.05. Report of the City Treasurer of His Operations Under the State-Aid Law for the Year 1866, dated January 1, 1867; NBCD, reel 2.

61. Address of Mayor John H. Perry, January 7, 1867; NBCD, reel 2.

62. More specifically, Pierce explained, New Bedford had paid nearly $9,500 in state aid to disabled veterans in fiscal year 1867, and with a previous balance of $1,149.74, the Commonwealth of Massachusetts owed the city a total of $10,646.05. Address of Mayor Andrew G. Pierce, January 6, 1868; NBCD, reel 2.

63. In this fiscal year, the Finance Committee introduced a more sophisticated and succinct accounting format that featured a one-page abstract that neatly summarized all major appropriations, balances, and alterations. Report of the Committee on Finance for Year Ending March 1, 1867; NBCD, reel 2.

64. Address of Mayor Andrew G. Pierce, January 6, 1868; NBCD, reel 2.

65. Address of Mayor George Howland Jr., January 2, 1865; NBCD, reel 2; Address of Mayor Isaac C. Taber, January 6, 1862; NBCD, reel 2.

9. "The Great Hope for the Future": New Bedford in the Postbellum Era

1. Address of Andrew G. Pierce, Mayor, January 6, 1868; New Bedford City Documents (hereafter cited as NBCD), reel 2.

2. Address of George B. Richmond, Mayor, January 3, 1870; NBCD, reel 2.

3. Herbert L Aldrich, "New Bedford," *New England Magazine and Bay State Monthly* 1, no. 5 (May 1886): 423–44; quotes on p. 442.

4. Report of the Committee on Finance for Year Ending March 1, 1868; NBCD, reel 2; Address of George B. Richmond, Mayor, January 2, 1871; NBCD, reel 2. Report of City Marshal For 1871; NBCD, reel 2.

5. Report of the School Committee For 1870; Report of Truant Officer for 1870; NBCD, reel 2.

6. Report of the School Committee For 1872; NBCD, reel 2.

7. Perry biographical sketch in Leonard B. Ellis, *History of New Bedford and Its Vicinity, 1620–1892* (Syracuse, NY: D. Mason & Company, 1992), 2:80–81, and business information in Massachusetts, vol. 17, 206, R. G. Dun Collection, Baker Library Historical Collections, Harvard Business School.

8. Pierce biography in Ellis, *History*, 2:120–21, describes an amazing rise through manufacturing businesses, as his directorships included the Grinnell Mills, the Morse Twist Drill Company, the Pierce Manufacturing Company, the Mechanics National Bank, and insurance companies. Pierce business information in Massachusetts, vol. 17, 131, R. G. Dun Collection, Baker Library Historical Collections, Harvard Business.

9. Richmond biography in Ellis, *History*, 2:106–7; business information in Massachusetts, vol. 17, 17, R. G. Dun Collection, Baker Library Historical Collections, Harvard Business School.

10. Address of George H. Dunbar, Mayor, January 6, 1873; NBCD, reel 2. Report from the New Bedford Orphan's Home, 1876, Boston Public Library, Rare Books, Mss. Acc. 844.

11. Thomas A. McMullin, "Overseeing the Poor: Industrialization and Poor Relief in New Bedford, 1865–1900," *Social Science Review* 65 (December 1991): 548–63. Also see Thomas A. McMullin, "Industrialization and Social Change in a Nineteenth-Century

Port City: New Bedford, Massachusetts, 1865–1900," (PhD dissertation, University of Wisconsin-Madison, 1976).

12. The Arctic disasters of 1871 and 1876, and whaling events through 1892, are covered in Ellis, *History* (1892), 425–35; Everett S. Allen, *Children of the Light: The Rise and Fall of New Bedford Whaling and the Death of the Arctic Fleet* (Boston: Little, Brown & Co., 1973); Eric Jay Dolin, *Leviathan: the History of Whaling in America* (New York: Norton, 2007).

13. Elmo Paul Hohman, *The American Whaleman: A Study of Life and Labor in the Whaling Industry* (New York: Longmans, Green and Co., 1928), 72, 73, 221, quotes on 300–1. Hohman's observations drew from earlier accounts such as George Brown Goode and Joseph W. Collins, "The Fishermen of the United States," section 4, The Fisheries and Fishery Industries of the United States, Senate Miscellaneous Documents, 47th Congress, 1st Session, 1881–82 (Washington, DC: Government Printing Office, 1887), 6–7; and James Templeman Brown, "The Whalemen, Vessels and Boats, Apparatus, and Methods of the Whale Fishery," in Goode and Collins, *Fisheries*, 218.

14. A solid overview is in Hohman, chapter 13, "Civil War, Petroleum, and the Arctic," in *American Whaleman*, 289–301.

15. See "Decline of Yankee Whaling," an excellent and succinct historical overview provided by the New Bedford Whaling Museum at http://www.whalingmuseum.org. Also see Lance E. Davis, Robert E. Gallman, and Karin Gleiter, *In Pursuit of Leviathan: Technology, Institutions, and Profits in American Whaling, 1816–1906* (Chicago and London: University of Chicago Press, 1997), and Dolin, *Leviathan*.

16. Zephaniah W. Pease and George W. Hough, *History of New Bedford: Its Industries, Institutions, and Attractions*, ed. William L. Sayer (New Bedford: Mercury Publishing Company, 1889), 187–88.

17. To my knowledge, there has been no focused analysis of claims paid specifically to New Bedford's whaling merchants. Claims were first laid out in *List of Claims Filed with the Department of State, Growing out of The Acts Committed by the Several Vessels, Which Have Given Rise to the Claims Generically Known as The Alabama Claims* (Washington, DC: Government Printing Office, 1871); see especially summary amounts, 243–47. A few sources explain the political and diplomatic machinations associated with the "Alabama Claims," including Adrian Cook, *The Alabama Claims, American Politics and Anglo-American Relations, 1865–1870* (Ithaca, NY, and London: Cornell University Press, 1975); James Tertius deKay, *The Rebel Raiders, The Astonishing History of the Confederacy's Secret Navy* (New York: Ballantine Books, 2002), 223–46; Tom Chaffin, *Sea of Gray, The Around-the-World Odyssey of the Confederate Raider Shenandoah* (New York: Hill and Wang, 2006), 368–70. New Bedford attorney William W. Crapo played an important role in legal wrangling; some of his correspondence is found through Inventory of the Correspondence of William W. Crapo Concerning the Alabama Claims Cases, 1870–76, MSS-98-3, Special Collections, University of Virginia Law Library, Charlottesville, VA. Also see extracts from Crapo's correspondence in Appendix D, *Documents of the Tribunal, Held at Geneva, Switzerland, 1871–1872, Collected and Arranged by John Chandler Bancroft Davis, Agent of the United States, and by Him Given to the Library of Harvard University, June 22, 1889*. At the National Archives, see George S. Ulibarri and Daniel T. Goggin, comps., *Preliminary Inventory of Records Relating to Civil War Claims, United States and Great Britain*, PI 135 (1962).

18. Hough, *Wamsutta*, 32–33, 38–41; Ellis, *History* (1892), 458–60.

19. McMullin, "Industrialization and Social Change," 19–20; Ellis, *History* (1892), 461; Pease and Hough, *History* (1889), 154. The best treatment of company housing is in Kingston William Heath, *The Patina of Place, The Cultural Weathering of a New England Industrial Landscape* (Knoxville: University of Tennessee Press, 2001); see especially 70–76 for Potomska Mill housing.

20. A company historian offered a benign view of various nationalities that comprised the manufacturing labor pool: "Here was modern America, coming together, working side by side, lending a hand not only at the mill business but at the greater business of becoming a nation." Hough, *Wamsutta*, 41–42. See Bennett Papers, ODHS Manuscripts, Mss. Collection 9, subgroup 4, series F, folder 3 for newspaper clippings relating to history of Wamsutta, including account of Bennett's resignation in 1874 and presentation of commemorative volume with signatures of 1,248 employees.

21. Pease and Hough, *History* (1889), 149–53; Pease, *History* (1918), 204; Ellis, *History* (1892), 460–61; Hough, *Wamsutta*, 43–44, 47.

22. In the 1870s, new directors included Edward D. Mandell (1870–98), Charles L. Wood (1871–81), Horatio Hathaway (1876–98), Edward W. Howland (1877–79), and Francis Hathaway (1879–95). Crapo information and quotations in Hough, *Wamsutta*, 45–47; directors through 1945 listed on 72. A short online chronology of William W. Crapo notes that he served as president of Wamsutta Mills between 1889 and 1918; director and then president of Potomska Mills, 1873–1923; and represented New Bedford in the US House of Representatives, 1875–83. See http://www.umflint.edu/library/archives/crapo.htm.

23. According to McMullin's figures, in 1890 twenty mills employed 7,694 people, plus six other manufacturing companies employed more than 100 workers each. McMullin, "Industrialization," 21–22, 221–24.

24. McMullin, "Industrialization," 21–22; George C. Avila, *Pairpont Glass Story* (New Bedford: Reynolds-DeWalt, 1968); Pease, *History* (1918) lists companies on 211.

25. Pease and Hough, *History* (1889), 6.

26. Hough, *Wamsutta*, 49–50. Leonard Bolles Ellis wrote glowingly in 1892 about New Bedford's textile factories that in their architecture, construction, equipment, and products "have no superior in this or any other country." Ellis, *History* (1892), 453. Robert Greive, ed., *New Bedford Semi-Centennial Souvenir: Containing a History of the City* (Providence, RI: Journal of Commerce Company, 1897). Kingston Heath explained the city's altered landscape: "Factory chimney stacks now replaced the mastheads of whaling ships that once were silhouetted against the sky. The visual presence of the chimney stacks separated these later mills, too, from the earlier mills of New England that were driven predominantly by water-powered technology." Heath, *Patina of Place*, 42.

27. McMullin, "Industrialization," 57–58, 78.

28. Ibid., 207–12.

29. Ibid., 215–20; quote on 220.

30. Ibid., 34–35.

31. See David Ward, *Poverty, Ethnicity, and the American City, 1840–1925, Changing Conceptions of the Slum and the Ghetto* (New York, 1989), 212–14.

32. Quoted in McMullin, "Industrialization," 182, 193–96.

33. Grieve, ed., Semi-Centennial Souvenir, 1. McMullin, "Industrialization," 248–49.

34. McMullin, "Industrialization," 237–47; "The 1898 Strike Scrapbook," NBFPL Special Collections.

35. Daniel DeLeon, *What Means This Strike? Address Delivered by Daniel DeLeon in the City Hall of New Bedford, Mass., February 11, 1898* (New York, 1898), 2; available online at http://tinyurl.com/deleon-strike.

36. Michael W. Santos, "Community and Communism: The 1928 New Bedford Textile Strike," Labor History 26, no. 2 (1985), 230–49; Seymour Louis Wolfbein, *The Decline of a Cotton Textile City: A Study of New Bedford* (New York: Columbia University Press, 1944).

37. Thomas A. McMullin, "Lost Alternative: The Urban Industrial Utopia of William D. Howland," *New England Quarterly* 55 (1982), 25–38, quote on 31. For the 1870

census, a database prepared by the New Bedford Free Public Library enumerates the names of 1,465 people of color.

38. Janette Thomas Greenwood, *First Fruits of Freedom: The Migration of Former Slaves and Their Search for Equality in Worcester, Massachusetts, 1862–1900* (Chapel Hill: University of North Carolina Press, 2009), 138–51. Greenwood pays attention to Irish and French Canadian immigrants who fared better than blacks; see 150. Bunch quoted in Margery Eagan, "Subtle bigotry halted black progress," *New Bedford Standard-Times*, February 22, 1980. Marilyn Halter's excellent work on Cape Verdeans in New Bedford offers a number of insights about "race" as a social construction and demonstrates this group's unique place within the region, particularly after the 1920s; see Marilyn Halter, *Between Race and Ethnicity: Cape Verdean American Immigrants, 1860–1965* (Urbana and Chicago: University of Illinois Press, 1993). Important works that compare native-born blacks with foreign-born immigrants in the late nineteenth century include Theodore Hershberg, ed., *Philadelphia, Work, Space, Family, and Group Experience in the Nineteenth Century, Essays Toward an Interdisciplinary History of the City* (New York: Oxford University Press, 1981) and Olivier Zunz, *The Changing Face of Inequality, Urbanization, Industrial Development, and Immigrants in Detroit, 1880–1920* (Chicago: University of Chicago Press, 1982).

39. Margery Eagan, "Subtle bigotry halted black progress," *New Bedford Standard-Times*, February 22, 1980; Ellis, *History* (1892), 564; Pease and Hough, *New Bedford* (1889), 305–9.

10. "On the Altar of Our Common Country": Contested Commemorations of the Civil War

1. A version of this chapter was published as "'A Different Civil War': African-American Veterans in New Bedford, Massachusetts," in Paul A. Cimbala and Randall M. Miller, eds., *Union Soldiers and the Northern Home Front: Wartime Experiences, Postwar Adjustments* (New York: Fordham University Press, 2002), 417–41. Address of John H. Perry, Mayor, January 1, 1866; New Bedford City Documents (hereafter cited as NBCD), reel 2.

2. Address of John H. Perry, Mayor, January 7, 1867; NBCD, reel 2. Zephaniah W. Pease and George W. Hough, *New Bedford, Massachusetts: Its History, Industries, Institutions, and Attractions*, ed. William L. Sayer (New Bedford: Board of Trade, 1889), 93. See also Report on the Committee on Finance for Year Ending March 1, 1867, and Fifteenth Annual Report of the Trustees of the Free Public Library, 1866; NBCD, reel 2. New Bedford was one of 233 cities or towns in Massachusetts that had built one or more Civil War memorials as of 1910, according to a survey by Alfred S. Roe, Commander of the Grand Army of the Republic in the Department of Massachusetts. See Alfred S. Roe, *Monuments, Tablets and Other Memorials Erected in Massachusetts to Commemorate the Services of Her Sons in the War of the Rebellion, 1861–1865* (Boston: Wright & Potter Printing Company, 1910), 20–21, 84. Following the lead of Governor John Andrew who issued General Order No. 1 in January 1865, Mayor Pierce urged his fellow citizens to repay their citizen-soldiers through patronage and employment "to repay in part the debt of gratitude we owe." Address of Mayor Andrew G. Pierce, January 6, 1868; NBCD, reel 2. Governor Andrew issued General Order No. 1 that encouraged the employment of veterans, especially disabled ones. See William Schouler, *A History of Massachusetts in the Civil War. vol. 1,* Civil and Military History of Massachusetts in the Rebellion (Boston: E. P. Dutton & Co., Publishers, 1868), 613.

3. A powerful and persuasive analysis of Civil War memory-making is David W. Blight, *Race and Reunion: The Civil War in American Memory* (Cambridge, MA: Belknap Press of Harvard University Press, 2001). By the time of the battle of Gettysburg's

fiftieth anniversary in 1913, Blight writes, "A segregated society required a segregated historical memory and a national mythology that could blunt or contain the conflict at the root of that segregation." A "reconciliationist" memory of the war trumped an "emancipationist" view propounded by black Americans. See Blight, *Race*, 2, 391, and *passim*.

4. The best overviews of "Memorial Day" or "Decoration Day" are by David W. Blight, chapter 3, "Decoration Day," in *Race and Reunion*, 64–97, and "Decoration Days: The Origins of Memorial Day in North and South," in Alice E. Fahs and Joan Waugh, eds., *The Memory of the Civil War in American Culture* (Chapel Hill, NC, and London: University of North Carolina Press, 2004), 94–129.

5. For provocative essays by accomplished historians, see James Oliver Horton and Lois E. Horton, eds., *Slavery and Public History: The Tough Stuff of American Memory* (New York: New Press, 2006), and Joan Waugh and Gary W. Gallagher, eds., *Wars Within a War: Controversy and Conflict Over the American Civil War* (Chapel Hill: University of North Carolina Press, 2009).

6. For American civil religious themes, the best starting point is Robert N. Bellah, "Civil Religion," in Robert Bellah, *Beyond Belief: Essays on Religion in a Post-Traditional World* (New York: Harper & Row, 1970), 171–82.

7. A number of scholars have addressed the unique aspects of African-American civil religion, most notably David W. Blight, *Frederick Douglass' Civil War: Keeping Faith in Jubilee* (Baton Rouge: Louisiana University Press, 1989); David W. Blight, "'For Something Beyond the Battlefield': Frederick Douglass and the Struggle for the Memory of the Civil War," *Journal of American History* 75 (March 1989), 1156–78; David W. Blight, "Frederick Douglass and the American Apocalypse," *Civil War History* 31, no. 4 (1985): 309–28. Blight's essays have been republished, with only minor changes, in David W. Blight, *Beyond the Battlefield, Race, Memory, and the American Civil War* (Amherst and Boston: University of Massachusetts Press, 2002). Other relevant sources include Charles V. Long, "Civil Rights—Civil Religion: Visible People and Invisible Religion," in Donald G. Jones and Russell E. Richey, eds., *American Civil Religion* (New York, 1974), 212–24; Mitch Kachun, *Festivals of Freedom: Memory and Meaning in African American Emancipation Celebrations, 1808–1915* (Amherst: University of Massachusetts Press, 2006); Kathleen Ann Clark, *Defining Moments: African American Commemoration & Political Culture in the South, 1863–1913* (Chapel Hill: University of North Carolina Press, 2005); Genevieve Fabre, ed., *History and Memory in African-American Culture* (New York: Oxford University Press, 1994); Elizabeth Bethel, *The Roots of African-American Identity: Memory and History in Antebellum Free Communities* (New York: St. Martin's Press, 1997); Earl Lewis, "Connecting Memory, Self, and the Power of Place in African American Urban History," *Journal of Urban History* (March 1995): 347–72.

8. See Blight, "For Something Beyond the Battlefield," 1156–78, and John Bodnar, *Remaking America: Public Memory, Commemoration, and Patriotism in the Twentieth Century* (Princeton, NJ: Princeton University Press, 1994). The scholarly literature devoted to "memory" is large, varied, and growing. Among the most influential works, see David Thelen, ed., *Memory in American History* (Bloomington: Indiana University Press, 1991); Michael Kammen, *Mystic Chords of Memory: The Transformation of Tradition in American Culture* (New York: Alfred A. Knopf, 1991); John R. Gillis, ed., *Commemorations: The Politics of National Identity* (Princeton, NJ: Princeton University Press, 1994); Barry Schwartz, *Abraham Lincoln and the Forge of National Memory* (Chicago: University of Chicago Press, 2000); Michael Frisch, "American History and the Structure of Collective Memory," *Journal of American History* 75 (March 1989): 1130–55; along with the journal *History and Memory*, published since 1989.

9. Eric Foner, "Ken Burns and the Romance of Reunion" in *Ken Burns's The Civil War: Historians Respond*, ed. Robert Brent Toplin (New York: Oxford University Press, 1996), 110–18, quote on 114; Kammen, *Mystic Chords*, 14.

10. Blight, *Race and Reunion*, is unsurpassed, but also see the important collection of essays in Fahs and Waugh, eds., *The Memory of the Civil War in American Culture* (Chapel Hill and London: University of North Carolina Press, 2004); Sanford Levinson, *Written in Stone: Public Monuments in Changing Societies* (Durham, NC, and London: Duke University Press, 1998); Cecilia Elizabeth O'Leary, *To Die For: The Paradox of American Patriotism* (Princeton: Princeton University Press, 1999); Kirk Savage, *Standing Soldiers, Kneeling Slaves: Race, War, and Monument in Nineteenth-Century America* (Princeton, NJ: Princeton University Press, 1997); Paul A. Shackel, *Memory in Black and White: Race, Commemoration, and the Post-Bellum Landscape* (Walnut Creek, CA: AltaMira Press, 2003). An entertaining assessment of battles over Civil War memorialization is Tony Horwitz, *Confederates in the Attic: Dispatches from the Unfinished Civil War* (New York: Vintage, 1999).

11. Gillis, "Memory and Identity: The History of a Relationship," in Gillis, ed., *Commemorations*, 3–24; quote is on p. 3.

12. *New Bedford Evening Standard*, May 31, 1866 (hereafter cited as *NBDES*).

13. *NBDES*, July 5, 1866. The Reverend Alonzo Quint served as chaplain of the Second Massachusetts Infantry from 1863 to 1864 when he was installed as pastor of New Bedford's North Congregational Church. Quint was the first New England man mustered into the Grand Army of the Republic and served as its Chaplain-in-chief for many years. See *One of a Thousand: A Series of Biographical Sketches on One Thousand Men Resident in the Commonwealth of Massachusetts, A.D. 1888–89*, Compiled under the Editorial Supervision of John C. Rand (Boston: First National Publishing Company, 1890), 497–98.

14. Barbara A. Gannon, "Sites of Memory, Sites of Glory: African-American Grand Army of the Republic Posts in Pennsylvania," chapter 7 in William A. Blair and William A. Pencak, eds., *Making and Remaking Pennsylvania's Civil War* (Pennsylvania State University Press, 2001), 165–87; see especially 174–84. See Gannon's more thorough account *The Won Cause: Black and White Comradeship in the Grand Army of the Republic* (Chapel Hill, NC: University of North Carolina Press, 2011). The subsequent examination of postwar parades is informed by Elsa Barkley Brown and Gregg D. Kimball, "Mapping the Terrain of Black Richmond," *Journal of Urban History* 21, no. 3 (March 1995): 296–346; Susan G. Davis, *Parades and Power: Street Theatre in Nineteenth-Century Philadelphia* (Philadelphia: Temple University Press, 1986; Berkeley: University of California Press, 1988); Mary Ryan, "The American Parade: Representations of the Nineteenth-Century Social Order" in *The New Cultural History*, Lynn Hunt (Berkeley: University of California Press, 1989), 131–53.

15. *NBDES*, May 30, 1868; May 30, 1876.

16. *NBDES*, May 30, 1876.

17. *NBDES*, July 5, 1867.

18. *NBDES*, July 6, 1868.

19. *NBDES*, July 5, 1870. For an account of the city's expenses, see Report of the Committee on Finance for Year Ending March 1, 1871, NBCD, reel 2.

20. For example, on the day before the Fourth in 1871, several establishments advertised "low carnival prices" and extended shopping hours to "accommodate the crowds of customers." *NBDES*, July 3, 1871. This pattern persisted of increased Irish Catholic visibility and African-American marginalization. For example, the St. Lawrence Temperance Band made its first official appearance in Fourth of July celebrations in 1874 and was posted prominently at the Soldiers' and Sailors' Monument. *NBDES*, July 6, 1874.

21. Reverend William J. Potter, "Soldiers' Memorial Sermon," May 23, 1880, handwritten manuscript, William J. Potter Papers, Special Collections, New Bedford Free Public Library (hereafter cited as NBFPL).

22. Blight, *Race and Reunion*; Andre Fleche, "'Shoulder to Shoulder as Comrades Tried': Black and White Union Veterans and Civil War Memory," in *Civil War History* 51, no. 2 (2005): 175–201, quote on 201; Gannon, *The Won Cause*.

23. My discussion of the Grand Army of the Republic (GAR) draws heavily upon Stuart McConnell's excellent history, *Glorious Contentment: The Grand Army of the Republic, 1865–1900* (Chapel Hill: University of North Carolina Press, 1992), along with Barbara A. Gannon's work cited previously, *The Won Cause*.

24. See *Proceedings of the Third National Convention and Proceedings of the Fifth National Convention* in *Proceedings of the First to Tenth Meetings 1866–1876 (Inclusive) of the National Encampment, Grand Army of the Republic, with Digest of Decisions, Rules of Order and Index* (Philadelphia: Samuel P. Town, Printer, 1877), 41, 117–18; Address of Department Commander John D. Billings, *Journal of Proceedings of the Nineteenth Annual Encampment*, Department of Massachusetts, G.A.R., held at Boston, 1885, in *Journals of the Encampment Proceedings of the Department of Massachusetts G.A.R. From 1881 to 1887 Inclusive* (Boston: E. B. Stillings & Company, 1902), 249–50 (hereafter cited as *Encampment Proceedings*); *Early History of the Department of Massachusetts G.A.R. From 1866 to 1880 Inclusive* (Boston: E. B. Stillings, 1895), iii–iv, 5–15.

25. *Early History of the Department of Massachusetts*, 8–9.

26. The Reverend Quint's address, extracted from the *New Bedford Evening Standard* of July 5, 1867, was printed as an appendix, "Post No. 1 Early Memorial Services in Honor of the Dead," in *Early History of the Department of Massachusetts*, 443–47.

27. William Logan Rodman Post Records, "Roll of Members," "Records," "Membership Roll," "Monument Fund," in GAR Records, Special Collections, NBFPL. Other publications included *Decoration of the Heroes' Graves by the G.A.R. Post #1, New Bedford, May 30, 1868* (1868), and *The Drummer Boy* (1870); see Charlene R. Burnett, "Checklist of New Bedford Imprints, 1866–1876," (MA thesis, American University, Washington, DC, 1964). Other printed sources found in Special Collections, NBFPL, include *By-Laws for the Government of William Logan Rodman Post, No. 1, Department of Massachusetts, Grand Army of the Republic* (New Bedford, 1870); *By-Laws and Roster of William Logan Rodman Post No. 1, Department of Massachusetts, G.A.R.* (New Bedford, 1894); "Old Post One." *Bulletin No. 4* (New Bedford, 1906).

28. *Old War Songs* (Syracuse, NY, n.d. [circa 1890]). GAR Records, Special Collections, NBFPL.

29. Committee members were to meet weekly with the authority to dole out money on an emergency basis, although no more than five dollars could be granted at any one time. Records of the Committee on Relief, GAR Rodman Post Number One, Special Collections, NBFPL.

30. Relief Committee Book, vol. 1, GAR Records, Special Collections, NBFPL. The first account book begins on January 10, 1870, and runs through 1899, although there are many chronological gaps in the ledger.

31. See especially Donald R. Shaffer, *After the Glory: The Struggles of Black Civil War Veterans* (Lawrence: University Press of Kansas, 2004), 70–171, and Gannon, *The Won Cause*. Richard Reid aligns with Gannon and Fleche that the GAR was more color blind than other organizations of the time, and he agrees with Gannon that a segregated GAR post comprised "an autonomous social organization within a larger interracial group." Richard M. Reid, *Freedom for Themselves: North Carolina's Black Soldiers in the Civil War Era* (Chapel Hill: University of North Carolina Press, 2008), 308–10.

32. See McConnell, *Glorious Contentment*, 213–18. Racial policies of the GAR in the South are outlined by Wallace E. Davies, "The Problem of Race Segregation in the Grand Army of the Republic," *Journal of Southern History* (August 1947): 354–72.

33. *Journal of Proceedings of the Sixteenth Annual Encampment, Department of Massachusetts, G.A.R., Held at Boston, 1882,* in *Encampment Proceedings,* 12, 20.

34. *Journal of Proceedings of the Seventeenth Annual Encampment, Department of Massachusetts, G.A.R., Held at Boston, 1883,* in *Encampment Proceedings,* 99, 101, 112–13, 138. Over 700 members belonged to the two white GAR posts at their peak. Writing in 1918, when their numbers had declined to about 200, Pease noted: "These two posts have included in their membership practically all the veterans in this city and vicinity; only a few scattered veterans have remained unaffiliated with either post, so that the membership to-day includes very nearly every veteran still living in this vicinity." In 1918 Post 190 claimed 96 veterans (from a peak membership of 390), while Post 1 enlisted 88, a decline from peak membership of 230. Zepahaniah W. Pease, ed., *History of New Bedford* (New York: Lewis Historical Publishing Company, 1918), 319–22.

35. Figures compiled from *Proceedings of the Department of Massachusetts Encampment, Grand Army of the Republic, 1881 to 1900.*

36. *History of the Department of Massachusetts Woman's Relief Corps, Auxiliary to the Grand Army of the Republic. From Date of Organization, February 12, 1879, to January 1, 1895. With Appendixes.* (Boston: E. B. Stillings & Company, 1895), 37, 205. For fundraising efforts, see ibid., 235–36. See also *Journal of Proceedings of the Seventeenth Annual Encampment,* in *Encampment Proceedings,* 85–86. The larger context of WRC growth and activities is covered by O'Leary, To Die For, chapter 6, "'Mothers Train the Masses—Statesmen Lead the Few': Women's Place in Shaping the Nation," 91–109. O'Leary writes that "members of the WRC ritualized memories of the Civil War by using Memorial Day to create a cultural bridge between the nation's past and its future," she notes the parallel but competing efforts among Northern and Southern women in memorializing the war. O'Leary, *To Die For,* 100–3.

37. *Massachusetts Woman's Relief Corps,* 271. For insights about black club women, including the WRC, see Francesca Morgan, *Women and Patriotism in Jim Crow America* (Chapel Hill: University of North Carolina Press, 2005).

38. The importance of Fort Wagner in overcoming negative stereotypes of black troops is noted by many, including Joseph T. Glatthaar, *Forged in Battle: The Civil War Alliance of Black Soldiers and White Officers* (New York: Free Press, 1990), 141–42. Emilio makes this point in his regimental history, based upon his reading of contemporary newspapers and magazines. See Luis F. Emilio, *A Brave Black Regiment, History of the Fifty-Fourth Regiment of Massachusetts Volunteer Infantry, 1863–1865,* 2nd ed., rev. (Boston, 1894; 1891).

39. Excerpts and clippings in volume 4, addenda, folder 8, The Civil War Records of the Fifty-Fourth Regiment, compiled by Luis F. Emilio, the Massachusetts Historical Society (hereafter cited as Fifty-Fourth Records, MHS). The efforts to award Carney the Congressional Medal of Honor nearly forty years after his act appear to have been spearheaded by Christian A. Fleetwood. See "Documents Relating to the Military and Naval Service of Blacks Awarded the Congressional Medal of Honor from the Civil War to the Spanish-American War," Microfilm M929, roll 1: Civil War, US Colored Troops, National Archives and Records Service. Also see the melodramatic account of Carney's actions in Irvin H. Lee, *Negro Medal of Honor Men* (New York: Dodd, Mead, 1967), 24–27, and list of "Negro Medal of Honor Men" in ibid., 127. Carney, and poetry in praise of him by Olivia Ward Bush Banks, are discussed in Alicia L. Moore and LaVonne I. Neal, "African Americans and the Civil War: Brave Standard Bearers," *Black History Bulletin* 73, no. 2 (Summer/Fall 2010): 4–7.

40. *NBDES,* April 27, 1870.

41. *Address of Gen. William Cogswell, of Salem, at the Grand New England Celebration of the Emancipation Proclamation, The Charge of the Mass. 54th, at Fort Wagner, and the Adoption of the 15th Amendment, Held under the auspices of the colored citizens of New*

Bedford, July 18, 1871 (Salem, Massachusetts: Office of the Salem Gazette, 1871), located in Special Collections, NBFPL.

42. *Boston Herald*, August 2, 1887; *Boston Journal*, August 2, 1887; vol. 4, addenda, folder 8; Fifty-Fourth Records, MHS.

43. William H. Carney folder, Black History, Special Collections, NBFPL.

44. Vol. 4, addenda, folders 5 and 6; Fifty-Fourth Records, MHS.

45. Carney folder, Black History, Special Collections, NBFPL.

46. Membership Roll, William L. Rodman Post Number One, vol. 3, 103, in GAR Records, Special Collections, NBFPL.

47. As early as the autumn of 1865, a number of Boston and Massachusetts' leaders met to consider a suitable memorial to Shaw. See Edward Atkinson, "History of the Shaw Monument," in *Exercises at the Dedication of the Monument to Colonel Robert Gould Shaw and the Fifty-Fourth Regiment of Massachusetts Infantry, May 31, 1897* (Boston: Municipal Printing Office, 1897). Luis Emilio noted that black troops had contributed substantial funds for a memorial to Shaw after receiving their first pay in September 1864. Emilio reprinted a letter from General Saxton to Colonel E. N. Hallowell in which Saxton acknowledges receipt of $1,545 contributed by black soldiers for a monument "soon to be erected in memory of their former colonel, Robert Gould Shaw, and those who fell with him in the assault on Fort Wagner." Emilio, *Brave Black Regiment*, 229. See David Blight, "The Shaw Memorial in the Landscape of Civil War Memory," chapter 7 in *Beyond the Battlefield*, 153–69. An excellent collection of essays is Martin H. Blatt, Thomas J. Brown, and Donald Yacovone, eds., *Hope & Glory: Essays on the Legacy of the Fifty-Fourth Massachusetts Regiment* (Amherst: University of Massachusetts Press, 2001). Also see Paul A. Shackel's chapter, "Saint-Gaudens's Shaw Memorial: Redefining the Role of the 54th Massachusetts Volunteer Infantry," in *Memory in Black and White*, 113–44.

48. *Boston Globe*, May 30, 1897; in vol. 4, addenda, folder 8; Fifty-Fourth Records, MHS.

49. Kirk Savage, "The Politics of Memory: Black Emancipation and the Civil War Monument," in Gillis, ed., *Commemorations*, 127–49. Blight, "The Meaning or the Fight," in ibid., 149–53. See also the essays by Gregory C. Schwarz, Ludwid Lauerhass, and Brigid Sullivan in *The Shaw Memorial: A Celebration of an American Masterpiece* (Conshohocken, PA: Pegasus Press, 1997).

50. *Exercises at the Dedication*, 24–35.

51. Ibid., 57–59.

52. Ibid. In his autobiography, Booker T. Washington reprints his address and a newspaper account of the moving festivities, then refers to Carney's impact on the audience; see Booker T. Washington, *The Story of My Life and Work, An Autobiography by Booker T. Washington* (Toronto: J. L. Nichols & Company, 1901), 201–12. David Blight refers to Washington's speech as a "brief rehash of *Up From Slavery*, combined with artful strokes of Southern sentimentalism and sectional reconciliation." See Blight, "The Meaning or the Fight," 149, and *Race and Reunion*, 338–40.

53. See the poem and photography from the *Boston Journal* of June 1, 1897, and letter from William Whitney Jr. to Luis F. Emilio, June 28, 1897, in folder 5; *Boston Globe*, June 1, 1897, in vol. 4, addenda, folder 8; Fifty-Fourth Records, MHS.

54. See David W. Blight, *Race and Reunion*, especially the "Epilogue," 381–97, and his earlier work, "Quarrel Forgotten or a Revolution Remembered? Reunion and Race in the Memory of the Civil War, 1875–1913," in David W. Blight and Brooks D. Simpson, eds., *Union & Emancipation, Essays on Politics and Race in the Civil War Era* (Kent, OH: Kent State University Press, 1997), 151–79; Chase quoted on p. 176. Cecelia O'Leary made similar points that "national amnesia had erased Emancipation from Civil War com-

memorations and history books." See Cecelia O'Leary, chapter 11, "Clasping Hands over the Bloody Divide," in *To Die For*, 194–219; quote on p. 195.

55. See accounts and minutes for meetings of 23 February 1897, 16 March 1897, and 30 March 1897; Sons of Veterans, John H. Clifford Camp, No. 130, New Bedford; Old Dartmouth Historical Society, Manuscripts, Mss. Collection 77, subgroup 1, series F, box 16, subseries 35.

Epilogue

1. "The elite culture of the city has assembled a public identity that seemingly speaks of shared experiences and common goals that affirm a cohesive public culture, devoid of economic inequalities and political conflicts," Heath argues. See Kingston William Heath, *The Patina of Place: The Cultural Weathering of a New England Industrial Landscape* (Knoxville: University of Tennessee Press, 2001), see especially 55–57. For information about the sculptor, Bela Pratt, and the city's payment to him, see William W. Crapo Papers, Mss. Collection 64 (Biographical), Old Dartmouth Historical Society, Manuscripts, series C, box 12, subseries 53, folders 4–8. Pratt was very grateful for Crapo's support, proud of his work, and happy to receive $25,000 for his handiwork. Marilyn Halter offered a detailed study of New Bedford's significant Cape Verdean community in Marilyn Halter, *Between Race and Ethnicity: Cape Verdean American Immigrants, 1860–1965* (Urbana and Chicago: University of Illinois Press, 1993).

2. Leonard Bolles Ellis, *History of New Bedford and Its Vicinity, 1620–1892* (Syracuse, NY: D. Mason & Company, 1892), 382. Henry Beetle Hough, *Wamsutta of New Bedford, 1846–1946, A Story of New England Enterprise* (New Bedford, MA: Wamsutta Mills, 1946), 51. For an evocative look at New Bedford in more recent times, see Rory Nugent, *Down at the Docks* (New York: Anchor Books, 2009). A long-time sailor who lived in New Bedford for nearly two decades, Nugent offers an unflinching look at the city's "riches to rags" story and shows how the New Bedford's maritime history informs the lives of people who live and work there today.

3. Seymour Louis Wolfbein, *The Decline of a Cotton Textile City: A Study of New Bedford* (New York: Columbia University Press, 1944), and Michael W. Santos, "Community and Communism: The 1928 New Bedford Textile Strike," *Labor History* 26, no. 2 (Spring 1985): 230–49.

4. Sidney Kaplan, "Lewis Temple and the Hunting of the Whale," *New England Quarterly* 26, no. 1 (March 1953): 78–88. Lisa Borders, "Statue is tribute to inventor—and sculptor," *New Bedford Standard-Times*, July 6, 1987; John H. Ackerman, "Temple changed whalers' fortunes," *Chowder* (*New Bedford Standard-Times* magazine), February 6, 1983. Emil F. Guba, "Lewis Temple and Contemporaries, New Bedford Blacksmith, Inventor of the Toggle Iron Headed Harpoon," in "Lewis Temple Folder," Black History, NBFPL.

5. Paul A. Shackel, *Memory in Black and White: Race, Commemoration, and the Post-Bellum Landscape* (Walnut Creek, CA: AltaMira Press, 2003), 209. Shackel devotes a full chapter to the Shaw/54th Memorial; see "Saint-Gaudens's Shaw Memorial: Redefining the Role of the 54th Massachusetts Volunteer Infantry," 113–44.

6. Other national efforts to "remember" blacks in the Civil War are seen in the African-American Civil War Memorial in Washington, DC, the National Gallery of Art's display of a plaster version of the famed St. Gaudens' sculpture, and the National Park Service sponsorship of the Civil War Soldiers and Sailors Project that began with computerized and searchable records of African-American veterans. See George M. Fredrickson, "From the OAH President: Shaw Monument Rededication Shows Value of OAH and NPS Collaborations," *OAH Newsletter* 25, no. 3 (August 1997): 9. Also see Martin H. Blatt, Thomas J. Brown, and Donald Yacovone, eds., *Hope & Glory, Essays on the*

Legacy of the Fifty-Fourth Massachusetts Regiment (Amherst: University of Massachusetts Press in association with Massachusetts Historical Society, 2001).

7. To explain the park's history and programs, the National Park Service published *New Bedford Whaling National Historical Park, the First Decade: A Retrospective, 1996–2006.* The park's mission statement reads in part: "New Bedford Whaling National Historical Park helps to preserve, protect, and interpret certain districts, structures, and artifacts located in New Bedford, Massachusetts, that are associated with the history of whaling and related social, economic, and environmental themes for the benefit and inspiration of this and future generations." The park is to function as a "source of community identity and pride." For relevant web sites see New Bedford Whaling National Historical Park: http://www.nps.gov/nebe/index.htm; New Bedford Historical Society: http://www.nbhistoricalsociety.org/index.html; New Bedford Whaling Museum: http://www.whalingmuseum.org/; City of New Bedford, Black Heritage Trail: http://tinyurl.com/bhtrail.

8. See http://tinyurl.com/nbnja.

9. For example, David Blight's *Race and Reunion* is the best historical scholarship that explains the development of Civil War memory, and Kathryn Grover's work on New Bedford, *The Fugitives' Gibraltar* provides a detailed overview of the city's antebellum black community.

10. Barbara A. Gannon, *The Won Cause: Black and White Comradeship in the Grand Army of the Republic* (Chapel Hill: University of North Carolina Press, 2011), see especially "Introduction," 1–11.

11. Gannon explains the term "Won Cause" on 146–47 and suggests its victory on 200 and 195, as follows: "While some scholars have been preoccupied with discrediting the Lost Cause, perhaps we should remember the Won Cause and the interracial blood sacrifice that redeemed, transformed, and made possible the modern United States—the living legacy of the black and white comrades of the Grand Army of the Republic."

12. See, for example, scholarly discussions of popular movies: Robert Brent Toplin, ed., *Ken Burns's The Civil War: Historians Respond* (New York: Oxford University Press, 1996), and Martin H. Blatt, "Glory, Hollywood History, Popular Culture, and the Fifty-Fourth Massachusetts Regiment," in Blatt, Brown, and Yacovone, eds., *Hope & Glory*, 215–35.

13. "We're inviting all kids to come and absorb their own history through the words, art and music of their peers," says Superintendent Jen Nersesian. "There's something really exciting going on around here." See "National park to showcase Young Ambassador Program," SouthCoastToday.com, August 19, 2010. For "New YAP! Single '54,'" see http://www.nps.gov/nebe/index.htm. The song itself is at http://soundcloud.com/yap-2/54yap.

Index

ABMC (American Baptist Missionary Convention), 44
accounting practices, 165–66
Adams, Virginia Matzke, 7
African Americans, 5, 6
  American civil religion and, 202
  antebellum New Bedford, 32–34, 40
  black enlistees, 7
  churches, 41, 42–43, 44–48
  coasting trade, 33–36
  economic transition and, 199
  enlistment, 99–100, 101–3 (*See also* black military service)
  GAR members, 209–10
  maritime commerce, 33–36
  militancy, 48–51
  occupational distribution, 39
  official memory inclusion, 202
  postbellum era, 121–22, 200
  professional class, 39
  skilled labor, 38–39
  soldiers, 91–92
  women's opportunities, 40
African Christian Church, formation, 42–43
AME (African Methodist Episcopal), 44–45
American Federation of Labor, 197–98
AMEZ (African Methodist Episcopal Zion), 45
Andersonville, 96
antebellum New Bedford
  African-American population, 32–34, 40
  church life, 41–45
  class divisions, 29
  crime, 29–30
  demographics, 33–41
  economy, 17–18, 21–23, 33–41
  religious life, 28

antislavery agitation, 5–6
  African-American churches, 45–48
  Young Men's Anti-Slavery Society, 46
arrest figures on home front, 73–75

backgrounds of soldiers, 85, 87
Bedford Commercial Bank, 22–23
Bender, Thomas, 4
Bennett, Thomas Jr., 19–21
Bethel AME church, 44–45
bicentennial celebration, 1–2
black enlistees, 7
black heroes, commemorations and, 212–15
black military service. *See also* Fifty-Fourth Massachusetts Volunteer Infantry
  Andrew, John A., 101
  Douglass, Frederick on, 99–100, 104
  Emancipation Day celebration, 114
  equal pay, 102–3, 107, 114–17
  equality in, 102–3
  financial results, 120
  fundraising, 112–14
  Harrison, Rev. Samuel, 106
  opposition, 103
  published accounts of, 104–5
  recruitment, 101–2
  state payments, lack of, 122–23
blacksmiths, antebellum New Bedford, 17
Board of Health establishment, 183
bounties paid for enlistment, 57–58, 87–88, 90
Burns, Anthony, 47
business community, 5
business leaders and textile industry, 199

capitalist networks, 21–23
Carney, William H., 110–14
  commemorations, 212–13, 214
  Congressional Medal of Honor, 212–13

financial assistance needs, 214–15
Glory (movie) and, 220
pension, 128–30
Post One Veterans photo, *129*
cask manufacture, antebellum New
    Bedford, 17
casualties, 95–97
    Fort Wagner, 109–10
    pensions and, 127–31
celebrations. *See also* commemorations
    American civil religion, 202
    centennial, 204–5
    deliverance theme, 202
    Fourth of July, 203–6
    Memorial Day, 203–6
    rebirth theme, 202
    Soldiers' and Sailors' Monument, 201
churches
    ABMC (American Baptist Missionary
        Convention), 44
    African American 41, 42–43, 44–48
    antebellum era, 28
    Christian denominations, slavery and,
        41–42
    Douglass, Frederick, 41–42
citizen soldiers, 7
Civil War
    memories, 9
    national war fought by local commu-
        nities, 3
    official beginning, 53–54
    social historians and, 3–4
Civil War cities, 2–3
class divisions, antebellum New Bedford,
    29
clustering of deaths, 96
coastal fortification, 71–72
coasting trade, African Americans and,
    33–36
commemorations. *See also* celebrations
    black heroes, 212–15
    Carney, William H., 212–13, 214
    of deaths, 96–97
    emancipation, 213
    segregated, 201–2
    Shaw Monument, 215–17
    Temple, Lewis, 220
Committee for the Relief of New Bedford
    City Guards, 67
Committee on Home and Coast Guard,
    67
Committee on Military Relief, 102

communities
    African American, 5, 6
    Bender, Thomas on, 4
    business, 5
    Mitchell, Reid on, 4
    within New Bedford, 4
    pension applications and, 131–34
    political, 5
    soldiers as cross-section, 83
Confederate attacks on whaling ships,
    142, 143–45
Congressional Medal of Honor, William
    H. Carney, 212–13
conscription. *See also* draft
    bounties and, 57–58
    deserters, 59–60
    percentages, 83
    property ownership and, 83
    public opinion, 63–64
    resistance to, 89
conservatism in postbellum era, policing
    moral order, 185
costs of war, 7–8
    federal funding, 70
    local responsibility, 169
    public concerns, 69
    reimbursable, 181–82
cotton textile industry growth, 195–96
    New Bedford Cotton Manufacturers
        Association, 199
County Street, *181*
Crapo, William W., 2
crime, antebellum New Bedford, 29–30
crimps, 15
Cruz, Carl, 220–21
CSS *Alabama,* 143–45
CSS *Florida,* 144–45
CSS *Shenandoah,* 145

death toll. *See* casualties
defenses
    coastal fortification, 71–72
    Committee on Home and Coast
        Guard, 67
    fear of attack, 66–70
    federal funding, 70
    forts, 68, 69
demographics
    antebellum New Bedford, 33–41
    Company C of Fifty-Fourth Massachu-
        setts Volunteer Infantry, 104
    draftees, 63

Irish soldiers, 94–95
MSSCW, 92–94
deserters, 59–60
disabled veterans, pensions, 127–31
Douglass, Frederick
    black military service, 99–100, 104
    churches, 41–42
    on New Bedford, 32
draft. *See also* conscription
    demographics, 63
    deserters, 59–60
    First District Board of Enrollments, 64
    media attention, 63
    New Bedford Recruiting Committee,
        65
    Potter, William J. sermon, 63, 65
    public opinion, 63, 64
    riot fears, 61–63

economic hardship in postbellum era,
        black soldiers, 121–23
economic opportunities
    African Americans, 38–41
    antebellum New Bedford, 33–41
    occupational distribution, 39
    Teamoh, George, 37
    Temple, Lewis, 37–38
economy. *See also* municipal spending
    antebellum, 17–18, 21–23, 33–35
    enlistment motives and, 83, 85–86
    Fourth of July celebration, 168
    manufacturing, 153–160
    petroleum, threat to whaling, 160
    PMG's office, 60
    post-war, 138–39
    retail prices, 162
    war bond sales, 168
    wartime, 146–47, 149, 150–51, 160–61,
        163
    Wing brothers (Joseph and William
        R.), 152–53
elections, incorporation and, 23–24
emancipation, commemorations and, 213
Emancipation Day, celebrations, 114
employment
    African Americans in postbellum era,
        199
    whaling industry, 11–14
enlightened attitudes of city government,
        24–27
enlistment. *See also* military mobilization
    1865 Army and Navy Register, 84–85

African Americans, 91, 100–3
    changing patterns, 91
    conscription, resistance to, 89
    economic motives, 83, 85–86
    effects on marginal families, 176
    Irish, 94–95
    MSSCW, 92–94
    promotions, 88
    volunteer, 57–58, 83, 87–88, 99–100
equal pay for black military service,
        102–3, 107
    fights for, 114–17
    legislation passed, 116–17
    nonpayment, family survival and,
        120–21
equality, black military service, 102–3
expenditures. *See* municipal spending

fear of attack, 66–70
federal funding, 70
    military pensions, 123–24
Fifty-Fourth Massachusetts Volunteer
        Infantry, 100
    appreciation for, 117
    Carney, William H., 110–14
    Company C, New Bedford men in,
        103–8
    demographics, 104
    equal pay, 107
    Fort Wagner, 108–10
    freedmen and, 107–8
    Grace, James W. on, 108, 111–12
    as model regiment, 106
    presentation of regimental flags, 106–7
    public aid applications, 122
financial inducement for recruits, 65
First District Board of Enrollments, 64
Fort Phoenix, *70*
Fort Wagner, 108–10
Fourth of July celebration, 68–69
    commercialization, 205–6
    defunding, 168
Freedmen's Relief Association, 107–8
fugitive slaves, 47–48
fundraising
    black military service, 112–14
    freed blacks, 107–8, 113–14

Gallman, J. Matthew, Civil War cities, 2–3
GAR (Grand Army of the Republic)
    African-American members, 209–10
    black veteran impoverishment, 210

ladies auxiliaries, 210–11
myth and memory, 206–12
parade march, *212*
Gooding, James Henry, 7
    capture, 117
    equal pay fights, 115–16
    letters, 105–6
governance
    Board of Health, 183
    enlightened attitudes, 24–27
    incorporation and, 23–24
    wartime, 166–75
    water system, 177–81
Grace, James W., 108, 111–12
Grimes, Rev. William, 106

Hall, Joseph, 124–27
Harrington, Rev. Henry F., 173–74
Harrison, Rev. Samuel, 106
Henson, Cornelius, 129–30
history glorification of New Bedford,
    219–20
home front
    policing, 72–76
    urban environment, 73–74
Horton, James and Lois Horton, 6
hospital building, 167
Howland, Abraham, 25
Howland, George Jr., 1–2, *78*
Howland, Sylvia Ann, 174–75

identity, memory and, 202–3
immigrants, 197
incorporation of New Bedford, 23–24
industrial development
    American Federation of Labor, 197–98
    consequences, 196
    immigrants, 197
    labor conflicts, 196–97, 196–99
    postbellum era, 187
    Social Labor Party, 197–98
inflation, wartime, 147, 149
interracial memory making, 222
Irish soldiers, 94–95

Jackson, Rev. William, 106
    pension, 133
Jackson-Grimes dispute, 106
Jacobs, Harriet, 107–8
Johnson, Ezra R., antiabolitionist
    movement, 46

Kelly, Patrick, 8
King, Isaiah, 127

labor conflicts, 196–99
labor market, racism in, 36–37
landsharks, 15
legislation for equal pay for black military
    service, 116–17
Leonard, Samuel, 16
Levi Starbuck, 143–45
loan interest payments, 169–70
localism, pensions and, 123–24
lodgers' during war, 73–74, 76

manufacturing
    1865 records, 157–59
    antebellum New Bedford, 17–18
    mechanical bakery, 154–55
    nonwhaling, growth, 155–56
    postbellum era growth, 193–200
    postwar rise, 9
    shoemaking, 154
    transition to, 153–60
    wartime inflation, 161, 163
    whaling and, 15–16
    women workers, 155–56
maritime commerce
    African Americans and, 33–36
    maritime workers, 85
martial citizenship, 8
mechanical bakery, 154–55
Melville, Herman
    Father Mapple, 26
    praising New Bedford, 10
Memorial Day celebrations, 203–6
memory work
    American civil religion, 202
    GAR and, 206–12
    identity and, 202–3
    interracial memory making, 222
    War Between the States, 202
    War of Northern Aggression, 202
militancy growth, 48–51
military mobilization
    cost responsibility, 169
    Council of War, 53–54
    draft, 59–60, 61–63, 64, 65
    funds appropriation, 54
    Minute Men of '61, 56–57
    New Bedford City Guards, 56
    Quakers, 54
    recruiting, 65

volunteer enlistment, bounties, 57–58
women's support, 54
militias, 48–51
Minute Men of '61, 56–57
Mitchell, Reid, community and, 4
mobilization of military. *See* military
   mobilization
model regiment of Fifty-Fourth, 106
monetary contributions to military, 102–3
monuments
   to dead, 96–97
   Soldiers' and Sailors' Monument,
      182–83
morality
   conservatism and policing, 185
   instruction in schools, 174–75
   pensions and, 135
mortality. *See* casualties
motivations of soldiers, 85, 87
MSSCW (*Massachusetts Soldiers, Sailors,
   and Marines in the Civil War*), 92–94
Mudge, Rev. Enoch, 26
municipal spending. *See also* accounting
      practices
   1850–75, 171
   expenditures and receipts 1850–75, 65
   Overseers of the Poor, 175–77
   postwar, schools, 174
   sanitation systems, 178
   school funding, 170, 172–73
   Soldiers' and Sailors' Monument,
      182–183
   wartime, 164–65, 166–70, 172–73
MVM (Massachusetts Volunteer Militia),
   professionals and merchants, 87

national debt, public concerns, 69
National Negro Convention Movement,
   49–51
naval ships
   CSS *Alabama,* 143–45
   CSS *Florida,* 144–45
   CSS *Shenandoah,* 145
   Levi Starbuck, 143–45
navy veterans, 134
New Bedford
   20th century developments, 219–22
   antebellum (*See* antebellum New
      Bedford)
   centennial celebration, 1–2
   civic identity, 2
   communities 5, 6

governance, 24–25
history glorification, 219–20
incorporation, 23–24
manufacturing rise, 9
prosperity, 10–11
richest city, 5–6
semicentennial anniversary (1897), 197
wartime, 6
whaling, 11–14
New Bedford City Guards, 56
New Bedford Ladies' Soldiers' Relief
   Society, 56
New Bedford Port Society, 26–27
New Bedford Protecting Society, 29
New Bedford Recruiting Committee, 65
New Bedford Whaling Museum, 221
nonpayment, family survival and, 120–21

occupational distribution (black/white),
   39
outdoor poor relief 1861–70, 177
Overseers of the Poor, 119–20
   applications for relief, 122
   funding jump, 168
   municipal spending and, 175–77
   outdoor poor relief 1861–70, 177
   postbellum era, 186

Parish, Peter J., 3
pensions, 120
   applications, 123, 125–26
   Carney, William H., 128–30
   casualties and, 127–31
   communities and, 131–34
   federal, 123–24
   Henson, Cornelius, 129–30
   heroes, 128–30
   Jackson, Rev. William, 133
   King, Isaiah, 127
   Lee, Harrison, 133
   localism and, 123–24
   modern welfare state, 123
   morality and, 135
   Phelps, Emery, 131–32
   political terms, 120
   Turner, Lucy, 124
   twentieth century, 124
   white widows *versus* black, 123
   widows, 135
petroleum's threat to whaling, 160
Phelps, Emery, 131–32
Phipps, Abner J., 170–75

Pierce, Missouri, 135–36
police force, 29–30
policing on home front, 72–76
political community, 5
Port Society. *See* New Bedford Port
    Society
postbellum era
    industrial development, 187
    manufacturing growth, 193–200
    mayors in, 185–86
    Overseers of the Poor, 186
    prohibition, 185
    textile manufacturing, 191–93
    transition state, 184
    Wamsutta, 191–93
    whaling decline, 187–89, 191
Potter, Rev. William J., 66
    The Voice of the Draft sermon, 63, 65
prison deaths, 96
privateer attacks on whaling ships,
    142–46
professional class African Americans, 39
prohibition in postbellum era, 185
property ownership, conscription and, 83
prosperity, mid-century, 10–11
Provost Marshal General's office, 58–60
PSHP (Philadelphia Social History
    Project), opportunity patterns, 41
public schools. *See* schools
    war's impact on, 173
public welfare system. *See* welfare system
public works, 27
published accounts
    black soldiers, 104–5
    Gooding, James Henry, 105–6

Quakers, 28. *See also* Society of Friends
    child's attire, 55
    military mobilization, 54
quotas and credits received, 169

racial tolerance, 5–6
racism, labor market and, 36–37
recruitment, 60–61
    African Americans, 101–2, 103
    demographics, 63
    expenditures, 168–69
    financial inducements, 65
    monetary contributions, 102–3
reimbursements
    postwar, 181–83

recruitment and, 168–69
    state, 169
relief. *See also* welfare system
    Carney, William H., 214–15
    GAR and, 208–9
    WRC, 210–11
religious life
    antebellum era, 28
    schools, 174–75
retail prices in wartime, 162
R. G. Dun credit reports, 149
    whaling valuations, 150–51
riot fears
    draft, 61–63
    Ricketson, Joseph and, 62
Rodman, William Logan, 77, 79–81, 82
    on African-American soldiers, 91
    funeral, 96–97
rope making, 16–17

salaries for government, 167
Salem Baptist Church, 43
schools
    adult, 172
    antebellum era attitudes, 170
    bequest from Sylvia Ann Howland,
      174–75
    budget cuts, 172–73
    evening, 172
    funding, 170, 172
    Harrington, Rev. Henry F., 173–74
    moral instruction, 174–75
    Phipps, Abner J., 170–75
    postbellum era, truant officer, 185
    postwar spending, 174
    reforms by first superintendent, 172
    religious values, 174–75
Second Baptist Church, 43
semicentennial anniversary (1897), 197
sewer construction, 177–81
Shaw Monument, 215–17
    rededication, 220–21
shoemaking, 154
skilled labor, 38–39
slavery
    black military service's effect on, 104
    Christian churches and, 41–42
    fugitives, 47–48
Snell, David, mechanical bakery, 154–55
social class
    among soldiers, 88–89
    immigrants and, 197

social effects of industrialization, 196
social historians, Civil War and, 3–4
social welfare, 7–8. *See also* welfare system
Socialist Labor Party, 197–98
Society of Friends, 28. *See also* Quakers
soldiers
    African American, 91–92
    backgrounds, 85, 87
    casualties, 95–97
    as cross-section of community, 83
    Irish, 94–95
    motivations, 85, 87
    social classes among, 88–89
Soldiers' and Sailors' Monument, 182–183
    as focal point, 201
Soldiers' Fund, 168
spending. *See* municipal spending
state reimbursements, 169
Stone Fleet, 139–42, *143*
    captains, *140*

tax rates, 169
Teamoh, George, economic opportu-
    nities, 37
Temple, Lewis, 37–38
    commemoration, 220
    Temple Toggle Iron Headed Harpoon,
    38
textile mills
    business leaders and, 199
    cotton industry growth, 195–96
    postbellum era, 191–93
    Wamsutta, 18–21
    wartime economy, 160–61, 163
"The Whaleman" (sculpture), 219
Third Christian Church, 43
Toussaint Guards, 103
transient persons during war, 73–74
transition of postbellum era, 184
    African Americans, 199
Turner, Lucy, 124–27

urban environment changes

veterans
    black, 120, 123, 125–26, 127–31, 204
    economic hardship, 121–23
    federal pensions, 123–24
    impoverishment, 210
    navy, 134
    pensions, 120, 122–24
Vigilant Aid Society, 47
Vinovskis, Maris, 3–4

volunteer enlistment. *See also* citizen
    soldiers; military mobilization
    African Americans, 91, 99–100 (*See also*
        black military service)
    bounties, 57–58, 87–88
    changing patterns, 91
    Irish, 94–95
    MSSCW, 92–94
    promotion, 88
    short-term infantry units, 83

Wamsutta textile mills, 18–21, *194*
    postbellum era, 191–93
    strike, 196
    transition to manufacturing and, 154
    wartime economy, 160–61, 163
War Between the States, 202
war bond sales, 168
War of Northern Aggression, 202
Washington, Booker T., Shaw
        Monument dedication and, 216
water system
    costs of new, 180–81
    crisis, 179
    deficiencies, 178–79
    necessity of, 180
    sewer construction and, 177–78
welfare system, 119. *See also* relief
    applications for relief, 122
    Civil War's effect on perceptions, 127
    modern, and Civil War system, 123
    Overseers of the Poor, 119–20, 175–77
    patterns of relief, 176–77
    rising costs, 169–70
    Turner, Lucy, 124–27
    war's effect on marginal families, 176
whaling
    Confederate attacks on ships, 142–46
    coopering, *190*
    crimps, 15
    decline in postbellum era, 187–89, 191
    employment, 11–14
    landsharks, 15
    manufacturing and, 15–16
    New Bedford Whaling Museum, 221
    petroleum threat, 160
    prosperity of New Bedford and, 11
    racial dynamics, 36
    related manufacturing, 156
    R. G. Dun valuations, 150–51
    richest city name, 5–6
    rope making and, 16–17

sperm oil, 16
Stone Fleet, 139–42
Temple Toggle Iron Headed Harpoon, 38
vessels, 14–15
wartime, 146–49, 152–53
whale oil, 16
wharves, 11
Wing brothers (Joseph and William R.), 152–53

women
  manufacturing jobs, 155–56
  New Bedford Ladies' Soldiers' Relief Society, 56
  support, military mobilization, 54
women's societies, 26–27
WRC (Woman's Relief Corps), 210–11
  African American, 211–12

Young Men's Anti-Slavery Society, 46

THE NORTH'S CIVIL WAR
Paul A. Cimbala, series editor

Anita Palladino, ed., *Diary of a Yankee Engineer: The Civil War Story of John H. Westervelt, Engineer, 1st New York Volunteer Engineer Corps.*

Herman Belz, *Abraham Lincoln, Constitutionalism, and Equal Rights in the Civil War Era.*

Earl J. Hess, *Liberty, Virtue, and Progress: Northerners and Their War for the Union.* Second revised edition, with a new introduction by the author.

William L. Burton, *Melting Pot Soldiers: The Union's Ethnic Regiments.*

Hans L. Trefousse, *Carl Schurz: A Biography.*

Stephen W. Sears, ed., *Mr. Dunn Browne's Experiences in the Army: The Civil War Letters of Samuel W. Fiske.*

Jean H. Baker, *Affairs of Party: The Political Culture of Northern Democrats in the Mid–Nineteenth Century.*

Frank L. Klement, *The Limits of Dissent: Clement L. Vallandigham and the Civil War.* With a new introduction by Steven K. Rogstad.

Lawrence N. Powell, *New Masters: Northern Planters during the Civil War and Reconstruction.*

John A. Carpenter, *Sword and Olive Branch: Oliver Otis Howard.*

Thomas F. Schwartz, ed., *"For a Vast Future Also": Essays from the Journal of the Abraham Lincoln Association.*

Mark De Wolfe Howe, ed., *Touched with Fire: Civil War Letters and Diary of Oliver Wendell Holmes, Jr.* With a new introduction by David Burton.

Harold Adams Small, ed., *The Road to Richmond: The Civil War Letters of Major Abner R. Small of the 16th Maine Volunteers.* With a new introduction by Earl J. Hess.

Eric A. Campbell, ed., *"A Grand Terrible Dramma": From Gettysburg to Petersburg: The Civil War Letters of Charles Wellington Reed.* Illustrated by Reed's Civil War sketches.

Herbert Mitgang, ed., *Abraham Lincoln: A Press Portrait.*

Harold Holzer, ed., *Prang's Civil War Pictures: The Complete Battle Chromos of Louis Prang.*

Harold Holzer, ed., *State of the Union: New York and the Civil War.*

Paul A. Cimbala and Randall M. Miller, eds., *Union Soldiers and the Northern Home Front: Wartime Experiences, Postwar Adjustments.*